a HISTORY of AMERICAN SPORTS in 100 OBJECTS

Also by Cait Murphy

*Crazy '08: How a Cast of Cranks, Rogues, Boneheads, and
Magnates Created the Greatest Year in Baseball History*

*Scoundrels in Law: The Trials of Howe and Hummel,
Lawyers to the Gangsters, Cops, Starlets, and
Rakes Who Made the Gilded Age*

a HISTORY of AMERICAN SPORTS
in 100 OBJECTS

CAIT MURPHY

BASIC BOOKS
New York

Books published by Basic Books are available at special discounts for bulk purchases in the
United States by corporations, institutions, and other organizations. For more information,
please contact the Special Markets Department at the Perseus Books Group, 2300 Chestnut Street, Suite 200, Philadelphia, PA 19103, or call (800) 810-4145, ext. 5000, or e-mail
special.markets@perseusbooks.com.

Designed by Jack Lenzo

Library of Congress Cataloging-in-Publication Data
Names: Murphy, Cait, 1961–
Title: A history of American sports in 100 objects / Cait Murphy.
Description: First edition. | New York : Basic Books, [2016] | Includes bibliographical
    references and index.
Identifiers: LCCN 2016012506 (print) | LCCN 2016013206 (ebook) | ISBN
    9780465097746 (hardcover) | ISBN 9780465097753 (e-book)
Subjects: LCSH: Sport—United States—History—Miscellanea.
Classification: LCC GV583 .M87 2016 (print) | LCC GV583 (ebook) | DDC
    796.0973—dc23
LC record available at http://lccn.loc.gov/2016012506

10 9 8 7 6 5 4 3 2 1

To the Asia crew:
You know who you are, and thanks.

CONTENTS

INTRODUCTION

How can I include Immaculata College and not Wilt Chamberlain? Why is Nancy Lopez in, but not Mickey Whitworth? Where are Mary Decker, Edwin Moses, and Al Oerter? Or Ty Cobb and Ted Williams? No Jerry West or LeBron James? Couldn't I have squeezed in something about wrestling or volleyball? Whither Tom Brady, Jim Brown, and Walter Payton? What in heaven's name is chunkey?

What kind of book is this?

Those are fair questions. Believe me, I would have loved to include all of the above, and many more. As a lifelong Mets fan, it hurt not to include either the Miracle Mets of 1969 or the infamous "Bill Buckner" game in the 1986 World Series. A veritable hall of fame of great athletes is absent. So let me explain.

CREATING THE LIST

This book is not about the 100 greatest moments in American sports, or the 100 greatest performances, or the 100 greatest athletes. If it were, of course Wilt Chamberlain and his 100-point game would make the cut. So would Cal Ripken's 2,632 consecutive games played, Michael Johnson's remarkable 200-meter/400-meter double in the 1996 Olympics, and Maureen Connolly's tennis Grand Slam in 1953. So would my Miracle Mets, damn it. But in each of those cases, the achievement was singular; the story was over when the game was won or the clock ran out.

Although these events are important threads in the fabric of American sport, one of the ideas behind this list is that history is not woven only by superstars. Social, political, global, and technological developments also play an important role. That is part of the fun of looking at sports through objects; it's not just the legends you know.

The Puritans, for example, may not have been world-class bowlers (who knows?). But the fact that they bowled at all says something important about them—that even a group as puritanical as they were needed to have some fun. So a wooden orb recovered from a seventeenth-century privy can tell us something interesting about America's early European settlers. The object tells a story.

Or consider the fight between Jack Dempsey and Georges Carpentier in 1921. This was not, in fact, a great fight (Carpentier got creamed). At best, it would be a footnote in boxing history, except that it marked the first time a sporting event was broadcast. The radio featured here therefore represents the moment sports and mass media first went out in public. Think of it as the direct ancestor of today's 24-hour sports coverage. The role of technology and innovation, whether it be installing lights to make night games possible, designing new medical procedures to restore careers, inventing an ice-surfacing machine, or extending sports to new outlets, such as video games, is another important thread. This list attempts to tell some of these larger stories.

Of course there are some people or events that muscle their way into any survey of American sports: think John L. Sullivan, Jim Thorpe, Bobby Jones, Jesse Owens, the 1980 Olympic hockey team, Michael Jordan, and Tiger Woods. So do dynasties like the Yankees and the Celtics. Win the most medals in a winter Olympics (Eric Heiden) or in the summer Games (Michael Phelps), and sure, you're in. Ditto for a woman who set an untouched world record in 1988—a period drenched in suspicions of performance-enhancing drugs—and was never suspected of anything but athletic brilliance (Jackie Joyner-Kersee). Great rivalries endure over time and say much about the athletes, their sports, and their times, such as Larry Bird–Magic Johnson, Chris Evert–Martina Navratilova, Auburn–Alabama, and UConn–Tennessee. (And yes, including rivalries means there are actually more than 100 objects; I didn't see the point in choosing one and not the other.)

Moments that become cultural touchstones qualify, even a largely forgotten one like the Great Match Race of 1823. In addition, certain events were critical in the development of American sports. These can be moments of origin, such as James Naismith creating the rules of basketball; the race that inspired the America's Cup; or the beginning of mixed martial arts. Or they can be turning points, such as the 1958 football championship or the 1960 US Open at Cherry Hills, at which Arnold Palmer and Jack Nicklaus first competed against each other, to stirring effect. I also wanted to make room for athletes who are legends in their own fields, but are not well known in general, such as Isaac Murphy, Tad Lucas, and Tommy Kono.

I had these principles in mind as I put together the list. In addition, with a few exceptions, I decided that each object had to exist somewhere; a photograph of something lost to history was not enough. I would have loved to include the gloves that John Carlos or Tommie Smith wore during their silent protest on the medal stand at the 1968 Olympics. These have disappeared. The death of Dale Earnhardt during the 2001 Daytona 500 may be the most important single moment in the modern history of NASCAR. Somewhat to my relief, however, I could find no artifacts of the tragedy. (The good people at the NASCAR Hall of Fame thought I was ghoulish even to ask.) In addition, I interpreted the idea of "object" liberally, to include such things as a building (Sportsman's Hall), a park (devoted to David Berger, the Israeli American killed at the Munich Olympics), and printed materials (Marvin Miller's contract).

I always kept in mind that sports are a source of both wonder and simple fun. So there is a good collection of great moments, such as Babe Ruth's (allegedly) called shot, Mary Lou Retton's perfect vault, and Armando Galarraga's "imperfect game." The Goal, The Drive, The Fight, The Play, and The Catch are all included.

Finally, I wanted a broad reach, in terms of sports, geography, and time. Football, baseball, and basketball have the most items because they loom largest on the American sports landscape. But combined, these account for less than half the total. Roughly three dozen different sports get an entry, including auto racing, cycling, gymnastics, rodeo, sharpshooting, and surfing. More than a third of the items date to before 1950. And yet . . . many more things are left out. There is no figure skating, snowboarding, triathlon, or diving. Curling missed the cut, too.

SPORTS AND SOCIETY

There are those who cannot resist seeing sports as a metaphor for history, or life, or character, or whatever. I am dubious about this. What can be said is that sports are part of the fabric of the society in which they are played—and always have been. I was intrigued to learn, for example, of the importance of lacrosse in many North American tribal cultures; it was play, of course, but could also be a spiritual ritual or a means of settling conflicts. The game of chunkey was one of the ways that the people of Cahokia spread their culture; it was central to their way of life in a way that cannot be recaptured in modern society.

In our own times, sports faithfully replicate many of the prominent features of American life, for good and ill. Drug problems in society? Cue Lance Armstrong and the Mitchell Report. Gambling? Say hello to Pete Rose. Poor leadership? In the last decade alone, incidents in baseball, cycling, football, the Olympics, the National Collegiate Athletic Association, soccer, tennis, and track-and-field have found their managements wanting in a sense of ethics and sometimes even of decency. America's troubled racial history appears in various forms, from Joe Louis to the "forgotten Hoosiers" of Crispus Attucks to the Tigerbelles to Muhammad Ali, Arthur Ashe, and the Williams sisters. And as the stories of the 10th Mountain Division and the 2013 Boston marathon remind us, sports cannot even be separated from war and terrorism.

But there is also a heartening tale to be told. Another theme that informs this book is that the joy of sport is simply more available to more people. When a modest 20-year-old amateur, Francis Ouimet, beat Britain's best pros to win the US Open in 1913, he took golf out of the exclusive precincts of the very rich and made it something that the middle class (or upper middle class, anyway) could play without irony. The nineteenth--century safety bicycle liberated middle-class American women only a little, but enough to know they wanted more. In recent years the opportunity to play sports has also been extended on a large scale to the physically and mentally handicapped. Taken as a whole, an unmistakable pattern is revealed. Decade by decade, sport by sport, more and more people have been able to participate in athletics, whether for pleasure, or as a profession, or as spectators.

The hoopsters of Immaculata have an honorable role in this evolution. A tiny Catholic women's college outside Philadelphia, the Mighty Macs were an unlikely dynasty. They were the first women's team to play in Madison Square Garden, the first to be televised, and the first to compete overseas. But they did all this in the 1970s, when women's basketball was not taken seriously.

A single generation later, the game had been transformed. Stars like Rebecca Lobo of the University of Connecticut were national figures. So the Mighty Macs represent not just on-court excellence, but women's sports on the cusp of change.

For an object, I've chosen the tunic the Mighty Macs wore when they won their first championship in 1972. The idea of playing serious hoops in wool dresses seems absurd now, and it was even at the time. Still, they did it. It doesn't matter where the tunic was sewn or what shade of blue it was or how many pleats it had. The point is that the tunic shows what kind of place Immaculata was and what the times were like.

THE OBJECT OF OBJECTS

Since the British Broadcasting Corporation pioneered the idea in 2010 with its brilliant *History of the World in 100 Objects*, there have been similar projects relating to many subjects, including American history, the Civil War, Ireland, Napoleon, New York, Shakespeare, and even bird-watching and retailing.

To apply this approach to sports seems particularly apt. It is no more possible to separate sports and their artifacts than it is to distinguish the blue from the sky. And because just about every fan has also played sports, there is a sense of familiarity. Few of us will ever approach Olympian greatness, but we may know the satisfaction of experiencing a moment when what we do exactly matches what we wanted to do: the hole in one, the perfectly hit ball, the marathon completed. That creates a kinship with those who do the same things, so much better.

And without getting too deep, there is also something deeper at work. Many religions enshrine relics with which to inspire devotees. Surely it is not ridiculous to wonder if the same impulse applies to sports artifacts. I know I experienced something like awe on a bleak midwinter day at the US Track and Field Hall of Fame in upper Manhattan. With the bemused permission of an official, I opened a file door, peeled back the tissue paper, and there it was: a hunk of aged brown leather, surpassingly soft and surprisingly light. I was stirred because I was in the presence of greatness. Babe Didrikson had worn this shoe when she won three medals at the 1932 Olympics.

And then we got to talking: about Didrikson's place in history, about how many medals she might have won if Olympic leaders (all of them male and deeply concerned about her fragile physiology) had allowed her to compete in additional events, about the development of women's sports.

That is the power of objects: a lump of leather provided a moment that still gives me chills and evoked a conversation that went well beyond the thing itself. Objects, whether they are as big as a ballpark (Camden Yards) or as small as a nail (from Secretariat's shoe), are a material connection between present and past. The best of them spark the imagination. Plus, they're fun to look at.

Another advantage of this approach is the unexpected connections that emerge. For example, Bill Bowerman was not only a veteran of the 10th Mountain Division; he was also the creator of the Nike Waffle Trainer and the coach of Steve Prefontaine. Frank Gifford was a halfback in the "greatest game" as well as one of the early stars of *Monday Night Football*. Joe Louis helped Jackie Robinson get his military commission. Robinson was the first Negro Leaguer to play in the major leagues; Hank Aaron was the last. There is clear continuity between the 1926 tennis match between Helen Wills and Suzanne Lenglen in France and the all-American hoopla of Billie Jean King versus Bobby Riggs in 1973.

Sports are supposed to be a simple pleasure. That they become something else can be deplored and sometimes cherished. Still, out of that awkward complexity come stories—in this book, 100 of them. Every single person who reads this book is going to wince at some omission or be incredulous at some inclusion, or vice versa. But save your outrage; it's only sports. And remember, I'm a lifelong Mets fan. Give me a break.

Circa 1100

STATUE OF A CHUNKEY PLAYER

On a flat field that could be as short as 100 feet or as large as several hundred acres, two men start to run. Then one of them rolls[1] a three- to four-inch-wide, concave stone disc.[2] The contestants maneuver their wooden spears, trying to place them through the ring. The winner is the one who comes closest.

The game was called chunkey, and it was a very big deal for hundreds of years. "All the American Indians are much addicted to this game," one British observer wrote in 1775, "which to us appears to be a task of stupid drudgery."[3] The American artist George Catlin, on the other hand, referred to a game he witnessed in North Dakota as one "of great beauty and fine bodily exercise."[4]

The game itself might have had a ritual purpose; some historians suggest that the rolling disc evoked the movement of the sun.[5] The stick and stone call to mind male and female and therefore the idea of sex and creation. Sometimes a cross would be etched into the stone, signaling the four directions.[6] Whatever the cosmology, it was a ton of fun. People would come from miles around to watch an all-day match, feasting and drinking along the edges of the playing field. There were rivalries between communities, and the players were local heroes. It all sounds a lot like tailgating at the Turkey Day classic, with a side of Vegas. Gambling was rife, with wives, children, and freedom sometimes staked. Committing suicide after a loss was not unknown.[7]

The 8.5-inch-high, red stone sculpture shown on the next page, was crafted near Cahokia, about five miles east of what is now St. Louis. Found in the early twentieth century, it shows a chunkey player with an oversized disc in his right hand; in his left he holds two somewhat undersized chunkey sticks. The figurine can also be used as a pipe.

Chunkey was played over much of the North American continent, but it was founded in Cahokia, a major urban center that used both sport and warfare to spread its culture.[8] At its peak around 1100, perhaps 10,000 people lived, worked—and played—in the meticulously planned Cahokia.[9] The largest city in North America outside

Mexico, it had huge buildings, pyramids, and a grand plaza for ceremonies—and chunkey games.

So what happened to Cahokia? No one knows. One theory is that the city may have become too large to sustain itself. Another is conflict. In addition to the 120 mounds, some with entombed human remains suggestive of ritual deaths, the Cahokians also built an elaborate wall around their most important sites; this suggests fear.[10] Drought and the onset of the "little ice age" around 1300 could have been factors. For whatever reason, by 1400, Cahokia was no more.[11]

Modernity played havoc with what was left. In the nineteenth century, some of the mounds were leveled to make railway beds. The biggest, known as Monks' Mound, had a footprint twice the size of the Colosseum in Rome.[12] Others were lost to farming.

The state of Illinois bought a large part of the area in the 1920s for a state park, but missed what had been the Grand Plaza (and probably the chief chunkey field); a housing development was planted there in the 1940s. In the mid-twentieth century, an interstate highway took another chunk. Since then the site has been treated better. The 2,200 acres are now a UNESCO World Heritage Site. Excavations continue. Parts of about 80 mounds still exist, the most visible remnants of America's first city.

Late 1600s

OLDEST AMERICAN "LAWN BOWLE"

The Puritans have a well-earned reputation as historic killjoys. They liked rules and considered it their godly duty to keep people from the fires of hell by telling them exactly how to live. Building what Governor John Winthrop called a "city upon a hill" that the world would watch in awe was not a job for libertarians, and certainly not for libertines.

Naturally, then, they disdained fun and games. Except they didn't—at least not entirely. As early as 1622, eight years before the founding of the Massachusetts Bay Colony, a sermon by a London-based Puritan clergyman advised that Puritans could perform their duties to God at all times, "yea, even in our eating and drinking, lawful sports, and recreations." Winthrop noted that "outward recreation," in the form of "moderate exercise," lifted melancholy and refreshed his mind.[1] Moreover, all Puritan villages had militias, whose training resembled a day camp, featuring horsemanship, jumping, weight lifting, wrestling, and races.[2]

And that brings us to Katherine Naylor's privy—an outdoor toilet and rubbish pit. Naylor, a late seventeenth-century resident of Boston whose father had been banished to what became New Hampshire for nonconformity with Puritan theology, became a successful businesswoman after she divorced her abusive second husband. Naylor was also a relative by marriage of the poet Anne Hutchinson, whom the Puritans banished in 1638.

Naylor was a woman of uncommon ability and of some prosperity. That is the evidence from a 1994 excavation done in preparation for Boston's Big Dig, the mammoth infrastructure project that reconfigured the center of the city. When archaeologists uncovered Naylor's centuries-old, three-seat toilet, they found a trove of artifacts, including silk, Venetian glass,[3] and the oldest known bowling ball in the country (see the following page). Made of oak and the size of a small grapefruit, this "lawn bowle" has flattened sides decorated with carved concentric circles, as well as a small hole where a weight would have been inserted.[4]

Boston's Puritan elders did not approve of bowling. A 1647 law forbade the activity at inns and taverns; another banned football in the "streets, lanes, and enclosures of this town."[5] In each case, the concern was that sport would infringe on public order. A complaint to the General Court noted that bowling was associated with "much waste of Wine and Beer,"[6] perhaps the first recorded mention of the association between sports and suds.

As historian Laurel Ulrich Thatcher wrote in her essay on the Naylor "lawn bowle," there would have been no need to legislate against bowling if the sport had not been popular. The lawmakers seemed concerned not about bowling per se, but rather its association with other vices, such as gambling, loose behavior, profanity, and breaking the Sabbath. Thus, it was legal for the Naylor family to bowl in the privacy of their own property; doing so in public was not.[7] In a sense, the Puritans were legislating against excess, not good clean fun.

But times change. The stern first generation of Puritans gave way to a less insular society. Many of the newcomers—sailors, merchants, and other ne'er-do-wells—didn't care about building a God-fearing city on a hill. By 1714 taverns were openly advertising their bowling facilities. When it came to sport, the Puritans were the first, but hardly the last, to learn that the great American public had a way of making its own rules.[8]

1823

SOUVENIR FROM THE GREAT MATCH RACE

The date: May 27, 1823.

The place: Union Course, eight miles from New York City.

The contestants: Eclipse versus Sir Henry.

The race: Best two out of three, at four miles.

The prize: $40,000 to the winner.[1]

The real stakes: Regional supremacy.

In addition to death and taxes, one thing was certain in the United States in the early 1820s: when it came to the horse, the South was superior. There were racetracks big and small all over the South, and the culture ran deep. Not so in the North, where there were few tracks, and there was deep suspicion of the sins that accompanied the sight of running horseflesh.

And then came Eclipse. He had won a couple of obscure events before being put to stud, but when racing was legalized in New York in 1821, he went back to work,

winning every race he entered, including four over southern-bred horses.[2] By 1822 northerners were bragging that Eclipse was "the greatest horse for bottom and speed in America."[3] Southerners had their doubts. In November 1822 Colonel William Ransom Johnson of Virginia—the self-described "Napoleon of the Turf"—issued a challenge: Eclipse versus a southern horse of Johnson's choosing. It was accepted.

After a series of trials, the southerners chose Sir Henry as their champion. Although he and Eclipse had never met before the day of what became known as the Great Match Race, they shared a bond. Both were grandsons of the great Diomed, an English champion who[4] was brought to stud in the United States. Diomed's blood coursed throughout American racing. Eclipse would carry 126 pounds; Sir Henry, the younger horse, only 108.[5] They would go four times around the one-mile oval, best two out of three, with only a short rest in between.[6]

It was the first modern-style sports spectacle. An estimated 60,000 spectators—New York had a population of 120,000[7]—made their way to the Union Course, where they could buy overpriced souvenirs such as the red-on-yellow cotton handkerchief (see previous page). About 20,000 of the attendees were from the South.[8] The newspapers covered the event extensively; the saloon talk was of little else, and the betting was outrageous.[9] Vice President Daniel Tompkins was there, as were future president Andrew Jackson and almost-president Aaron Burr. The New York Stock Exchange closed for the day.[10]

Sir Henry won the first heat in a record time of 7:37.5.[11] Eclipse raced bravely, but his young jockey, William Crafts, rode him cruelly, lashing him bloody down the stretch. One of the horse's legs and a testicle were cut. In the 30 minutes between heats, the call went up for Samuel Purdy, Eclipse's regular jockey, who at age 49 had been deemed too old for the big race. Some of Eclipse's backers tracked him down: Would Purdy ride? Yes, he said, and ripped off his overcoat. He had worn his racing silks underneath, just in case.[12]

In the second heat, the old pro showed how it was done, coaxing Eclipse to the rail in a nifty move on the inside to take the lead in the last mile, then holding off a game Sir Henry. Eclipse finished in 7:49, two lengths ahead.

So it would come down to the third heat; neither horse had ever had to run three in a day. They were exhausted but had the competitive spirit of true athletes. Eclipse took the lead at the start and hung on the whole way, winning in 8:24. Over the three heats, a distance of 12 miles, the difference between the two was no more than a length.

Although the Great Match Race was a conflict contested by animals, the humans involved were acutely aware that it was something more. "It was the first great contest between the North and the South," Josiah Quincy, a member of the Adams family, would write in 1881, "and one that seems to have foreshadowed the sterner conflict that occurred 40 years afterwards."[13]

Pre-1845

LACROSSE STICK

The first written reference to lacrosse, North America's oldest continuously played team sport, dates to 1636, when a French missionary, Jean de Brébeuf, witnessed a competition in present-day Canada between Indian tribes.[1] De Brébeuf, one of Canada's patron saints, spent 15 years among the Huron; he appreciated their culture and became fluent in their language. Still, he was appalled by the spectacle.[2] As a compatriot later complained of the sport, "Almost everything short of murder is allowable."[3]

In some ways, that was the point. There was a spiritual component to the game, which might be played to honor the Creator or as a plea to heal the sick; it was also used to train young men and to mediate disputes. The Creeks and Choctaws once played a match to decide rights to a beaver pond.[4] The Mohawk version of the game was known as "tewaarathon," meaning "little brother of war," which is telling. French priests, for their part, thought the stick resembled the ceremonial crozier carried by Catholic bishops—thus, "la crosse." Tribes along the east coast, and as far south as northern Mexico, played slightly different styles; in one form, the competitors used two sticks. The balls were made of wood or stuffed leather. The goals could be miles apart, and dozens or hundreds of young men might play for days.

Many non-native observers disapproved of such aggressive frivolity; missionaries in particular didn't like the game's non-Christian religious element. They didn't take it seriously enough to write detailed descriptions of the play, but clearly, the spectacle was enthralling, a fact that Indians could use to their advantage. In June 1763, for example, during Pontiac's war against the British, several hundred Chippewas and Sauks staged a version of lacrosse known as baggataway outside Fort Michilmackinac, near present-day Mackinaw City, Michigan. The British soldiers, including the commander (who had a big bet on the Chippewas), became so interested that when a player pushed a ball through the door of the fort, the soldiers were unprepared for the teams that rushed through, picked up weapons that their women had stashed, and killed half the garrison.[5]

European settlers began playing lacrosse in the early 1800s, and a group of Canadians organized the first club in 1844. This stick, made of hickory with a calfskin net, hails from that era. Crafted by a Cayuga artisan, it is particularly beautiful, with geometric carving along its length; the top of the webbing emerges from the nose of a carved dog head. At the butt, a human hand grasps a ball; just below, there are two clasped hands.[6]

For many years lacrosse was a regional sport in the United States, prominent mostly in the mid-Atlantic. It also continued to play an important role in the cultural life of a number of tribes. Today it has become one of the nation's fastest-growing sports. In 2015 the University of Denver won the National Collegiate Athletic Association men's title, the first championship for a school west of the Mississippi. And in a reminder of the sport's roots, the trophy given to the year's best collegiate player features an Indian player with stick held high, poised for action.

1851

STERN ORNAMENT FROM THE *AMERICA*

John Cox Stevens was one of the great sports impresarios in American history. He introduced cricket to the United States; backed Eclipse in the Great Match Race (see the 1823 entry); and owned the Elysian Fields, where the first organized baseball game was played (see the 1853 entry).[1] In 1851 he turned his attention to a bigger goal: beating the British.

In that year he formed a syndicate of six men, including James A. Hamilton, son of Alexander, to pay for the construction of a yacht to sail to Great Britain during the Great Exhibition of 1851. Called the *America*, it was designed by George Steers, who had made his name as a crafty designer of the pilot boats that sailed New York waters. These boats had to be fast to outrace the competition, and they had to be robust and maneuverable in all kinds of water.

Steers took all of his experience working with pilot boats and applied it to the *America*; 171 tons of Yankee ingenuity, she had a hollow, concave bow, with sails made of closely woven cotton that could be set relatively flat. It carried no topsails, giving it a simple profile; its hull was wedge-shaped and its rudder rounded. The center of displacement was aft of the beam rather than forward.[2] All of this, noted the *Illustrated London News*, was "rather a violation of the old established ideas of naval architecture."[3] This large gilt eagle, about eight feet wide, was placed on the stern, keeping wooden watch on all that passed.[4]

As the *America* approached the Isle of Wight on August 1, 1851, the English cutter *Laverock* challenged its crew to a race. If there was dust on the high seas, the *Laverock* would have been left in it. The *America* won easily.[5] Prior to this spanking, the British press had been characteristically patronizing regarding the unconventional Yankee yacht. Now, however, Stevens's call for a race met with silence from the British. The *Times* of London noticed and scorned "the pith and courage"[6]—or lack thereof—of British yachtsmen.

Stung, the Royal Yacht Squadron invited Stevens to take part in an open regatta on August 22, a 53-mile circumference of the Isle of Wight, with the winner to be awarded a Cup of One Hundred Sovereigns.[7] Stevens accepted. At 10:00 a.m. the 15 yachts sailed. The *America* got off poorly, but took the lead shortly after the first mark and never lost it, even when it lost its jibboom and had to pause to clear the wreckage. By the time it reached the vicinity of the royal yacht, the second-place *Aurora* was literally miles behind. This led to a famous exchange, which sounds too good to be true and therefore probably isn't: "Which is first?" Queen Victoria asked an officer.

"The *America*."

"Which is second?"

"Ah, Your Majesty, there is no second."[8]

The *Aurora* narrowed the gap when the wind died down, but the *America* still won by 18 minutes. A week later the yacht left the speedy *Titania* in its wake, proving that the victory in the regatta was no fluke. Stevens sold the *America* and returned home via steamship, carrying the Cup of One Hundred Sovereigns. This 27-inch-high ewer, of high Victorian design, would become known as the America's Cup, the oldest trophy in international sports and the most prestigious prize in yachting. That, of course, was not known at the time; the first America's Cup race would not take place until 1870. But it was recognized on both sides of the Atlantic that something important had happened. The *America* revolutionized maritime design and forced others to take the young country's capabilities seriously.

Life after the regatta was picaresque for the *America*. For the next decade, it was sold and re-sold to various Englishmen. During this period, the eagle ornament pictured on the previous page was removed and found a new calling above the door of a pub, The Eagle, on the Isle of Wight.[9] (The Royal Yacht Squadron got it back and presented it to the New York Yacht Club in 1912.)[10]

Returning stateside in the early 1860s and fitted with a few guns, she was re-named the *Memphis* and served as a Confederate blockade runner until Union forces finally caught up. Scuttled in Florida, she was later raised and then joined the Union's blockading fleet off Charleston and served as a training vessel at the US Naval Academy.[11]

A former Union general, Benjamin Butler, bought the yacht in 1873. In the South, Butler was known as "the beast" for his harsh rule during the occupation of New Orleans and Norfolk—and also, perhaps, for being remarkably ugly. Although Butler made a mysterious fortune during the war and rigged the sale to buy the former *America*,[12] the famous yacht could not have landed in better hands; he pampered her rotten. But after his death in 1893 his heirs neglected her until she was sold, battered but still historic, in 1916 to a group of yachtsmen who wanted to keep her in the United States. The *America* returned to the Naval Academy in 1921; she was towed from New England to Maryland, stopping at yacht clubs all along the way. Two thousand midshipmen welcomed her back to Annapolis,[13] where she lived until a snowstorm in 1942 damaged her beyond repair.

There was no formal epitaph for the *America*; the most apt tribute had been penned in 1851, not long after her famous victory. *Punch*, the British humor magazine, offered a new verse to a well-known song:

> *Yankee Doodle had a craft,*
> *A rather tidy clipper,*
> *And he challenged, while they laughed,*
> *The Britishers to whip her.*
> *Their whole yacht squadron she outsped,*
> *And that on their own water;*
> *Of all the lot she went ahead*
> *And they came nowhere arter.*[14]

1853

SOIL FROM THE ELYSIAN FIELDS

In Greek mythology, the souls of the heroic dead enjoyed paradise in the Elysian Fields. It's fittingly poetic, then, that perhaps the first organized baseball game took place on the Elysian Fields of Hoboken, New Jersey.

The aptly named Alexander Joy Cartwright has long been credited with devising the first modern rules; it is on this basis he is often referred to as "the father of baseball." There is some truth to the legend; in September 1845 he wrote 20 rules and regulations for his Knickerbocker Base Ball Club. Among them are some familiar concepts, such as three strikes for an out, three outs to an inning, and foul territory.[1]

But Cartwright was more like Moses, setting down familiar practices for what became known as the "New York game" (as opposed to the "Massachusetts game").[2] As one early baseball historian, John Ward, put it in 1888, "They recorded the rules of the game as they remembered them from boyhood, and as they found them in vogue at that time."[3] But others did as much or more; for example, not only did Daniel "Doc" Adams create the shortstop position,[4] but he also led the legislative effort in 1857 that set the bases 90 feet apart and established nine innings as the standard. These "Laws of Base Ball" sold at auction in April 2016 for $3.26 million.[5] Adams, too, was associated with the Knickerbockers.

Over time the New York game, itself derived from "town ball," which was a fairly primitive and informal pastime derived from the English game of rounders, evolved into the much more challenging one that became baseball. There is a nice symmetry to the fact that Cartwright, Adams, and their Knickerbocker cronies often played in the open area around Madison Avenue and East 27th Street, the future location of the first Madison Square Garden.

Looking for more space and less congestion, the gang began to take the ferry to the Elysian Fields, an expansive park on the other side of the Hudson River. It was there, on June 19, 1846, that the Knickerbockers played the New York Base Ball Club in what could be considered the first formal game played under modern rules.[6] The Knicker-bockers lost 23–1.[7]

This modest chunk of soil comes from that field; some of the original Knicker-bockers might have slid on these exact ounces of dirt.[8] In 1853 on a visit to the area, a young man named James Orr attended a ball game there. Orr was so taken with the new sport—he would call watching this game one of the most sublime moments of his life[9]—that he dug up a piece of the field to remember the occasion. He put the soil in a box with a note explaining where it was from and why it was important to him. The family kept it for generations.

Three years after Orr's sublime experience, an English-born sportswriter named Henry Chadwick—confusingly, he is also often referred to as the "father of baseball"—visited the Elysian Fields and had a re-action not unlike Orr's. This, he said, was "just the game for a national sport for Americans." Chadwick became a tireless publicist for baseball. He also invented the box score,[10] reason enough for his inclusion in the Hall of Fame.

Modern scholarship has cast some doubt on whether Cartwright was quite as important as he has been made out to be; indeed, his Hall of Fame plaque is riddled with errors (he didn't set the bases 90 feet apart, for example). Unlike the silly myth of Abner Doubleday inventing the game on a rainy day in Cooperstown, however, there is a solid basis of fact related to Cartwright. He was an early player, in every sense of the word, on the Elysian fields of baseball.

1860

ABRAHAM LINCOLN'S HANDBALL

In his early days in New Salem, Indiana, Abraham Lincoln made his name among the tough Clary Grove gang by wrestling their leader, Jack Armstrong, to a draw.[1] That was the first of many matches; Lincoln lost only once in 12 years, as far as the US Wrestling Hall of Fame can determine. Indeed, young Lincoln was known for two things: his character and his strength.

Like many an accomplished sportsman, Lincoln had attitude. After winning one wrestling match with indifferent ease, he is said to have shouted to the crowd, "Any of you want to try it, come on and whet your horns!"[2] Lincoln was also an excellent runner and jumper, the latter no doubt helped by his unusual height.[3] His friends were awed by his strength; one contemporary described him as "a Hercules."

As a grown man in Springfield, Illinois, Lincoln's favorite athletic activity was a handball game known as "fives," played against a brick wall in an alley near his law office. One of his opponents described the scene: "Here is where 'Old Abe' was always champion, for his long arms and long legs served a good purpose in reaching and returning the ball from any angle his adversary could send it to the wall."[4] Another observer was less complimentary, saying that Lincoln's "suppleness, leaps, and strides to strike the ball were comical in the extreme."[5]

Lincoln was not out for style points, however. He liked the competition, and a rousing game of fives was also a good way to relieve the stress of life with his wife, Mary Todd; the law; and politics. So it is not altogether surprising that in May 1860, with the presidential nominating convention going on in Chicago, he went down to the alley for a game. On the first ballot, William Seward of New York took the most votes, with

Lincoln second. On the second ballot, Lincoln narrowed the gap. The suspense must have been excruciating.

When the messenger came with the results of the third ballot, Lincoln opened the telegram, read the news, and didn't finish the game. Instead, he headed home, saying, "There is a little woman down on Eighth Street who will be glad to hear this news."[6]

The ball in this picture may not be the exact one Lincoln played with as he waited for word from Chicago, but it certainly could be. It was found in a dresser in his home, and when Lincoln left Springfield after the election, he never returned alive.

SPORTSMAN'S HALL

Animal sports such as bearbaiting and cockfighting were popular in the nineteenth century. Dogfighting, in which specially trained canines fought to the death, was a more specialized taste. The same was true for dog versus rat fights, in which a squirming bag of rodents was dumped in the pit and officials timed how long it took the dogs to kill them. There are also records of man versus rat fights, but not many: even nineteenth-century New York had its limits.[1] This was all legal; there were no animal cruelty laws until 1868, and even then prosecution was uncertain. One judge threw out a case on the grounds that there was nothing wrong with "the fine sport of dog-fighting."[2]

Owned by Kit Burns, a former notable in the notorious Irish American Dead Rabbits gang, the 25-square-foot basement hall in the building on lower Manhattan's eastern waterfront known as Sportsman's Hall was the city's most popular venue for such contests. "Nowhere," wrote one disapproving observer, "could the moolahs and thugs find such delectable divertissement as Burns' pits."[3]

Public attitudes began to change, though, and in late 1870 the police waded into the middle of a heated bout between two dogs, Slasher and Old Rocks, and arrested 34 spectators. The cops also took away a cage of 150 rats meant for entertainment later in the evening, dumping them in the East River. Burns died before the trial, but his successors agreed not to hold any more dogfights; they told the *New York Times* that from then on, they'd stick to selling "rum and rats." And by the way, Burns's widow argued, she wanted compensation for those 150 rats.[4]

Built in the 1770s, this is one of the oldest buildings in New York City. It started as a home for a sea captain and has also served as a residence for fallen women, an apothecary, and a shoe store. In the late 1990s it was in such terrible condition that the city government gave it to a developer, on condition that the exterior be preserved. It now houses luxury apartments. Kit Burns would be appalled.

JOHN L. SULLIVAN'S DUMBBELL

John L. Sullivan, America's first sports superstar, was also the first athlete to earn $1 million. He pioneered other types of action, too. He dabbled in show biz and willing women. He drank too much. He had a posse of hangers-on. And he died destitute.

Remarkably, he managed all this even though at the height of his fame, his sport was illegal in every state.[1] Today, boxing and prizefighting are synonymous. In the nineteenth century, however, they were distinct. Boxing, which gentlemen like Theodore Roosevelt did as a hobby at Harvard, was socially acceptable; prizefighting, which tough guys did for money, was not. Even so, prizefights took place all over the country, supported by a public that loved the action and a gambling culture that provided an economic base.

John L. was the best fighter in the land and had been regarded as such since at least 1882, when he pummeled Paddy Ryan to the canvas in 11 minutes. He hadn't lost since, dispatching his challengers with contemptuous ease.

Jake Kilrain, who had made his name fighting around Boston, was good enough that Richard Fox, owner of the *National Police Gazette*, which covered the sport thoroughly, had proclaimed him champion. No one beyond Kilrain's friends really believed this assertion (if they did). But if Kilrain could beat John L., he could turn that claim into reality, as well as pick up the $20,000 stake, the biggest purse ever.[2]

Sullivan's people were sure that at his best, he could lick Kilrain with the proverbial one hand tied behind his back. The problem was that when they made the deal for a title match against Kilrain in early 1889, their man was suffering from the aftereffects of a particularly prolonged period of debauchery that had him seeing phantom rats.[3] But the fight was set for July 8, 1889, six months away, more than enough time to dry him out. With two months left before the big fight, though, Sullivan's backers were desperate; he was still a sodden mess. So they made a bet with Billy Muldoon, a famous trainer and reigning Greco-Roman wrestling champion.[4] They would pay him $10,000 to get Sullivan in shape—to be paid only if he won.

Sullivan was shipped to Muldoon's farm in an isolated part of upstate New York. Muldoon was ready for him. He told the only two bars in town not to serve Sullivan and banned the champ's friends.

Sullivan hated it. He loathed Muldoon. And he wanted a drink. Despite Muldoon's warning, a local bartender gave him one, or maybe three or four. Who was going to say no to the heavyweight champ? Muldoon hauled Sullivan out and wrestled him to the ground. With that, Sullivan got serious. Over the next seven weeks, he did whatever Muldoon asked, including milking cows, and was in bed by 9:00, with Muldoon asleep in the same room. He even bathed in brine to toughen his skin. After a few weeks, Sullivan was doing eight to ten miles of roadwork in the morning; in the afternoon, he worked out in a barn Muldoon had converted into a gym. Pictured here is one of the weights he used.[5]

Sullivan and Kilrain would fight under London Prize Ring rules. There were no gloves, and a round lasted as long as one man was on his feet; wrestling and grabbing were legal. The fight would end when one man could not go on. On a blistering hot day, a series of trains took spectators from New Orleans to a farm in Richburg, Mississippi, where a 20-foot-ring had been built. A little after 10:00 in the morning, the two stepped into the ring. Kilrain wore black knee breeches; Sullivan his famous green ones. Both were around 5 foot 10. Kilrain, 29, weighed in at 195 pounds. Sullivan, 30, was 207 pounds of superbly conditioned muscle.

One glance at Sullivan's trim figure told Kilrain he couldn't outslug the Boston Strong Boy; his strategy was to tire him out. But Sullivan was well able to chase Kilrain, even if he didn't much like it. In the fourth round, which lasted 15 minutes, Sullivan became exasperated: "Why don't you stand and fight like a man, you sonofabitch?"[6] When there was an actual exchange of blows, he got the better of the action. As the fight wore on, Kilrain tired, not Sullivan, and he began to land thudding blows at will. In the seventy-sixth round, Kilrain's seconds wouldn't let him come out. Sullivan had won. Kilrain was devastated but philosophical; his telegram to his wife read: "Nature gave out. Not hurt, though licked. Your husband."[7] Various authorities came after the two for fighting illegally, and it took a lot of time and money to settle the charges.

The battle at Richburg was the last bare-knuckle heavyweight championship prizefight. Sullivan himself always preferred fighting with gloves and began to insist on it.[8] With his stock as high as it would ever be, his opinion carried weight. In 1892, in the first title defense to be contested with gloves, Sullivan lost to 26-year-old Jim Corbett, crushed by a left to the jaw in the twenty-first round. It was the only loss of his career. Corbett's deft use of feints and jabs and movement was altogether more sophisticated than the pounding rushes characteristic of Sullivan and his peers. Corbett is sometimes called the "father of modern boxing."

This was also the first legal title fight; Louisiana had decriminalized the sport in 1890.[9] For that, Sullivan must get a large share of the credit. While he was at times a rake and a drunk, he was also hugely popular. He lifted the sport from being a spectacle for lowlifes to one that also attracted the middle and upper classes. It was their support that successfully got the sport legalized in state after state.[10] The first and last great champion of bare-knuckle boxing, Sullivan embodied one era and helped usher in a new one.

1890

ISAAC MURPHY'S SILK PURSE

The best jockey of the nineteenth century and perhaps of all time, Isaac Murphy won a record 34 percent of his 1,538 mounts.[1] When the Racing Hall of Fame was founded in 1955, he was the first jockey to be inducted. His is a story of grit and athletic genius. But because Murphy was black, it is also more complicated than that. He was the greatest of the long line of great black jockeys and had the highest profile; he might well be thought of as the first black superstar athlete.

Murphy was born in Kentucky in 1861 to enslaved parents. His father joined the Union Army and died shortly after the end of the Civil War; his mother moved to Lexington. At age 12, Murphy was apprenticed to a stable.[2] For a black male, this was an excellent career choice. Historically, slaves had run the day-to-day work of racing—everything from breeding to foaling to training to riding—earning themselves unusual status and sometimes a degree of autonomy.[3] After emancipation, the tradition endured. Racing was an area in which the opinions of black Americans were valued. Some even moved into the ranks of ownership.

The first time Murphy got on a racehorse, though, it threw him, and he was in tears at the thought of having to remount.[4] But he did. More important, he began to understand the half ton of nervous energy beneath his saddle. Murphy rarely had to use the whip; he could ride "to hand," communicating through touch and something like telepathy. He rode his first winner in 1876, as an 87-pound 15-year-old. By 1879 he had begun to be noticed.

In 1884 he separated himself from the pack, winning the three biggest races in the state: the Kentucky Oaks, the Kentucky Derby, and the Clark Stakes. He earned about $10,000 that year,[5] making him one of the most affluent black men in America. He might also have been the country's highest-paid athlete.[6]

For the next six years, Murphy was the finest jockey in the land. He was known for being able to pace his mounts with uncanny precision and for winning by just enough;

these close finishes were known as "Murfinishes."[7] Self-assured but reserved in public, Murphy rode that way, too, with total control and stillness in the saddle. And in a field rich in skullduggery, "Honest Ike" was considered incorruptible.[8]

In 1890 he had his finest year, but it ended on a troubled note. At Monmouth Park in August, Murphy ran an inexplicable race aboard the favorite, Firenze, pulling him this way and that. Firenze finished last, and Murphy looked much the worse for wear. The papers diagnosed drunkenness, and the authorities suspended him. Murphy denied the charge. In later months he wondered if he had been poisoned, and some evidence supports that idea. In the immediate aftermath, he simply said he was unwell.[9] Although the executive committee that looked into the incident concluded that Murphy "wasn't and couldn't have been drunk,"[10] he had already been convicted in the court of public opinion. Murphy would never ride quite as high again.

He won the Kentucky Derby again in 1891—in a race so slow that it became known as the "Funeral Procession Derby."[11] The winnings were presented in this silk purse.

The victory made Murphy the first jockey to win two Derbies in a row, but at age 30, making weight had become increasingly difficult, and half a lifetime of crash diets and purging had undermined his health. His career was sinking. Murphy won only a handful of times in 1892 and 1893, and not at all in 1894. Shortly after his last race in 1895,[12] he caught pneumonia; he died in February 1896.

There may have been another factor in his decline. Black jockeys were being systematically squeezed out of the profession, just as black Kentuckians in general were being constrained. In 1892 the Kentucky legislature passed a bill segregating train cars, the first formal expression of Jim Crow laws. For jockeys, the most important year was 1894, when the National Jockey Club put in place formal licensing requirements for jockeys and trainers—and then denied licenses to blacks.[13] White jockeys did their bit, too; they attacked their black colleagues so often during races that owners began to think that having a black jockey aboard constituted a danger to their horses.[14]

As racial attitudes hardened, opportunities narrowed: No black jockey has ridden a winner in a Triple Crown race since Jimmy Winkfield in the 1902 Kentucky Derby. That is particularly ironic, since Kentucky was a historic source of black racing talent, and the Derby was their race. In the first Derby, in 1875, 14 of the 15 jockeys were black,[15] and black jockeys won 15 of the first 28[16] races. It didn't help that in one of the country's spasms of righteousness, many states began to shut down racecourses; there were only 25 left by 1908.[17] When a number of them reopened, it was easy to exclude blacks.[18]

1891

JAMES NAISMITH'S ORIGINAL RULES OF BASKETBALL

Even young men training to be Christian missionaries are young men, with the limited attention span not uncommon to the species. And that presented a problem to James Naismith, a Canadian chaplain working at the International YMCA Training School in Springfield, Massachusetts. He faced a rambunctious class of future administrators; the students enjoyed football in the fall and baseball in the spring but were vocally unhappy with the winter options available to them.[1] Swedish drill, marching, and mass calisthenics failed to appeal, and the men flatly refused to play "drop the handkerchief."[2] They had already chewed through two instructors.

In December 1891 it was Naismith's turn. His orders were to invent a noncontact indoor sport that the boys wouldn't loathe. But his attempts at indoor football, lacrosse, and soccer had all failed, and the "class of incorrigibles"[3] was more fractious than ever. Thoroughly discouraged, Naismith sat at his desk to think.

The men liked ball games, so any new game must use a ball, a big one so that it could not be hidden and could be easily caught and thrown. If there was no running with the ball, there would be no need for tackling. So that was another rule. What, then, to do with the ball? Well, pass it—in any direction. To what end? Some sort of a goal was required.

Inspiration struck again. If the goal was placed high, the players could not cluster around it, and the ball would be lofted, rather than thrown hard. Naismith knew he had something here; he dreamed of the game that night.[4]

The next morning he nailed two peach baskets to the lower rail of a balcony, 10 feet above the gym floor. Then he asked an assistant to type up his 13 rules, which she did, on the two pages shown here. Naismith tacked them up to the bulletin board and went out to face the class of 18 incorrigibles. In fewer than 500 words, Naismith had sketched the outlines for what became one of the world's most popular sports.[5]

Naismith would hardly recognize the above-the-rim theatrics of today's hoops, but the game is clearly visible in and between these lines. It is still true, for example, that the ball can be passed in any direction (rule 1), that running with the ball is forbidden (rule 3), and that scoring occurs by putting the ball in the basket (rule 8). The game evolved quickly, with specialized balls and free throws introduced in 1894; five-man teams were standard by 1897. Other rules have disappeared, such as the rule against three straight fouls. Still, if a team were to play strictly by the 1891 rules, the result would look like basketball.

The sport spread far and fast. For that, the YMCA can take all the credit. Founded in London in 1844, the Y came to the United States before the Civil War and spread quickly in the rapidly urbanizing young country. Luther Gulick, Naismith's boss, was one of the more eloquent apostles of the idea of "muscular Christianity," which was a response to the prevailing impression that Christianity was becoming feminized, dominated by strong women and weak men. "Body and soul are both so closely related that one affects the other," Gulick argued. "Christ's kingdom should include the athletic world."[6] The Y used sports to draw young men away from the lures of city streets; in addition, its leaders believed that sports themselves could teach character and ethics. In effect, the Y helped to legitimize sports as a constructive activity,[7] even if that was not its sole intention.

A month after the first game, the Y's newspaper, *The Triangle*, printed the rules, and branches all over the country began to play. There was an international dimension almost from the start. By 1893 a French graduate had introduced the game there.[8] Overseas missionaries trained by the Y spread the game. Hoops was being played in parts of China before it penetrated some areas of the United States.

Women took to basketball remarkably quickly. The game was no more than a month old when women began to play. They must have looked odd, in their street shoes and leg-of-mutton sleeves, but they kept coming back. In a few weeks there were enough females with some skill to play a game against each other. Naismith was impressed; in fact, he married one of the participants.[9]

Senda Berenson,[10] a young Lithuanian-born physical education instructor at Smith College, about 20 miles from Springfield, came to take a look a few weeks after Naismith posted his 13 theses. She liked what she saw. After a few weeks of practice, she arranged a game between her first- and second-year students, in March 1892.[11] "The girls went wild," according to one account, "and the spectators yelled and cheered at the top of their lungs."[12]

Berenson was both pleased and unsettled. She believed that exercise was important for women and had no patience with the types who "thought fainting interesting and hysterics fascinating."[13] Nor did she share the view of much of the medical profession that physical exertion would imperil women's reproductive capabilities by depleting their "vital force." But she did think that competition would lead to rough play that was unwomanly and harmful to the female psyche. On that basis, she refused to allow Smith to play other schools.[14] For reasons of both aesthetics and principle, then, girls gone wild is not what Berenson had in mind.[15]

She decided to feminize the game, forbidding swatting the ball away and dividing the court into three zones that no player could stray across. Some form of this idea would be common in women's basketball for more than 75 years. Another Berenson rule was that no player could hold the ball for more than three seconds; this made for a game in which passing and ball-handling were at a premium. Berenson wrote the first book of women's rules in 1899 and edited it for the next 18 years.

After leaving the Y, Naismith got a medical degree and then became a physical education instructor at the University of Kansas, where he worked from 1898 to 1937 (with a hiatus for service in World War I). He started a basketball team, of course; ironically, he is the only coach in Kansas history to post a losing record (55–60). His successor was Phog Allen, who coached the Jayhawks from 1907 to 1909 and 1919 to 1956 and helped to create the National Collegiate Athletic Association end-of-season hoops tournament. Allen taught both Adolph Rupp of Kentucky (876 wins) and Dean Smith of North Carolina (879 wins). Their protégés include such coaches as Larry Brown, Joe B. Hall, Pat Riley, and Roy Williams. In short, Kansas is the wellspring of college hoops. The Jayhawks play on the James Naismith Court in the Allen Fieldhouse, which is on Naismith Drive. It is appropriate, then, that in 2010, a Kansas graduate bought the 13 rules for $4.3 million and donated them to the university.

1892

RECORD OF PAYMENT FOR FIRST PROFESSIONAL FOOTBALL PLAYER

I t's just two lines on a loose-leaf page: "Game performance bonus to W. Heffelfinger for playing (cash) $500.00." But that entry for the November 12, 1892, game between two Pittsburgh teams, shown in this photo, marks the first time a player was

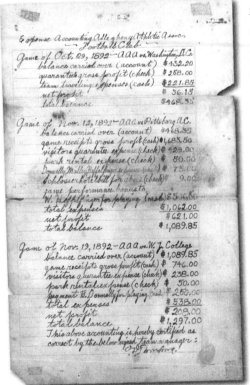

openly paid. That makes William "Pudge" Heffelfinger the first pigskin professional. Considering the average American was making around $700 a year at the time, it was an excellent payday for the all-American guard from Yale, who was recruited to play for the Allegheny Athletic Association as a ringer against the Pittsburgh Athletic Club. The ploy worked: Heffelfinger scored the game-winning touchdown. He helped at the box office, too; at the time, he might have been the most famous player in the country.[1]

To put his pay in context, consider that it accounted for almost half the day's total expenses ($1,062) and almost as much as the day's profit ($621). Those figures look comically small; the day's revenues totaled just $1,683.50. But the beginning of any enterprise is as much an act of imagination as of economics, and that is what this receipt represents.

1892

SAFETY BICYCLE

Social change can occur through war or revolution. It can come from the genius of inventors tinkering in a garage or from people peacefully crossing a bridge. And it can come, entirely unexpectedly, on two wheels. That is the story of the safety bicycle, a device that, no less an authority than Susan B. Anthony boasted, "has done more to emancipate women than anything else in the world."

The first popular bicycle dated to the 1860s. Known as the velocipede, the penny-farthing, or the "boneshaker,"[1] it had one huge and one small wheel; it was heavy, unsafe, undignified, and perilous to mount. Women found the temptation to climb aboard easy to resist.

The safety bicycle, which debuted in 1885,[2] solved all those problems; its wheels were the same size, making the bike much more stable. The chain-gear drive made it easier to pedal. And the development and improvement of the pneumatic tire made for a smoother, faster ride.[3] The final innovation was the "drop frame," which made it possible for women in skirts to hop on with grace and modesty. By the mid-1890s the bike was recognizably modern[4]—and women took to it with verve.

At a time when it was an entirely settled matter that the middle-class woman's place was in the home, the bicycle allowed them to expand their geographic boundaries. Many chaperones could not keep up with their charges, and it became possible, even acceptable, for young couples to go cycling together. Even with the drop frame, riding in ankle-length skirts and corsets was problematic, and this dovetailed with the "dress reform" movement, which called for less constricting attire. Many women switched to comfortable footwear, shook off their bustles and corsets, and adopted (slightly) shorter, divided skirts.

There was pushback against all this freedom. One female physician warned that cycling could lead to everything from gout to tuberculosis to epilepsy and cancer.[5] A more general concern was that straddling the bike saddle could damage the "feminine organs of matrimonial necessity," as one European put it.[6] Another worry, difficult to put into print, was that women would experience new feelings and, in a sense, become debauched by the bike. Clergymen despaired that girls and women were skipping church in favor of riding into the countryside. With males. Unescorted. Where would it all end? "Bicycling by young women," charged the Women's Rescue League, "has helped more than any medium to swell the ranks of reckless girls, who finally drift into the army of outcast women."[7] They were willing to risk it.

So the first important consequence of the bicycle for women was that, in an astonishingly short time, it became conventional wisdom that exercise was good for them,

and would help to "rid them of vapors and nerves."[8] The *British Medical Journal* concluded: "There is no reason whatever why any sound woman should not ride either a bicycle or a tricycle." No racing though, and not during menstruation or for at least three months after giving birth. Still, this was progress. The idea that exercise would not undermine women's femininity or make them unfit mothers was revolutionary.[9]

In 1890 there were about 150,000 Americans riding bikes; by 1896, there were four million.[10] Perhaps a third were women. Just as quickly as it started, however, the bicycle craze crashed. By 1902 production was down to 250,000 a year.[11] The novelty had worn off, and manufacturers who had proven so innovative a decade before had lost their creative spark.

But the influence of the bicycle did not end with the death of the craze. For one thing, the bicycle literally paved the way for the car, as the shocking condition of American roads became all too obvious. Bicyclists pushed, successfully, for improvements, in the form of smoother surfaces, better lighting, and increased signage.[12] This was critical to making roads fit for cars.

In addition, bike manufacturers were in the vanguard in the use of the assembly line, the development of precision manufacturing, and the standardization of components.[13] Henry Ford was a former bicycle mechanic; so were several of the pioneers of aviation, including the Wright brothers. The early automobile and aviation industries borrowed copiously from the bicycle, including the use of pneumatic tires, differential gears, ball bearings, and chain and shaft drives. The Wrights rode a specially fitted bicycle through a wind tunnel to test lift and drag.[14]

The safety bicycle pictured on the previous page was owned by Frances Willard—largely forgotten now, but famous and influential in her day. A temperance reformer who was also active in the suffrage, public health, and labor movements, Willard was the first woman to be featured in the Statuary Hall in the US Capitol.[15] In 1892, at age 53, depressed and grieving after the death of her mother, she decided to learn to ride a bike. She adored it, and wrote a short book in 1895 that is still in print, *A Wheel Within a Wheel: How I Learned to Ride a Bicycle.*

The book suffers from a surfeit of earnestness, with too much deep meaning ascribed to a two-wheeler. But Willard's delight in Gladys, the name she gave to her metal steed, is endearing. Gladys, she wrote, was "as full of kinks as the most spirited mare that sweeps the course." However overwrought her extended essay, Willard appears to be entirely sincere: "I found a whole philosophy of life in the wooing and winning of my bicycle."[16] Her last words to her readers ring with the fervor of the convert: "Moral: Go thou and do likewise."[17]

THE YARD OF BRICKS AT THE INDIANAPOLIS MOTOR SPEEDWAY

Although the practice dates to the mid-1990s, it seems that racers have been "kissing the bricks" in Indianapolis forever. The tradition started after NASCAR's Dale Jarrett and his crew chief, Todd Parrott, lowered themselves to their knees, turned their caps around, and did just that after winning the Brickyard 400 in 1996. They were saying thanks—both for the victory and for the history that is paved into every turn of the 2.5-mile oval that is the Indianapolis Motor Speedway.

Every Brickyard winner since has followed suit, and starting a few years later, so have winners of the Indianapolis 500, who pucker up after drinking the traditional glass of milk on the same track. Sometimes drivers kiss the bricks alone; usually, it's a moment for team and family, too.

The 9.5-pound bricks themselves date back to the earliest days of American motor sports. Carl Fisher, a successful bicycle salesman,[1] was transitioning to the auto business. He envisioned Indianapolis as "the world's greatest center of horseless carriage manufacturing." But it would need a track for testing. "What could be more logical than building the world's greatest racetrack right here?"[2]

Fisher missed on the first part of the prediction; Detroit, not Indianapolis, became the horseless-carriage hub. But the Speedway is still the world's largest sports venue, seating more than 257,000 people. And Fisher himself helped to pave the United States, by promoting the first cross-country road suitable for cars, the New York to San Francisco Lincoln Highway,[3] as well as the Chicago to Miami Dixie Highway.

The first track on the site opened in August 1909, but its tar-gravel-oil surface was unforgiving to vehicles and deadly to their drivers, who couldn't keep the cars steady on the slippery track. Several competitors and spectators died in the first few days of racing, and the American Automobile Association said it would boycott the Speedway unless a safer surface was installed. Brick, which was durable and offered better traction, was a natural choice. It took 3.2 million bricks to cover the original track, over a base of sand. The track reopened in December, and by the time the first Indianapolis 500 took place, it was already referred to as the Brickyard. Over time, asphalt replaced the brick, first on the turns, and then on the rest of the track. Except, that is, for the three-foot strip at the start/finish line shown in the picture opposite, known as the "Yard of Bricks."[4]

1910

ANNIE OAKLEY'S RIFLE

Forget the anthem from *Annie Get Your Gun*, the Broadway musical, that "You can't get a man with a gun." That was way too easy a target. The real Annie Oakley could nail the edge of a playing card. Backward. With either hand. And she got the man, too.

Five-foot-nothing, with big eyes and a quiet voice, Annie Oakley acted like a lady. She could also shoot out a cigarette held between Kaiser Wilhelm's fingers. Or the pips on a playing card. Oakley literally made her name (she was born Phoebe Ann Mosey) in Buffalo Bill's Wild West extravaganza. But that should not obscure the fact that she was also an extraordinary athlete in an era when the idea of a woman making a living through sports was unknown. And she is one of the few women, then or since, who not only competed with men on an equal basis, but creamed them. Her fellow sharpshooters had to concede her excellence. Before she was 20, she was barred from local turkey shoots because she won them all. Later she was regarded with awe in both Europe and the United States, where she instructed army sharpshooters. Although Oakley's heyday was in the 1880s and 1890s, she was still shooting well into the twentieth century; in her sixties, she could hit a hundred clay targets in a row. This deluxe .22 caliber target rifle dates from around 1910.

For those who still aren't sure that Annie Oakley counts as an athlete, consider the following feat. She would put her shotgun on the floor about 10 feet away from a table. When her husband, Frank Butler, released the clay target, she would jump over the table, pick up the shotgun, and blast the target before it hit the floor. She could also pick off glass balls with her shotgun while standing on the back of a running horse.[1] Looked at this way, Annie Oakley might be America's first great female professional athlete—and 120 years later, still one of the finest.

1912

JIM THORPE'S RESTORED OLYMPIC GOLD MEDALS

In July 1912 Sweden's King Gustav V told Jim Thorpe: "Sir, you are the greatest athlete in the world."[1] Few would have disagreed. Thorpe had just won the pentathlon and decathlon in the 1912 Stockholm Olympics, breaking the world record in the latter.

Back home in the United States, he was the country's most famous football player as the star of the Carlisle Indians (see the 1925 entry on the modern football). If the Heisman Trophy had existed, he probably would have won it in both 1911 and 1912. And the year after Stockholm, he began a seven-year career playing baseball for the New York Giants. Beginning in 1915 he also played pro football; he was one of the early stars of the National Football League—and its first commissioner. In 1928 he played his last pro football game, which marked the end of his athletic career.

Those are the highlights. Contemporary observers also said that Thorpe was accomplished at swimming, wrestling, lacrosse, boxing, hockey, shooting, and handball; he even won a ballroom dancing title.[2] In 1950 sportswriters named him the greatest American athlete of the half century.[3] To look at photos of Thorpe in his prime is to see a body of such beauty and perfect proportion that it would have made Renaissance painters swoon.

Thorpe's American Indian name was Wa-Tho-Huk, meaning "Bright Path,"[4] but off the field, his journey was marked with shadows. One of the worst blows came in January 1913, when a Massachusetts newspaper revealed that he had played a few months of pro baseball in North Carolina in 1909.

To the Amateur Athletic Union (AAU), the matter was straightforward. Thorpe had earned money for playing a sport; therefore, he was a professional. Case closed. In this narrow sense, the facts are not in question. But there were extenuating circumstances. For a start, the sport was baseball, not track, and there is no evidence that Thorpe was thinking about the Olympics at the time. That is one reason he competed under his own name, not a pseudonym.

In addition, the legalities are murky. Under Olympic rules, any such objection was supposed to be lodged within 30 days of the close of the Games. Moreover, the Swedish Olympic Committee, which might have taken a softer view of the infraction, was supposed to make the decision. The court of appeal was never consulted. Ironically, the founder of the modern Games, Pierre de Coubertin, was not troubled by the apparent infraction of the tenets of amateurism: "Such a lot of blame for a peccadillo!"[5] The European press was also sympathetic. But the AAU wasn't, and its opinion sealed Thorpe's fate. At its behest, the International Olympic Committee stripped him of his gold medals.[6]

Thorpe was publicly stoic about the decision, but privately devastated. Many years later, one of his teammates with the Giants, fellow American Indian John "Chief" Meyers, recalled how Thorpe woke him up in the middle of the night, crying, "They're mine, Chief, I won them fair and square." The decision, Meyers concluded, "broke his heart."[7]

Beginning in the 1940s, there were efforts to reconsider the decision. By that time, though, the most committed apostle of the amateur creed, Avery Brundage, was in power. Brundage had also competed in Stockholm: He finished fifteenth in the decathlon and fifth in the pentathlon. Despite not winning a medal, the experience changed him. "Here was no commercial connivery or political chicanery," he recalled. "The rules were the same for everyone, respected by all, and enforced impartially."[8] For the rest of his life, Brundage would see the Olympics through these rose-colored perceptions.

A self-made man who built a successful construction business, Brundage's heart was in sport. Named to the International Olympic Committee (IOC) in 1936, he led it from 1952 to 1972, retiring at age 84. Brundage's views on amateurism were so exalted, and so rigid, that they curdled idealism into a legality that was simultaneously crabby and inconsistent. Somehow, he could overlook the obvious fact that Eastern-bloc athletes were full-time employees of the state. "I have yet to see any evidence that the Russians are not amateur," he declared in 1960.[9] But he was so bothered by the omnipresence of ski companies that he questioned whether the Winter Olympics should be held at all.[10] In 1972 he forced swimmer Mark Spitz, in the middle of his seven-gold performance, to write a groveling apology after he was photographed holding his Adidas shoes.[11]

Once Brundage was out of the picture, things began to move in Thorpe's favor. In 1973 the US Olympic Committee restored Thorpe's Olympic status and in 1981 the word "amateur" was struck from the Olympic charter, signaling a major change in official thinking. Eventually, this led to today's more open rules, in which athletic federations set the standards for participation—and most are happy to have professionals compete. In 1982 good sense and belated compassion prevailed, and the IOC voted to rehonor Thorpe's achievements, 29 years after his death. He is now recorded as cowinner of the events. The two medals in these pictures were struck from the original molds and sent to his family.

Members of the Thorpe family are fighting one last battle. After his death in 1953, Thorpe's third wife interrupted the Sac-and-Fox tribal burial rites and placed his body in a crypt. Then in 1954 she sold it to Mauch Chuck and East Mauch Chuck, in northeastern Pennsylvania. The two towns agreed to merge, rename the new municipality Jim Thorpe, and create a suitable final resting place for the athlete. The town has kept its word. The red granite mausoleum, set atop a knoll and flanked by statues of Thorpe at play, is attractive and dignified. But it still seems more than a little strange that Thorpe, in death, lies in a place where he never set foot in life. Some of his surviving children believe that his remains should rest in the land of his forbears in Oklahoma. In late 2015, however, the US Supreme Court refused to settle the matter,[12] so it looks like Jim Thorpe will stay in Jim Thorpe.

1913

FRANCIS OUIMET'S IRONS, BALL, AND SCORECARD FROM THE US OPEN

The story of the humble unknown who prevails against the odds is a cliché. In the pantheon of underdogs, though, the story of the 20-year-old amateur who beat two of the world's most dominant golfers—Britain's Harry Vardon and Ted Ray—to win the 1913 US Open continues to impress. Francis Ouimet came out of nowhere to win the country's most prestigious tourney and to change golf in America.

Born in 1893 across the street from The Country Club in Brookline, Massachusetts, Ouimet got his first club by trading in balls he collected from the course. He and his brother carved a primitive three-hole layout in a backlot, sinking tomato cans for cups.[1] He began caddying at age 11 and snuck onto The Country Club before dawn to practice. Over time, Ouimet built a consistent, all-purpose game.

Six weeks before the US Open in 1913, he had shown what he was capable of, shooting six birdies in a row down the stretch[2] to win his semifinal match in the Massachusetts Amateur. He went on to win that title and then performed brilliantly in a match-play loss at the US Amateur.

Those performances earned Ouimet a last-minute invitation to the US Open, basically as a token local; with The Country Club hosting the Open, no one was more local than young Francis. Golf officials didn't expect much. Neither did Ouimet, for that matter. Worried about missing work, he had to be coaxed to enter.

The tournament schedule called for four rounds over two days. After 54 holes, Oumet found himself tied with Vardon and Ray. An excellent performance, but no one thought he could sustain it. And he didn't. He shot a wretched 43 on the front nine, then doubled-bogeyed the tenth and bogeyed the twelfth. But Vardon and Ray had also faltered. As Ouimet stood on the thirteenth tee, he was only two strokes behind.

Assessing the situation, he realized that if he could birdie two holes and par the other five, he could tie the British pros. He got the first birdie on the thirteenth, chipping in from the edge of the green. Then he picked up a straightforward par on the fourteenth and a brilliant one on the fifteenth, getting up and down from a gnarly position in the rough. The sixteenth looked like birdie bait; it was a short par three that he had deuced dozens of times. Not today, though. He had to sink a tough nine-footer just to make par. Two holes left.

The seventeenth hole, a tricky 370-yard par four with a dogleg left, was the hole Ouimet knew best: he could see it from his bedroom window. A good drive and an excellent approach put him about 20 feet from the pin; if he made the putt, he would be tied. He stroked it home almost too vigorously; the ball fell into the hole, then popped up before settling down.[3] Watching from the perimeter, all but swamped by 5,000 cheering, gasping, incredulous spectators, Ted Ray analyzed the moment with precision: "That," he said, "was a great putt for America."[4]

On the eighteenth hole, Ouimet coolly sank a five-footer for par. The 20-year-old clerk/caddy had tied two of the world's best. An 18-hole playoff would determine the winner.

September 20 dawned miserably; gray skies and drizzle dampened the already wet grounds. Even so, a record 10,000 people turned out to watch.[5] At the turn, all three players were tied at 38. While the contest was close for several more holes, Ouimet never trailed after the tenth, beating Vardon by five and Ray by six. The seventeenth again played a crucial role. Only a stroke behind, Vardon decided to try to cut the corner of the dogleg on his tee shot; instead, he drove his ball into the front edge of a protective bunker. He ended up with a bogey. Ouimet drained an 18-footer for birdie. To this day, that patch of sand is known as "Vardon's Bunker." The eighteenth was a formality. Thus ended what golf sage Herbert Warren Wind called "the most momentous round in the history of golf."[6]

Ouimet's upset made golf front-page news. The *New York Tribune* called it "easily the most thrilling and spectacular event seen on a golf course in this country." And it made Francis Ouimet an exotic species: a golf hero. Self-confident but humble, gracious but competitive, this son of working-class immigrants[7] was a Horatio Alger hero with a driver.

The rulers of golf had shown little interest in promoting the game outside the narrow precincts of wealth and status they inhabited. Ouimet's victory changed that. In the decade following the 1913 Open, two million Americans began to play,[8] and hundreds of new courses were built, including such classics as Pebble Beach and Winged Foot. Ouimet's victory had a particular influence on a gifted 11-year-old in Atlanta. Reading about the final rounds, young Bobby Jones "began to feel that golf was a real game." Thenceforth, he took it more seriously (see the 1930 entry on him).[9]

Ouimet returned to win the US Amateur in 1914, but then, in one of the true travesties of sports administration, he was banned from amateur golf. His crime: investing his life savings in a sporting-goods store. This, the wealthy stewards of the game decreed, smacked of professionalism. Ouimet was not forgiven the sin of needing to earn a living until 1919.[10] When he was reinstated, he ran into Bobby Jones. Three times during the 1920s, the two would duel in the US Amateur. Jones won every time.

Still, Ouimet had his moments. He won a second US Amateur in 1931, the year after Jones retired, and was a Walker Cup stalwart. A favorite in Scotland for his sportsmanship and love for the game, in 1951 Ouimet became the first American to be elected Captain of the Royal and Ancient Golf Club of St. Andrews.

The 1913 US Open did not make American golf. The game had been advancing steadily for a dozen years; at the time, there were about 350,000 players, and a working infrastructure of courses, teaching, and competition. But Ouimet's victory pushed the game to another level, much faster than would have happened otherwise.

RADIO BROADCAST OF THE DEMPSEY-CARPENTIER FIGHT

As a fight, it wasn't much. As a spectacle, it was considerably more. And as a precedent, it was decisive, the beginning of the marriage between sports and broadcasting.

The event was the fight between heavyweight champ Jack Dempsey and the pride of France, Georges Carpentier, on July 2, 1921. Dempsey, known as the Manassa Mauler (after his Colorado hometown), had pummeled Jess Willard for the title in 1919, knocking him down seven times in the first round. Dark-haired, with deep-set eyes, Dempsey made his boxing bones in the mining camps of the West. He bobbed and weaved with deft subtlety; what made him famous, however, was his unrelenting ferocity. His left hook was devastating.

Carpentier had won European championships in four weight divisions before World War I; during the war he won the Croix de Guerre and the Medaille Militaire for his bravery in combat. There was also a certain je ne sais quoi about the Frenchman. The scribes of the era swooned at his blond tresses, his lean torso, his aquiline features, and his overall élan. "Michelangelo would have fainted for joy with the beauty of his profile,"[1] wrote one breathless *New York Evening World* reporter. Heywood Broun of the *New York Tribune* said he had "one of the most beautiful bodies the prize ring has ever seen." His nickname was the "Orchid Man," for the flower he wore in his lapel.[2]

Unfortunately he was only 172 pounds of perfect beauty, compared to Dempsey's 188. Moreover, Dempsey had a better record against stronger competition. Even rumors that the Frenchman's manager could cast hypnotic spells did not sway the judgment of the cold-eyed pros: Carpentier, they said, didn't have a chance.

That was a conviction fight promoter Tex Rickard shared, but quietly. To make the kind of money he had in mind, people needed to believe the war hero with the fabulous legs had a chance. One strategy was to create a good versus evil story line. Dempsey wore the black hat. Accused (and acquitted) of draft dodging, the faint whiff of cowardice clung to him. No one ever compared him to a Greek god.

The bout became one of those events that caught the spirit of the time. Leasing an empty lot in Jersey City known as Boyle's Thirty Acres, Rickard built a ring and temporary stands for 50,000 people. As the hoopla grew, he added more. Eventually, there was room for more than 90,000 people—the largest audience to ever witness a sporting event in person to that time[3]—with seats costing from $5 to $50.[4] The event brought in almost $1.8 million.[5] Ringside seats were filled with names like Astor, Ford, Guggenheim, Fairbanks, Rockefeller, Roosevelt, and Vanderbilt. Forevermore, boxing would mix seamlessly with high society and show biz.[6]

France was also caught up in the spirit. Six military planes were deployed to fly over Paris. When the results were relayed via the telegraph, they would flash red lights for a Carpentier victory, white for Dempsey. Carpentier was Europe's finest fighter. But still—this was the Manassa Mauler versus the Orchid Man.

Rickard had no doubts, murmuring to Dempsey, "Don't kill the son of a bitch." He didn't, but left no doubt about who the superior fighter was. He broke Carpentier's nose in the first round. Carpentier got in a good blow in the second but broke his hand in the process. (Dempsey professed not even to remember the swat.) In the fourth round, Dempsey decided enough was enough. He knocked Carpentier down. The Frenchman stayed down for a nine count, bounced up, then caught Dempsey's right fist with his chin. There was no getting up this time.[7]

So that was that, a fairly routine Dempsey pummeling. But what made this match historic was the audience. It was not just 90,000 people in Jersey City. Less than a year after the first commercial radio station began broadcasting, a ringside, round-by-round account of the fight could be heard in real time over the radio, like this Westinghouse Aeriola Senior shown opposite. The Battle of Boyle's Thirty Acres was the first time a sporting event had been widely broadcast. Listeners tuned in as far away as Vermont.[8]

All told, *Wireless Age* magazine estimated that some 300,000 people heard the fight, some in theaters and other public places, some at home. It's difficult even now to estimate audiences, so the 300,000 figure can only be regarded as a guess, no doubt on the high side. But it was certainly the biggest radio audience to that date.

Other sports took notice. Tennis had its first on-air moment a little over a month later,[9] and in 1922 broadcasters called their first live World Series.[10] This Westinghouse radio cost $65 in 1921,[11] the equivalent of $861 in 2015 dollars. At the time, radio was still a boutique technology. But that would change fast, as costs fell and coverage improved. By 1927, when Dempsey fought Gene Tunney in a bid to retake his title in the fight famous for the "long count," some 60 million Americans could listen in.[12]

THE MODERN FOOTBALL

To see the pigskin hurled down the field to a streaking receiver is one of the thrills of sports. It was also impossible for decades. Not because the athletes weren't good enough, but because the ball wasn't. The early footballs were round rather than spherical and therefore difficult to throw far. The early game was ground-and-pound; teams sometimes punted on first down just to establish field position. In addition, the rubber bladder inside the ball would deflate under the stress of the game, making its already nonaerodynamic shape even worse; play would be stopped to fill it with air.

The forward pass wasn't even legal until 1906, when rule makers unveiled a slate of reforms to reduce fatalities. Gang tackling was outlawed, and the yardage necessary for a first down was increased from five to ten yards. The Carlisle Indian School, coached by Pop Warner, soon showed the potential of passing. In 1907 the team completed eight passes, including one to a first-year player named Jim Thorpe (see the 1912 entry), to beat and befuddle a previously unscored-upon Penn, 26–6.[1] On the second play of the game, end William Gardner caught a 40-yard heave on a dead run. "It was," argues sportswriter Sally Jenkins, "the sporting equivalent of the Wright brothers taking off at Kitty Hawk."[2]

Even so, few teams were about to change how they played just because Carlisle had showed them a better way.[3] The regulations about the pass were punitive; an incompletion meant loss of possession of the ball. So its use was still limited. Over the next few years, however, rules evolved to favor the pass. In 1912 it became legal to catch the ball in the end zone. Three years later the points awarded for a field goal dropped from four to three, and for a touchdown rose from five to six.[4] An incompletion now led only to a loss of down, and a fourth down was added.[5]

In a higher-profile game, on November 1, 1913, Notre Dame's Fighting Irish beat a powerhouse Army team that included Dwight Eisenhower and Omar Bradley, 35–13. Passes featured in all the scoring,[6] including a 25-yarder to senior end Knute Rockne.[7]

That was the first time the obscure Indiana school had made a splash in the game's eastern heartland, and Notre Dame's exploits woke people up to the possibilities of the new rules. "Football men," reported the *New York Times* the following day, "marveled at this startling display of open football."[8] Rockne would always credit Pop Warner and others as the true innovators,[9] but the victory of the Fighting Irish caught people's attention. Over the next decade the forward pass became integrated into the game; still, it was deployed more to keep defenses on their toes than as a sustained offensive strategy. Few quarterbacks could throw the watermelon-shaped[10] football well, particularly for long yardage.

Finally, technology and design caught up to the action on the field, in the shape of the Wilson KR. In 1925 Wilson developed the football in the picture above in consultation with Rockne (hence the KR). The ends were discernibly more tapered,[11] and because it had an interior valve, it did not have the lumpy exterior stem that hampered handling.[12] The double-lined, internal bladder ensured that the ball kept its shape. These qualities improved the ball's aerodynamics, making it possible for athletes less gifted than those at Carlisle to throw wobble-free spirals. In effect, the Wilson KR took the "foot" out of football; the kicking game became a sideshow rather than the main event.

The Wilson KR became the official ball of college football, and the passing game came into its own. The ball continued to be refined, until it eventually reached its current shape, known as a prolate spheroid. In addition, rule changes over the years have gone in the direction of protecting the passer and giving receivers more room to maneuver. The result is the aerial display that rules the game today.

TAD LUCAS'S RIDING BOOTS

Tad Lucas picked up where Annie Oakley (see 1910 entry) left off. She was tiny, a fraction over five feet tall, and had the charisma of the born performer. But Lucas's tool of choice was the horse, not the gun. During the golden age of rodeo in the 1920s and 1930s, she was the unquestioned first lady of the sport.

Born Barbara Inez Barnes in 1902 to a ranching family in western Nebraska, Lucas was breaking colts and riding calves by the time she was seven. By age 15 she was performing professional rodeo, and at 20 she was doing it full time, sometimes competing against men. She toured all over the United States and Mexico and also appeared in London and Sydney. Lucas was an accomplished bronc rider, relay racer, and snappy dresser ("best dressed" was an award category then and sometimes now). But she really made her name as a trick rider, winning the event eight straight times at the Cheyenne Frontier Days.[1]

The red leather boots shown here were made specifically for trick riding, and Lucas used them for years. The heels are flat, making it easier to stand in the saddle, and the rubber vamps are flexible to enable her to move in and out of the stirrups.

Her success was unmatched. Lucas won the all-around cowgirl championship at Madison Square Garden six times in seven years (the other year she was pregnant)[2] and every major rodeo at least once. In the teeth of the Great Depression, she earned more than $10,000 a year.[3]

When the rodeo circuit dropped women's events in the 1940s, Lucas continued to perform in trick-riding exhibitions. She would vault into the saddle, then go on to the "Cossack drag"—learned from an actual Cossack family she had befriended at a Wild

West show—in which she would keep one foot in a stirrup, then hang upside down along the flank of the horse, trailing her fingers in the dirt. She would conclude by standing on the saddle, arms raised in farewell.

Lucas was one of the founders of the Girls' Rodeo Association in 1948 to promote all-female rodeos. The GRA had seventy-four members at the start; now known as the Women's Professional Rodeo Association, it has about 2,500,[4] and the best can earn more than $300,000 a year.[5]

STATISTICS FROM RED GRANGE'S NFL DEBUT

The numbers on the scorecard for this Thanksgiving Day game—6 first downs, 29 punts, 4 completions, zero points—describe a dull contest. Even so, this was one of the most important games in National Football League history, because it was the first time Harold "Red" Grange took the field as a pro.[1] The NFL had much to be thankful for.

Nicknamed the "Galloping Ghost" for his elusive running style, Grange was a legend at the University of Illinois at a time when the college game ruled. His greatest performance took place when he was a junior, against Michigan on October 18, 1924. On the opening kickoff, Grange started up the middle, broke right, and cut back across the field and into the end zone 95 yards away.[2] Then he made touchdown runs of 67, 56, and 45 yards. In the first 12 minutes, Grange scored as many touchdowns as the Wolverines had given up in their previous 20 games.[3] Widely broadcast over radio and featured on newsreels, the game made Grange a national phenomenon. He joined the golden-age pantheon of sports stars, along with Ruth, Dempsey, Tilden, and Jones.

Two days after his last college game in 1925, Grange dropped out of college (he was well short of a degree)[4] and signed with the NFL. The decision was controversial. To call the NFL fledgling[5] in 1925 would be generous. Conceived in a car showroom in Canton, Ohio, five years earlier, the professional game was considered déclassé and more than a little disreputable, played by and for a rough element. Attendance ranged from a few hundred to a few thousand per game. "I'd have been more popular with the colleges," Grange later said, "if I had joined Capone's mob in Chicago."[6] His Illinois coach was so furious at his decision that the two didn't speak for years.[7]

Part of the credit for getting Grange to the NFL altar goes to C. C. "Cash and Carry" Pyle, one of the first sports agents (see the 1926 entry on Helen Wills). The rest goes to George Halas, owner/coach/trainer/publicist of the Chicago Bears. A fellow Illinois alum, Halas thought Grange could take the NFL to the next level. He and Pyle negotiated a per-game salary (for at least 30 minutes of play) for Grange, plus half the gate.[8] Grange made more money in 1925 than everyone he played against—combined. He was worth every cent.

The Ghost's first game against the Chicago Cardinals drew 36,000 people; legend has it that Halas wept as he counted the receipts.[9] The Bears played one more game that season, then embarked on a two-part, coast-to-coast tour over 66 days. The highlight was a game played before a record 70,000 people in the Polo Grounds that saved the New York Giants franchise from going under. "For the first time," Halas wrote, pro football "took on true national stature."[10] As for Grange, he made more than $100,000. Off-field earnings—a doll, a brand of ginger ale, movies, sporting goods, an outboard motor, even a meatloaf[11]—boosted that figure nicely.[12]

It was not all glory; when Grange played poorly in Boston near the end of the first part of the tour, the crowd let him have it.[13] At one point he played 10 games in 17 days. Still, the modest ice-hauler from Wheaton, Illinois, enjoyed the money and didn't mind the fame. Sixty years later he recalled, "After I became a pro, if something I ordered didn't cost $20, I didn't want it."[14]

Not everyone got caught up in the glow of Grange's burgeoning celebrity. When Grange and Halas were introduced to Calvin Coolidge as being with the Chicago Bears, the president replied politely, "Glad to meet you fellows. I've always enjoyed animal acts."[15]

A financial dispute kept Grange out of the NFL the following year; he and Pyle started a rival league that folded after one season. He rejoined the Bears, but after tearing a knee ligament in 1927, he was a ghost of his former galloping self, probably better on defense than with the ball. His greatest moment as a pro came in 1933, when he saved the first NFL title game with a last-second tackle. He retired the next year.

Red Grange did not make the NFL on his own. What he did was hasten the sport's acceptance by introducing it to hundreds of thousands of Americans and pushing it onto the sports pages. His prime was short—but it was transcendent.

1926

HELEN WILLS'S LEATHER TRAVEL BAG

Before a boxing match at Madison Square Garden on February 15, 1926, the crowd bowed their heads for a moment of silence. They were being asked to send good thoughts over the ocean to Helen Wills, the 20-year-old American tennis star who would be playing the match of her life the next morning against France's Suzanne Lenglen.[1] Wills had been traveling the Riviera for weeks, lugging this bag and a dozen rackets, in the hope of playing Lenglen.

Now she would.

The consensus was that Wills would need all the positive thinking she could get. Lenglen had dominated tennis for years, and at 26 she was at her peak. Her breakthrough came in 1919, when she saved two match points to win a thrilling three-set Wimbledon final against Dorothea Douglass Chambers, 10–8, 4–6, 9–7. It was a passing of the generations. Chambers, a 40-year-old mother and seven-time champion, played in traditional attire: ankle-length skirt and long-sleeved buttoned-up top, with her long hair piled up.[2] The bob-haired Lenglen looked practically naked by tennis standards, wearing a knee-length skirt and a loose, sleeveless blouse. If Lenglen had done nothing else, she would have done a great deal by liberating sportswomen from the fashion police.

Her style went well beyond her apparel. Lenglen was known to sip cognac and brandy between sets, and she favored an aesthetic of play that drew on the ballet. To imagine Lenglen is to see her in flight, her silk skirt swirling to form an abstract pattern—and then she would cream the ball. Lenglen played with a power and aggression never seen from a woman before. She treated all of tennis with imperious charm, and with occasional bolts of temper. Think of "Suzanne Lenglen" as French for diva, and that gets the idea across.

She got away with it because she was so good. From 1919 to 1926, Lenglen went 269–1 and lost just two sets.[3] She never lost a singles match at Wimbledon,[4] which she won six times. Even the male-dominated sports press couldn't help but notice. Lenglen became the first internationally celebrated female athlete; in her prime, she might have been the most famous athlete in the world.[5]

Six thousand miles away, Helen Wills of California was building her own reputation. She won the US national championship in 1922, 1924, and 1925 and made the finals of Wimbledon in 1924. Unlike Lenglen, the drama queen, Wills was stoic on the court. Like Lenglen, she was fiercely competitive, dismissive of other players, and determined to be regarded as number 1.

She and Lenglen were by far the world's best female tennis players, and when Wills decided to play the Riviera circuit in 1926, everyone looked forward to watching them play each other. But Lenglen played hard to get. The two women were rarely in the same place at the same time. With little other sporting action, a large number of sportswriters had the hellish duty of following Wills all over the Riviera. So the suspense grew.

By the time the two made their way to the final at the Carlton Club in Cannes, the match had become a full-blown sensation. Newspapers all over the world sent reporters; in California, where the match began at 2:00 a.m., there were all-night parties to listen to it.[6] For the first time, a contest featuring women was top of the sports news.

Perhaps no match could have lived up to the hoopla, but this was an excellent one. Lenglen won 6–3, 8–6, her closest match in years, and the level of play was impressive.[7] This mattered. A sluggish, error-filled contest would have brought scorn on women's tennis, which didn't get much respect. The little coverage there was tended to emphasize the players' looks or clothes.

Helen Wills and Suzanne Lenglen were both beyond that. Individually and together, their game was so good that they were impossible to patronize. They may have been the first women to command respect as athletes. Six months after their match in Cannes, though, another emerged; Gertrude Ederle was the first woman to swim the English Channel, besting the men's mark by two hours. She came home to ticker-tape parades. These breakthroughs didn't earn women's sports consistent attention, but at least they began to get a little.

Wills credited Lenglen with being the better player on the day, which was true.[8] But it was also true she had given the French goddess all she could handle. Many a knowledgeable spectator—including, perhaps, Lenglen—saw the younger American as a real threat to her hegemony. Jean Borotra, one of the famous "four musketeers" of French tennis, called it "a heartbreaking victory"[9] for Lenglen.

The two never played each other again. Wills missed action for a few months due to medical issues, and then Lenglen turned professional. Under the rules of the era, not only did that bar her from all the national championships, but amateurs like Wills could not even play against her.

Wills picked up right where Lenglen left off. From 1927 until mid-1933, she didn't lose a set. While the press praised Wills for her girl-next-door looks, her peers saw something else. "I regard her as the coldest, most self-centered, most ruthless champion ever known to tennis," her fellow champion, Bill Tilden, remarked (see the 1930 entry on him).[10] Wills might have been pleased with the description. While lacking Lenglen's flamboyance, the economy of her style had its own appeal; Charlie Chaplin would say that the most beautiful thing he ever saw was "the movement of Helen Wills playing tennis."[11] By the time Wills concluded her career, she had won 19 singles majors (in 22 attempts), including eight at Wimbledon, a record that lasted until Martina Navratilova won her ninth in 1990.

Wills called the match against Lenglen the most important of her career because it showed her a level of play to which she could aspire.[12] Not that she was going to emote over it. "No tennis match," she wrote, "deserved the attention which this one received."[13]

AMELIA EARHART'S GOGGLES

In the years immediately before and after Charles Lindbergh's 1927 transatlantic crossing, flying was a sport and entertainment, as well as a form of transportation. Americans flocked to air shows to gawk at the sight of wing-walkers and loop-the-loops. Aviators were local heroes and national celebrities.

Among them were more than a few women. Just as they had done with the bicycle, women seized the chance to fly before it could be forbidden to them. Pancho Barnes, Jacqueline Cochran, Bessie Coleman, Ruth Elder, Amy Johnson, Anne Morrow Lindbergh, Beryl Markham, Ruth Nichols, and Phoebe Omlie all wrote excellence in the sky. In 1928 Elinor Smith showed the kind of audacity pilots of all kinds appreciate, flying under four New York City bridges. She was 17.[1] To be an aviatrix was considered the epitome of cool, modern womanhood—and Amelia Earhart was the most famous of this elite corps.

In 1929 air racing was a full-fledged sport, with big crowds, rules, and regular newspaper coverage. It was also for men only. Some of the more imaginative aviation leaders recognized that a women's race could bolster public confidence. If the weaker sex could negotiate thousands of miles all by themselves, that would be an excellent advertisement for the industry. The women pilots loved the idea of testing themselves—and perhaps taking home as much as $3,600 in prize money.

That August, before 20,000 spectators, 19 women took off in the National Women's Air Derby, a race from Santa Monica to Cleveland, with overnight stops along the way. Will Rogers called it the "Powder Puff Derby."[2] But the powder-puffs, Earhart among them, put women's aviation on the front pages of newspapers all over the country for nine days. Not all the news was good: one pilot died, probably from carbon monoxide poisoning;[3] another ventured into Mexico. One plane was totaled.

Critics cited these events as proof that women should not fly. But they didn't have much of a case. One competitor put out a midair fire, then calmly landed her plane,

proving that she certainly had the right stuff. Sixteen planes finished, a higher percentage than any similar race among men.[4] Earhart finished third. She wore these goggles at the start of the race; they were lifted from her plane at an early stop.[5]

In the years after the Derby, Earhart set an altitude record, in 1931; became the first woman (and second person) to cross the Atlantic solo, in 1932; and was the first to fly solo from Hawaii to California.[6] By 1935, women were competing against men on equal terms in some air races. Earhart was the first to do so, finishing fifth in a cross-country event.

Flying was high risk. The death rate for pilots was high, and engines conked out in midair on an alarmingly regular basis. So Earhart knew the danger when she and her navigator, Fred Noonan, prepared for a west-to-east, around-the-world journey. The hazards multiplied in the vast expanse of the central Pacific, where they had to navigate from speck to speck. With three-quarters of the flight behind them, on July 2, 1937, they disappeared, leaving behind a haunting mystery: What happened?

Before she left on her final journey, Earhart wrote to her husband, George Putnam: "Women must try to do things as men have tried. When they fail, their failure must be but a challenge to others." Her life, and death, bore witness to those words.

1930

BILL TILDEN'S TENNIS RACKET

Great athletes are a joy to behold, carrying with them a sense of destiny that makes people want to participate, if only by watching. The first man to bring that spirit to American tennis was Bill Tilden.

From 1920 through 1925, he competed in eight Grand Slam tournaments and won them all.[1] He also led the United States to seven Davis Cups, from 1920 to 1926.[2] In 1924 he won 95 straight matches.[3] He was the first man to win 10 Grand Slams.

Tilden was a late bloomer; at college, he failed to make the team. But he steadily built his game. By 1918, at age 25, he had reached the finals at Forest Hills, and he did so again in 1919. He spent that winter refining his backhand drive and studying the game with the analytic intensity of a Talmudic scholar, a scientist, or an artist.

Tilden would have appreciated the analogies. He saw tennis as many people see religion: something that gave meaning to his life. He brought his considerable intellect to bear on teasing out the intricacies of the game. His 1925 book, *Match Play and the Spin of the Ball*, was a great leap forward in terms of sophisticated analysis; future tennis greats Jack Kramer and John Newcombe swore by it.[4] And he brought an artistry and showmanship to men's tennis that had never been seen before.

In a sense, "Bill Tilden" is American for "Suzanne Lenglen" (see 1926 entry). Both had temperament, style, and charisma in buckets. Both made fortunes, and lost opportunities, by going pro. Both had arrogance leavened with charm. Both were adored for their play, but alone in life. Both could be imperious on the court; Tilden's glare was legendary. Lenglen attracted royalty and decayed aristocrats; Tilden attracted Hollywood. Naturally, they detested each other.

Most important, both lifted their sport to new heights on the basis of otherworldly play and blazing personality. Lenglen drew so many fans to the cozy little grounds on Worple Street that the All-England Club created a new facility down the road in Wimbledon.[5] Tilden did the same in New York, leading the West Side Tennis Club to build the Forest Hills complex, which would host the American championships until 1978.[6] In spite of his WASPy Main Line Philadelphia roots, Tilden made people see tennis as a sport that demanded mental and physical excellence, not as a genteel pastime for rich dilettantes.

Tilden used this racket below at his last Wimbledon triumph in 1930, at age 37. He is still its oldest champion.[7] The victory came almost exactly a decade after he won his first, and over those 10 years, Tilden stamped his game and his personality on the sport.

At the end of 1930, he turned professional. Well into his forties and fifties, he was capable of taking sets off the likes of Don Budge and Bobby Riggs in their prime.[8] Tilden made a good deal of money after he turned professional; one estimate is $500,000 in the first six years.[9] It disappeared in good living, greedy friends, legal woes, and bad stage plays. As his competitive career wound down, he turned to giving lessons, including to the likes of Charlie Chaplin and Douglas Fairbanks.[10]

But when he died of a coronary in a small walk-up apartment in Hollywood in 1953 at age 60, poor financial management and scandal had left him just about destitute.[11] What he left behind—besides the few trophies he had not yet pawned—was a reputation as the greatest player of his time. In 1950 an Associated Press poll of sportswriters named him the greatest tennis player of the first half century, and the vote wasn't close. Don Budge, the next American to dominate the sport, put it simply. Big Bill Tilden, he said, was "the only genius tennis has produced."[12]

1930

BOBBY JONES'S PUTTER, CALAMITY JANE

Probably the most famous club in the history of golf, Calamity Jane helped Bobby Jones complete the game's only Grand Slam.

Today, the Slam refers to the British and US Opens, the PGA, and the Masters. In 1930 it meant the British and US Opens and the British and US Amateurs. The latter two, by definition, were restricted to nonprofessionals, so the fields were not as strong. Because of this, Ben Hogan's three major wins in 1953 and Tiger Woods's four in a row in 2000–2001 might well be considered greater accomplishments.

But that does not diminish what Jones did. He set out to win the four biggest events on the golf calendar. He did it—and then quit, at age 28. He had achieved all he could in golf, Jones said, and competing took too much out of him. So he retired to his life in Atlanta as a husband, father, lawyer, mentor, and founder of Augusta National, the home of the Masters.

Jones first came to national attention in 1916 as the 14-year-old "Dixie Wonder" who won two matches at the US Amateur at Merion. If there was a prize for the category, he might also have won for most clubs thrown. But for the next six-plus years, he never won on the biggest stages. The low point came in 1921, when he was playing poorly in the third round at the British Open—and quit. Though he later finished the round, he would be forever ashamed of himself for that lapse, which he considered an insult to the game.[1]

Jones broke through in 1923, when he won the US Open. It didn't come easily; he blew a lead in the fourth round. Jones was distraught, keening that he had played "like a yellow dog." Francis Ouimet (see the 1913 entry), who had taken a fraternal interest in the decade-younger man, consoled him, took him out to dinner, sang to him, and all but tucked him into bed.

The next day, Jones won on the final hole of the 18-hole playoff.

Confident now that he had both the mental and physical qualities to excel, from then through 1930 Jones won five US Amateurs, four US Opens, three British Opens, and a British Amateur. Over that period, he contested 21 majors and won 13 of them. No one has ever come close to that kind of dominance. In 1926, when Jones became the first man to win the US and British Opens in the same year, he got a ticker-tape parade down Broadway. In 1930, when he became the first man to win both the British Open and Amateur in the same year, he got another. He is still the only person to be thus honored twice.

He also became known as a great sportsman; his example did much to establish the high standard of behavior that continues to be a welcome feature of the game. In the 1925 US Amateur, for example, he called a one-shot penalty on himself when his ball moved as he addressed it. He later lost in a playoff. He accepted no praise for his act: "You might as well praise me for not robbing a bank."[2] The British golf writer, Bernard Darwin (grandson of Charles), was not known to gush. But he said of Jones, "Even the golf ball cannot help but like him."[3]

About 33 inches long, with eight degrees of loft and a hickory shaft, the putter pictured here is the second Calamity Jane. The face on the first Calamity, which was battered and might have been 20 years old when Jones bought it in Scotland in 1923, eventually wore out.[4] He replaced it with this one in 1926.

During his march to the Slam in 1930, Calamity Jane II served Jones well. At the British Amateur, for example, a match-play tournament that comprised the first side of the quadrilateral, he used it to drain a nasty eight-foot uphill putt on the famous Road Hole, number 17. In the semifinal, he had to do the same—this time an 18-footer to stay even. He won the match on the next hole, and the tournament shortly after.[5] At the US Open at Interlachen, he used Calamity Jane to drop a 40-footer on the eighteenth; that gave him a two-shot cushion.

Bobby Jones not only recorded the only Grand Slam in golf history, but when he retired, he closed the door on an era when amateurs routinely competed with the pros. John Goodman would win the US Open in 1933, but no amateur has taken a major since. In part because of the visibility Jones brought to the game, more men could make a living as touring pros—something that Walter Hagen had become the first to do only in 1919. Jones was also one of the last competitive players to use hickory-shafted clubs.[6] His Slam, then, ended an era in several ways.

Even after Jones retired from competition, he stayed connected to the game. He made a small fortune starring in a series of sometimes corny, sometimes funny, always instructive short films, *How I Play Golf*, teaching Hollywood stars like W. C. Fields and James Cagney.[7] He worked with Spalding to design a set of mass-market irons. He also consulted with the Works Progress Administration during the Great Depression to build and repair some 600 golf courses.[8] He could have played golf exhibitions during World War II; instead, he insisted on active duty, and landed on Normandy shortly after D-Day.[9] In 1950 a sportswriters' poll named the 1930 Slam the most notable sports achievement of the half century.[10]

By that time Jones had been unwell for years. In 1956 he was diagnosed with a rare and painful degenerative spinal disease, syringomyelia. It turned his hands into claws and confined him to a wheelchair, and eventually his bed. By the time he died in December 1971, his once-magnificent physique was down to 90 pounds. When the birthplace of golf, St. Andrews, got the news of his death, play stopped in honor of the man Scotland had grown to love as "our Bobby."

1932

BABE DIDRIKSON'S UNIFORM

Mildred "Babe" Didrikson was the finest female athlete of the first half of the twentieth century and one of the best ever, male or female. A first-class competitor in three sports—basketball, track-and-field, and golf—she probably could have added more to that list if she had tried. Part of the reason for her wide-ranging excellence, it has to be said, is that the competition was thin. But mostly she was just brilliant.

The daughter of Norwegian immigrants, young Mildred grew up in Beaumont, Texas, surrounded by boys and oil rigs. After hitting five home runs in a sandlot game, she became known locally as "Babe," a nickname she embraced.[1] At an early age, she knew she wanted to be a professional athlete. The problem with that ambition was that there was no such thing for women.

Other than high school basketball, softball teams, and athletic clubs, girls and women who wanted to play sports didn't have many options. One reason for this was general disdain for the idea of women competing against each other. But another, surprisingly, was that much of the women's sports establishment agreed. The biggest objection was medical. Tennis, swimming, and golf, in mild doses, were acceptable. Maybe archery. But strenuous exercise, many authorities asserted, would weaken women and quite possibly displace their uteruses or otherwise jeopardize their reproductive capacity.[2] Plus, it just wasn't nice for females to sweat and grunt and do all the things they needed to do to become good athletes.

The International Olympic Committee, which could usually be relied on to be small-minded, wasn't entirely so in this regard. Having banned women from track-and-field since the founding of the modern games in 1896, the IOC was startled when an enterprising Frenchwoman, Alice Milliat, drew enthusiastic crowds to the Women's World Games in 1922 and 1926, which featured a dozen track-and-field events. The international athletes performed well, setting numerous world records.

Not willing to see its athletic monopoly eroded, the IOC agreed to add 10 women's track-and-field events to the 1928 Olympics. (Then it reneged, and offered only five—a breach of faith that so infuriated the British that they refused to send a women's team.)[3] America's female sports establishment, the Women's Division of the National Amateur Athletic Federation, was disgusted at the "sacrifice of our school girls on the altar of an Olympic spectacle."[4] The Women's Division would later campaign against *any* women's participation in the Olympics. The group lost that battle, but did manage to banish a great deal of women's intercollegiate athletic competition in the 1920s in favor of intramurals and insipid "play days." One does wonder what the good ladies of the Women's Division were thinking. After all, millions of American women endured endless hours in farms and factories—labor considerably more taxing than, say, throwing a javelin.

Didrikson was probably unaware of all this byplay; Beaumont was several worlds away from the rarefied air of women's sports politics. Instead, she found her way to the industrial leagues, in which company-sponsored teams played unapologetically competitive sports. These leagues were particularly popular in the South and Midwest. In 1930 the Employers' Casualty Insurance Company of Dallas hired Didrikson, then 19, mostly to play basketball for the Golden Cyclones (the firm specialized in cyclone insurance). Dressed in sleeveless tops and satin shorts,[5] the team drew up to 4,000 spectators to their games. She was an all-American in 1930–1932 and led the team to the national championship in 1931. The company also started a track program, and Didrikson took up the sport with characteristic enthusiasm, training in event after event.

Track was a good fit for Didrikson, whose ego was as prodigious as her talent. She was an accomplished trash talker, with a line of Texas crude that could startle even the grizzled male sportswriters who would later chronicle her career. At this point, however, she was relatively unknown. That would change forever at the Amateur Athletic Association national meet in 1932, which also served as the Olympic qualifying meet. Employers' Casualty had entered a team of one, Babe Didrikson. Wearing the uniform shown opposite, she entered eight events, won five, tied for first in another, set three world records—and won the team standings easily, all by herself.

At the Los Angeles Olympics, she could only contest three events; women couldn't stand any more strain than that, the IOC had decided. One reason for this protective attitude was the 800-meter final at the Amsterdam Games in 1928. One eyewitness reported that "knocked out and hysterical females were floundering all over the place"[6] at the end of the race. Another reported seeing "11 wretched women, five of whom dropped out before the finish, while five collapsed after reaching the tape."[7]

Film of the race, however, shows nothing of the kind. Of the nine runners (not eleven), eight finished; one tripped near the end. There was no flopping or floundering. Three runners broke the world record. "The sensational descriptions are much exaggerated I can assure you," noted Harold Abrahams, the 100-meter winner in 1924 (of *Chariots of Fire* fame).[8] No matter. The mass collapses of 1928 became conventional wisdom; the 800-meter race was not restored to women until 1960.

So Didrikson entered the 80-meter hurdles, the javelin, and the high jump—a curious combination of events that shows her remarkable athletic range. She won the first two, setting two more world records, and came in second in the high jump, though she also broke the world record in that. (The judges ruled that Didrikson had violated jumping technique; perhaps they, too, wanted to take the braggart down a peg.) Nevertheless, she was the breakout star of the Olympics, crowned as such by no less than famous sportswriter Grantland Rice, who dubbed her "the most flawless section of muscle harmony, of complete mental and physical coordination the world has ever known."[9]

To make a living, Didrikson turned to exhibitions and vaudeville, sometimes running on a treadmill to show her speed; she also played a mean harmonica. She toured with the semi-pro House of David baseball team, whose shtick was that they all had beards. It was pretty small-time, but it paid the bills, while keeping her in the public eye.[10] And she began to play golf.

Golf may be the sport that least rewards the natural athlete; raw ability will only get a player so far. Didrikson's golf education began in earnest in 1935, when she went on an exhibition tour with Gene Sarazen, then the top male pro. She pleased the crowds by booming her drives farther than any woman they had ever seen; more important, she soaked up Sarazen's golfing wisdom. And she practiced—more than anyone, said Sarazen, except maybe Ben Hogan. But she was still stuck. There was no pro tour, and she wasn't allowed to compete as an amateur because she had already made money from golf (and other sports).

Marriage in 1938 to George Zaharias, a handsome and rich professional wrestler, provided some breathing space. By sitting out paid golf for a while, she could reclaim her amateur status, which she did in 1943. That gave her access to the most prestigious tournaments. After the war, she began to win—and win and win. In 1946–1947, she won 17 of 18 tournaments.[11] Perhaps her favorite was in 1947, when she became the first American to win the British Women's Amateur, held in Scotland. Something about the brash Texan appealed to the Scots, and when she did a Highland fling after the last round, they were entirely won over.

Didrikson went on to become one of the founders of the Ladies Professional Golf Association in 1948, and for a while, her star power was the only thing that kept it going.[12] As the tour grew, she made more money than friends, an inevitable consequence of her voluble arrogance.

But the public loved her. She would banter with spectators between shots, and in her broadest Texas drawl say things like "I couldn't hit an elephant's ass with a bull fiddle today."[13] Asked how she managed to drive the ball so far, her much-repeated response was: "I just loosen my girdle and let 'er fly!"[14]

Her success couldn't last forever, but it ended horribly. In 1953 Didrikson was diagnosed with colon cancer. Showing a courage and determination that left even her detractors awed, she won the US Women's Open in 1954 by the record margin of 12 strokes—while wearing a colostomy bag under her skirt. But she couldn't lick cancer. It came back in 1955, and she never played again. She died the following September.

Babe Didrikson might not have been the greatest golfer of her era—a good case can be made for Britain's Joyce Wethered. And Glenna Collett-Vare, an American whose heyday was in the 1920s, was more dominant than Didrikson for longer.[15] Nor was she the first great multisport female athlete. In the early twentieth century, Eleanora Sears, a daughter of Boston privilege and a direct descendant of Thomas Jefferson, played good tennis and was an excellent horsewoman; she was also a race-walker and a squash player. In a unique double, Mary K. Browne reached the semifinals of the US Amateur in both tennis and golf in 1924; she lost to Helen Wills in the tennis and Glenna Collett in the golf. Ora Washington was an eight-time singles winner of the American Tennis Association's national tournament for African American tennis players; she was also a spectacular basketball player whose team, the Philadelphia Tribune, lost only a handful of games in 18 years.[16]

Didrikson was gifted, funny, and arrogant. What she wasn't, was a role model. Many women looked at her muscles and chiseled features and saw a living stereotype of all the awful things sports could do to the female form. Men didn't like that she was so much better at sports than most of them would ever be. One male pundit quipped that Didrikson played sports because "she cannot compete with other girls in the very ancient and honored sport of man-trapping."[17]

The fact that Didrikson was decidedly out of the mainstream meant that her feats did little to draw more women into sports or to change the negative perceptions of athletic women. In 1953 the IOC even considered eliminating all women's events.[18] The evolution in attitudes, women's among them, toward talented sportswomen, would take decades. What Babe Didrikson did, however, was important. She forced people to recognize that women could be great athletes. And she had a whale of a time doing it.

1932

BABE RUTH'S "CALLED SHOT" BAT

It was a legendary moment in a legendary career.

In the fifth inning of the third game of the 1932 World Series against the Chicago Cubs, the score was tied 4–4; the Yankees were up two games to none. The Chicago bench was riding Ruth hard, and the fans had joined in. Two had thrown lemons at him, and a whole bunch had laughed a little too hard when a fly ball skipped past him for two bases.[1] Ruth tipped his hat after the miscue. But the fans had also been rude to his wife, Claire, and the insults might have been getting to him. At age 37, Ruth could still turn anger into pulverizing action. During the regular season, he had hit 41 home runs, batted in 133, and hit .341.

Another lemon rolled to his feet, as Ruth clutched his bat near the knob, his feet close together. He took strike one from pitcher Charlie Root, then waved his hand in the general direction of center field. He watched two balls go by. After a called strike two, he repeated the gesture. Root threw his fifth pitch, a curveball that didn't curve—and Babe clouted it well beyond the center field fence for his fifteenth (and last) World Series home run. He dropped the bat shown opposite, and as he trotted past first base, made rude gestures toward the Cubs bench and some kind of pushing motion as he approached third.[2] The Cubs dugout had gone silent.

The next day, the legend began. While many accounts of the game noted the byplay between Root and Ruth, the most widely circulated write-up[3] stated that the Babe had pointed to center "so as to call his shot." It didn't take long for the tale to become an accepted truth.

Root, of course, said it never happened. If the Babe had been doing any such thing, the pitcher said, the slugger would "have ended up on his ass."[4] Eyewitness testimony was divided. The video evidence is ambiguous.

Ruth himself did not clarify matters. In his 1948 autobiography, he said he hit the ball "in exactly the spot I had pointed to."[5] But in 1933, he was equally definitive: "Hell no," he told a reporter who asked if he had called the shot. "Only a damn fool would have done a thing like that."[6] In other instances, the Babe was uncharacteristically coy, neither confirming nor denying his intent.

In a sense, it hardly matters. In a sport that treasures its myths, this one was too good to cross-examine. Perhaps the best summation came from Tom Meany, an early biographer: "Whatever the intent of the gesture, the result was, as they say in Hollywood, slightly colossal."[7] Not that Ruth needed the publicity. Widely regarded as the greatest baseball player ever,[8] he fundamentally changed the game. Consider: in 1920, his first season with the Yankees, Ruth hit 54 home runs—or more than all but one *team*.[9] And on May 25, 1935, the day he hit his 714th and last home run—the ball featured on the cover of this book—he was hundreds in front of his nearest rivals, Lou Gehrig (378) and Rogers Hornsby (302).

Recognizing the power of power to put runs on the board and fill seats, management and players began to go for the home run in a way that had never happened before. No other player has had that transformative an influence. Ruth still ranks first in slugging percentage and on-base plus slugging percentage; he also has more home run titles (12) and RBI titles (6) than anyone else. Nor has any other player been as versatile. Ruth was a pitcher before he was a slugger, posting a league-best 1.75 earned run average (ERA) in 1916. He compiled a career record of 94–46, with a 2.28 ERA. If he hadn't made the Hall of Fame as a slugger, he might well have got there as a pitcher. That can be said of no other player.

1935

PROGRAM FROM THE FIRST NIGHT BASEBALL GAME

The Negro Leagues did it. The minor leagues did it. Football did it. But long after night play was routine in other contexts, major league baseball would not allow the lights to go on.

The reasons given were ludicrous. Games couldn't start until the sky was pitch black. Teams would have to pay two sets of players, one for day, one for night, because no one could be expected to play under such different conditions.[1] "The disturbed and misanthropic fan," argued the *Sporting News*, "will not sleep well after a night game."[2] Most important, though, was that baseball's leaders just didn't like the idea. If God had intended baseball to be played under the lights, the Almighty would have let them know. The only good reason not to do it came from outfielder and bon vivant "Turkey Mike" Donlin back in 1909, when the idea was first floated: "Jesus! Think of taking a ballplayer's nights away from him!"[3]

In 1935, however, night baseball debuted for reasons that trumped theology, tradition, and even the sanctity of the family dinner: money. The Great Depression had hit the game hard. In 1929, the 16 major league teams drew 4.7 million fans; by 1933, that was down to 2.9 million.[4] The owners were hurting.[5]

Larry MacPhail, president of the Cincinnati Reds, had seen how night baseball had saved the minors.[6] With the Reds attracting fewer than 5,000 fans per game, it was time to shake things up. So on the night of May 24, 1935, with the middling Reds playing the even-worse Philadelphia Phillies, President Franklin D. Roosevelt pushed a button to light a million watts—and sparked the biggest change to baseball since pitchers were allowed to throw overhand. That night's program (which cost 10 cents) marked the moment, with a prominent advertisement on the cover from the company that provided the light (see the photo). The Reds, remember, were desperate for revenue.

That first year, Cincinnati was allowed one night game against each of the other National League teams. In those seven contests, it attracted an average of 18,571 fans.[7] MacPhail estimated that one night game alone, which attracted 33,468 fans, brought in almost enough revenue to offset the entire cost of installing the lights.[8]

By any standard, the experiment was a success; there were no complaints about the quality of light, and the play was sharp. But there was still a sense that it was a little undignified. It was not until June 1938 that a second team installed lights—the Brooklyn Dodgers, also run by MacPhail. It worked there, too—39,000 fans saw Johnny Vander Meer throw a second consecutive no-hitter in Brooklyn's night debut. The American League flatly banned night play through 1938, but the Philadelphia Athletics and the Cleveland Indians gave it a go the following year; Cleveland drew 55,000 fans its first night. In 1940 the St. Louis Browns joined the queue.[9]

By 1941, 11 of the 16 teams were playing night games,[10] and during the war, the number allowed was increased to serve day-shift workers in defense industries.[11] After the war, the remaining holdouts gave in—with one exception. The Cubs had light towers all but ready to go in 1942. Then management donated them to the war effort. It would take another 46 years for the lights to go on at Wrigley Field.[12]

Circa 1935

DUKE KAHANAMOKU'S SURFBOARD

When Captain James Cook and his crew floated into the Hawaiian islands in 1778, one of the many things that astonished the Englishmen was how the locals were "so perfectly masters of themselves in the water."[1] Big waves scared the Europeans; to the Hawaiians, they were playthings. Most of all, the Europeans were fascinated by seeing them surf.

Surfing was imbedded in every part of Hawaiian culture. There were rituals associated with building a surfboard, and a strict social order regulated who got to ride which waves. Royal boards were longer (12 to 14 feet) and made of olo wood.[2] Surfing was also part of courtship. In a society where the mixing of the sexes on land was strictly regulated, sharing a wave was decidedly erotic. And it was fun. Whole communities would catch waves together, old and young, male and female. "The boldness and address, with which we saw them perform these difficult and dangerous maneuvers," wrote Lieutenant James King, "was altogether astonishing, and is scarcely to be credited."[3]

Cook's crew were among the last Europeans to see surf culture in all its glory. When outsiders came to harvest Hawaii's sandalwood and to plant rice and sugarcane, they converted what had been a comfortable subsistence-plus economy into a wage-driven one. Hawaiians had less time to surf; they had schedules to keep. Christian missionaries, who began arriving in 1820, mildly discouraged the practice.[4]

The largest reason for surfing's decline, however, was the decline of *kapu*, the traditional value system of which it was a part, as Hawaiian communities withered away from imported diseases. By 1898, the year Hawaii officially became a US territory, the population of the islands had dropped at least 80 percent from Cook's time.[5]

But the sport never quite died, and in the early twentieth century a native Hawaiian named Duke Paoa Kahanamoku led its renaissance, becoming, in a sense, a surfing missionary. Born in 1890, Kahanamoku grew up on the beaches of Waikiki and at an early age was recognized as the most gifted waterman around, skilled at swimming, surfing, and paddling. As a teenager, he and some friends started the first surf club, Hui Nalu, or Club of the Waves,[6] which is credited as an important influence in reviving the sport. Kahanamoku was the acknowledged leader, which is why he is often referred to as the father of surfing.

In 1911 Hawaii held its first organized swim meet. Kahanamoku not only won the 100-yard race, but broke the world record by 4.6 seconds.[7] He broke two other records in the same meet.[8] The Amateur Athletic Union, which governed swimming and selected athletes for the Olympics, refused to sanction the records, finding the times literally unbelievable. But it was enough to get Kahanamoku invited to the Olympic trials.

On arriving in California, he gave a number of surfing demonstrations. Making his way cross-country, he easily qualified for the Olympics; he also benefited from coaching that improved his technique at diving and turning, areas the open-water swimmer needed to master.[9] He did so, winning the 100-meter freestyle in Stockholm, and a silver medal as part of the 4 x 200-meter freestyle relay. Back in the United States, he gave swimming and surfing demonstrations on both coasts, before returning to acclaim in Hawaii.

Invited to Australia and New Zealand in 1915, he performed in dozens of swimming exhibitions. Near the end of his stay he crafted a nine-foot board. Then he took to the waves at Sydney's Freshwater Beach, showing hundreds of screaming spectators what surfing was all about. Once he came in while standing on his head; another time with a 14-year-old girl on his shoulders.[10] The Aussies loved it.

Kahanamoku returned to Hawaii, which was beginning to build a surfing economy. He made a living teaching the sport, including to a "frightfully keen" Prince of Wales.[11] At the 1920 Olympics in Antwerp, Kahanamoku took two more golds, and then a silver in Paris in 1924 at age 34, just behind "Tarzan" Johnny Weissmuller. Kahanamoku remains the oldest man ever to win an Olympic swimming medal.

In the 1920s he became involved with the Hollywood in-crowd, befriending the likes of Charlie Chaplin, Babe Ruth, and John Wayne. He appeared in some 30 silent movies, albeit in typecast roles such as an American Indian chief, Hindu priest, or Turkish warrior.[12] At the same time, Kahanamoku used his popularity to promote surfing, an effort that he bolstered in the best possible way in 1925, when he rescued eight people from a capsized fishing boat.[13]

Returning to Hawaii in 1930, he became the sheriff of Honolulu and taught and surfed as much as he could. The photo on the previous page dates from the 1930s; he stands in front of Waikiki beach, where he had learned to surf and swim as a boy, and Diamond Head can be seen in the background. Shortly after Hawaii became a state in 1959, Kahanamoku was named its "Ambassador of Aloha"[14]—the perfect title for this gentle man with the bright smile and magnificent physique.

Kahanamoku was never rich, and he sometimes struggled financially. Unlike many other athletes, though, he was appreciated during his life and has never been forgotten. In 1990 a statue of Duke Kahanamoku in his prime, standing in front of a surfboard, was unveiled on Kuhio Beach in Waikiki. Four years later, the Sydney waterfront did the same. In 1999 *Surfer* magazine named him the "Surfer of the Century." And in August 2015, Google designed one of its doodles in honor of the modern father of surfing. He is a member of the swimming, surfing, and US Olympic halls of fame.[15]

Duke Kahanamoku's is a unique set of accomplishments. He was world class in one sport (swimming) and became the face of another (surfing), all while negotiating two cultures. He surfed into his sixties and had the satisfaction of seeing the sport he loved fill the beaches of Waikiki again. When he died in 1968, 15,000 admirers lined the beach as his remains were given to the ocean.[16]

1936

JESSE OWENS'S BATON FROM THE 4 X 100-METER RELAY

The story is familiar. Jesse Owens faced down a hostile Germany, winning four gold medals at the 1936 Olympics. In so doing, he shocked the Nazis and humiliated Hitler, who refused to shake his hand and stormed out of the stadium in anger. Owens had been snubbed, but in the process, this great African American athlete gave the lie to the idea of Aryan superiority.[1]

It's a great story, and there's even a bit of truth to it. But it is best seen as a myth—that is, a tale that speaks to a society's sense of itself. The Owens saga is more complex and more interesting than that simplistic morality tale.

About 5 foot 10 and 160 pounds, Owens was not a big man, but he was perfectly proportioned. Well coached since high school, his form was exquisite in its economy, with no wasted motion. Even at peak speed, his head barely moved, his upper body stayed still, and his feet hit the cinders with unfathomable lightness. Owens had the ability to accelerate smoothly, late in a race, into a gear unavailable to lesser mortals. Going into the Berlin Games, the 22-year-old from Ohio State was considered one of the country's finest athletes.

So let's dispose of myth number 1, that his performance shocked the Nazis. Not so. From 1934 on, the only people who had seriously challenged Owens were fellow Alabama-born African Americans Ralph Metcalfe and Eulace Peacock; no one else was in the same zip code. Metcalfe finished second to Owens in the 100 meters at the Games. Peacock did not compete. After beating Owens five times in a row in 1935–1936, he injured his hamstring and did not make the team.

In Berlin, Owens tied one world record (in the 100 meters); set one Olympic record (in the 200 meters);[2] and was part of the world-record 4 x 100-meter relay. Then there was the thrilling long-jump duel with one of Hitler's favorite athletes, Luz Long. When Long jumped a personal best, Owens warmly congratulated him, then jumped just a little farther to win. Long was equally sportsmanlike, rushing over to embrace him. There is a lovely picture of the two of them shortly after the competition, lying on their stomachs, obviously comfortable in each other's company.[3]

Great as Owens's Olympic performance was, it was not his best. That had taken place some 15 months before, at the 1935 Big Ten championships in Ann Arbor. Competing for Ohio State, Owens broke three world records (in the long jump, the 220-yard hurdles, and the 220-yard dash) and tied a fourth (in the 100-yard dash). No one had ever before broken two world records in a day; Owens did all this in less than *an hour*.[4] So, no, Owens shocked no one in Berlin. Rather, he affirmed his own brilliance.

That brings us to myth number 2: he performed in a hostile environment. Owens did have reason to be concerned about his reception. The run-up to the Olympics had been tempestuous. When Berlin was awarded the Games in 1931, the Nazis were not yet in power. When Hitler became chancellor in 1933, a number of organizations,[5] including a significant minority of the black press,[6] argued that the United States should boycott the games if Germany did not treat its Jewish athletes fairly. The Amateur Athletic Union agreed, and since it was the AAU that certified US athletes, this was serious.

The head of the American Olympic Committee, Avery Brundage, traveled to Germany in 1934 to assess the situation, and Nazi leaders managed to say just enough of the right things to win his support. Not that Brundage needed much persuading; he suggested privately that the boycott threat was just a matter of Jews being noisy and quite possibly unpatriotic.[7] Eventually, the AAU acquiesced.[8]

Still, Owens was aware of Germany's toxic racial environment. In the weeks prior to the Games, Nazi Party newspapers had taken to picturing him next to an ape. As he prepared himself for his first heat in the 100 meters, his coach advised him, "Don't let anything from the stands upset you. Ignore the insults and you'll be all right."[9]

When he peeled down to his shorts and singlet, the crowd did begin to stir—not in abuse, but in a spontaneous roar: "Jess-say! O-wenz! Jess-say! O-wenz!" From that beginning to the end of the Games, he was showered with Teutonic affection. Other African American athletes were also pleasantly surprised. "They idolized us," 400-meter gold medalist Archie Williams[10] said of the German fans. "They wanted to take us to their house to meet their family."[11] Jimmy LuValle, who won bronze in the 400 meters,[12] agreed: "The German people were as nice as they could be."[13]

Myth number 3: Hitler was so enraged by Owens's performance that he stormed out of the stadium rather than shake his hand.

This just didn't happen. Here is the chronology of events.

Germany got off to a great start. On the first day of the Games, Tillie Fleischer won the country's first-ever women's gold medal in a field event (in the javelin), and Hans Woellke won the first-ever men's gold (in the shotput). Three Finns swept the 10,000 meters. In each case, Hitler greeted the victors cordially, shaking their hands. The final event was the high jump. Two African Americans took the top spots—Cornelius Johnson, who had not lost a competition since 1932, and Dave Albritton, Owens's fellow Buckeye. Hitler left the stadium shortly before the medal ceremony. No insult intended, German officials asserted. The great man just wanted to beat the traffic. Well, maybe. But it is hardly a stretch to suspect other reasons played a role.

At any rate, the omission was noticed, and the head of the International Olympic Committee (IOC) was not pleased. He told Hitler to greet all winners, or none. The Fuhrer agreed on the latter—except for Germans, whom he would congratulate privately. And in fact, Hitler did not shake anyone's hands in public after that conversation.

On the second day of the Games, Owens won the 100 meters, tying the world record (10.3 seconds) despite bad weather and a chewed-up inside lane. "No one ever ran a more perfect race," the *New York Times* reported.[14] The crowd roared its approval. Metcalfe was a tenth of a second behind. The closest quasi-Aryan, Martinus Osendarp of the Netherlands, took third.[15] Owens made a short and graceful speech, then took the podium, saluting smartly during the US national anthem. Hitler made no effort to shake his hand, creating a stir back in the United States.

But Hitler shook no one's hand that day (or any subsequent day), not even that of Karl Hein, the German who won the hammer throw. And he did not storm out of the stadium. For years afterward, Owens shrugged off the alleged snub. In the 1964 documentary *Jesse Owens Returns to Berlin*, he pointed out that "the real snub" was to Johnson, the high-jumper, the day before.

No matter; the idea that Hitler had gone out of his way to insult Owens took hold. When Owens returned to a divided and still-battered West Berlin in 1951, Mayor Walter Schreiber told him, "Hitler wouldn't shake your hand; I give you both hands." Once again, the crowd roared.

While the facts say Owens was not directly snubbed, that is not to say that Hitler was being polite, only politic. "The Americans ought to be ashamed of themselves for letting their medals be won by Negroes," he told a Nazi Youth leader some days later. "I myself would never shake hands with one of them."[16]

Myth number 4: the Nazis were humiliated because their theories of Aryan supremacy were so vividly debunked.

Not at all. While Nazi racial philosophies were vicious, they were also infinitely flexible; to believers, the results of the Berlin Olympics proved they were right. In 1932 Germany had won just 20 medals, 3 of them gold; in 1936, the country won 89 medals (33 gold), far ahead of the second-place United States. Nazi leaders could and did point to Germany's success as a vindication of the ideals of the Third Reich.[17]

The United States outperformed Germany on the track (12 gold medals to Germany's 3), in large part due to the excellence of its African American athletes.[18] But this could be explained away. Hitler's favorite architect, Albert Speer, stated that the boss was "highly annoyed" by Owens's success, but not surprised: "People whose antecedents came from the jungle were primitive, Hitler said with a shrug; their physiques were stronger than those of civilized whites and hence should be excluded from future Games."[19]

To sum up: when Aryans do well, it's because they are superior; when blacks do well, it's because they are inferior.

Far from a humiliation, the Games were a triumph for the Nazis. Visitors came away with a sense that there was a true connection between Fuhrer and (non-Jewish) Volk. The *New York Times* observed a "deep-seated adoration of Hitler [that] gave all German athletes an inspirational lift that no other country could match."[20]

As politics, sport, and spectacle, it worked, attracting a record number of countries (49) and spectators.[21] The Berlin Games were the first to sponsor a torch relay from Olympia, the first to be reported on global radio, the first to be broadcast on television (in special screening venues),[22] the first to feature photo-finish technology, and the first to use electric apparatus to record hits in fencing.

The Olympic Village, which housed 3,500 male athletes, was a marvel. The 140 buildings were laid out in the shape of Germany,[23] and each residence was named after a German city. Art students contributed work that reflected the landscape or culture of that city.[24] In addition to a sauna, cinema, post office, bank, and training facilities, the kitchens provided cuisine adapted to the different tastes of the competitors.[25] The IOC was certainly impressed. In late 1938, Switzerland decided not to host the 1940 Winter Games. At that point, there was no longer any doubt about the nature of Nazism. Even so, as a replacement, the IOC chose . . . Germany.

Jesse Owens performed brilliantly in Berlin, but he did not smash or even weaken the notion of Aryan supremacy: People who believed in that idea before the Olympics believed in it after. Moreover, the way the Owens's story is generally told, as the noble American triumphing over nasty Nazis, elides some uncomfortable truths.

It was not only Nazis who needed to learn (and didn't) that racial superiority was a fallacy. Owens could live in the Olympic Village with other athletes; he could not live on campus at Ohio State, a ban confirmed by the Ohio Supreme Court in 1933.[26] He could sit in any seat on a Berlin bus or train (except that he would have been smothered in love); he could not do that in his birthplace of Alabama.[27]

The "Legend of the Snub" has become so firmly established because it serves a variety of interests. For the West Germans, "I shake both your hands" was a way of separating postwar democratic Germany from the Third Reich. For the United States, it provided a comfortable way to affirm truth, justice, and the American way. For Olympic leaders, it allowed them to present the Games as a force for good, a highly debatable point.

Owens used this baton to win his fourth gold medal—the most ever in a single Games by a US track athlete at the time, and because of that, in a sense, the one that made him a legend.[28] A hollow length that weighs next to nothing, the baton is signed by the four winning runners—Owens, Ralph Metcalfe, Foy Draper, and Frank Wykoff. But there is another story behind those signatures. Neither Owens nor Metcalfe had been scheduled to run the relay. Just a few hours before the competition began, the US coaches, Lawson Robertson and Dean Cromwell, ordered them to take the places of Marty Glickman and Sam Stoller, who had been named to the relay team at the Trials and had been training for weeks with their teammates. The Germans, the coaches claimed, were hiding secret super-athletes.

This was, of course, ridiculous; world-class athletes cannot be stowed away. The suspicion, then and now, is that the US coaches were pressured not to allow Glickman and Stoller to compete because they were Jewish. That's possible, but it's hard to see how replacing two Jewish athletes with two African American ones placates Nazi sensibilities. Another possibility is that having decided to add Owens and Metcalfe, just in case, Cromwell expelled Glickman and Stoller in favor of his own runners from Southern Cal (Draper and Wykoff). At any rate, the four duly set a world record, 39.8, a time that would last for twenty years. Germany, of course, had no secret weapons in spikes; it finished third, 1.4 seconds behind.

There can be no definitive answer to why the coaches made this decision; what can be said is that it smelled, even at the time. Robertson would later apologize to Glickman and Stoller for what he called "a terrible injustice."[29]

After the Games, Germany swapped Olympic flags for ones with swastikas. Anti-Jewish posters, graffiti, and harassment reemerged immediately. The Olympic Village became an infantry training center before World War II,[30] a hospital during it, and a KGB interrogation center after. It is now a ghostly ruin, with the exception of Jesse Owens's room, which has been restored.[31]

Almost three years to the day after the closing ceremonies, Hitler unleashed the war that would kill tens of millions of people, including dozens of Olympic athletes. Among them: Foy Draper, a bomber pilot lost over North Africa, and Luz Long, killed in action in Sicily.

1936

THE *HUSKY CLIPPER*

This is a simpler story from the Berlin Olympics. Call it the Miracle on Water. Or Hoosiers West.[1] It's that kind of story.

In 1936 an eight-man boat from the University of Washington, with a crew composed almost entirely of the sons of lumberjacks, miners, farmers, and laborers, dominated their archrivals at the University of California, went east and won the national championship, then triumphed at the Olympic trials. Then they got the bad news. If they couldn't pay their own expenses, a team from the University of Pennsylvania would be happy to take their place in Berlin. Penn had no lumberjacks among its crew.

There was no way the boys from Washington could come up with anything near the $5,000 required. There were no rowing scholarships, and most of them worked tough jobs just to stay afloat. So the entire state rose to the challenge;[2] newspapers publicized their plight and clubs and individuals all over raised the money in a couple of days.[3]

The boys repaid this generosity with style, setting a world record in their first 2,000-meter heat in Berlin. That got them noticed. But just as the United States owned the track in 1936 (see the 1936 entry on Jesse Owens), Germany owned the water, winning five races and coming in second in another. Hitler, who attended the finals along with top lieutenants Hermann Göring and Joseph Goebbels, was delighted. So were the 75,000 spectators, whose cries of "Deutschland, Deutschland," called in the cadence of each German boat,[4] must have been unnerving.

The 2,000-meter race was the last of the day. The Americans were not intimidated, but neither were they in the best of shape. Their stroke, Don Hume, had risen from his sick bed to race, and their number three, Gordon Adam, was also feeling weak. In addition, the Olympic authorities had put the slower qualifiers, including Germany, in the better lanes. The Americans were in the worst, farthest from the starting gun, and most vulnerable to the crosswinds. Then they got off to a bad start, losing half a length before they had taken a single stroke.[5] "We didn't start slow, we just didn't start, period," said crew member Joe Rantz.[6]

At 1,000 meters, the United States was in last place, five seconds behind.[7] With 800 meters left, Hume gathered his strength "and by golly, away we went," recalled coxswain Bob Moch.[8] At 500 meters, the boat had moved into third; at 300 meters, it was a close second. At 100 meters, it had pulled even, and the eight-man crew took the tempo up to an unprecedented 44 strokes a minute.[9] It was just enough. The United States finished about eight feet ahead of Italy, which beat Germany by even less.[10] A single second separated the three.[11] The crew was so exhausted it couldn't muster the energy to follow Washington tradition and throw the cox overboard.[12]

This is the boat, the *Husky Clipper*, that the boys rowed to victory. It is 60 feet long, 2 feet wide, and less than half an inch thick, and weighs about 235 pounds. Designed by craftsman and rowing mystic George Pocock, it is made chiefly of western red cedar. Pocock would lather the underside with whale oil to reduce friction.

Today's boats, by contrast, are composed of space-age composites that do not require the use of whale by-products, and the oars weigh a third as much as in 1936. But though the technology of rowing has changed, the place of the *Husky Clipper* in Washington's history has not. The shell hangs from the ceiling of the university's boathouse; it is tradition for each new cohort of rowers to be told the story of 1936 as they stand under it. And to this day, Husky rowers use white blades—just as the boys in the boat did.[13]

TOWEL THROWN INTO THE RING AT THE FIGHT BETWEEN JOE LOUIS AND MAX SCHMELING

On the night of June 22, 1938, something unprecedented happened. Sixty million Americans sat by their radios and rooted for a black man to triumph. He did, in 124 seconds of savagely beautiful boxing.

In one corner was America's Joe Louis, the heavyweight champion; in the other was Germany's Max Schmeling, the only man who had ever beaten Louis as a pro. This was more than a fight. It was truth, justice, and the American way against a Nazi regime of unmistakable viciousness. "Joe," President Roosevelt had told Louis a few weeks before, "we need muscles like yours to beat Germany."[1] Louis himself recognized the heavy symbolism of the occasion. "I knew I had to get Schmeling good," he wrote in his autobiography. "The whole damned country was depending on me." He also appreciated the irony of the moment, noting that he had solid support even in regions that were lynching fellow African Americans.[2]

Two years earlier, in a shocking upset, Schmeling had knocked Louis down in the fourth and out in the twelfth. To many Americans, the fact that Schmeling was white meant more than that he was foreign, and they were happy that Louis had lost. At news of Louis's defeat, there was cheering in the House of Representatives.[3]

By 1938, however, as the news out of Germany had become progressively darker, opinions had changed. Now this was not just Louis versus Schmeling, but democracy versus fascism. Black Americans in particular were absorbed with every detail. To many, Louis was hope in boxing gloves, an inspiration and possibly a promise of better days ahead. "As a kid, Joe Louis was everything," recalled Charles Rangel, the longtime US Congressman from Harlem. "He just was the epitome of racial pride."[4] No previous event had ever so consumed black America. America as a whole was only slightly less engaged and was largely united behind Louis.

Germany, of course, was solidly behind Schmeling. Although never a member of the Nazi Party, his victory over Louis in 1936 had made him a national icon of Aryan superiority. As many as 100 million people tuned in on radio worldwide, making the rematch the biggest sporting event in history to that date.

Shortly after 10:00 pm the opening bell rang, and Louis all but sprinted across the ring to attack. A few seconds later, he landed a solid left jab, and then a few more. A right to the jaw staggered the German. Clinging to the ropes, Schmeling absorbed punch after punch. At about 1:20 into the fight, Louis unloaded. Schmeling hung onto the rope with one glove; his body was open, and Louis drove his fists in again and again, alternating with blows to the head. A thudding right to the jaw dropped Schmeling. Brave but dazed, Schmeling rose off the mat at the count of two—to be met by another flurry of blows he could not defend against. He stumbled but didn't quite go down. Louis backed off briefly, then went at his almost defenseless opponent, raining blows at will, climaxed by a crushing right to the jaw. Schmeling went down again, and this time would not get up. His handlers threw in this towel just two minutes and four seconds into the fight.[5]

Black America was beyond thrilled. "The black race is supreme tonight," read a banner in Harlem.[6] Poet Maya Angelou, then a 10-year-old girl, remembered listening to the fight in her grandmother's Arkansas store: "Champion of the world. A Black boy. Some Black mother's son. He was the strongest man in the world."[7]

When America entered World War II, Louis donated several substantial purses to war-related funds—then he joined the army. "There's a lot wrong with America, but nothin' Hitler could fix," he explained his decision to enlist.[8] Assigned to a segregated unit, he offered boxing exhibitions to boost morale, but with one stipulation: the audience must be integrated. He also used his influence to help African American soldiers apply to officer candidate school. (Among them was Jackie Robinson; see 1947 entry.) By the end of the war, Louis was regarded by both blacks and whites as an American hero.

This is the towel thrown in by Max Schmeling's handlers in his return match with Joe Louis at Yankee Stadium, New York City, June 22, 1938, and thrown out of the ring by Arthur Donovan, Referee, because it is a rule of the New York Boxing Commission that seconds cannot throw a towel in the ring to stop a fight. This towel was thrown in during the first minute of boxing in the first round.

Time and lack of real competition had eroded his boxing skills, but persistent tax troubles kept Louis in the ring. In October 1951, after a young Rocky Marciano knocked him through the ropes, he called it quits. Louis retired with a record of 66–3, with 52 of the victories by knockout. He holds the record for the longest reign as champion—11 years and 10 months—and the most title defenses (25).

His larger achievement was a more subtle one. Louis was the first black man to be widely accepted by American society. That was a complicated matter. The previous black heavyweight champion, Jack Johnson, had positively reveled in irritating white America, with his gold teeth and white women. Promoters used Johnson's controversial reign as an excuse to keep blacks out of the highest ranks of boxing.

Louis's first fight, then, was to get a chance not only to fight, but to fight honestly. He tread cautiously. His managers advised him never to smile when he beat a white boxer and never to be seen with a white woman; they also groomed his table manners and coached him on how to speak in public. While Louis could turn a memorable phrase—"he can run but he can't hide" is one of them—his public utterances were cautious to the point of banality. To some members of a later generation of black athletes, such discretion would be regarded with contempt; Muhammad Ali (see the 1975 entry on the Thrilla in Manila) called him an "Uncle Tom."[9]

That is unfair. Louis showed what black Americans could achieve, given the chance. His success helped prepare the way for the general integration of sports and also allowed him to negotiate, and expand, the treacherous public space open to black Americans. When the black Jack Johnson beat the white Jim Jeffries in 1910, it touched off white-on-black violence all over the country[10] that left 19 dead and 249 injured.[11] When Louis beat Schmeling, most of the country celebrated with him. "White Americans," concluded historian Gerald Early, "accepted Joe Louis as a sort of emblem of the US, an emblem of American democracy."[12] That had never happened before.

While Louis's later years were deeply sad, punctuated by money, health, and marital troubles, they should not obscure his greatness as an athlete and the depth of his legacy as an American. Joe Louis, said author Richard Wright, "was the concentrated essence of black triumph over white."[13] At the end, the country that had humiliated and hounded him finally offered him the respect he deserved: Louis was buried with full military honors in Arlington National Cemetery.

HANDBOOK FROM THE ALL-AMERICAN GIRLS PROFESSIONAL BASEBALL LEAGUE

In the first half of the twentieth century, baseball was the undisputed national pastime for women as well as men. There were industrial softball leagues and tournaments and national organizations. By the early 1940s there were tens of thousands of women's softball teams.[1]

During World War II this pool of talent found a new outlet. The need for military manpower hurt professional baseball; dozens of minor league teams closed down, and major league rosters were filled with near-middle-aged has-beens and never-wases. With factories hiring Rosie the Riveters to fill in for male factory workers, Cubs owner Philip Wrigley saw an opportunity for something similar: an all-women professional baseball league in case the majors had to be shut down. Scouts recruited from the extensive softball network, and in 1943 a four-team league debuted: the Kenosha Comets, the Racine Belles, the Rockford Peaches, and the South Bend Blue Sox.

The All-American Girls Professional Baseball League (AAGPBL), as it became known, lasted 12 seasons, under three different ownerships. It eventually expanded to as many as 10 teams, all in the Midwest. That's a pretty good run for a women's team sport; many an effort since has gone under much faster. Salaries were not startling—$60 to $85 a week at first—but well above that of most munitions workers.[2] The managers were men, including a number of former major leaguers, such as Bill Wambsganss, who turned the only unassisted triple play in World Series history in 1920, and Hall of Famer Jimmy Foxx.[3]

At first the women played softball, but the game evolved; it's best to see the sport the women played as a hybrid between softball and baseball that got closer to the latter over time. By 1948 they were pitching overhand, using a hardball. The women showcased an energetic brand of baseball, running wild on the base-paths and sliding head-first, on account of their uniforms—a one-piece dress, cut four inches above the knees.

At a time when many physical educators of both sexes thought that competition coarsened girls, the league's management placed an emphasis on femininity. Players took mandatory etiquette lessons and had to follow strict rules of conduct. The handbook pictured below, created by the league, gave advice on everything from speech ("no slang or slurry words")[4] to beauty routines and hygiene (shower after games and dry thoroughly) to sportsmanship and stretching. "You have certain responsibilities," the guide noted, because you "are in the limelight."[5]

On-field makeup was compulsory; one player recalled that a chaperone held her back from going to the plate in a tense situation until she refreshed her lipstick.[6] The team chaperone had to approve all social engagements.[7] In each town, there was a list of places not to go.[8]

All of this sounds both curious and condescending, but it was a calculated choice to make these athletes less threatening to the social mores they were so enthusiastically flouting. For these jocks, if the price of playing for real was makeup lessons and stupid rules, so be it.[9] And drawing on talent from all over the country, Canada, and even Cuba—but no African Americans, even after Jackie Robinson had debuted[10]—the AAGPBL teams gave a chance to some 545 athletes.[11] Wally Pipp, the man Lou Gehrig displaced at first base, called Dottie Kamenshek of the Rockford Peaches the "fanciest-fielding first baseman I've ever seen, male or female."[12]

A GUIDE FOR

ALL AMERICAN GIRLS

HOW TO ○○○○○

LOOK BETTER

FEEL BETTER

BE MORE POPULAR

Although the AAGPBL was a wartime innovation, the league hit its peak after the fighting was over, attracting nearly a million fans in 1948.[13] By the early 1950s, though, it was declining. Baseball was back, football was on the rise, and television was providing a different form of family entertainment. The league was also not managed as well as it had been under Wrigley and his successor. Spending on promotion and publicity plummeted, and so did attendance. The league died with a whimper in 1954.

But it had a very American resurrection, courtesy of Hollywood. In 1988 the Baseball Hall of Fame opened its "Women in Baseball" exhibit, and dozens of league alumni attended. So did filmmaker Penny Marshall.[14] Four years later, Marshall released one of the few great baseball movies, *A League of Their Own,* about the AAGPBL during World War II. The film is not historically precise, and too many of the actors throw like girls; they would never have made the cut. But it captures the spirit of the enterprise, and the players, forgotten for decades, became hometown celebrities.

The movie also added a phrase to the game's rich lexicon of clichés when the manager, played by Tom Hanks, barked at one of his players: "There's no crying in baseball." Of course there is. The players of the AAGPBL knew that as well as anyone. But to a woman, they also recalled their years as professional ballplayers as among the most joyous times of their lives.

1945

10TH MOUNTAIN DIVISION PARKA

The story of America's most famous ski troops begins in Finland. During the Winter War of 1939–1940, the tiny country of fewer than four million people used its expertise in the snow to inflict more than 300,000 casualties on the Soviet invaders. The Finns could never win, but it took almost four months to subdue them; their unexpectedly effective resistance showed the potential of unconventional warfare on skis.[1] An American named Charles Minot Dole, founder of the National Ski Patrol, took note. He argued that such a unit could also be useful to the US military. Army leaders were dubious, but a few weeks before Pearl Harbor, the War Department decided it was worth a try. That was the beginning of what became the 10th Mountain Division.[2]

The 10th had a number of great athletes in it, including Norwegian-born world ski-jumping champion Torger Tokle; Swiss championship downhiller Walter Prager; Austrian-born Toni Matt, who won two US downhill titles; and US Olympic field hockey player Bill Boddington. As those names suggest, the 10th was remarkably international; it was also conspicuously well educated. Skiing, at the time, was an elite sport embedded most prominently in eastern colleges; Dartmouth alone sent dozens of men. There were also lumberjacks, cowboys, ranchers, and outdoorsmen of all kinds. What drew them together was their love of the mountains. The division's weekly newspaper, *The Blizzard*, featured pinups of slopes, not women.[3] On leave, many would head to the hills, not the saloon. Those who did the latter were known to rappel down hotel walls for the heck of it. The 10th had style.

The romance of the "ski commandos" was irresistible. They got a spread in *Life* and the cover of the *Saturday Evening Post*. Warner Brothers released what can only be called a Technicolor panegyric, *Mountain Fighters*. "And what men they are!" the narrator gushed. "There they go, the hard-hitting mountain troopers, the daredevils of the heights. They conquer mountains and men that liberty might live forever as they fight on to victory!" Fade to flag.[4]

In military terms, however, the 10th was a puzzle. The first officers knew a lot about the military but next to nothing about skiing or mountaineering; their men knew a lot about the outdoors and next to nothing about the military. The turning point was the establishment of a dedicated training center in late 1942, 9,250 feet above sea level, in Pando, Colorado, about 114 miles west of Denver. There, at Camp Hale, the three regiments that made up the division—the 85th, 86th, and 87th—trained for the better part of two years, in skiing, rock-climbing, winter survival, and mountain rescue and combat. Gradually, men and officers refined their equipment, including the first snow-mobiles and snowcats.[5]

But when American troops hit the beaches of France on D-Day, Hollywood's hard-hitting daredevils stayed in Colorado. No one quite knew what to do with them. Their firepower was light, and there was some skepticism about a division that was just so . . . different. In June 1944, much to the 10th's dismay, they were relocated to the snakes, scorpions, and sweltering weather of Camp Swift in Texas.

Later that year they got their chance. Although Rome had surrendered to the Allies in 1943, Germany still held large chunks of northern Italy. The Nazis' "Winter Line" stretched east to west, just below the top of the Italian boot, including a strong position on the tops of a series of ridges that were part of the Apennine Mountains. These blocked access to the Po valley and the route to Bologna and on through to Austria and southern Germany. Four times the Fifth Army tried to dislodge them; four times it was beaten back.[6] Perhaps, the thinking went, this was a job for trained mountain troops.

The 10th got into position in January 1945 and sent out patrols, sometimes on their white-painted skis, to explore their surroundings—the only times the ski equipment saw use in Italy.[7] On these missions, the troops would wear parkas like the one opposite; one side was snow white, the other olive, adaptable for use in different kinds of terrain.

As the patrols scouted the area, they determined that the key to breaking through the Winter Line was a series of peaks that became known as Riva Ridge. These overlooked the approaches to Mount Belvedere, which protected the road to Bologna. If the Allies could take Riva Ridge, they could move on to Mount Belvedere, but not vice versa—something the Fifth Army had learned at great human cost.

There was just one problem: getting up Riva Ridge. The Germans had fortified their positions with mines, barbed wire, and bunkers. Night after night, the men of the 10th probed and explored. Eventually, they mapped five routes up the lightly defended eastern face. Variously steep and muddy or steep and icy, the Germans considered it unclimbable.

The plan was simple. Climb 1,500 feet up the eastern face, in force, at night. Then surprise the Germans, establish a position, and hold it. At 7:30 on the evening of February 18, eight hundred men of the 86th regiment stalked silently up. They even unloaded their weapons lest an errant shot betray their positions. None of the trails required advanced mountaineering skills, but two of them were tricky enough to require ropes, which had been hammered into the rock a few days before. Negotiating even the easier terrain with full packs was a feat of conditioning that might have overwhelmed soldiers who lacked the 10th's training.

If a single German had looked over the ridge, the men could have been picked off easily. But no one looked, and no dogs were on patrol. A providential fog descended. This made climbing more difficult, but much safer. Before dawn broke on February 19, everyone had reached the summit.

There the men of the 10th loaded their weapons, set up communications, and prepared for battle. Surprised but determined, the Germans counterattacked all along the crest of Riva Ridge. The 10th held them off. Supplies came up and the wounded went down via mules, men, and an ingenious portable tram.[8] Allied forces also moved into Mount Belvedere. Less than a week after the 10th's climb up Riva Ridge, the Germans fell back.

Over the next three months the 10th, supported by other American forces, as well as allies from Brazil, Italy, New Zealand, and Poland, chased the Germans off Belvedere, then across the Po valley, then over Lake Garda. In one case, the 10th advanced so fast that when they stumbled across the headquarters of the German 90th Panzer division, there was a fresh slice of bread and jam left on the table, with one bite gone.[9] Allied forces were in sight of Austria when the German armies in Italy surrendered on May 2, six days before V-E Day. The 10th spent the following months enjoying themselves in the Alps. They were home by August.

The climb up Riva Ridge was the signature moment for the 10th—the only time the men had to use their special skills. But without that ascent, nothing else they did would have been possible. During its 114 days in combat, the 10th was credited with neutralizing five German divisions. It paid a heavy price: 975 dead and 3,871 wounded.[10]

Though it was part of the last division to enter the war, the 10th fought with an improvisational flair characteristic of more seasoned troops, never losing a battle. In his journal, the German general who surrendered to them called the 10th his "most dangerous opponent."[11]

After the war, the story of the 10th continued to exert a hold. These troops were an especially interesting bunch. Two of the sons of the Trapp Family Singers fought with the 10th; so did Morley Nelson, who brought his goshawk with him to Camp Hale and then became Hollywood's in-house falconer.[12] Bill Bowerman went on to coach track at Oregon and cofound Nike (see the 1974 entry on the Waffle Trainer and the 1975 entry on Steve Prefontaine). Don Coryell was a National Football League head coach, leading the "Air Coryell" teams of the San Diego Chargers.[13] Bob Dole, who came to the 10th as a wartime replacement, lost a kidney and the use of his right arm leading a patrol; he later was a US Senator from Kansas and the Republican presidential candidate in 1996.

Appropriately, the greatest postwar influence of the 10th was a collective one: the veterans helped to create the modern American ski industry. Five members were on the 1948 US Olympic ski team and a sixth was its coach. Members of the 10th founded almost two dozen ski areas, including Snow Valley in California; Arapahoe Basin, Aspen, Steamboat Springs, and Vail[14] in Colorado; Waterville Valley (New Hampshire); Mount Bachelor (Oregon); and Sugarbush and Pico (Vermont). They managed or ran ski schools in dozens more; they made ski films, designed equipment, and organized competitions. Veterans of the 10th founded *Skiing* magazine. Don Goodman invented one of the first safety bindings.[15] Monty Atwater became an expert in avalanche control. Jim Winthers began ski programs for the disabled. Robert Heron, the civilian engineer who designed the portable tram used to ferry supplies up Riva Ridge, designed generations of chairlifts.[16] "We wanted to teach the country to ski," said veteran Dick Wilson. "And we did."[17]

1947

JACKIE ROBINSON'S JERSEY

This jersey is made of flannel, redolent of sweat—and full of stories.

One story is about 60 years of segregation. When Jackie Robinson donned a Dodgers jersey and took the field at Ebbets Field on April 15, 1947, he was the first black man to appear in a major league game since 1887.

A second story is about social change. Martin Luther King Jr. would say that Robinson was "a pilgrim that walked in the lonesome byways toward the high road of Freedom. He was a sit-inner before sit-ins, a freedom rider before freedom rides."[1]

A third story is that of a man. Jack Roosevelt Robinson was born to a sharecropping family in south Georgia; his mother moved her five children to Pasadena, California, when he was an infant.[2] After excelling in sports in high school, Robinson went on to the University of California at Los Angeles, where he was the first student to letter in four sports.[3] After the attack on Pearl Harbor in December 1941, he joined the military and was eventually sent to officer candidate school (see the 1938 entry on Joe Louis). In Fort Hood, Texas, he had his own Rosa Parks moment, 11 years before her challenge to segregation, when he refused to move to the back of the bus while traveling to base in 1944. Acquitted after a court-martial, he left the army (or perhaps vice versa) and joined the Kansas City Monarchs in the Negro Leagues.

At the same time that Robinson was playing second base for the Monarchs, the general manager of the Brooklyn Dodgers, Branch Rickey, was thinking about how to bring African Americans into the major leagues. In this he had the quiet support of the baseball commissioner, Happy Chandler, who noted that if blacks could die for their country in combat overseas, "they can play ball in America."[4] But Rickey also faced the quiet opposition of the 15 other major league clubs.[5]

An innovator who had pioneered the modern farm system and the use of statistical analysis, Rickey was both idealistic and shrewd. He genuinely felt it was long past time that black Americans be part of the national pastime; a devout Methodist, he refused to play baseball on Sunday during his conspicuously inglorious major league career (120 games over four years, with a career .239 batting average).

Rickey also knew there was a wealth of black talent that could improve his team and draw black fans to Dodgers' games. And he knew it had to be done carefully. Before taking any action, he sought the advice of black leaders about what kind of player to recruit and how to manage the transition.[6] To provide cover as he evaluated the talent, he floated the possibility of starting a new Negro League. Reports began to come back about an infielder named Robinson. Rickey sent his favorite scout, Clyde Sukeforth, to check him out.

In Jimmy Breslin's happy phrase, Sukeforth "could go out for coffee and come back with a second baseman."[7] He was a shrewd judge of character as well as skills, and he liked what he saw and heard of Robinson. In August 1945 Rickey called Robinson in for a chat: "You were brought here, Jack Robinson, to play for the Brooklyn organization."[8] In October 1945, to no fanfare, Robinson signed a Brooklyn Dodgers contract. He spent the 1946 season with the Montreal Royals, where he was spectacular, and made the big team out of spring training in Havana the following year. "My purpose," said Rickey on the announcement of the signing, "is to be fair to all people, and my selfish objective is to win baseball games."[9]

Even in retrospect, it is difficult to imagine a better choice to play the role of pioneer than the 28-year-old Jackie Robinson. With his college and military background, whites could not patronize him (though some tried). With his reputation for challenging racism, earned in both the military and the Negro Leagues, blacks respected him. With a loving and tough-minded wife, Rachel, he had a solid emotional foundation. And his own athletic abilities and strength of character allowed him to excel even as he faced vicious abuse.

While the white press certainly noticed the moment, the black press had a surer appreciation of its importance. For example, the edition of New York's *Amsterdam News* that came out after his debut featured no fewer than 14 articles on Robinson,[10] covering everything from his play (good) to how people should behave (no "loud and uncouth jokes"). Columnist Earl Brown was ahead of the game when he predicted that "Rickey will be remembered by posterity more for breaking the color bar in the big leagues than he will for any of the many other epochal things he has done in baseball."[11]

It's worth remembering, too, just how good a player Robinson was. Under extraordinary pressure, he had a career batting average of .311 and an on-base percentage of .409; he won the Rookie of the Year award in 1947 and Most Valuable Player in 1949. He was a dynamic base-runner who helped move the game away from its station-to-station lethargy. Most important, he was a competitor, who would steal home or lay down a bunt or break up a double-play to win a game. "He came to beat you," said manager Leo Durocher. "He came to stuff the damn bat right up your ass."[12] Bill James, the baseball historian and statistical genius, ranked Robinson the 32nd best player ever.[13]

And Robinson did all this under a kind of pressure no other player has ever faced— from vicious bench-jockeying to isolation from his teammates[14] to the extraordinary expectations of other black Americans. Infielder Ed Charles, who would have a solid major league career from 1962 to 1969, remembered how as a boy, he and his friends followed Robinson to the train station after watching him play in Florida: "When the train pulled out, we ran down the tracks listening for the sounds as far as we could. And when we couldn't hear it any longer, we stopped and put our ears to the track so we could feel the vibrations of that train carrying Jackie Robinson."[15] Hank Aaron put it simply, "He gave us hope; he was the Dr. King of baseball."[16]

Robinson was the first black American to excel in a white-dominated pro team sport. Previous African American stars, such as Jesse Owens and Joe Louis, had made their names in individual sports. Being part of a team, with all the implications of physical proximity and mutual dependence—that was different. Robinson's success, playing side by side with white teammates, proved that he was equal to the moment. And it didn't take long before his skills and character earned the Dodgers' respect. When Philadelphia players were particularly abusive to him about six weeks into the 1947 season, other Dodgers rallied to Robinson's defense. By 1949 Robinson would say that "racial tensions had almost completely dissipated" on the team.[17] He and other black Dodgers, such as Roy Campanella and Don Newcombe, would play key roles in Brooklyn's only championship in 1955.

All this raised an interesting question: If blacks could excel while competing with whites at the highest level of baseball, and also become acknowledged leaders in the clubhouse, what else might they be capable of? Historian Cornel West put it this way: "More even than either Abraham Lincoln and the Civil War, or Martin Luther King, Jr. and the Civil Rights movement, Jackie Robinson graphically symbolized and personified the challenge to the vicious legacy and ideology of white supremacy in American history."[18]

Baseball likes to pat itself on the back for integrating a year before the military and many years before other major institutions. To some extent, it deserves that pat. But remember, too, how slowly it went; in 1953 most teams still didn't have a single black player, and in 1960 the American League had all of six.[19] Moreover, the baseball establishment also proved remarkably myopic about how it went about integration. For almost two decades after his debut, Robinson and the black Americans who followed frequently could not stay at the same hotels as their teammates. Well into the 1960s, teams were sending talented young black players to get minor league experience in the South Atlantic League, an experience that embittered everyone it touched (see the 1974 entry on Hank Aaron). There was next to no progress for 40 years in terms of bringing blacks into the business or management sides of baseball.

This speaks to a larger issue. While the integration of the major leagues was an important and positive historical moment, no substantive change comes without losers. In this case, the loser was the Negro Leagues. Blacks had been playing baseball for as long as the game existed. Beginning in the early 1900s, they played exhibition games against white teams, and often beat them. These contests regularly disproved the lie, peddled for years by baseball Commissioner Kenesaw Mountain Landis and others, that the reason there were no blacks in major league baseball was because none had proved good enough.

With the founding of the Negro National League in 1920, African American players had an organized outlet for their talents. The pay wasn't great, but not bad either, and the conditions of play were often less so. Teams had to play a lot of exhibitions to pay the bills, and sometimes played three games in a day; many franchises were on fragile financial ground. But players could make a living, the Negro Leagues became an important component of African American life, and the players had high status. Over time, the league did find a degree of stability; its best year was probably 1946.

After Robinson's debut, white baseball skimmed off the best talent—often with limited or no compensation. The Negro Leagues could not survive. And with the end of the Negro Leagues came the end to many things: black coaches and managers; black vendors; black suppliers; black promoters, marketers, and accountants.

For his first two years in the major leagues, Robinson had turned the other cheek to abuse, at Rickey's urging. In 1949, his third year, he began to showcase his outspoken and combative nature. Not everyone liked what he had to say. After Rickey left the Dodgers in 1950, Robinson's relations with the team's management grew testy and then toxic. It didn't help that he suffered the blow that comes to all athletes: age. After the 1956 season, the Dodgers announced that they had traded Robinson to their detested rival, the New York Giants, for the baseball equivalent of a ham sandwich. Robinson resigned instead. Elected to the Hall of Fame in 1962, he paid tribute in his speech to his wife, his mother—and Branch Rickey,[20] but not to the Dodgers, whom he never worked for again after he turned in his uniform. He had moved on to a career in business and a crusade of civil rights activism.

In 1972, on the twenty-fifth anniversary of his debut, a new generation of Dodger ownership sought to heal the breach. Robinson traveled to Los Angeles for a ceremony that retired his number. He also threw out the first pitch at that year's World Series— and publicly rebuked the game for the lack of black coaches and managers. He died a few weeks later of a combination of diabetes and heart disease. Six athletes served as pallbearers: five fellow Dodgers, both black and white, and Bill Russell of the Celtics (see the 1962 entry). He was buried a few blocks from Ebbets Field.[21]

Jackie Robinson was an exceptional man, and his story is exceptional. It is the one clear instance in which sport did not just reflect society but helped to change it. When he died at age 53, he was eulogized as a great American, and the accolades have kept coming. In 1984 he was posthumously awarded the Presidential Medal of Freedom,

America's highest civilian honor. In 1997 major league baseball retired his number, 42, from all teams. The ballpark for the New York Mets, an homage to Ebbets Field that opened in 2009, features the Jackie Robinson Rotunda.

Robinson earned every bit of these honors. But to the end of his days, his sense of anger and injustice burned deep. He would always feel a place apart in his own country because, he wrote, he was "a black man in a white world."[22]

ORIGINAL ICE-RESURFACING MACHINE

After a Great Depression and a world war, Americans were ready to have some fun. Postwar innovators delivered, with new or improved products that made it easier, and cheaper, for people to play.

The first commercial ski lift, for example, debuted in Sun Valley in 1936,[1] when a railroad engineer working at the resort adapted a technology he had seen at work on banana plantations.[2] After the war, the first double-chair went to work, and by the 1950s, chairlifts were ubiquitous, allowing operators to move more people up the mountain than the primitive rope tows ever could.

In bowling, the pinsetter went through a similar evolution. Before the war, a bowler and engineer named Gottfried Schmidt, with the help of a few friends, had built a crude prototype in a turkey coop.[3] Schmitt continued to work on his invention when he joined AMF—still an important name in bowling—but the firm took a break for war duty and didn't produce one it was ready to show the public until 1946.[4] A two-ton behemoth, it proved unreliable and never reached the market. By 1952, after many more trials and errors, the first recognizably modern and efficient pinsetter was hard at work.[5]

Without needing to wait for humans to set pins, games went faster and more pleasantly. That was better for bowlers and also improved the economics of running an alley. Both factors were critical to the bowling boom of the 1950s; by the end of the decade, 10 million people a week were bowling, and 9 out of 10 alleys were using automatic pinsetters.[6] Of course the boom turned into a bubble, which burst, but that is a different story.

Another postwar innovation was the golf cart. There were a few efforts putt-putting around in the 1930s, but these went nowhere commercially. Things changed in the early 1950s when reliable and quiet versions entered the market. Initially, these served a specific need, helping the old or injured; at some courses, a physicians' note was required to rent one.[7] That changed quickly when course operators realized that carts made for faster games. That meant more golfers on the course, and more greens fees, as well as new revenues in the form of rentals. Now about two-thirds of all rounds use a cart.

Then there is the eponymous Zamboni® ice-resurfacing machine—another tale of persistence and ingenuity. Beginning in the 1920s, brothers Frank and Lorenzo Zamboni made a nice living producing block ice for the food industry. But as refrigeration improved, the ice market melted away. So in 1940 they opened a skating rink, the Paramount Iceland, about a dozen miles from Los Angeles.[8] Maintaining a quality surface was almost impossible. Resurfacing was expensive and time-consuming, requiring several workers to shave the ice, haul the scrapings away, squeegee the surface, and then spray water and wait for it to freeze. Skaters either moved through sludge on bad ice, or waited. And waited. The process took about 90 minutes.

Frank Zamboni, who never graduated from high school but was an inspired tinkerer—he got his first patent, for an electrical resister, in 1928—figured there had to be a better way. Beginning in 1942, he experimented with idea after idea, using different configurations of water, heat, chassis, storage, and engines.

In 1949, he cracked the code.[9] This was the Model A (pictured below). Built on a Jeep platform, a wooden box held the snow shavings; water dropped from a tank to wash the ice and was pumped back into the bucket. Then another layer of water was

laid down for a fresh, clean surface. The vehicle looked ungainly, but it worked, resurfacing the rink with a clean sheet in 15 minutes.[10]

Restored by the company in 1998,[11] the Model A still works, though it mostly enjoys a well-deserved retirement at the Paramount rink. The second Zamboni® machine, the Model B, was created in 1950, at the request of figure skater Sonja Henie, who saw the Model A and had to have one for herself. The machine earned a patent in 1953 and began its long, if lumbering, march across American ice. A Zamboni® machine was first used in an NHL game in 1954, and one scraped the ice at the Olympics for the first time at Squaw Valley in 1960.

Growth was slow at first; only 32 machines were built through 1956. As with the other inventions, though, there emerged a symbiosis between the product—good, clean ice—and the times, as many municipalities and schools began to build rinks. More than 10,000 have been sold.

But the Zamboni® ice-resurfacer is more than another example of ingenuity. It is a cultural touchstone. There is the rock song, "I Want to Drive the Zamboni®," by the Gear Daddies, and the machine has been featured in television shows ranging from *CSI* to *David Letterman*. There are license plate frames that read, "My other car is a Zamboni®," and a Zamboni® token in a hockey-themed version of Monopoly.[12] The late Charles Schultz, an avid hockey player, had two of them at his home rink, and the machines made several appearances in his *Peanuts* comic strip.[13] Snoopy drove one. Charlie Brown, as usual, got it exactly right when he mused: "There are three things in life that people like to stare at: a flowing stream, a crackling fire, and a Zamboni® clearing the ice."[14]

1952

TIGERBELLE MAE FAGGS'S SHOES
FROM THE HELSINKI OLYMPICS

At its height, the women's track team at Tennessee State University[1] may have been the most dominant athletic program in history, winning 12 straight national titles in the 1950s and 1960s. The secret to TSU's success was simple: it was one of the few colleges where black women could get both a solid education and real coaching.

Not that it was easy. When Coach Ed Temple was hired in 1950, he recalled, the program consisted of "a partial track ending at a dump, no budget to speak of, three or four fellows, and two girls."[2] At the time, amateur clubs provided opportunities for some women athletes to compete, but few were based in the South. On the collegiate level, Tuskegee was the power at the time, winning 11 national titles between 1937 and 1948.[3] Alice Coachman, the "Tuskegee Flash," was the biggest star. She dominated US track for a decade and was the first African American woman to win Olympic gold, in the high jump in the 1948 Olympics.

But the TSU Tigerbelles were about to push the Tuskegee Tigerettes into second place. In 1952 Temple recruited a talented New Yorker, Mae Faggs, who had competed in the 1948 Olympics as a 16-year-old. Faggs would become the first American woman to compete in three Olympics. She wore these shoes in Helsinki.

Segregated Tennessee was a shock to Faggs, a New Yorker: "I was almost struck dumb by the situation in the South," she recalled.[4] But she stuck it out, in part because of her admiration for Temple, and in part because she was able to get work-study financial aid. Coach Temple was TSU track's undisputed leader—benign dictator might be the better description—but Faggs was an enduring influence, known as "the mother of the Tigerbelles."[5]

The Tigerbelles won their first Olympic gold in 1952, with Faggs and Barbara Jones comprising half the 4 x 100-meter relay team. That was the beginning of a remarkable run. Between 1952 and 1984, 40 Tigerbelles competed in the Olympics (35 of them for the United States), earning 27 Olympic medals, 15 of them gold.[6] The Tigerbelles also succeeded off the track. Thirty-nine of the Olympians graduated from TSU, and the other earned her degree elsewhere;[7] 28 got advanced degrees.[8] Sprinter Wyomia Tyus was 15 when she first met Temple and some of the athletes at the summer clinic he ran. "To me, the Tigerbelles were everything that I could see a woman should be," she said. "It was not only that they were great athletes, but they were also women that were doing something to make careers for themselves when they were told, 'No.'"[9]

Seven Tigerbelles made the 1960 US track team. Temple was the coach. (He made headlines by issuing a no-dancing edict that the Italian press found highly amusing.) And Wilma Rudolph was the star. The twentieth of 22 children, Rudolph was raised without electricity or indoor plumbing. Enduring polio, pneumonia, measles, whooping cough, and numerous other childhood illnesses, she wore leg braces until she was 12.[10] No one could have predicted that she would become one of the most powerful, and elegant, sprinters in history.[11]

Rudolph had competed in the 1956 Melbourne Olympics as a fast but raw 16-year-old, running the third leg on the bronze-medal-winning relay team. (Faggs, whom Rudolph revered as a mentor and second coach, led off.[12]) In Rome, Rudolph was a well-trained athlete in her prime. With an ease that belied the years of hard work, Rudolph won the 100- and 200-meter races. "The sensuality of her sprinting was in that stride," wrote a British track journalist. "Those legs running seemed to induce hydraulic elevation."[13]

Her favorite event, however, was the 4 x 100-meter relay; all four runners were Tigerbelles. They broke the world record in a heat, then won the gold in heart-stopping fashion, with Rudolph coming from behind after almost dropping the baton. "My relay medal meant the most to me," Rudolph later said. "I won it with my college teammates, for my coach." An unknown before the games, Rudolph's three gold medals—a record haul for an American woman—made her the belle of the Olympics. She was much more sought after than the gold-medal boxer, Cassius Clay, who desperately sought the attention Rudolph attracted without even trying.[14]

When her hometown, Clarksville, Tennessee, wanted to honor Rudolph, she agreed, on one condition: the celebrations could not be segregated. It was the first integrated parade in the town's history.[15] Two years later, she retired from competition. But the Tigerbelles kept rolling.

In 1964 Wyomia Tyus and Edie McGuire, fellow Tigerbelles (and high school teammates), went 1–2 in the 100 meters. McGuire won the 200 in world record time, and two Tigerbelles won silver in the 400-meter relay. In 1968, six Tigerbelles ran for the United States, and one more for Jamaica. Tyus became the first sprinter (of either sex) to repeat as 100-meter champion. Tigerbelle Madeline Manning became the first American woman to win the 800 meters.

The Tigerbelle record was astonishing, but their achievements barely registered, even on campus. Football was king at TSU. The track, located between a cow pasture and a pigpen, was an abbreviated dirt oval; sometimes the athletes lined it themselves. And yes, it smelled. "You ought to be down here when the temperature is 105," Temple said in 1960. "Between the rocks on the track and the pigs, let me tell you, it is rough around here."[16] He regularly had to get out a shovel and clear the cow patties. After complaining to the governor, the team got its first scholarships in 1967; it didn't have a complete track until 1978, after a Nashville newspaper featured photos of the giant potholes that pockmarked the old one. As Temple quipped, "Talk about Title IX? Shoot, we started at Title I."[17] (See 1972 entry on Immaculata.) The indifference was hardly unique to TSU, whose record was better than most; after all, it did at least field a women's team. In 1958 the US track coach, George Eastment, estimated that fewer than 200 American women were seriously training in track-and-field.[18]

The irony is that the Tigerbelles got a track worthy of their talents just as their glorious run was ending. Though TSU sent several athletes to the 1972 and 1976 Olympics, and the team was nationally competitive into the early 1980s, the writing was on the wall. After being ignored and ridiculed for decades, women athletes of all races were being wooed by larger, richer schools, thanks to Title IX. The last Tigerbelle to win Olympic gold was Chandra Cheeseborough in 1984; she is now the coach at TSU.

In a sense, TSU's relative decline can be seen as good news. Thanks to positive social changes in regard to both African Americans and women, by the 1970s TSU was no longer the only game in town for gifted black female athletes. They had more choices, and they exercised them.

Consider Evelyn Ashford, the premier American sprinter of the 1980s. She would have been a natural for the Tigerbelles, and Temple tried to recruit her,[19] but in 1976 she accepted one of the first female athletic scholarships to UCLA. The university was close to home and offered training, travel, equipment, and facilities far superior to those of TSU. In 16 years of competing at a world-class level, Ashford qualified for five Olympics. She won four golds and one silver medal; she was also chosen to be the flag-bearer for the American team at the 1988 Games in Seoul. Jackie Joyner-Kersee (see the 1993 entry on her), who considered Wilma Rudolph her role model,[20] also went to UCLA, and won six medals in four Olympics. These are not the kinds of careers even the greatest Tigerbelles could have imagined. But they helped to make them possible.

MAGAZINE COVER FEATURING TOMMY KONO

One of the redeeming qualities of sports is that they can offer structure and even purpose. Think of the child with indifferent parents who finds a mentor in a coach. Or the teenager who stays away from trouble to stay on the team. Or the people who train for charity runs in honor of a loved one.

Or think of Tamio "Tommy" Kono, sent to the Tule Lake internment camp in northern California as a 12-year-old for the crime of being a Japanese American during World War II. Ironically, the camp was actually good for his health; the dry desert air helped his asthma. And when a neighbor showed him how to use barbells and dumb-bells,[1] the boy took to it. Though his parents were concerned the activity was too strenuous,[2] he worked out in secret and developed new muscle—and confidence.[3]

Among others who were interned at Tule Lake were Pat Morita, the star of the *Karate Kid* films; George Takei of *Star Trek* fame; Bob Matsui, who would serve 13 terms in Congress; and Emerick Ishikawa, a well-known weight-lifter who would compete for the United States in the London Olympics in 1948, finishing sixth. Kono regarded Ishikawa with awe. The older man's weights, he recalled, "looked like train wheels to me."[4] But Kono's career would far eclipse that of his boyhood hero; for a time, he was the biggest star in his sport.

Released after the war, Kono's family set-tled in Sacramento, where he finished high school—and kept lifting. He began training seriously in the late 1940s. By 1952 he was on the army weightlifting team and ready to compete internationally.

More than ready; Kono didn't lose for the next eight years. That included two Olympic gold medals, one at Helsinki in 1952 (competing at 67.5 kilograms) and the other in Melbourne in 1956 (competing at 82.5 kilograms). He also won the world championships every year from 1953 to 1959. He slumped to a silver in Rome in 1960 (competing at 75 kilograms), and medaled in two more world championships (bronze in 1961, silver in 1962). Over this period, he set 26 world records in four different weight classes;[5] the latter is an achievement no one has matched. In 2005, the International Weightlifting Federation named him the greatest lifter of the previous 100 years.[6]

While weightlifting has never been a sport that attracts much attention, Kono's excellence could not be overlooked. Not only did he routinely make the magazine covers of the sport's press, such as in the photo on the previous page, he was also an eight-time finalist for the Sullivan Award, given to the nation's best amateur athlete, finishing second four times—behind shot-putter/discus thrower Parry O'Brien in 1959, sprinter Wilma Rudolph in 1961, miler Jim Beatty in 1962, and pole-vaulter John Pennel in 1963.[7] He also had a successful career as a bodybuilder, winning the Mr. Universe title in 1955, 1957, and 1961.

After retiring from competition in 1964, Kono became a coach, working with the Mexican, West German, and American men's teams, as well as with the first US women's weight-lifting teams in the late 1980s. He published several books on weight lifting and designed weight-lifting equipment, such as knee and waist bands. Unfortunately, Kono saw US performance decline over this period; no American man has won an Olympic medal in the sport since 1988, and only one woman has done so.

Kono sometimes wore glasses when he competed, and he was highly regarded for his humane approach to the sport and generosity with young lifters. But in the heat of competition, he was an intimidating presence. When he "looks at me from the wings," said a Soviet rival, "it works on me like a python on a rabbit."[8]

MILAN HIGH SCHOOL LETTER JACKET AND OSCAR ROBERTSON'S CRISPUS ATTUCKS JERSEY

Sometimes life imitates art, sometimes art imitates life, and sometimes the two are so close together as to make no difference. That is the case with the stories of Milan and Crispus Attucks high schools. In 1954 Milan (enrollment 161) became the smallest school ever to win the Indiana state basketball championship. The following year Crispus Attucks became the first all-black team to win. The two schools weave together the two strands of Indiana's hoops culture: one rural and predominantly white, the other urban and mostly black.

Milan's victory made the team of crew-cut farm boys local heroes, and they became national legends in 1986, thanks to the movie *Hoosiers*, which was based on the Milan miracle. The Milan Indians were no fluke, however. They had reached the state tourney's Final Four in 1953 and had gone 19–2 during the regular season. Milan, about 50 miles west of Cincinnati, was home to 1,100 people at the time; the school also served nearby communities like Pierceville (population 45), birthplace of the star guard, Bobby Plump. When a new coach, 24-year-old Marvin Wood, came to town in 1952, bringing both modern tactics and a serious case of the fundamentals, he clicked with a critical mass of boys who had been playing together for years.[1]

The game was different in 1954, in ways that made it possible for teams that looked overmatched to compete. Most important, there was no shot clock. If Milan got ahead, Wood called for the "cat and mouse"—that is, the stall. In one game in the 1953 tournament, Plump held the ball for eight interminable minutes.[2]

The cat and mouse played a major role in the 1954 championship game against much bigger, much taller Muncie Central, which had won the title in 1951 and 1952. This was not a great game, on the merits; both teams shot poorly, and at critical times, the play was sloppy. As the fourth quarter opened, the score was 26–26. With six-plus minutes left and Muncie leading 28–26, Wood called for the cat and mouse. If the Indians were fouled, they could sink free throws. Otherwise, the idea was to keep the game close and take their chances at the end. So Plump stood near center court, cradling the ball and occasionally looking over at Wood for guidance. For more than three minutes, nothing happened. It is not the most thrilling hoops sequence ever filmed, but it is oddly compelling.[3]

With three minutes left, the action resumed. Plump missed a shot from the top of the key; Muncie rebounded, but turned the ball over. Milan scored to tie, 28–28, with a little more than two minutes left. Plump drew a foul and sank two free throws. Milan up two. Muncie took the ball in, and on yet another careless pass, Milan took it back.

No cat and mouse here. Milan's Ray Craft found himself in position inside, went for it—a basket would give them a decisive four-point lead—and watched his shot curl out. Muncie tied it up with a backdoor layup. Forty-five seconds left. Plumb got the inbound pass, dribbled in place—the lack of defensive pressure is astonishing—then made his move with six seconds to go. Dribbling with his right hand, Plumb drove, faked left, stepped right, and drained a 14-footer as time expired. Final score: 32–30 for Milan. A legend was born. A few weeks later, the players were rewarded with letter jackets; this one belonged to Gene White, the 5-foot-11 center.

A 32–30 victory betokens something less than a masterpiece, but there was a lot more to Milan's play than strategic standing around. The team could certainly score, putting up 60 against Terre Haute in the semis and 39 in the first half against Crispus Attucks High School in the quarterfinals.

Crispus Attucks was founded in 1927 to segregate black Indianapolis students; they were not allowed to attend any other public high school. Then, because Crispus Attucks by definition was for blacks only, state basketball authorities barred it from entering the state tournament on the grounds that it was not open to all.[4] That catch-22 was dissolved in 1942, but a number of Indianapolis schools continued to refuse to play the Tigers. Ray Crowe, who became coach in 1950, used to tell his players that they were playing five against seven—the team could expect no close calls from the all-white referee crews.[5]

Talent has a way of asserting itself, however, and the Tiger teams of the 1950s were stuffed with talent, including two future Harlem Globetrotters. The biggest star of all was Oscar Robertson, who was a sophomore when Milan beat the Tigers in 1954. The next year, Crispus Attucks was ready to break through. After losing just one game during the regular season, it beat Gary Roosevelt 97–74, becoming the first all African American team to win the championship. Robertson wore this jersey in the final, in which Crispus Attucks set a record that still stands for most points scored—a style of play a world away from Milan's hold-and-hope strategy.[6]

In 1956 Crispus Attucks did itself one better, going undefeated and repeating as state champions.

It would be pleasant to report that all of Indianapolis embraced the Tigers, the first team from the city to win the tourney. The team did make the traditional parade, riding a fire truck from Butler Fieldhouse to Monument Circle downtown. But unlike the teams in every other year, the Tigers were not allowed to get off and take pictures. Instead, the truck made a circle and headed to the black side of town.[7] The players suspected, bitterly and probably correctly, that the authorities feared they would make trouble.[8]

There can never be another Milan miracle. Hundreds of small schools disappeared through consolidation, and in 1997 Indiana eliminated its single-class state tournament. Now schools of similar size play only against each other. But *Hoosiers* keeps the story alive—and also pays quiet homage to the history of Indiana hoops. In the climactic scene, the hero from Hickory High takes his final shot from the exact same place on the floor that Plump did.[9] And in another art-imitates-life moment, the coach of the other team is played by Ray Crowe—Crispus Attucks's longtime coach.[10]

1955

PAINTING OF STILLMAN'S GYM

Dirty, smelly, clouded in a fog of tobacco, filled with characters straight out of Damon Runyon, and run by a crusty lifer with a foul mouth: that is the stereotype of the midcentury boxing gym.

It is also a precise description of Stillman's, the "University of Eighth Avenue," as boxing writer A. J. Liebling called it.[1] The second-floor gym was a few blocks from Madison Square Garden, *Ring* magazine, and the Neutral Corner, the saloon of choice.[2]

As the capital of American boxing for three decades, Stillman's was as famous as its fighters. Outsiders paid 50 cents for the privilege of watching the workouts and of getting abused by proprietor Lou Stillman. Everyone paid, even Frank Sinatra and Tony Bennett, who were known to go to the gym for a break between sets. Marlon Brando took in the place to prepare for his role as a washed-up pug in *On the Waterfront*.[3] The gym itself had a major role in *Somebody Up There Likes Me*, the 1956 film starring Paul Newman as fighter Rocky Graziano.

There were rules, of course. "No rubbish or spitting on the floor, under penalty of law," read one sign,[4] above the gobs of spittle and litter. For Stillman, the grime was a matter of principle: "I keep the place like this for the fighters' own sake. If I cleaned it up, they'd catch a cold from the cleanliness." Featherweight champ Johnny Dundee noted of fresh air, "Why, that stuff is likely to kill us."[5]

Naturally, Stillman was not Stillman's real name. Born Lou Ingber, he was a beat cop before he went to work for an eccentric philanthropist, Alpheus Geer, who ran something called the Marshall Stillman movement, designed to reform burglars through boxing.[6] Ingber became so identified with the establishment that he changed his name; everyone called him "Stillman" anyway. The do-gooders abandoned the program when their equipment was stolen. Stillman decided to keep it going as a business, eventually moving it from uptown Harlem to midtown Manhattan.

His trusty sidekick was Whitey Bimstein, the inspiration for the trainer in the *Rocky* movies. Bimstein figured he trained more than 7,500 boxers;[7] he was also one of the great cutmen. When Graziano got nailed above the eye during a middleweight championship fight, Bimstein lanced the hematoma with a silver dollar in less than a minute. Graziano won three rounds later.[8]

Georges Carpentier (see the 1921 entry) trained at Stillman's when he was in the United States. Primo Carnera, Joe Louis, and Gene Tunney dropped in on occasion.[9] Jack Dempsey, Lou Ambers, James J. Braddock, Billy Conn, Kid Gavilan, Billy Graham, Willie Pep, Sugar Ray Robinson, Jersey Joe Walcott—champions all—were

regulars. Tough but democratic, Stillman described his management philosophy this way: "Big or small, champ or bum, I treated 'em all the same way—bad. If you treat them like humans, they'll eat you alive."[10]

At its peak, some 375 boxers paid a monthly fee to Stillman's, and the place was so crowded fighters could get hurt shadowboxing. But time and television took a toll. Instead of going to the Friday night fights, fans stayed home and watched them. That meant fewer fights, and thus fewer fighters, and thus fewer people training. "The racket's dead," Stillman said in February 1959,[11] estimating that only 75 fighters were enrolled in his school of hard knocks. The gym closed a few weeks later.

This painting is by John Cullen Murphy, the author's father. Murphy's early career was in sports illustration; he then began drawing *Big Ben Bolt*, a comic strip featuring a college-educated boxer that ran from 1950 to 1978. In the image above, painted around 1955, Murphy captures the dingy camaraderie of the place. There is, however, a glaring flaw. Light didn't flow into Stillman's with such golden brilliance. The windows were never cleaned.

1956

YOGI BERRA'S CATCHER'S MITT

Yogi Berra participated in 19 World Series as a player, manager, and coach. He was a 15-time all-star and a three-time most valuable player (1951, 1954, 1955).[1] The number Berra liked most, however, was 10. That's how many World Series–winning teams he played on—more than anyone else in baseball history.[2]

If there was an award for most likable athlete, Berra might have won that, too. And he certainly would have won the prize for being the most quotable. Among the jewels in the Yogi lexicon are the following:

> "It ain't over 'til it's over."
> "It's deja vu all over again."
> "When you come to a fork in the road, take it."
> "You can observe a lot by watching."[3]
> "You got to be very careful if you don't know where you're
> going because you might not get there."[4]

His geniality, combined with his unique command of language, sometimes made Berra the butt of patronizing comments. That was to underestimate the man greatly. Almost every Yogism had the truth of a mystically inflected epigram. That was appropriate: Lawrence Peter Berra did not get his nickname—the best ever, hands down—from a cartoon bear. It dated, he said, from his boyhood, when he and a friend saw a film that featured a yogi; for some reason the figure evoked young Larry. From then on, to everyone but his immediate family, he was Yogi.[5]

In every important way, this son of Italian immigrants was not just a winner but a man of wisdom and character. As a seaman second class, he manned a machine gun on a rocket boat to Omaha Beach on D-Day, ahead of the landing forces.[6] He had a happy, 64-year marriage. He was financially shrewd; indeed, he was one of the first players to hire an agent. Berra dropped out of school after the eighth grade, but in later life gave his time, money, and attention to a well-regarded learning center in New Jersey. His calm dignity made people like Yankees owner George Steinbrenner look small.

The glove pictured here is from Berra's eighth World Series, in 1956, which the Yankees won in seven games against the Brooklyn Dodgers. Berra used this glove to catch journeyman pitcher Don Larsen's perfect game—the only one in World Series history. Larsen, who had lasted less than two innings in his first Series start, would later say he didn't shake off Berra once during his 97-pitch masterpiece,[7] a tribute to the catcher's hard-won baseball savvy.

Berra had struggled defensively as a young player, so manager Casey Stengel asked Hall of Fame catcher Bill Dickey to tutor him. Berra soaked it all in, and in his prime he was regarded as one of the smartest backstops in the game.[8] Ted Williams said that more than any other catcher, Berra noticed when he or other hitters shifted their feet—a subtle sign of their intentions.[9] "Talking to Yogi Berra about baseball," baseball commissioner A. Bartlett Giamatti once said, "is like talking to Homer about the gods."[10]

As an individual, Berra became a cherished national institution who was willing to poke gentle fun at himself. As a player, he is best understood as a key Yankee in the team's most dominant era. From his first full season in 1947 to his last, in 1963, Yankee teams won 15 pennants.

This was not the only Yankee dynasty. Love them, or more likely, loathe them, they are by far baseball's most successful team. The Yankees won their first pennant in 1921, after trading for a certain George Herman Ruth, and their first World Series in 1923. Since then, they have racked up 26 more. St. Louis ranks second, with 11.

The Yankee championships have occurred over several distinct dynastic eras. There was the Age of Ruth (1923–1928), when the team won its first three championships. Then there was the Age of DiMaggio (1936–1943), when they won six more, followed by the Berra-Mantle era (1947–1964). After a pause for mediocrity—call them the Horace Clarke years—there was the Age of Crazy. From 1976 to 1981, the Yankees went 2–3 in the World Series. Finally, there was the Age of Jeter (1996–2001), in which the teams managed by Joe Torre chipped in four more, plus another in 2009.

Yogi Berra was not the greatest player the Yankees ever had. But he was the greatest winner—and the most beloved. Shortly before his death in September 2015, at age 90, he summed his life up in his own inimitable way: "If I had to do it all over again, I would do it all over again."

1958

FIRST MODERN ARTHROSCOPE

"Arthroscopic surgery" does not describe a procedure, but rather the device that enables it: the arthroscope, whose name derives from the Greek *arthron* (meaning joint), and *skopein* (to look at). An arthroscope, then, looks at joints.

In medical terms, this is not a new instrument. A primitive kind of scope was found at Pompeii, the Roman city destroyed by a volcano in AD 79. The first remotely modern arthroscope dates to the early 1800s, when a German doctor illuminated two tubes with a candle to examine the inside of the bladder. The instrument slowly grew in sophistication, though it still seems a case of the examination being worse than the illness. (One French doctor ignited a mixture of turpentine and gas to create light that would bounce off mirrors to provide a view of the bladder.)[1]

In 1912 a Danish physician used a scope to examine the inside of the knee joint; he also coined the term "arthroscopy," which stuck. Arthroscopy advanced steadily from there, and after World War II a Japanese doctor, Masaki Watanabe, continued the work. He designed scope after scope, adapting electronics and optics to create the finest arthroscopes in the world. His masterpiece, completed in 1958 and known as Watanabe number 21, is considered the first modern arthroscope.[2] The twenty-first-century version, shown here, does not look much different from Watanabe's finest.

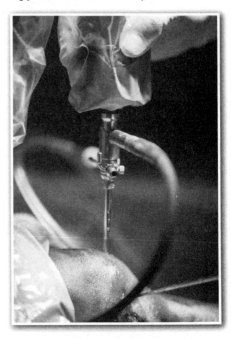

So what does all this have to do with sports? For centuries, the arthroscope had satisfied curiosity and helped in diagnosis. But with Watanabe's version, it also became a means of treatment. He performed the first arthroscopic knee surgery on a 17-year-old who had twisted his knee playing hoops. The young man went home that day and was back on the court weeks later. American surgeons began cautiously using the procedure in the early 1970s; by the end of that decade, it was routine.[3]

For his work, Watanabe is routinely referred to as the "father of modern arthroscopy."[4] But he could be also be called the "father of second chances," because that is what arthroscopic surgery, the most common orthopedic procedure in the country,[5] has offered to thousands of athletes.

Its great advantage is a small one. Rather than carving up a whole joint to see the problem, in arthroscopic surgery, the doctor makes a small incision—as short as a quarter of an inch—into which the scope can be inserted to look and operate through. That means less trauma to the body and a swifter recovery.

In late 1981 downhill skier Steve Mahre underwent arthroscopic surgery on both knees; five weeks later, he became the first American man to win a World Cup race.[6] Gymnast Mary Lou Retton (see the 1984 entry) was back in the gym the day after her operation.[7] In both cases the surgery was relatively minor. Not so Adrian Peterson's. The Minnesota Vikings running back ripped up his anterior cruciate ligament (ACL) in December 2011. After arthroscopic surgery, he was back on the field, at full speed and strength, at the beginning of the next season.

Arthroscopy can be done on any joint, including hips, wrists, and ankles.[8] But along with the knee, the most famous kind has to do with the elbow—better known as Tommy John surgery. In a fairer world, it would be known as Frank Jobe surgery, for the doctor who invented it. In this procedure—officially "ulnar collateral ligament reconstruction"—an elbow ligament is replaced by a tendon from another part of the body. Tommy John was the first pitcher to try it; he pitched for another 14 years.

Like any medical procedure, there is risk involved, but arthroscopy has proved its mettle. As of 2015, more than 500 major league pitchers had undergone Tommy John surgery;[9] about 80 percent made it back to the majors,[10] and two-thirds pitched to the same standard as before.[11]

For sports fans, arthroscopic procedures have brought longer careers for great athletes, but also a sense of wistfulness. Red Grange, Billie Jean King, Sandy Koufax, Mickey Mantle, Joe Namath, Bobby Orr, Gale Sayers, Smoky Joe Wood, and many others—what more could they have achieved if arthroscopy had been available for them?

1958

ARTIFACTS FROM THE "GREATEST GAME"

This wasn't the greatest game in history, not by a long shot. There was too much sloppy play and not enough of the really stirring big moments—the downfield bomb, the broken-field run—that make for a classic. The kicking was appalling.

But that is to look at a beautiful landscape and see only the litter. If a great game is one that gets people so involved that they won't leave the couch to get another beer, the label fits. And even though this contest wasn't the greatest game in pro football history, it is undoubtedly the most important.

The date was December 28, 1958. The place was Yankee Stadium. The occasion was the twenty-sixth National Football League championship. The teams were the New York Giants and the Baltimore Colts. Fifteen Hall of Famers were involved.[1] The first football championship to be televised nationwide, it was watched by 45 million people, the largest viewing audience for an American sporting event to that time. When it ended, the NFL had broken through in a way it never had before.

For three quarters and 13 minutes, the game was good, but slipshod. Both teams missed chances and gave away opportunities; there were two missed field goal attempts. The Giants fumbled four times; two of these fumbles, by the normally sure-handed halfback, Hall of Famer Frank Gifford, set up two Colts touchdowns and a 14–3 half-time lead.

In the second half, the Colts had a first and goal from the three and didn't score. The Giants defense would not let them pass, twice stuffing fullback Alan Ameche.[2] Given new heart, New York's offense stepped up and capitalized on their limited opportunities to score two touchdowns. The Giants could have sealed the deal late in the fourth quarter with one more first down, but Gifford was stopped just short. After a punt, the Colts took possession on their own 14, with 1:56 left, down 17–14.

It was the kind of situation that Colts quarterback Johnny Unitas, 25, was born for. Rejected by Notre Dame and Pitt, then cut from the Pittsburgh Steelers without throwing a pass, he knew the hard knocks of football life. He had been playing semipro ball for $6 a game when a fan tipped the Colts to give him a shot. This was his second year as a starter. Even though he hadn't played particularly well thus far, with a fumble and an interception, Unitas had the essential quality of the true leader: he could inspire others to believe in him and in themselves. Hall of Fame tight end John Mackey would say that at moments like these, it was "like being in the huddle with God."[3]

In the cool and misty early evening air, as patches of ice began to appear on the field, Unitas picked apart the Giants' secondary, informed by the game plan featured in this photo. After a first-down pass to flanker Lenny Moore, three straight throws to wide receiver Raymond Berry, who would have 12 catches on the day, moved the Colts 62 yards. Forty years later, Giants Hall of Fame linebacker Sam Huff would say that "Unitas to Berry," the phrase he heard so often that day, "still rings in my ears."[4]

With seven seconds left, Steve Myhra used this shoe to kick this ball through this goal post for a 20-yard field goal to tie the score 17–17. For the first time in NFL history, a game went into overtime. The first team to score would win the game—and the title, and the $4,718.77 winners' share.[5]

The Giants won the toss to get the first possession and could do nothing with it. Unitas, playing with complete cool, could. He directed a 13-play, 80-yard drive of such precision and unpredictability that the Giants defense was befuddled. "When you thought he'd call a running play, he'd pass," Huff would recall, "and when you were sure he was going to pass, he'd call a run."[6] The famous image of the final play tells the story. It shows Ameche running in the game-winning touchdown from the one-yard line. The hole

he is running through is, quite literally, big enough for a truck to go through.[7] The Giants had been expecting a pass.[8]

Even at the time, people realized that this game had meant something special. Commissioner Bert Bell was overcome: "This is the greatest day in the history of professional football!"[9] The Associated Press would write the day after, "It seems pro football has come of age." The prescience of that announcement would become apparent the following year, when football telecasts began to rack up much bigger numbers.

Watching from a hotel room in Texas, the son of a wealthy oil family watched the game and thought, "Well, that's it. This sport really has everything. And it televises well. Who knew what that meant?"[10] Lamar Hunt would draw his own conclusions—and change the course of football history (see the next entry).

1959

STATUE OF LAMAR HUNT

In the late twentieth century, professional athletes in many sports earned two things: money and power. Lamar Hunt had as much to do with that as any other individual. He was a force in three sports: football, soccer, and tennis. In each case, he disrupted the status quo and in the process helped to build something better. That is why he is a member of the halls of fame for all of those sports, a unique achievement.[1] Oh, and he was also one of the founding partners of the Chicago Bulls basketball team. Remarkably, Hunt did all this while retaining the respect of almost everyone he dealt with. In a field with more than its share of sharks, he was known as a good man and a loyal friend.

Hunt, a member of the Texas family that made serious money in oil and commodities, had little interest in drilling for more dollars. While his two older brothers stayed in the family business (and almost lost it all in a failed attempt to corner the world silver market), all Lamar Hunt wanted was to get into sports. Even as a college student, he set up a batting cage and miniature golf course.[2] As an adult, he would think bigger.

He made his biggest mark in football. When the National Football League rejected his bid to start a new team in Dallas, the 27-year-old Hunt brought together eight other men who also wanted to break into the NFL. In 1960 he was the first among equals in the founding of the American Football League. The AFL struggled but prevailed, in large part because Hunt insisted on revenue sharing among all the teams, a principle that stabilized franchise finances. In 1966 Hunt was one of the AFL owners who negotiated the merger with the NFL, including a championship game between the two. How about calling it the Super Bowl, he mused? Hunt was also the one to suggest naming the Super Bowl trophy after Vince Lomardi. The Packers coach was no friend of the AFL, but Hunt thought the gesture would help unify the sport.[3]

His team, the Kansas City Chiefs (moved from Dallas in 1963), lost the first Super Bowl to Lombardi's Packers, but it won the fourth (or IVth), Hunt's proudest moment in sports. It was Hunt who suggested that the Super Bowls be numbered with Roman numerals,[4] a rare lapse into pretentiousness for a zillionaire who flew coach. The Hunt family still owns the Chiefs; this statue outside the team's Arrowhead Stadium honors him.

Then Hunt turned to tennis, helping to found and largely bankrolling the World Championship Tennis tour for men. Until 1968, when "open tennis" began (see the 1968/1975 entry on Arthur Ashe), pro players were banned from the four majors (Wimbledon and the Australian, French, and US championships). The WCT forced the issue when it recruited the "Handsome Eight," a group that included five premier amateurs, John Newcombe and Tony Roche among them. This further stripped the amateur game of top players. The mandarins of tennis were forced to give in; the major tourneys were running perilously short of major talent.

After a difficult start, the WCT signed up a large share of the best players to healthy contracts, ran tournaments in major cities, and established a ranking system and a year-end championship. It also was the first tour to use the tie-breaker and to allow players to perform in something other than white attire. By 1970 almost all the top players had joined.

The International Lawn Tennis Federation (ILTF) was the established tennis organization—essentially, the equivalent of the NFL. While it had mismanaged the game into near-irrelevance, it had the possessiveness and sense of entitlement of most monopolists. It saw the WTC, quite rightly, as competition for its own Grand Prix, which included three of the four majors. In 1971 it banned WCT players from Grand Prix events. That meant that John Newcombe could not defend his Wimbledon title, and Rod Laver, Ken Rosewall, and Arthur Ashe could not compete. The situation was both ridiculous and untenable.

Tennis politics is more boring than most; the upshot is that the WCT and ILTF managed to negotiate a semipeaceful coexistence for some years,[5] but the WCT was marginalized in the 1980s as the players gained more power.[6] In 1990 it was dissolved. But by establishing a well-run, well-funded circuit, the WCT had accelerated the formation of the open era, improved the financial standing of the players, and generally raised the game. Stan Smith, a first-rate player who turned pro in 1969, wrote to Hunt that he "would always consider you and your organization as the founders of our modern professional game."[7]

While the WCT was getting started, Hunt also had an interest in the Dallas Tornado, the Texas entry in the obscure United Soccer Association. In 1968 that league merged with another obscure one to form the North American Soccer League. The NASL flared brilliantly, and briefly, on the back of the incomparable Pelé (see the 1975 entry on him), as well as on Hunt's money. Then it fizzled just as dramatically. Hunt lost millions, but never gave up on soccer. He helped to put on the men's World Cup in 1994[8] and was one of the founders of Major League Soccer two years later. MLS has not joined the athletic big time, but it is growing steadily. For a time, Hunt owned three MLS teams—Columbus, Dallas, and Kansas City—and the league may not have survived without his constant support. Hunt died in 2006, but he leaves a substantive legacy in three sports. Don Garber, the longtime commissioner of MLS, put it simply: "There's no American soccer today, without Lamar Hunt."[9]

1960

PETE ROZELLE'S TYPEWRITER

This is a mid-1940s Royal, the kind of clunker one could imagine a hard-bitten reporter pounding away at in a postwar noir flick. From the man behind its keys, however, came something rather different: a sports revolution. From 1960 to 1989, Pete Rozelle used this typewriter to transform the American sports landscape. On Rozelle's watch, football became the country's favorite sport, and the Super Bowl became an unofficial civic holiday celebrated rather more seriously than many official ones.

"Pete who?" That was the reaction when, out of exhaustion more than anything else, the 12 National Football League (NFL) owners named Rozelle commissioner in January 1960. They had deadlocked on their first 22 votes[1] and needed a compromise candidate. As the general manager of the Los Angeles Rams, Rozelle had proven his ability to herd cats by working with four fractious co-owners—two of whom wouldn't even ride in the same elevator together.[2] This, and the fact that no one disliked him enough to veto him, were his main qualifications. Rozelle himself called the idea "ludicrous."[3]

Nevertheless, he took the job. The grand old men of the NFL were sure that the "boy czar" would just follow orders. Washington Redskins owner George Marshall called him a "good boy"; the less polite used the term "amiable mouse"[4] or the "boy wonder."

That was a colossal miscalculation. Rozelle became the most consequential commissioner in the history of American sports. He gave notice early on that he was willing to act with the authority of a czar, even to his elders. In 1962 he fined one of the NFL's founders, George Halas of the Chicago Bears (see the 1925 entry on Red Grange), for intemperate remarks about officiating.[5] In 1963 he exercised his czarist prerogative again,

suspending two stars, Paul Hornung of the Green Bay Packers and Alex Karras of the Detroit Lions, for gambling.

Rozelle's signature moment occurred in 1961. When he took over, the game was healthier than it had ever been; average attendance had risen from 23,356 in 1950 to 43,617 by the end of the decade.[6] But Rozelle sensed that there was a much bigger market to be tapped, and that television was the way to do it. Taking a page from Lamar Hunt of the detested American Football League (AFL; see 1959 entry), Rozelle coaxed the NFL's owners to agree to a unified, league-wide television contract—and to divvy up the loot equally. It took an act of Congress to make this structure legal, and he got that, too. In the first deal negotiated on these terms, the league got $9.3 million from CBS, a quantum leap;[7] two years later, the figure was almost $28 million.[8]

This agreement, as well as other forms of revenue sharing, established the foundation for the NFL's financial stability and competitiveness. Every time a contract was due to be renewed, Rozelle won better and better terms. The boy wonder was now the golden boy. Pittsburgh Steelers owner Art Rooney dubbed him "a gift from the hand of Providence."[9]

An even bigger challenge was the formation of the AFL, which shook up the elder league's complacent hegemony. Initially, Rozelle sought to throttle the infant league. There is no doubt that his desire to kill the AFL in its crib was genuine; the bad feelings between the two leagues ran deep. A by-product of the battle, though, was to keep football in the news even when it was not on the field.[10] When the AFL failed to fail, Rozelle accepted that there needed to be a truce; players' salaries were rising fast, and the owners in both leagues were feeling some pain. That would never do.

While negotiators settled the terms of the merger of the two leagues in 1966, Rozelle worked out a deft quid pro quo with two powerful Louisiana lawmakers, Senator Russell Long and Representative Hale Boggs. The duo slipped in some language authorizing the merger in an unrelated bill;[11] New Orleans got a franchise 11 days later.[12] The merged entity, which Rozelle led, had strong teams, rich owners, natural rivalries, and national reach. It was ready to take over American sports, and did. By 1964 a national poll found that football had overtaken baseball as the country's favorite sport,[13] and the margin has widened since. The seven most-watched television shows are all Super Bowls.

ARNOLD PALMER'S VISOR FROM THE US OPEN

Whice the beginnings and endings of a golf era cannot always be established with precision, it's broadly true that Ben Hogan was The Man for much of the 1950s, that Arnold Palmer had taken over by the end of that decade, and that Jack Nicklaus assumed the role by 1965. And for a few hours on June 18, 1960, on the back nine of the US Open at Cherry Hills, the past, present, and future of golf battled it out. The present, in the form of Palmer, won. But the past, Hogan, was tied for the lead at the seventy-first hole, and the future, Nicklaus, was two strokes ahead with six holes to play.

Going into the last round, Palmer was seven strokes behind, in fifteenth place. When he mused that a 65 would bring him to 280, a competitive score for the US Open, even his good friend, golf writer Bob Drum, was dismissive: "You're too far back."[1] Palmer was nettled by the response. Also, he felt that while his first three rounds of 72, 71, and 72 were pedestrian, he was just a bump here and a putt there from going seriously low. There just might be a 65 for the taking.

The place to make a dent was on the front nine. Located in the mile-high city of Denver, Cherry Hills was a great course, but its relatively short 7,004 yards played even shorter because of the altitude. The front nine was just 3,316 yards.[2] There were birdies for the taking, and Palmer took 'em—six in the first seven holes. He made the turn in 30. A good start, but a long way to go; at this point, there were 11 players within three strokes of the lead.[3] Two of them were Hogan, 47, who wanted very much to win a record fifth US Open, and Nicklaus, a student at Ohio State with a rising reputation.

By the twelfth hole Nicklaus was five under and in the lead. Palmer, Hogan, and two others trailed by a stroke. But Nicklaus three-putted the thirteenth to drop into a tie. Then he three-putted 14, to go one back, tied for second with Palmer and Hogan. Hogan birdied 15, making a nice 20-footer, and now *he* was tied for the lead with

Palmer; a par on 16 kept him in position. Always known for his precision as a ball-striker, Hogan had hit every green in regulation—as he had in the third round as well.

At the seventeenth then, Hogan and Palmer were tied for the lead, at four under, with Nicklaus one back. Two pars would bring Hogan home in 280 and put some pressure on Palmer to match that or risk doing one better. The man the Scots approvingly called the "wee ice mon" for his cool and steady play could surely find two pars. Maybe he could have, but he decided to play aggressively. On his third shot of the par five, he went for the pin, which was sited perhaps 15 feet from a pond. Using his wedge, Hogan landed the ball almost exactly where he intended. "Almost" was not good enough; the ball spun and then splashed. Bogey. Angry but still fighting, Hogan again went for birdie on the eighteenth, but his effort to rip a big drive backfired, and he found water again. Triple-bogey. It must have been heartbreaking to watch, but Nicklaus was busy making his own mistakes, playing the last six holes in three over.

When Nicklaus and Hogan finished, Palmer was on the seventeenth, aware that he needed two pars for victory. And that seemed both doable and appropriate. After his electric start, Palmer had spent the back nine racking up par after par (plus one birdie) while all the other contenders imploded. So he now collected two more—and hit the magic number he had speculated would win, 280. His 65 was to that point the lowest round ever shot by the winner in the final of the Open. He jumped, whooped, and threw this visor into the air.

Nicklaus was second, two shots behind, the best showing for an amateur since 1933; six men tied for third, and Hogan tied for ninth. He would never come so close again; he could see the future coming. Hogan would tell the press he had played "with a kid who should have won this Open by 10 shots"—a compliment with a sting in the tail, and one Nicklaus never forgot.[4] Palmer went home with a check for $14,400[5] and notions of winning the Grand Slam.

The idea of a modern Grand Slam was relatively new; it didn't exist in 1953, when Hogan won the first three legs but couldn't compete at the PGA because it overlapped with the British Open. But the idea had been coalescing; in fact, Palmer published an essay in the *Saturday Evening Post*, "I Want That Grand Slam,"[6] in which he maintained that a professional Slam should be the US and British Opens, plus the Masters and the PGA. Like everything he did at that time, it got people's attention. Having won the 1960 Masters in dramatic fashion (birdieing the last two holes) and now the US Open, Palmer was halfway there. Next stop: the British Open, which he would play for the first time.

Today, of course, The Open is a highlight on every US pro's calendar. In 1960, it wasn't. Plane fares were expensive, and the British courses had been known to befuddle, even embarrass, American pros. St. Andrews had humbled Bobby Jones himself (see the 1930 entry on him). In addition, players had to survive two qualifying rounds to get any share of a small pot; in 1960, the winner took home just $3,500.[7] The Brits even used a smaller ball. In 1959, no American golfer bothered to compete.[8]

As the son of a golf pro, however, Palmer had a strong sense of history,[9] and the 100th anniversary of the British Open, to take place at the birthplace of golf, St. Andrews, was as historic as things get. Moreover, money was fast becoming no object to him. Since his breakout year, 1958, Palmer had become what was then a rare thing—a golf superstar. It was apparently impossible to write about the man without using the word "charisma" in the first paragraph, but this was a cliché with the force of truth. He had it, as well as rugged good looks, a powerful game, a flair for the dramatic, a warm personality, and a ton of sex appeal. When TV began covering golf, the camera could not take its mechanical eye off him.

Palmer, Nicklaus would say, "took golf from being a game for the few to a sport of the masses."[10] In 1960 he led the tour with $80,738 in winnings,[11] a tidy sum for the era, and he earned almost twice as much[12] from his various off-course activities, ranging from exhibitions to endorsements (ketchup, golf clubs, apparel) to a piece of a golf cart company. Palmer was the first golfer to professionalize his nontournament life—and he did (and still does) enormously well out of what became a corporate empire.

At St. Andrews in 1960 he came, he saw—and came one shot shy of conquering. He shot a wonderful 68 on the last round to tie the course record, but Australia's Kel Nagle broke it, to finish one ahead. Still, Palmer made a lot of friends, and he reignited interest in the British Open, among both fans and other players. When he won in both 1961 and 1962, bringing tons of media and tourists in his wake, the tournament became an essential stop on the golf calendar.

BILL RUSSELL'S 10,000-REBOUND BALL

Bill Russell is the greatest winner in team sports. From 1957 to 1969 his Boston Celtics won 11 championships; he was the only player to be part of all of them. In addition, he won two national titles at the University of San Francisco and, in 1956, an Olympic gold medal. He also won five most valuable player awards.

Russell played defense like no one before him, and in a way that influenced everyone who came after. Psychologically intimidating, he dominated games from the defensive end, something that came as a revelation. His offensive statistics were useful but not gaudy, an average of 15.1 points per game for his career. But he didn't need to pour in points for the Celtics to win, which is all that mattered to him.

When Russell joined the pros for the 1956–1957 season, pro hoops was still in its awkward phase, just seven years past the merger that created the National Basketball Association. There were franchises in Rochester and Fort Wayne, but not in Chicago or Los Angeles. Teams often played in low-rent venues and traveled on the cheap.

Russell quickly became the game's first black superstar, in a league with only about 15 African American players.[1] His was not a cuddly or anodyne public face. He frequently refused to give autographs and was frosty to the press. He once called basketball "the most shallow thing in the world"[2] and was openly critical of America's—and Boston's—racial hypocrisies.

Russell would have been great anywhere, but he could not have landed in a better place than Boston. His previous relationships with coaches had been unfriendly and adversarial,[3] but he clicked right away with Red Auerbach, who recognized his strengths. The Celtics had the core of a great team, including Bob Cousy and Bill Sharman, but it is no coincidence that they didn't win a title until Russell arrived to anchor the defense.[4] The next year, when he injured his ankle in the final, they faltered. Then they reeled off eight in a row. No one else, before or since, has won more than three straight. "We don't fear the Celtics without Bill Russell. Take him out and we can beat them," Lakers coach

John Kundla said after the 1959 finals. "He's the guy who whipped us psychologically. Russell has our club worrying every second."[5]

The Celtics had only seven set plays; the offense revolved around getting turnovers or taking the ball off the boards. That was Russell's specialty; he had a PhD in the geometry of basketball, as well as excellent timing and anticipation. This enabled him to out-rebound even bigger men. In 1962 he grabbed the ball shown here for his 10,000th rebound; for his career, he had 21,620 (an average of 22.5 per game)[6] and recorded 9 of the top 20 seasons.[7]

Russell made the defensive rebound an offensive weapon. Before he even hit the floor, he could get the ball to the outlet, and the fast break would be on. This style of play required a high degree of intelligence, teamwork, and trust. Auerbach therefore sought, and found, men who were great teammates as well as great players. As a result, the Celtics became that rare organization anywhere in the 1950s and 1960s—multiracial and harmonious. There were no divas and no black or white cliques;[8] the locker-room ribbing was both merciless and color blind. Russell remembered how one of his teammates mocked his brooding reputation: "I'd find him hunched over in the locker room with his fist on his chin, like Rodin's *Thinker*, scowling ridiculously." When Russell came in from the showers, he might see players sashaying around the locker room, modeling his stylish clothes.[9]

That attitude came from the top. Owner Walter Brown was genuinely beloved.[10] The Celtics believed in Auerbach, who said he made decisions based only on what would help the team win. His actions proved it. In his first year as the Celtics coach, in 1950, Auerbach drafted the league's first black player, Charles Cooper.[11] In 1965 the team was the first to play five black starters, and three years later he named the first black head coach in any pro sport: Russell, who led the team to two titles in three years.

Russell's prickly relationship to the game continued after his retirement. When the team wanted to raise his jersey to the rafters, he told Auerbach he would do it only in an empty Boston Garden, with a few teammates present.[12] Three years later, he made it clear he did not want to be inducted into the Hall of Fame (he was anyway). But when it came time for the Celtics to honor Auerbach in 1985, Russell did return for that. Why? "Red Auerbach is my friend."[13]

The NBA's Coach of the Year Award is named after Auerbach; the MVP award for the finals is named after Russell. And that seems right. Together, they made the Celtics great and the NBA better.

1966

MARVIN MILLER'S UNION CONTRACT

Two men transformed postwar baseball: Jackie Robinson (see the 1947 entry) and Marvin Miller. Robinson opened the game to people of talent, regardless of color. Miller enabled that talent to have a say in their destiny—and to profit from their skills.

When someone says, "It's not about the money," it's reasonable to assume that it is. In the case of the baseball players' union, however, it was not entirely about the money. The players had justified grievances that went much deeper. Specifically, due to the reserve clause, they had no say in where they played, and because of custom, they had almost no say in anything else.

The reserve clause, which dated to 1878 and eventually became a mandatory part of every contract, stated that players were the property of the team that signed them. Forever. Simply by enduring, the clause gained a kind of legitimacy. In congressional hearings in 1951, for example, a number of players, including Jackie Robinson, actually testified in favor of it.[1] They had absorbed the idea that baseball would collapse in a heap without it.

There were other concerns, however, including the pension plan and working conditions. In 1954 the players started the Major League Baseball Players' Association (MLBPA). This had a few minor successes, but it had only one part-time executive and acted as an interest group rather than a full-blown union.

On July 1, 1966, that changed forever, when the MLBPA hired a longtime labor executive, Marvin Miller, as its first paid, full-time executive director. The picture on the following page shows that first contract; his confident signature is on the lower right. Miller had two great advantages. First, he knew labor law cold. Second, he was an outsider. Where baseball people saw practices such as the reserve clause as engraved on horsehide tablets, for example, Miller considered it "the most abominable thing I'd ever seen."[2]

He was schooled in the facts of baseball life early on, when the owners summoned him a few weeks after he started, to inform him that they were changing the basis of

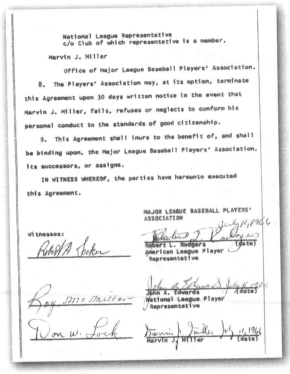

their pension contributions. No discussion, no negotiation; here's the deal, thanks for coming. Then it was Miller time. He proceeded to school them in the facts of labor law. You can't do that, he told them. The MLBPA is a duly empowered collective bargaining agent—and that means you have to talk to me. Round 1 to Miller, by a technical knockout.[3]

In 1968 he negotiated the first collective bargaining agreement (CBA), winning a substantial increase in the minimum salary (from $7,000 to $10,000)[4] and establishing some rules of engagement. It wasn't easy. The owners, in the words of the MLBPA general counsel, Dick Moss, were both "hostile and patronizing"; they fought tooth and nail over everything, from meal money to baseball card fees.[5] In 1970 Miller negotiated another CBA. Although this did not deal directly with the reserve clause, it contained a bomb, hidden in plain sight in the language of Article X, that would later explode the owners' comfortable superiority. This was the establishment of binding arbitration to resolve player grievances.[6]

For a time it didn't seem to matter. Management saw off Curt Flood's courageous challenge to the system when he opposed his trade from St. Louis to Philadelphia before the 1970 season.[7] In June 1972 the Supreme Court rejected Flood's argument, on antitrust grounds, that he had the right to negotiate with teams other than the one that had signed him once his contract expired. The justices described the sport's antitrust exemption as an "established aberration" that it was up to Congress to change.[8] Between the lines, they advised baseball to play nicer. The owners failed to take the hint.

Nor did they appear to recognize how the game had changed with regard to the MLBPA. In early 1972 the players went on strike, mostly over pension issues. The owners didn't believe they would do it, but they did. Then management was sure they would fracture. They didn't. After 13 days and the loss of 86 regular season games, the owners blinked—and got their first inkling that the union was for real.

Although Flood's lawsuit had failed, it was a useful failure that told Miller he could not look to the courts for action on the reserve clause. The case also brought the issue to public attention, and many people began to question, like Flood, the decency of a system that looked in all essentials like indentured servitude.

And Miller kept chipping away, improving conditions bit by bit while waiting for the right moment to strike at the reserve clause. One break came in 1974, when Catfish Hunter, the Hall of Fame pitcher, won a grievance against the Oakland A's owner, Charles Finley, for failing to fund an annuity promised in his contract.[9] The game's independent arbitrator, Peter Seitz—the human form of the arbitration time bomb planted in Article X—ruled that Finley had indeed violated the contract, and that Hunter could sell his services on the open market. This he promptly did, signing with the Yankees for $3.75 million for five years, about seven times what he was making with the A's. That opened players' eyes to the reality that their market value—if a market could be established—was much higher than their pay.

With the authority of the arbitrator established, the next step was to figure out how to challenge the reserve clause itself. The language of the standard player contract read that if a player refused to sign, the club could "renew the contract for a period of one year." Baseball had always interpreted this as one year, year after year, a perpetual renewal machine. Miller thought otherwise. Pitchers Andy Messersmith and Dave McNally agreed to play out their contracts and thus provide the basis for a test case.

Again, the case went to Seitz. The owners argued that baseball would descend into chaos and certain ruin without the reserve clause staying exactly the way it was.[10] Miller and the MLBPA argued that a year meant 365 days, not forever. Again, Seitz agreed with the union. He had barely finished reading his decision when he was handed a note telling him that baseball no longer needed his services, but the decision stood. Messersmith, who became baseball's first true free agent, promptly signed for more than double what the Dodgers had been offering.[11]

In the next CBA, the players and owners worked out a structure to allow players free agency after six years of service. It was a compromise that rewarded clubs for developing talent while allowing players to control part of their professional destiny. In its essentials, this system still exists.[12]

Settling a framework for free agency did not, of course, herald an era of good feelings. There have been numerous strikes (1980, 1981, 1985, 1994–1995) and lockouts (1973, 1976, and 1990).[13] The loss of the entire 1994 postseason disgusted fans and probably killed the Montreal Expos. And while the MLBPA was surely on the right side of history in its first decade, it has not always been so since, such as in its approach to steroids (see the 2007 entry).

Marvin Miller set baseball players free—and set an example for football (free agency in 1992) and basketball (1996). For almost a century, the negotiating position of the owners was "take it or leave it." Thanks to Miller, players forged a third option. It was the difference, Miller would say, "between dictatorship and democracy."[14]

And the money wasn't bad, either. In 1966, the year the players hired Marvin Miller, the average salary in baseball was $17,664. By 1982, the year he retired, it was $245,000,[15] and in 2015, it was $3.4 million.[16] The changes Miller provoked also made the owners much richer. In 1973 George Steinbrenner led a consortium that bought the Yankees for $8.7 million.[17] In 2015 the market value of the team was estimated at $3.2 *billion*.[18] The least valuable team, the well-run but largely unloved Tampa Bay Rays, was worth $625 million.

Like many prophets, Miller was not honored in his own time. Three times before his death in 2012, he was up for induction into the Hall of Fame. Three times the vote fell short, as did another try in 2014. His lack of a plaque in Cooperstown is almost incomprehensible—until one remembers it was just such stubborn blindness that he fought, and usually conquered.

1967

KATHRINE SWITZER'S BIB FROM THE BOSTON MARATHON

Kathrine Switzer was not the first woman to run America's oldest marathon; at least one woman, Roberta Gibbs, finished it as an unregistered "bandit" in 1966, after hiding in the bushes near the start.[1]

But Switzer is much better remembered because she was the first woman caught *trying* to run it. In 1967 she registered for the race under the name K. V. Switzer. It was a cold, blustery Patriots' Day. Instead of running in her lovingly prepared burgundy shorts and top,[2] Switzer ran in baggy sweats (and lipstick).[3] Her fellow runners could have been under no illusions about her sex. To a man, in fact, the 740 other runners welcomed her.[4]

A few miles in, however, a race official in an overcoat and fedora planted himself in the middle of the road and reached out to stop her. Switzer dodged and went on. A few moments later, she heard the thud of leather chasing her from behind. The marathon codirector, Jock Semple, had spotted her figure and semi-bouffant hair and diagnosed her as female. Outraged at this feminine mistake, he lunged at Switzer and yelled, "Get the hell out of my race and give me those numbers," as he tried to rip her bib off; a slight tear on the upper right of the bib is visible evidence of the effort.[5] With the help of friends, Switzer shrugged him off and finished in 4:20:02. (Gibbs, running as a bandit again, finished in 3:27:17.)[6]

The Semple/Switzer picture made front pages all over the country. Semple did himself no favors by continuing to open his mouth: "My wife is so mad at me over this," he said at one point, that "she gave my roast beef to the dog and made me buy my own Swanson's."[7] His colleague Will Cloney chirped, "If that girl [Switzer] were my daughter, I would spank her." Curmudgeons, yes, and the butt of much richly deserved ridicule, but the two had their allies. The Amateur Athletic Union stripped Switzer of her membership for, among other things, running in a competition longer than the 1.5 miles then allowed for women.

Women runners would have the last laugh. Over the next four years a few more ran the marathon unofficially, and in 1972 Boston allowed them to register. Male runners had no problem sharing the roads with women, and there was no rule or law to bar them. Resistance was futile.

In the end, Semple displayed a puckish graciousness about the whole thing. Spotting Switzer at the starting line before the 1973 race, he grabbed her and said, "C'mon lass, let's get a wee bit o' notoriety." And kissed her soundly.[8] The two became friends, finding common ground in their love of running. Semple respected Switzer once he saw that she was a serious athlete; Switzer respected Semple for keeping the Boston Marathon going through some very lean decades. She ran Boston eight times, finishing second in 1975 with a personal best of 2:51:37. She also organized races all over the world and played a role in the addition of the women's marathon to the Los Angeles Olympics in 1984.

One thing Switzer couldn't do was to keep up with the competition. As more women took to the sport, they got much better. Nina Kuscsik won the 1972 Boston marathon in 3:10:26. In Los Angeles in 1984, Joan Benoit Samuelson, a proud daughter of New England, won the first women's Olympic marathon in 2:24:52.

<u>1967</u>

BENCH FROM THE ICE BOWL

It introduced the phrase "the frozen tundra" to the football lexicon. It provided the coda to what may be the best football book ever written, *Instant Replay*. It was the end of the Green Bay Packers dynasty. The game forever known as the Ice Bowl, played on December 31, 1967, was terrific sport. What made it the stuff of legend were the conditions. At game time, the temperature was minus 13 degrees; with the wind chill, it felt like minus 48.[1]

It also featured two of the greatest coaches in National Football League history, Tom Landry of the Dallas Cowboys and Vince Lombardi of the Green Bay Packers. From their days on the New York Giants in the 1950s, when Landry ran the defense and Lombardi the offense, the two had mixed respect and rivalry. Landry was a quiet stoic from Texas. Lombardi was a passionate loudmouth from Brooklyn. In other ways, their characters were similar: they were both religious, intense, and driven.

Lombardi was the first to leave New York, taking over the browbeaten Packers in 1959; the team hadn't had a winning season in 11 years. From then through 1967, he led it to a record of 89 wins, 29 losses, and four ties,[2] winning six conference titles and five championships, including the first two Super Bowls.

Landry took over the expansion Cowboys in 1960 and didn't have a good team until 1966, when the team lost a heartbreaker to the Packers in the conference championship, 34–27. But the Packers were beginning to age, while the Cowboys were a team on the rise. Going into this game, Lombardi had ulcers; Landry had the sense his time had come.

Neither man had anticipated the arctic front that drove temperatures down 30 degrees overnight. It was so cold that the electric coils beneath Lambeau Field, installed to keep the field playable, also froze. The teams played on a rock-hard field, with a layer of ice on top. The officials could not use their whistles because they stuck to their lips. Several players got frostbite, and one fan died of exposure. Before the game, announcer Frank Gifford set the tone with the comment, "I think I'll take another bite of my coffee."[3]

One end of this bench, used by the Packers, was popular because it was adjacent to the warmer—which then ran out of fuel.[4] There was no respite.

The Packers forged a 14–0 lead early in the second quarter, but the Cowboys turned two turnovers into 10 points and trailed at the half only 14–10, a score that held up into the fourth quarter. Then, showing some razzle-dazzle, the Cowboys ran an option play in which running back Dan Reeves, who had taken a handoff, found wide receiver Lance Rentzel for a 50-yard touchdown. With 4:50 left, Dallas was ahead for the first time, 17–14.

Starting from their own 32, the Packers began The Drive. "This is it," quarterback Bart Starr told his teammates. "We're going in."[5] Mixing short passes and runs, the Pack marched down the field with relentless efficiency. All 11 men knew exactly what they needed to do and did it. Lombardi emphasized fundamentals and execution; The Drive exemplified both. With less than a minute left, if was first and goal from the one. Twice, the Packers tried to run it in. Twice, the Cowboys held.

With 16 seconds left, Starr took the final timeout. The percentage play was to try a pass; if it fell incomplete, there would be time to kick a field goal to tie. But the pass protection had been poor all day. Starr's idea was to lunge into the end zone between the center and the guard.[6] "Let's run it," Lombardi agreed, "and get the hell out of here."[7] In the huddle, Starr called "31 wedge and I'll carry the ball."[8] The key was for right guard Jerry Kramer to push Jethro Pugh out of the way. He did, hitting him low, while center Ken Bowman pushed Pugh back. Starr slipped through, and the Packers won, 21–17.

In the winners' locker room, Kramer said of Lombardi, "This is one beautiful man."[9] Kramer did not love Lombardi all the time, something that comes across in his book, *Instant Replay*. But he realized that it was Lombardi who had instilled in the Packers the will, and the capabilities, to compete the way they had.

Player bench from last game Vince Lombardi coached at Lambeau Field. Green Bay, Dec. 31, 1967

In the losers' locker room, Cowboys' quarterback Don Meredith expressed pride in his teammates and mused that in a sense there was no loser in the game, because all involved had displayed such courage. His eloquence was impressive and played a role in ABC calling him a couple of years later to join a new show, *Monday Night Football* (see the 1970 entry on *MNF*). There he would be Dandy Don, class clown; on December 31, 1967, he was Don Meredith, Cowboy poet.

The Packers would beat the Raiders in the Super Bowl and become the first (and still only) team to win three championships in a row.[10] Landry's time would indeed come; he would win two Super Bowls with the Cowboys in the 1970s.

1968

STATUE OF TOMMIE SMITH AND JOHN CARLOS

In November 2005 San Jose State University unveiled this 22-foot-high statue featuring two of its former students, Olympic medalists Tommie Smith and John Carlos. The statue, and the photo on which it is based, not only freeze a moment in time but wordlessly crystallize the complicated problems that exist at the intersection of race, sports, and society. Those problems have not been resolved; only the details have changed. That is why the moment has retained its power. The photo has become one of the most iconic moments of Olympic history, indeed of twentieth-century American history.

In broad terms, this silent gesture was the end result of a lifetime of racial insult. More narrowly, it was the culmination of about a year of activism among a wide range of black American male athletes.

In late 1967 San Jose State professor Harry Edwards founded the Olympic Project for Human Rights (OPHR).[1] The group had some local successes, forcing a number of universities to take black grievances seriously and disrupting what would have been the New York Athletic Club's 100th-anniversary celebrations, when many of the best black athletes (and a good many white ones) refused to compete at the all-white, all-Christian club. But the OPHR's Olympic goals—the resignation of leader Avery Brundage and the banning of South Africa and Rhodesia, in particular—seemed destined to fail. In February 1968, after a five-year absence, South Africa was readmitted to the Games. That decision reinforced the idea that black Americans should boycott the Mexico City Olympics in October,[2] not only in protest against apartheid South Africa, but also against racial inequities at home.

The idea was controversial, not only among Brundage and the Olympic establishment, but also among the black athletes themselves. When South Africa was banned again in April, much of the momentum went out of the boycott movement.[3] Most of the male African American athletes surveyed wanted to compete.[4] Interestingly, black women were not even asked for their opinion; Wyomia Tyus (see the 1952 entry on the Tigerbelles) was more than a little ticked, saying later that she was "appalled . . . that the men simply took us for granted," assuming that the women would do "whatever we were told."[5] The point became moot. In the end, even the leaders of OPHR, such as John Carlos, Lee Evans, and Tommie Smith, went to Mexico City to compete.

But while the boycott had imploded, the idea of using the Olympics as a platform had not. Carlos and Smith decided that after the 200-meter race—they were confident that they would both medal—they would make the podium "a festival of visual symbols to express our feelings."[6] When the race started, Carlos took the lead, but near the bend, Smith turned on what had become known as the "Tommie jets" and surged past him. Australian Peter Norman nipped Carlos with a few meters left to take second. Smith set a world record 19.83 seconds that lasted for more than a decade.

Exhilarated and relieved, the two men changed into their warm-up suits, then prepared themselves. They each put on one black glove and took off their shoes; Smith wore a scarf and Carlos some beads. Norman, in solidarity with the two sprinters, whom he had come to like and respect, wore an OPHR button.[7] The three stepped up to their respective places, and when the "Star Spangled Banner" began to play, Smith, an army reserve officer, straightened his back and raised his black-gloved right arm straight up while he bent his head.[8] Carlos, in a more relaxed pose, raised his left arm. In stillness, they listened to the anthem of a nation to which they were profoundly connected but from which they were also deeply detached.[9] The crowd, too, was still, or in Carlos's memorable phrase, "you honestly could have heard a frog piss on cotton." Then came the boos, as well as a scattering of cheers. The two were hustled out of the stadium.

Shortly afterward Smith explained the symbolism of their act. His raised right hand was for the power of black America; Carlos's left was for the unity of black America. The black scarf was for black pride; the black beads represented the history of lynching[10] and the black socks and no shoes the prevalence of poverty. "The totality of our effort," Smith concluded, "was the regaining of black dignity."[11]

Avery Brundage did not see it that way. One of the most consequential Olympic figures of the twentieth century, he is also the most controversial. On almost any subject of substance, he could be relied on to do the wrong thing, in the wrong way. This was one of those times.

The members of the US Olympic Committee (USOC), while not happy with the protest, were inclined to do nothing about it.[12] As far as they were concerned, it was over. Brundage and the International Olympic Committee, however, were enraged. The protest violated the "universally accepted principle," the IOC stated, that politics "play no part whatsoever" in the Olympics.[13]

Perhaps this is the place to spike the idea that politics and sports don't mix. They do, and in the case of the Olympics, they always have. Greece agreed to host the first modern games in 1896, for example, in part to bolster the standing of its not-very-robust monarchy.[14] The IOC dealt only with national committees, the Games began with the parade of nations, athletes performed as members of national teams, and victors heard their national anthems.[15] Somehow, none of that counted as political.

The USOC was ordered to expel the two from the Olympic Village and the American team,[16] or the whole US track team would be kicked out.[17] The US officials complied and also offered an apology. For Carlos and Smith, the sanctions were meaningless; they were already moving out of the Village, and they had no more events.[18] They were not stripped of their medals. The ban from international competition hurt, however. Smith's athletic career ended on that podium. As *New York Times* sports columnist Red Smith (no relation) would later note, the IOC's heavy-handed reaction turned a simple gesture that might have been forgotten into an international incident.[19]

Carlos and Smith were not the only ones to bring protest politics to the podium in 1968. There was also Vera Čáslavská. The great Czech gymnast had been an outspoken advocate of the Prague Spring, the effort to diminish Soviet influence and liberalize the country. After the Soviet invasion in 1968, she fled to the mountains, where she trained by lifting sacks of potatoes and swinging from trees.[20] At the last minute, she was allowed to go to Mexico City, where she won six medals, including a tie for gold in the floor exercise with a Soviet athlete. When the Soviet anthem played, Čáslavská turned her head down and away, a subtle, sad Cold War Pietà.[21] The IOC imposed no punishment for her unmistakable gesture. Perhaps it knew it wouldn't have to. On her return to Czechoslovakia, Čáslavská was essentially banned from sports and public life for the next 17 years.[22] Nor did anyone in the Olympic movement see fit to protest the treatment of Emil Zátopek, a triple gold winner in the 1952 Olympics. Also a supporter of the Prague Spring, Zátopek was expelled from the Communist Party; fired from his job; stripped of his military rank; and required to work as a garbage collector, street sweeper, and miner.[23]

And that was not even the worst of it for poor Czechoslovakia when it came to the dangerous intersection of sports and politics. That low moment came in March 1950, when the secret police convicted all but one member of the country's ice hockey team[24] on charges including treason, espionage, and slander. Their real crime was that the authorities thought some of them were considering defection. After months of brutal treatment,[25] the players were sentenced to terms ranging from 1 to 15 years in prison. Most were amnestied in 1955, having spent years as forced laborers, some of them down uranium mines. The IOC had nothing to say about this, either, though many of the players had competed on the 1948 silver-medal Olympic team.

These are examples of individuals and governments taking action, but in terms of things over which the IOC has sole authority, politics are still ubiquitous. In 1908, for example, Finland was allowed to have its own team, but not to show its flag. Serbia, which was then part of the Austria-Hungary empire, had its own two-man team in 1912, a privilege accorded to none of the other bits and pieces that made up that empire. The decision not to invite Germany and its World War I allies (Austria, Bulgaria, Hungary, Turkey) to the 1920 Games in Antwerp was clearly political; nor was Germany welcome in 1924, 1948, or 1952. The winner of the 1936 marathon, Sohn Kee-chung, ran under the Japanese flag and under a Japanese name, Son Kitei. Sohn was, in fact, Korean, which was an unhappy colony of Japan and not allowed to compete in its own right.[26] After the war the highly political question of how many Germanies to allow, and under what flag and banner, was not settled until 1972. And that was comparatively simple compared to the endless wrangling over what to call Taiwan, once the People's Republic of China decided to reenter the Olympic arena at the 1980 Winter Olympics.[27] Puerto Ricans are American citizens, but not when it comes to the Olympics; they compete independently. In the 1992 Winter Olympics, there was still a Yugoslavia, but also a Slovenia and Croatia, which had not yet been recognized by the United Nations at that point.

In this context, then, the outrage directed at Tommy Smith and John Carlos appears both ridiculous and hypocritical. Sending an Olympic team down the uranium mines is met with indifferent silence, but when two black Americans make a peaceful, purposeful, and dignified gesture, the outrage is instant.

Sometimes, though, the arc of the universe does indeed bend toward justice, or at least vindication. Over the last couple of decades, Carlos and Smith have put their critics behind them. Rather than the misspelled and frightening death threats they endured for years, now their mail is more often made up of speaking invitations. Most Americans, white and black, appear to accept their stand on the podium for what Smith says it was: "a cry for freedom, not a cry for hate."[28]

To an extent that might have astonished their younger selves, Carlos and Smith have even been embraced by the Olympic establishment: a poster of them in their most famous moment features prominently on the walls of the US Olympic Training Center.[29]

1968/1975

ARTHUR ASHE'S RACKETS

These two rackets represent two of the transformations in modern tennis: money and technology.

Arthur Ashe used the wooden racket on the left to win the first US Open in 1968. From 1881 until 1968, America's national tournament was for "amateurs" only. The quotation marks refer to a secret that was so open that it was no secret at all: that the best "shamateurs" were making a lot of money under the table.

Meanwhile, tennis pros led a hardscrabble existence, staying in sponsors' homes and playing one-night stands. Official tennis treated them as if they smelled. The situation was absurd, and had been so for decades. Golf, hardly the most wild-eyed of institutions, had sponsored open tournaments for decades, featuring both amateurs and professionals. Civilization had survived. It made no sense that most of the best tennis players were unable to play in the most prestigious tournaments (see the 1959 entry).

After Wimbledon indicated in late 1967 that it would accept professionals, the tide turned. "Open" tennis—tournaments in which both professionals and amateurs could play—hit the courts in 1968.

Ashe, a UCLA graduate then serving as a US Army officer, was an amateur when he won the first US Open. If he had been a professional, he would have taken home $14,000. (The women's winner, Virginia Wade, earned $6,000.)[1] Ashe missed the era of outrageous money—in 2015, the US Open singles champions earned $3.3 million each[2]—but he did well, earning almost $1.6 million[3] in prize money and 33 singles titles during his career.

His best year was 1975, when he won nine tournaments and was ranked number 1 for a time.[4] That year he also recorded his greatest victory, upsetting Jimmy Connors at Wimbledon. Few thought that Ashe's power game could prevail against Connors's abilities as a counterpuncher. Ashe, 31, didn't disagree; he had lost to the 22-year-old Connors the only three times they had played.[5] So Ashe changed tactics, feeding Connors low off-speed forehands, luring him into the net, and then lobbing him to death.[6] He won in four sets.

It was a popular victory. A great and passionate player, Connors was also often vulgar, grabbing his crotch and bellowing profanities. Ashe, by contrast, wore his dignity like armor. There were other differences that fed into the frank dislike between the two. Ashe was a Davis Cup stalwart; Connors couldn't be bothered. Ashe was one of the founders and longtime president of the Association of Tennis Professionals, created to protect players' interests. Connors was the only leading player not to join. For all these reasons, Ashe's victory "spread happiness and satisfaction," wrote British tennis journalist Richard Evans, "because it had turned a good man into a great champion."[7]

The racket on the right on the previous page, a Head Competition, is the one Ashe used to beat Connors. It is so obviously different from the other that it is remarkable that only seven years separate the two. The 1968 racket is made of wood and not all that different than what Bill Tilden would have used during his career (see the 1930 entry on Tilden). The 1975 racket is a composite made of glass fiber and aluminum with a foam core,[8] and a longer, sleeker shape.[9] Ashe had been working with aluminum or composite rackets since 1969, making him a very early adopter of advanced technology.

For that, thank (or curse) Howard Head, an aircraft engineer who revolutionized two sports. Skiing was first. When he picked up the sport, Head found wooden skis difficult to use. Aircraft materials, he thought, might be better. So he went to work and figured out how to combine aluminum, adhesives, and other materials to create a ski that made turning easier and that never warped. Purists nicknamed them the "cheaters";[10] everyone else called them a godsend. Head skis were being sold by 1950 and quickly dominated the market.[11]

Retiring in 1969, Head took up tennis and had a similar experience: he wasn't very good. Again he looked at the equipment, and again, he thought modern technology could improve on wood (or steel, which Jimmy Connors's famous T2000 was made of). Composite materials were lighter and more flexible than wood, but could be strung tighter and so delivered more power. The year after Ashe's Wimbledon triumph, the Head-designed Prince Classic came out. The first oversized racket, it had a "sweet spot" of 110 square inches, compared to 65 for the average wooden racket.[12] Weekend warriors took to the oversized composites immediately, and the pros were not far behind.[13] Players won big tournaments using wooden rackets into the early 1980s, but by the middle of the decade, wood was gone forever, banished to museums and tag sales.

While all this matters in terms of the evolution of tennis, to speak of Ashe in terms of only money and science is to miss the point. Tennis gave him a platform, but as an African American and a man of the world, he used his fame to build a much more substantive legacy.

Beginning in the 1970s, he became a committed opponent of apartheid. He visited South Africa several times that decade, after being rejected for a visa repeatedly—a reproof that became a high-level diplomatic issue. He insisted that the events he played in be integrated (the South African government reneged), and he visited townships and held clinics that included black children. After the massacres during the 1976 Soweto uprising, in which hundreds were killed, his attitude hardened. In 1983 he cofounded Artists and Athletes Against Apartheid, which encouraged them not to perform in South Africa.

Ashe always made a distinction between the South African regime and South Africans. For example, he favored banning the country from the Davis Cup but opposed excluding individual South Africans from tennis.[14] He worked with such sustained commitment that when reporters asked Nelson Mandela who he would like to meet after his release from prison in 1990 after 27 years, he responded, "Arthur Ashe." They did meet, in 1991.

Back home, Ashe was a forceful and sometimes controversial voice on social issues. When the National Collegiate Athletic Association imposed academic standards on athletes, for example, critics opposed them on the grounds that they were set too high for many black high schoolers to meet. Ashe opposed them because he thought the standards were too low.[15] He often endured boos when he criticized what he saw as the self-inflicted wounds of certain aspects of African American society.[16] But he didn't back down. Instead, he backed up his words with his money and time, founding urban health and education programs. And when he was teaching a course on the black athlete, he realized that there was almost no material on the subject. So he spent six years researching *A Hard Road to Glory*, a three-volume history that came out in 1988.

Ashe retired from tennis in 1979 due to heart problems; during a 1983 operation, he was transfused with infected blood, and he was later diagnosed with AIDS. He made the diagnosis public in 1992—and then, naturally, began fund-raising and outreach about the disease. He spent much of his last year working on his autobiography, *Days of Grace*, in which he wrote this extraordinary sentence: "I am a fortunate, blessed man. Aside from AIDS and heart disease, I have no problems."[17] He died a week after the book came out—and 15 months before Mandela was elected president of South Africa.

On his death in 1993, Virginia ordered the state flags flown at half-mast, and his body lay in the governor's mansion, the first man to be so honored since Stonewall Jackson in 1863. In 1997 the main stadium at the USTA National Tennis Center was named for him. And in a gesture he might have appreciated even more, his hometown of Richmond, where he saw "no colored" signs as a child, paid him its ultimate homage. The city's famed Monument Avenue, which is lined with statues of Confederate heroes, added a new one: Arthur Ashe. A scholar-athlete who always thought about the next generation, in the statue Ashe is ringed by children. He is carrying books in one hand and a racket in the other.

ROBERTO CLEMENTE BASEBALL CARD

Baseball players are not saints. So at first blush, it seems odd that there is a sincere if quixotic effort to canonize one as such. But when that ballplayer is Roberto Clemente—well, the idea is still quixotic but not quite laughable.[1] Clemente died on New Year's Eve in 1972, taking supplies from his home in Puerto Rico to earthquake victims in Nicaragua. In 1973 the game's award for charitable work was named after him in honor of his death and his life. During his 18-year career, Clemente was one of the most respected players in the game. With the perspective of history, he can be seen as a living bridge between a game whose players were all-American to one that fully embraced talent born outside the United States.

Clemente, who was signed by Branch Rickey shortly after the general manager left Brooklyn (see 1947 entry on Jackie Robinson), toiled in the relative obscurity of Pittsburgh. At first the Pirates were bad, and when they got good, they were still in Pittsburgh. Most fans could see the Bucs on television once or twice a year, if that. During the 1971 World Series, though, Clemente emphatically made his presence known. Then 37 and the oldest player on either team, he batted .414, getting at least one hit in every game, and won the MVP. But those bald facts do not convey the reality of this athletic and aesthetic tour de force, in which he also displayed his arm and his base-running skills. "He was just magic to watch," said teammate Steve Blass.[2] In the locker room after the final victory, Clemente politely interrupted an interview to send a message home to his parents, in Spanish. He wanted to share his moment with the people and place that he loved.

The 1971 Series was Clemente's finest athletic hour, but he had already clocked a brilliant career. Known as a bad-ball hitter, he didn't walk much, but had such a shrewd sense of his own strike zone that he rarely struck out, either; his career batting average was .317. His arm was remarkable. For this, he credited two things: throwing the javelin in high school, and his mother, who was apparently a gamer.[3] He was an excellent base-runner who ran everything out and took the extra base with controlled aggression.

Using a complicated metric that combines everything that happens on the field, plus some other statistical razzle-dazzle, Clemente is the highest-rated right fielder in history based on the number of runs he was worth over his career.[4] He won the MVP award once—beating out Sandy Koufax in 1966—and from 1960 to 1972 finished among the top dozen nine times. He also won 4 batting titles and 12 straight Gold Gloves. In his last regular season at-bat, he clubbed a double for his 3,000th hit, becoming the eleventh man to reach that milestone.

Athletically and culturally, Clemente was more than the sum of his statistics. While there had been Latin American players before, including from Puerto Rico,[5] he was the first great one. And in important ways, he set the template for how Latin players should be treated—the same, he insisted, as anyone else.

This baseball card represents a small point in that evolution. For years, writers, broadcasters, and even baseball cards, as this one from 1968 proves, referred to Clemente as "Bob" or "Bobby," even though he had made it clear his name was Roberto.[6] By the time of his death, he was definitively and only Roberto. He had made his point, and that meant the many Latin Americans who followed never had to explain themselves that way again. The poet Enrique Zorrilla caught Clemente's spirit when he said that he had "the fire of dignity."[7]

It was a fire heated in harsh conditions. When Clemente made the majors in 1955, at age 20, a number of teams still had no black players, and segregation during spring training and in certain cities was the norm. Clemente was black; in addition, at the time his English was limited. Sportswriters took cruel pleasure in reproducing his speech along the lines of "Next time hup I heet ze ball" and "I no play so gut yet."[8]

Over time he earned everyone else's respect, then a great deal of affection, and eventually

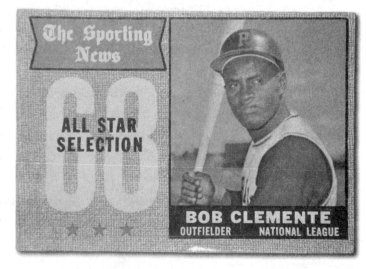

something like reverence. By 1960 the Pirates' popular radio announcer, Bob Prince, was shouting "¡Arriba!, Roberto!"[9] when he did something great, and fans made the phrase their own. Clemente took the lead in insisting that the Pirates delay opening the season until after the funeral of his friend and hero, Martin Luther King Jr. In 1971, when Three Rivers Stadium opened, Roberto Clemente Night in July was one of the biggest occasions of the year. The place was packed—and the ceremony was in both Spanish and English.

Clemente was considered temperamental (not without cause)[10] and seemed to positively revel in feeling misunderstood. He complained early and often of not getting the credit he deserved,[11] which was true. He turned these grievances into performance; pride and anger were fuel for his competitive fire. As his confidence grew, in both his game and his English, he matured into a leader, not only among his Pirates teammates and other Latin players but in general. He was a forceful voice in the emerging players' union.[12]

In addition, there was a basic decency to the man that may not reach to sainthood, but is still far from common. He would apologize for shortness of temper or when he misunderstood someone else. In 1972, long established as one of the greats, he still stayed in the dorms at Pirate City, where young players hung on his every word.[13] Remember those stories of ballplayers quietly visiting kids in hospitals? Clemente actually did.

After his death, Puerto Rico declared three days of mourning. The Pirates retired his number. Major league baseball waived the five-year waiting period, and Clemente was voted into the Hall of Fame in 1973. Having played his entire career in Pittsburgh, he may be the player most closely associated with the team. When the Pirates endured 20 straight losing seasons from 1993 through 2012—tied for the longest such streak in North American sports history—many people choked at the idea of a twenty-first, which would associate epic failure with their hero, who wore number 21. (The Pirates escaped that fate, going to the playoffs in 2013.)

Clemente's unusual combination of athletic and human gifts has ensured he is not forgotten. There are Roberto Clemente schools and parks everywhere, as well as hospitals and sports leagues. Best of all, though, may be the yellow Roberto Clemente Bridge over the Allegheny River. On game days it's closed to cars, and fans can walk across it, step past a Roberto Clemente statue, and see a ballgame.

1969

GAME BALL FROM SUPER BOWL III

After an act of Congress and several brutal negotiating sessions, in 1966 the long-established National Football League came to terms with the upstart American Football League, founded in 1960 (see 1959 entry on Lamar Hunt). The details, the two sides agreed, would be worked out, and the rivals would be one big happy family by the 1970 season. That was the idea, anyway.

There were just two problems. The first was that the respective owners didn't like each other. The AFL owners were men who had tried to get into football, but had been rejected; this stung their egos, which were large. The NFL owners had little respect for the nouveau AFL, which played a glitzier game and had an edgier feel altogether than the crew-cut, meat-and-potatoes ethos of the senior circuit.

The other problem was the perception that the AFL was distinctly inferior. While the leagues didn't play each other during the regular season, in the first two Super Bowls the AFL's Kansas City Chiefs and Oakland Raiders both lost badly to the Green Bay Packers (by scores of 35–10 and 33–14, respectively). This was not looking like a merger of equals.

That was the conventional wisdom, and it was repeated so often that it passed for truth. The AFL probably did not have the depth of the NFL, but it had excellent players and teams, and the overall gap was closing; this was no minor league. The New York Jets exemplified the AFL's ability to develop talent; only six of their players had any NFL time. But perceptions matter, particularly when an institution is on the cusp of remaking itself, as football was. If the third Super Bowl was another blowout, mused commissioner Pete Rozelle (see 1960 entry on him), it might be necessary to rethink not just the championship game but also the entire structure of the league. It wouldn't be tenable to field one division that was clearly superior to the other.[1]

A blowout was expected. The Colts had gone 13–1 and outscored their opponents by 258 points. The Jets had gone 11–3 and were not nearly as dominant against a weaker schedule. Their defense had given up almost twice as many points as the Colts, who happened to have the game's best offense. Though Colts legend Johnny Unitas (see 1958 entry) had missed the season, his substitute, Earl Morrall, had won the NFL's MVP award. The cold-eyed analysts in Las Vegas made the Colts a 19.5 point favorite, 7–1 on a straight win-lose bet.[2]

The Jets didn't see it that way. Head coach Weeb Ewbank had been the coach of the Colts during the "greatest game" in 1958, and he knew what a championship team looked and felt like. From his perspective, quarterback Joe Namath was playing as well as anyone,[3] and so was the defense. The players had spent hours watching film of the Colts and were not all that impressed. They saw a team that was old, stodgy, and blitz-happy. The Jets ate blitzers for breakfast. And they had their own MVP in "Broadway Joe" Namath, who had signed a big contract with the Jets out of Alabama and took to New York nightlife like a natural. Namath shared his teammates' confidence. A few days before the game, he boasted, "The Jets will win Sunday. I guarantee it."[4] Now regarded as a Very Important Phrase in NFL history, at the time it was ignored, because it was so absurd.[5] "We believed what we heard," Colts tight end John Mackey would recall ruefully, "that the NFL couldn't lose to an AFL team."[6]

But of course they did. The Jets won authoritatively, 16–7. There wasn't any Broadway in Namath's performance, just intelligence and cool judgment (17 for 28 passing for 206 yards and no interceptions). The offensive line kept his uniform clean. Calling audibles frequently, he sliced and diced the Colts defense with the clinical dispassion of a surgeon; the ball pictured here was the instrument of his work. The Jets defense picked Morrall off four times. An injured Unitas came in during the second half, but it was the same story.

The NFL executives were distraught and incredulous. But Rozelle, who was as taken aback as anyone, was quick to see the bigger picture. "Don't worry," he said, "this may be the best thing that ever happened to the game."[7]

It was. The Jets victory changed perceptions of the AFL and made reaching the final decisions on how to structure the game much easier than they would have been. After a series of all-night bargaining sessions, the Baltimore, Cleveland, and Pittsburgh owners agreed to join the American Football Conference in the realigned league. If the Jets had lost badly, such a deal might have been untenable—and Joe Namath would never have become a legend.

1970

BOBBY ORR'S KNEE BRACE

In the most famous image in pro hockey, Bobby Orr is flying, almost perfectly parallel to the ice, his arms extended in a swan dive. He has just scored the winning goal in overtime to bring the Stanley Cup to the Boston Bruins for the first time in 29 years. The team unveiled a bronze statue of that frozen moment on May 10, 2010, the fortieth anniversary of what is known as "The Goal."

No one has had more influence on hockey, both on and off the ice, than Bobby Orr. As a scrawny boy, Orr learned to use speed and guile to maneuver his way on the ice. He signed a pro contract with the Bruins at age 14[1] and made the National Hockey League four years later. Boston needed him badly; the team had missed the playoffs seven straight years and had been proclaiming Orr the franchise's savior since before he could drive. He started well, winning the Rookie of the Year in 1967 for a bad Bruins team and performing brilliantly the next two years as the team improved.

In 1969–1970 the 22-year-old Orr, and the Bruins, put it all together. He notched 33 goals and 87 assists to become only the second man to break the 100-point mark. He also became the only man ever to be named best defensive player (for the second of eight straight times), most valuable player, highest scorer, and postseason MVP in the same year. Orr is still the only defenseman to lead the league in scoring, and he did it twice.

Orr's play and presence—by this time, he was endorsing everything from snowmobiles to soap[2]—made him the first hockey player to become a superstar in the United States. Even Boston's strippers showed their appreciation, imitating on their bodies the single strip of black tape Orr used on his stick. The decorative motif was known as the "Bobby Orr."[3]

The Bruins also won the Cup in 1972, but lost in the finals in 1974. Orr's last great season was 1974–1975, when he broke his own record for scoring by a defenseman. But his knees were already scarred by multiple operations; he was wearing the brace pictured on the following page when he scored The Goal. After two miserable seasons in Chicago, where he played only 26 games, he retired in 1978, at age 30. The Hockey Hall of Fame waived the usual three-year waiting period to induct him in 1979.

On the ice, Orr redefined his position; no less an authority than the great Gordie Howe would say, "He changed the game of hockey forever."[4] Orr was the first defenseman to become an offensive force, electrifying crowds with his end-to-end rushes and then using his speed and anticipation to get back into position. In 1970–1971 he set the single-season record for "plus-minus" rating (goal differential while on the ice), proof that his offensive brilliance did not come at the expense of his defensive responsibilities. His style opened up the game. Play became more fluid now that the defenseman was part of the action, not parked behind the blue line.

Orr had a modest, small-town Canadian demeanor. He was always uncomfortable with the golden-boy persona thrust on him—a reputation, he knew, that would do him no good with the hard men of the NHL. In an era when even practices were notably rough, Orr proved his cred quickly. Goalies loved him for blocking shots however he could, and teammates valued his ability as a fighter. "Oh, boy, this guy would fight," remembered hockey journalist Red Fisher.[5] "They tested him the first year. They didn't test him in year two."

Off the ice, Orr was the first NHL player to use an agent to negotiate his contract. Rookies of that era were lucky to get $10,000 a year and a handshake.[6] Lawyer Alan Eagleson negotiated something like four times that figure, making Orr one of the game's highest paid players before he had skated a single line—and changing the economics of the NHL forever.[7] Veterans like Gordie Howe took notice and demanded more money. The following year, Eagleson started the first successful NHL players' union.

There was, of course, a conflict of interest in Eagleson's status as both an agent (for as many as 150 players)[8] and the head of the union. But it also made him the most powerful man in hockey. Power corrupted him, and he defended himself with a rudeness and vulgarity that came to disgust his star attraction.[9] In 1980 Orr publicly broke with the man he used to refer to as a brother[10] for catastrophic financial mismanagement. The worst? That would be Eagleson telling Orr in 1976 that the Bruins didn't want him anymore; in fact, the owners were offering him an 18.6 percent stake in the team.[11]

In the early 1990s the truth came out: Eagleson had mishandled the players' pension and disability funds.[12] Eventually convicted on related criminal charges in both Canada and the United States, he was fined, imprisoned, disbarred, and disgraced.[13] The Bernie Madoff of hockey, Eagleson had used his standing as Orr's friend and manager to put himself in a position to damage the lives and futures of those he was supposed to be protecting. "Shame on him," was Orr's verdict. "Just, shame on him."[14]

YELLOW BLAZER FROM *MONDAY NIGHT FOOTBALL*

B eing a loser can be liberating, and in the late 1960s ABC was the biggest loser on American TV. The advantage of that position, though, was that it could take more risks. And it got the chance of a generation when NFL commissioner Pete Rozelle (see 1960 entry) pitched the idea of a regularly scheduled prime-time game.

It was not an easy sell. Since the end of the Friday night fights in 1959,[1] sports had only occasionally been seen after dinner; Rozelle had managed to shoehorn in a handful of prime-time games on a one-off basis, with middling results.[2] He was sure there was a market. Under the terms of the NFL's antitrust agreement with Congress, the league could not show games on Friday night. Saturday was for college; Sunday was already full of games, and midweek was out because players needed to recover. That left Monday.

CBS wasn't interested. "What?" cried one aghast executive. "Pre-empt Doris Day?"[3] NBC had a good thing going with *Rowan and Martin's Laugh-In*; also, Johnny Carson had not been amused when his show was delayed by a game that ran long.[4] NBC was not going to mess with Johnny.

That left ABC. Its president of sports, Roone Arledge, saw all kinds of possibilities. Other executives saw only problems. Women wouldn't watch; the affiliates wouldn't like their evening newscasts interrupted; most fans wouldn't have a rooting interest; and so forth. Fine, Rozelle said, Howard Hughes's new sports network would take it. That got ABC's attention, and with great reluctance, it paid $8.6 million for Monday night rights for the 1970 season.[5]

With that, Arledge took charge. He saw, before anyone else, that sports were not just about the game, but also about the people who played it and those who watched it. He wanted to show emotions as well as the score, and he wanted to bring a less reverent sensibility. "Sport is a business, not a religion, and there is no sacred way things must be done," he said.[6] "The games aren't played in Westminster Abbey."[7]

With *Monday Night Football* (*MNF*), Arledge had a template to test his vision. Again, ABC's low status was helpful. Because it didn't have any other football games, it could put all its energy into this one. ABC threw everything at it: slow motion, split screens, instant replay, handheld cameras, sideline mikes, closeups, and graphics.[8] The network deployed nine cameras, compared to the more typical four or five, and two production units, one exclusively for replays.

Arledge wanted *MNF* to be interesting, and that meant the people calling the games had to be. With that in mind, he hired Howard Cosell, who was already known as one of the more provocative voices in sports. To provide contrast, he hired Don Meredith, the former Dallas Cowboys quarterback (see 1967 entry on the Ice Bowl), who did a nice line in cornpone. Veteran sportscaster Keith Jackson would do the play-by-play. It was the first time there had been three announcers in the booth.

Jackson was a capable professional, but it was the Cosell-Meredith dynamic that defined the show. Cosell was pedantic; Meredith punctured him with down-home darts. Cosell was ponderous; Meredith was funny. Referring to a receiver with the fabulous name of Fair Hooker, Meredith mused, "Fair Hooker—I haven't met one yet."

Right from the beginning, it worked. The first game, on September 21, 1970, between the Jets and the Cleveland Browns earned a stellar 34 percent share.[9] Meredith won an Emmy for his work. The following year, Frank Gifford (right) replaced Jackson; he, Cosell, and Meredith, made *MNF* a national phenomenon. Movie theaters reported that sales slumped on Monday nights; bars began to offer customers a chance to throw bricks at a television featuring Cosell's face.[10]

Football was already America's favorite sport when *MNF* debuted, but the show helped to bring it to a new level, expanding the football audience. The show also proved that the appetite for sports was much bigger than anyone had thought and not as rigidly defined by traditional schedules. The year after *MNF* debuted, the World Series had its first prime-time game, and the National Collegiate Athletic Association basketball tournament followed a year later. Between 1975 and 1981 network sports coverage increased by a third, and new cable stations added many more hours.[11] In 1979 ESPN launched; it was by no means certain there was a market for 24-hour sports at the time, but given the post–*MNF* sports boomlet, the idea was credible enough to attract backers.

Even when the personnel changed, *MNF* kept going. Meredith left in 1973 for NBC, then came back for a four-year stint in 1977. Cosell left in 1983. Arledge began devoting more of his time to ABC News in 1977, where he also made important contributions, including starting *Nightline*. Even so, Arledge, who died in 2002, seven years after Cosell, is best remembered as the most important person in the development of television sports (sorry, Howard). As for *Monday Night Football*, the voices in the booth keep changing, but the games go on and on. And the money gets bigger and bigger. The most recent deal, signed with ESPN in 2011, called for about $15.2 billion over eight years.[12]

GOLF CLUB USED ON THE MOON

Give Bob Hope an assist. The comedian was taking a tour of the National Aeronautics and Space Administration, and as he bounced on the moon walk simulator, he clung to his driver for balance. Hope's tour guide, Alan Shepard, had an epiphany: "I have to find a way to hit a ball on the moon."[1] Shepard, the first American in space in 1961, was one of the only men on Earth for whom such a thought was not sheer fantasy. He was scheduled to ride Apollo 14 to the moon in February 1971.

Very discreetly, Shepard brought an expandable instrument designed for collecting moon samples to a golf pro, who fitted a number 6 club head to it.[2] Voila: the first moon club. After nine hours on the lunar surface, moments before leaving the moon forever, Shepard took out his unique 6-iron and a couple of balls. Swinging one-handed, he shanked his first shot. On Earth Shepard was a duffer, and even on the moon, the first rule of golf technique holds true: keep your head down. "That looked like a slice to me, Al," chirped a NASA critic. Addressing the second ball, Shepard hit it nicely, sending it perhaps 200 yards.[3] At the time, the astronaut described it as going "miles and miles and miles," thus uttering the first and so far last golf lie from space.[4] To the end of his life, when he looked at the moon, Shepard would muse, "I wonder where my golf ball is."[5]

1971

PING-PONG DIPLOMACY SOUVENIR PADDLES

Modern China has never pretended that sports are separate from politics: Mao Zedong's first published essay was about how sports could help to build a new China.[1] The Beijing Olympics in 2008 were an assertion of China's rising status on the world stage. And in one of the most iconic moments of the Cold War, China chose a sporting event to make a political statement of enormous consequence. In 1971 Mao invited the American Ping-Pong team to visit the mainland.

Beijing was a Ping-Pong power. The men had won the world title in 1961 and 1963; the women joined them as champions in 1965. Upon the team's return, China's top leaders hosted a party in honor of these symbols of the nation. But this status was not to last. During the Cultural Revolution, which Mao (a keen player, by the way) launched in 1966, denunciation and terror replaced Ping-Pong as the national sport, and China skipped the world championships in 1967 and 1969. By 1971, with the worst of the Cultural Revolution chaos over, China was beginning to consider how it could reengage with the world, a consideration made more acute by its recent border conflict with the Soviet Union. Being friendless in a dangerous world was increasingly unappealing.

In the United States—which was not a global Ping-Pong power—President Richard Nixon was also eager to change the status quo; there had been no American diplomatic mission in China since 1949. In 1970 both countries made approaches to each other of such exquisite subtlety that neither recognized them for what they were.

That was the context for one of the major questions the Chinese leadership was considering in early 1971. Should the national team go to the world Ping-Pong championships in April, to be held in Nagoya, Japan? Premier Zhou Enlai favored the idea, but the only opinion that really mattered was Mao's. He eventually agreed. Before the players left, though, they were given strict guidance. If they had to play the Americans, no shaking hands. No talking with them first. No exchange of flags. Report back three times a day.[2]

The Chinese players performed and behaved impeccably in Nagoya, even chanting quotations from Mao to psych themselves up before playing.[3] But they found it difficult to stay away from the Americans, who kept trying to introduce themselves. At a reception, the leader of the Chinese delegation found himself sitting next to his American counterpart, who promptly angled for an invitation to visit. On a sightseeing tour, players from the two countries were thrown together; again, the Americans said they would love to come. All of this was reported back to Beijing. The US players were just hoping for a fun trip. Beijing saw something more serious at play: a signal from the White House. That put a different spin on matters. On reflection, though, China decided it wasn't the right time to invite Americans, even innocents like these.[4]

Then on April 4 one of the American players, Glenn Cowan, jumped on the Chinese team bus—whether inadvertently or mischievously is not clear. But it was certainly a surprise to the Chinese, who were stunned. Three-time world champion Zhuang Zedong broke the silent tableau. Gesturing to the long-haired American—Cowan liked to see himself as a hippie—Zhuang gave him an embroidered silk banner. When the bus stopped, journalists noticed Cowan; he explained what happened and had a picture taken with Zhuang. The incident got enormous coverage, most of it positive. Zhou and Mao, however, were still cautious.

And then one evening Mao woke up—literally. He had been intrigued by the coverage of the bus episode, and on the evening of April 6 he awakened and murmured to his attendant to tell the Foreign Ministry to invite the American team. The situation was awkward. For one thing, Mao had given instructions not to act on anything he said while under the influence of sleeping pills. For another, the tournament ended the next day. Mao drifted off, and when he realized the attendant hadn't moved, became irritated. He affirmed that yes, he wanted the team to come.[5] The message got through, and Nixon was quick to give the players the go-ahead.

Three days later they landed in Beijing—the first American group since 1949. The unexpectedness of the visit made it a global sensation. Gracious hosts, the Chinese teams even managed to lose a game or two to the deeply inferior American players.[6] They met Zhou, went to the Great Wall, and saw a revolutionary ballet. Every step of their trip was exhaustively chronicled, and when the team returned home, they were hailed as heroes.

The members of the American team could not have been better ambassadors—for Beijing. They reported happy peasants, productive collective farms, freedom of movement, and a sense of unity and content. Maoism, said one player, was "beautiful."[7]

All of this would have been surprising to the people of China—not least to the table tennis team, which had been devastated by the Cultural Revolution. Accused of following the capitalist road, espionage, anti-Maoism, and trophyism, they had been sent to the countryside, along with hundreds of other athletes, to cut wheat, build aqueducts, and read Mao's Little Red Book.[8]

Zhuang, for example (the man who had greeted Cowan), had been jailed, beaten, and exiled; not heard from for three years, he was feared dead. The coach of the national team, Fu Qifang, was driven to suicide, and the same was said of the country's first world champion, Rong Guotan, though he might have been beaten to death. Even as the American players were touring China, many leaders of the National Sports Commission were literally up to their elbows in muck, hauling manure in rural Shanxi.[9]

The US Ping-Pong players would not be the last visitors to see and hear only what China wished them to. But their positive impressions, however erroneous, helped to change the way Americans saw China. During their trip Nixon lifted trade sanctions and travel restrictions, to little opposition, and in the immediate aftermath, for the first time, polls found that a majority of Americans favored admitting the mainland to the United Nations,[10] which occurred in October. In February 1972 Nixon visited China. Three months after that, the Chinese Ping-Pong team came to the United States, the first official delegation from the People's Republic since 1949. With capitalist vigor, the free market produced all kinds of mementoes, such as these commemorative paddles. From now on, the two nations would negotiate business in the normal back-and-forth of international relations.

The United States and China would have figured out a way to connect; the world's most populous country and the world's most powerful one could not ignore each other forever. But as a way to break the ice, Ping-Pong worked beautifully: it was a nonthreatening, and to Americans, somewhat amusing little diversion that they didn't mind the Chinese being much better at. However unlikely, Ping-Pong truly did help break China's diplomatic isolation and by doing so, changed global geopolitics.

At a human level, though, there was also tragedy—one taking a particularly Chinese form, and the other characteristically American. Zhuang Zedong became a political symbol and aligned himself with Jiang Qing, the widely despised wife of Mao, and with her allies, the "Gang of Four," who were blamed for many of the excesses of the Cultural Revolution. Zhuang enthusiastically led denunciation meetings, including against his former teammates; he also attacked both Zhou and future leader Deng Xiaoping as toadies to foreign powers. When Mao died in September 1976, the political winds shifted. The Gang of Four was arrested, and so was Zhuang. He was himself denounced, then spent four years in solitary confinement, followed by a stint in Shanxi as a street sweeper. Allowed to return to Beijing in 1984, he taught at a sports school and then started a Ping-Pong club in 2005.[11] He died in 2013, full of history and regrets.

Glenn Cowen's downfall was distinctly capitalist. He believed his role in Ping-Pong diplomacy would bring him fame and fortune. When that didn't happen, he was unmoored and began to suffer mental health and drug problems. Every April, around the anniversary of his visit to China, he would break down. Eventually, Cowan was reduced to hustling for paddle-tennis games and living in his car on Venice Beach. He died of heart disease in 2004, a man long broken.

1972

MEMORIAL TO DAVID BERGER

David Berger was an all-American boy. A gifted student athlete in high school in Ohio, he was a collegiate weightlifting champion at Tulane, then earned an MBA and a law degree. Realizing that he was unlikely to make the US Olympic team, he emigrated to Israel[1] and qualified for the 1972 Games in Munich. Though he was eliminated from the light-heavyweight competition quickly,[2] he stayed on to enjoy the Olympic experience.

And that was easy to do. The Germans had created a fun, relaxed atmosphere. Police were armed with bouquets of flowers to defuse tension; security was in the care of 2,000 unarmed men known as Olys, dressed in light blue suits. At one point night patrols were cut back because "nothing happens."[3]

Then, around 4:30 in the morning on September 5, eight members of Black September, a Palestinian terrorist group, invaded the Israeli living quarters at 31 Connollystrasse. They went into apartment 1, where the coaches were, and then proceeded to invade apartment 3, which Berger was sharing with other weightlifters and wrestlers. Berger suggested in Hebrew that the team attack the intruders: "We have nothing to lose."[4] But one of the gunmen understood, and the opportunity was lost; all the men were herded into apartment 1. Two Israelis, Moshe Weinberg and Yossef Romano, resisted and were killed on the spot; two escaped. All told, the terrorists had captured nine Israelis. What they wanted, they told stunned authorities, was the release of 234 prisoners in Israel, as well as Germany's most infamous terrorists, Andreas Baader and Ulrike Meinhof.

At first the athletic events went on as normal, in the hope that the situation would be resolved quickly. About 11 hours later, though, continuing what had been billed as the "Serene Games"[5] became unconscionable, and the remaining events of the day were canceled. And so the athletes, like the rest of the world, watched the awful ending.

Israel had ruled out complying with the demands; the Germans had failed to budge the terrorists. The offers of money and even the German interior minister[6] in exchange for the Israelis were turned down flat. After several extensions, the terrorists agreed to take the hostages to Cairo. The Germans had no intention of letting that happen.

At 10:35 pm,[7] helicopters took everyone to the Fürstenfeldbruck military airport, about 15 miles away, where the security forces hoped to mount a rescue. But everything went wrong. The Germans did not have enough snipers, and the snipers did not have night-vision goggles or bulletproof vests. A slapdash ambush had to be scrapped when the police officers assigned to it walked off, refusing to participate in what they saw, with justification, as a suicide mission.[8] The lighting was bad. Armored personnel carriers got stuck in traffic. Fundamentally, the Germans didn't know what they were doing, and they refused the help of the Israelis, who did.

Shortly after midnight the terrorist in Berger's helicopter opened fire on the hostages; Berger was wounded but not killed. Then the Palestinian tossed a hand grenade into the cockpit, killing Berger and his Israeli comrades.[9] All nine hostages died in the ensuing two-hour firefight, as well as five terrorists and one German police officer. Three Palestinians were captured. All were back home by the end of the year, released in return for a hijacked Lufthansa airliner.

On the morning of September 6, a memorial service was held in the Olympic Stadium for the dead Israelis, and then the Games resumed. It was not an easy call to go on, but it was a defensible one. Stopping the Games would, in a way, honor the dead athletes, but it would also please those who sympathized with the terrorists. Resuming them could seem callous, but could also be seen as a sign of determination and a different way of honoring fellow Olympians.

The memorial itself was well attended and well done. Until, that is, IOC president Avery Brundage's speech. He got off to a good start, mourning the Israeli victims in simple terms. But then he kept talking: "It is a sorrowful fact in our imperfect world that the greater and more important the Olympic Games become, the more they become the victim of economic, political, and now criminal pressure. The Games of the XXth Olympiad have been the target of two terrible attacks because we have lost the struggle against political repression in the case of Rhodesia."[10] To conflate his hobbyhorse of pure amateurism with Black September, or the banishment of Rhodesia with 11 dead Olympians—even for Brundage, it was an almost pathologically ill-judged moment.

The five dead assailants were flown to Libya, where their caskets were greeted with acclaim. At almost the same time, a US Air Force jet returned David Berger's body to his parents; Ohio's state flags flew at half-mast. This memorial is located outside Cleveland, not far from Berger's childhood home. About 14 feet high and made of steel alloy,[11] it shows the five Olympic rings broken by the tragedy. The rings rest on 11 segments, one for each dead Olympian.

The Olympics have never been particularly innocent. These festivals of sport can be glorious, but greed, cheating, and venality of all kinds have also been regular visitors. The tragedy of Munich, however, was of an entirely different order of evil, and the events of those 20 hours represent a profound loss. Today, every Olympics has to design and budget with security uppermost in mind. A spectacle intended to showcase international goodwill is now shaped in large part by the profound lack of it.

SILVER MEDAL FROM THE US–USSR MEN'S BASKETBALL FINAL

For Americans, the 1972 US–Soviet basketball finals might be the most infamous controversy in Olympic history. It featured a game that was made in America (see 1891 entry on James Naismith) and was played against the Soviet Union in the teeth of the Cold War. Also, it was just so bizarre.

Team USA went undefeated in the first Olympic hoops tournament in 1936—James Naismith himself was in the stands—and never lost a game over the next 36 years. But starting in the 1950s, the Soviets had put enormous resources into international sport, seeing it as "one of the best and most comprehensible means of explaining to people the advantages which the socialist system has over capitalism," in the words of one state-run publication.[1] The Soviet hoops team had done well on a recent tour of the United States and had the advantage of having played together for years. The US coach, Hank Iba, who had also led the 1964 and 1968 teams, recognized that the gap between the United States and the rest of the world was closing.

The US teams had always been composed of college players; that had long been more than enough. But the 1972 team was young and inexperienced; it had played just 12 exhibition games together. Also, for various reasons, it was missing such elite college players as Julius Erving, David Thompson, and Bill Walton.[2]

Even so, the Americans made it through the preliminary rounds without too much trouble and met the Soviets on the night of September 9 for the gold medal. Iba had coached the team to play deliberate, slow-paced basketball. That had worked fine so far, but against a good team—and the Soviets were very good—it wasn't effective. The Americans also shot poorly—only 33 percent for the game—and at halftime, they trailed 26–21. "We had young deers," recalled a guard on the team, Tom Henderson. "We should have run them back to Russia."[3]

With 6:07 left and the Soviets up eight, the American players decided to do just that. The Soviets mustered only one field goal the rest of the game against the pressing American defense. Meanwhile, the Americans chipped away. With 10 seconds left, and the Soviets up one, Doug Collins picked up a loose ball, drove to the basket, and got clobbered. Three seconds left, two free throws, one woozy point guard. He swished the first. As Collins began to shoot the second, a horn blew. The Soviets were trying to call a time-out.

This is the tricky bit; if the Soviets were late making the call, as it appeared at the time, then too bad. But it is also possible that the time-out device the seasoned Soviet coach used was not working, or that the scorekeepers missed his signal. At any rate, Collins drained the second shot. With three seconds left, then, the United States was ahead for the first time, 50–49.

And that's when things got interesting. A Soviet player grabbed the ball and flung an inbounds pass. At midcourt, the Brazilian referee saw the Soviet coaches waving and jumping around in something like a panic. Confused, he stopped play. (The ref could have also called a technical, as several Soviet coaches were on the court, which is a no-no.) The Soviets explained they had been trying to call a time-out, but the signal hadn't got through; that's why the buzzer had sounded right before the second free throw. Sorry, the ref decided, there had been no time-out. Play would continue, with one second left. Even that was something of a break. After all, if there was no time-out, play should not have been stopped.[4] That point was now moot. The Soviets had the ball at midcourt with one second left. Simple enough.

Not so simple. William Jones, the head of the international basketball federation, entered the scene. He had been sitting in the stands and had no jurisdiction, any more than the commissioner of baseball decides safe or out calls in the World Series. No matter; Jones gestured that the time-out that may (or may not) have been called should have been granted and ordered the clock set to three seconds. Essentially, he ordered a do-over from the time Collins made his second foul shot. The seconds in between vanished into the Olympic ether.

The Soviet passer, guarded closely by 6-foot-11 Tom McMillen, could only get the ball to the top of the key, and the desperation heave from there missed. The buzzer sounded, and the Americans celebrated. Not so fast. This time, the problem was that the scorekeeper had not reset the clock correctly. It is true that the clock was wrong; it is also true that the Soviets had made their play, and it failed. At this point, Iba was in a rage. He would not send his players out again, he stormed. Yes, you will, Jones told him—yes, Jones was back—or the game would be forfeited and the US team could be barred from international competition.[5]

So there were three seconds left—again. McMillen again defended against the inbound pass, but the referee made a gesture to back him off—although he was perfectly within his rights to stick right where he was. But McMillen didn't want to risk a technical, so he moved almost to the foul line. That gave the Soviet passer much more room to maneuver. He lofted a pass—it is known in Russia as the "golden toss"—to Aleksandr Belov, who was parked in the paint, and Belov put it in. This time, the game really was over, 51–50 to the Soviets.

The United States appealed the decision—or rather, the several decisions—that had determined the outcome. The appeal failed, with Cuba, Hungary, and Poland forming the 3–2 majority. Captain Kenny Davis said the team voted unanimously against accepting a silver medal.[6]

The medal pictured here, then, is strictly symbolic—what the US team would have taken home had it chosen to. The members of the team have neither forgiven nor forgotten. Davis even made it a condition in his will that his heirs "never accept a silver medal."[7]

The Soviets were and are unapologetic. "We unquestionably deserved the victory," Alzhan Zharmukhamedov said in 1992.[8] The Soviets have a case. Remember, they did lead for at least 39:57, and they simply played the game as it was called. But the Brazilian ref had it right when he later called the result "completely irregular and outside the rules of basketball";[9] he thought the Americans deserved the victory.[10] Making time vanish, twice, is not part of the game.

The next time the US men's basketball team lost a game was in 1988—to the Soviets again. This time, it was straightforward: The Soviets simply played better, and the Americans had to settle for bronze. With that result, the world had officially caught up, and the Olympics changed the terms of engagement, allowing National Basketball Association and other professionals to compete. That led to the famous "dream team" of 1992, which included Charles Barkley, Larry Bird, Magic Johnson, Michael Jordan, Karl Malone, David Robinson, and John Stockton. The dreamers won easily, by an average of almost 44 points. Though the United States won again in 1996 and 2000, it never got easier, and in 2004 the team lost three games on the way to a disappointing bronze. With a renewed sense of urgency and commitment, the United States returned to gold-medal form in 2008 and 2012.

But no one assumes a gold medal for Team USA anymore. With the globalization of the game, its dominance has diminished. And that's not a bad thing. In fact, given the enthusiasm of America's basketball missionaries to spread the game, going all the way back to the 1890s, one could even call that a different kind of victory.

<u>1972</u>

IMMACULATA MIGHTY MACS UNIFORM

Made of wool, worn with bloomers, and accessorized with a rope-like sash, these uniforms were considered hideous even in the early 1970s, when most fashion was hideous. Plus, they itched. But however old-fashioned their kit, the Immaculata College Mighty Macs were anything but quaint on the basketball court. They won the first three women's national basketball championships (1972–1974), then went to two straight finals (in polyester skirts and tops) and a Final Four (in shorts).

It was a different time, and not just because today's players don't wear uniforms almost as old as they are.[1] Elite hoopsters also don't have to sell toothbrushes to raise money to get to the finals, as Immaculata did. And when a team repeats as champions, it gets a little more notice than the single paragraph the *New York Times* offered in 1973. (Most newspapers chose not to waste even that much ink on a bunch of girls.) The tunic in these photos, then, is not just an artifact; it is also a reminder of how far women's sports has come.

That the first national champion came from a Catholic liberal arts college near Philly shouldn't come as a surprise. Philadelphia had a dense network of single-sex parochial schools, almost all of which fielded hoops teams for both boys and girls. As early as the 1920s, nice Catholic girls were encouraged to play ball. In official games, they had to play the turgid, six-a-side, two-dribble, stay-in-your-zone game designed to "protect" them from exertion. But they also played the real thing in parks, recreation centers, and driveways, often against boys. Catholic parents might not have approved if their girls took to shot-putting or rugby, but they loved basketball. On Friday nights girls routinely played before packed houses, and the high-school championships sold out Penn's famous Palestra arena.[2]

Immaculata benefited from this tradition. The small women's school, run by the Sisters, Servants of the Immaculate Heart of Mary (IHM), had fielded varsity hoops teams since 1939. And that, too, is not surprising. Women's schools were much more likely to field teams and to treat athletes with respect; they are the unsung heroes who kept college sports going. "We were encouraged to believe that anything was possible," recalled the Macs nifty point guard, Marianne Crawford Stanley.[3]

The same could not be said of many, perhaps any, coed schools. When it came to sports, the men simply would not share the sandbox. Well into the 1970s, it was not unusual for them to hog 99 percent of the athletic budget.[4] At the University of Washington, men's sports got $1.3 million; the women's, $18,000.[5] At Arkansas, the calculation was simpler: $2.5 million for men, zero for women.[6] *Sports Illustrated* estimated in 1973 that in the entire country, women accounted for fewer than 50 athletic scholarships—less than the number allotted to a single Division I football team.[7] And then there were the small daily humiliations and inequities: not having a trainer, or being kicked out of the gym, or having to panhandle for travel money.[8]

Things began to improve in the early 1970s. In 1971, having been ignored by the National Collegiate Athletic Association forever, a group of female educators organized the Association for Intercollegiate Athletics for Women in 1971. The AIAW ran on a tiny budget, but it did its best, and in 1972 it arranged the first national basketball championship;[9] after regional qualifying rounds, there would be a 16-team final tournament at Illinois State.

The timing was fortuitous; the five-on-five game had become standard only a year earlier, after a research study confirmed that playing full court posed no health risks to women.[10] Really. Immaculata's Cathy Rush, hired as a part-time coach in 1970 for $450, seized the moment. At the time, the Macs didn't even have a gym; their court had burned down, and the nuns were still raising money to replace it. But the Macs had some seriously good players, schooled on the Philly playgrounds. Also, the 22-year-old Rush was married to a National Basketball Association referee and conversant with the full-court game. She drilled her players in a fast-break offense and a trapping, tenacious defense.[11]

When the Macs made it through the regionals, the school was both delighted and dismayed: it didn't have the cash to send them to Illinois. So the players sold toothbrushes to raise money;[12] other clubs at the school chipped in what they could, and the college scraped together some cash, too. Even so, there was only enough to send eight players. They shared two rooms and washed their uniforms in the sink between games.[13] The Macs were seeded fifteenth out of 16 teams. But they beat South Dakota State, Indiana State, and then top-seeded Mississippi College for Women to reach the finals—against their rival and neighbor, West Chester State. The Golden Rams had thumped the Macs, 70–38, two weeks earlier. But this time the Macs played a patient, sure-handed game, and won, 52–48. When they arrived home—a Catholic benefactor flew them back first class because they missed their original flight—almost the entire school was waiting for them at the airport.

After winning national titles again in 1973 and 1974, the little school with the big game became a phenomenon. The Macs were the first women's college team to play internationally (in Australia, in 1974); the first to play in a nationally televised women's game (against Maryland, in 1975); and the first to play at Madison Square Garden (against Queens, in 1975), drawing 12,000 spectators.

Much of the credit for Immaculata's aura must go to the nuns. The president of the school in 1972, Sister Mary of Lourdes, a former Philly high school star herself, would shoot around with the Macs on occasion and always found a way to get the team what it needed. The old and sick nuns who lived in a home on campus had the games piped in. If the Macs were losing, an announcement would go out, "Sisters, the Mighty Macs are in trouble!" And they would take to their walkers and wheelchairs, and hustle as well as they could to the chapel.[14]

A cohort of nuns attended every game, clustered near the floor in their dark blue-and-white habits. They were not always images of serene grace. The father of one of the players handed out metal buckets and sticks, which the nuns would bang with such religious fervor that they were eventually banned (the buckets, not the nuns). The sisters didn't trash talk, but they did visibly deploy their rosary beads, which might have been more intimidating. And they had game. A sportswriter was stunned during a tense moment when he heard a sister shout, "Watch the pick and roll!"[15] The whole thing was irresistible.

And doomed. In 1972 a part of the education bill known as Title IX stated, in effect, that schools that took federal money had to accommodate the interests of all students, even those who lacked a Y chromosome. This didn't mean spending had to be equal; it did mean that women had to get a fair share of time, money, and other kinds of support—something more than 1 percent, or zero.

Over time Title IX has evolved, due to legal challenges and new interpretations. In the process, it has become more complicated, and more controversial, than it needs to be. As written, the rule was not meant to impose quotas. But it is also true that the surest way to stay out of court is to keep a keen eye on the numbers. If a school has, say, 45 percent female students, and 45 percent of its athletes are also women, then compliance is assumed. As a federal judge put it in a landmark case regarding Brown University, "a university which does not wish to engage in extensive compliance analysis may stay on the sunny side of Title IX simply by maintaining gender parity between its student body and its athletic lineup."[16] As part of its settlement, Brown University was required to deviate no more than 3.5 percentage points between female students and female varsity athletes.[17]

The problem is that the use of such metrics has led to unintended consequences, in which the need for compliance has trumped equity and even common sense. In one famous example, in 2001 Marquette cut its wrestling team—which cost the school nothing, because it was funded by outside sources—in order to hew closer to the right gender proportionality.[18] The action closed athletic opportunities for Marquette men while creating no new ones for women, a lose-lose situation that was not unique.[19]

These are real issues, but they are also narrow ones. Title IX is the single most important and positive thing that has ever happened to women's sports in the United States. In 1970 there were only 16,000 female college athletes; by 2012, there were more than 200,000. The figures for high school are just as dramatic, from 294,015 girls playing sports in 1971 to almost 3.2 million in 2012.

In a larger sense, Title IX helped to make it socially acceptable for girls to be competitive and athletic—to take pride in their bodies for their function as well their looks. In 1932 Babe Didrikson Zaharias's muscles were considered off-putting, even freakish. In 1999, when Brandi Chastain ripped off her shirt at the end of the 1999 World Cup (see entry) to reveal her stellar abs, her physique was celebrated.

While Title IX greatly accelerated the pace of change, it's not as if women were waiting around for the men in Congress to give them permission to play. Even before Title IX, many were getting involved in sports, and the AIAW was working to raise the level of competition. Ironically, then, the NCAA, which fought against Title IX bitterly, ultimately benefited from it. The AIWA, which fought for Title IX, was destroyed by it. Once women's sports gained traction, the NCAA became interested and put the squeeze on the AIAW, which was gone by 1982.

The women of the AIAW had been trying, sometimes awkwardly, to develop a different model of sports—more participatory, less exploitive, more student-centered, and run by and for women—that would not replicate the mistakes of the NCAA.[20] They might not have succeeded. Still, it's a shame they never got the chance.

Title IX also spelled the end of schools like Immaculata as national powers. In 1977 Cathy Rush retired with a career record of 149–15; in 1978 UCLA won the national championship, ushering in the era of big-school dominance. The nuns gave in. "We do not want an image of a sports college,"[21] President Sister Marie Antoine said. Knowing it could not compete with bigger, richer universities, Immaculata wisely decided not to try. Today, the school competes in Division III. But the Macs are not forgotten. In 2008 Cathy Rush was elected to the Naismith Basketball Hall of Fame, and Immaculata, as a team, joined her in 2014.

How good were the Mighty Macs? Well, they would certainly be creamed by any Division I program. Compared to today's top teams, the Macs' perimeter shooting was not as precise; their play was slower and less sophisticated. But forget the temptation to patronize these working-class Catholic girls in the funny tunics: the Macs were good. One player at the 1972 tournament recalled seeing the Macs for the first time and marveling at the skills of these "fast, sharp-eyed, hard-elbowed easterners." That was Pat Summitt, who would go on to lead Tennessee's women to eight national championships (see 1995/2009 entry).

A number of Macs stayed with the sport after graduation and helped it grow. Marianne Crawford Stanley coached Old Dominion to three national titles and also coached at the University of Southern California, the University of California/Berkeley, and in the Women's National Basketball Association. Rene Muth Portland coached Penn State for 27 years. Teresa Shank Grentz, once described by *Sports Illustrated* as the "Bill Walton of the East," coached the US national team to a bronze medal in the 1992 Olympics. One of her players was Muffet McGraw, now the women's coach at Notre Dame. Tina Krah directs the women's national championship tournament for the NCAA.

In her Hall of Fame induction speech, Cathy Rush recalled that she told her mother of her Immaculata teams, "These girls start with a prayer, and then play like hell."[22] The nuns would have approved.

NAIL FROM SECRETARIAT'S SHOE

When Secretariat came roaring down the stretch at the Belmont, Jack Nicklaus (see 1986 entry on the Masters) was watching the race at home. As the horse flew toward the finish, visibly exulting in the glory of his power, the two-legged golf legend found himself pounding the floor—and weeping.[1] Secretariat that day was athletic perfection: form and function and will coming together to create a moment of pure beauty.

A foal is hope on four legs. When Secretariat was born on March 30, 1970, hopes were particularly high, as his sire and dam were both highly regarded. With his bright chestnut coat, deep chest, and well-formed knees and ankles, the colt impressed from the start. The farm log noted four months later, "You just have to like him."[2]

Like many young males, though, Secretariat was temperamental and undisciplined. For a time, his nickname was "ol' Hopalong" because he was fat, slow, and clumsy.[3] (He was also known as Big Red.) When his groom, Eddie Sweat, first saw him, he was unimpressed: "Too pretty! Too big an' fat."[4] And then one morning Secretariat decided to grow up. He went five furlongs in 57.6 seconds—an excellent time. "We have a race horse on our hands," trainer Lucien Laurin told owner Penny Chenery.[5]

Imperious but playful, Secretariat drew people to him with a personality that seemed more than strictly equine. Once he nipped a reporter's notebook from his hands with his teeth, then tossed it into his stall, as if to say, "Come and get it."[6] Another time, Secretariat took his groom's rake and dragged it around his stall as if to clean it.[7] Secretariat was extraordinary; he was not, however, a comedian. But what these stories speak to is that there was a presence, an ease of manner, even a playfulness that made people love Big Red, even as they were awed.

Coming off a phenomenal season in which he won seven of nine races as a two-year-old,[8] there were high hopes for Secretariat as the 1973 racing season began. But two weeks before the Kentucky Derby, he came in a sluggish third at the Wood Memorial. Secretariat had just been syndicated for a record $6.1 million, but people began to have doubts about him. He had bad knees, went one rumor. His jockey, Ron Turcotte, wasn't up to the task. The horse was moody—just like his sire.[9]

The Derby would tell. Secretariat broke poorly and was running last at the first furlong. Then he began to pick off the other horses. Running on the outside down the stretch, he accelerated. The other horses "were rolling," Turcotte would recall. "We were flying."[10] Secretariat finished the 1¼-mile course in a record 1:59.4, two-and-a-half lengths ahead of Sham. Incredibly, Secretariat ran each quarter faster than the one before, meaning he was still accelerating at the end. As racing commentator Heywood Hale Broun put it: "Another quarter of [a] mile and he might have taken to the air and flown."[11]

At the Preakness two weeks later, Secretariat broke last again. A few strides into the first turn, he veered to the outside and swept past the other five horses before the straight. Strategically, owner Penny Chenery would note, that went against all the books. But Secretariat had imposed his will, taking Turcotte along for the ride as he cruised to another course record.[12] Sham again finished second.

Going into the Belmont, Secretariat was a full-blown star. Not only was he on the cover of *Sports Illustrated*, but he had pushed both Watergate and the Vietnam War off the covers of *Time* and *Newsweek*. He was one race away from being the first Triple Crown winner since Citation in 1948. But this, the smart money said, would be his toughest race.

The one knock on Big Red was that he was the son of Bold Ruler, who was known as a good sprinter who couldn't win at the longer distances.[13] At 1.5 miles, the Belmont was the longest of the Triple Crown races. Sham's owners thought if he could stay close, he might be able to take advantage if Secretariat faltered.

Sham was a brave horse. He even had his head in front for a few seconds. But halfway through the race, Secretariat broke him. He covered the mile in 1:34.2, a time so fast that sportswriter William Nack, Secretariat's muse, began furiously shouting at Turcotte, "You are going to kill the horse! You are going to lose the Triple Crown!" And still, Secretariat kept going, 1,155 pounds[14] of perfect form to the end. He finished an incredible 31 lengths ahead. (Poor Sham finished last, 45 back.) "He was running because he loved it," said Chenery. He was "glorying in his own ability." It remains the greatest

performance ever seen on a racetrack. Secretariat's time of 2:24 smashed the track record by 2.6 seconds and still stands—as do his other Triple Crown marks.

Greatness happens when many things break correctly—or don't break. If one of Secretariat's shoes had come off or become damaged, he could not have shown his true colors. So every nail in every shoe mattered—like the one pictured here, which did its small but important job at Belmont.

Was Secretariat the greatest horse ever? There is certainly a case to be made for Man O' War, who won 19 of 20 races in 1919 and 1920, a better record than Secretariat's record of 16 wins, 3 seconds, 1 third, and 1 fourth. At his best, Citation would have given either of them a run for their money. But let's give this one to Secretariat by a nose, if only because, with a few clicks on a keyboard, it is possible to call up his races, watch him fly—and feel a lump in the throat.[15]

BILLIE JEAN KING'S DRESS AND BOBBY RIGGS'S JACKET FROM THE "BATTLE OF THE SEXES"

In 1973 Margaret Court had a great year, winning 18 of 25 tennis tournaments and 3 majors. But it is a year that must also evoke a wince. In what became known as the Mother's Day Massacre, she played quite possibly the worst match of her life when she lost to Bobby Riggs in less than an hour, 6–2, 6–1.[1]

Riggs was a former Wimbledon champion and world number one. He was also a 55-year-old misogynist with a big mouth who had made what Court thought would be a nice little payday into a national event, played out on network television. The whole thing was humiliating for Court and embarrassing for women's tennis. When Billie Jean King, 29, heard the result, her response was immediate: "Now I'm going to have to play him."[2]

In July she and Riggs agreed to a best-of-five-set match to be played September 20 in Houston's Astrodome for a stake of $100,000. Nine weeks of nonsense ensued, mostly due to Riggs. King had competitive tennis to play, and while she was not averse to helping stir up publicity, it was Riggs who hustled all over the country saying outrageous things and raking in cash.

He did everything but prepare for what was, after all, an athletic event as well as a spectacle. To beat Court, he had trained rigorously and spent hours analyzing her play.[3] Facing King, he was too busy being a blowhard to bother. "There's no way that broad can beat me," he told friends the day before the match.[4]

King did not make that mistake. She respected Riggs and took a couple weeks off from the tour to prepare. Seeing how Riggs had dinked and lobbed Court to distraction, King practiced her overheads and decided to take something off her serve so that Riggs could not leverage her pace. She would pick on his backhand and extend points to wear him out.[5]

She also got in touch with tennis couturier Ted Tinling—make me a dress, she told him, a wonderful dress. With sequins (always appropriate for evening wear) and color.[6] And she told Adidas she wanted blue suede shoes to match. She even agreed to enter the arena on a feather-bedecked palanquin manned by four toga-clad male college athletes. Riggs, dressed in the jacket (see above) of one of his sponsors, the Sugar Daddy candy, came in on a rickshaw pulled by six beauties in tight shirts that read "Bobby's Bosom Buddies."

The hushed civilities of Wimbledon this wasn't.

There were more than 30,000 people in the Astrodome and maybe 50 million more watching on US television,[7] plus satellite feeds to 36 countries. The betting had been huge, with Riggs the 5–2 favorite.[8] Even King's female colleagues on the tour bet against her.[9]

Fit and focused, King was primed to play. Riggs was not. He double-faulted to lose the first set and simply wilted as King hit crisp winners and moved him around the court. There was no gamesmanship or comedy. King won easily, 6–4, 6–3, 6–3. "She was too good," Riggs confessed.[10]

The year after the Battle of the Sexes, King wrote that the match proved two things: a woman could beat a man, and tennis could be a big-time sport. By 2013 King was arguing that, with Title IX rules being debated and the tenor of the times, a loss would have set women's rights back 50 years and ruined women's self-esteem:[11] "Two things came out of that match for women," she said in a 2015 TED talk—"confidence [and] empowerment."

Yes, the match mattered. It introduced many people to great female athleticism, boosted the women's tour, and helped sustain the tennis boom of the 1970s. Men would have been insufferable had Riggs won. But little girls would not have hung up their cleats in shame if King had lost, any more than they did after Court's poor performance. All the factors that were encouraging girls and women to get into the game would have continued. As for the idea that Title IX would have been jeopardized had King lost, the subject never came up in the voluminous coverage of the event.[12] And confident women did not need a tennis match in the Astrodome to bolster their self-esteem.

In a way, the fame of the Battle of the Sexes obscures a fuller appreciation of Billie Jean King's achievements. She is the most consequential female athlete in history and would have been so if she had never played Riggs.

In 1968, when open tennis began, the game was run by and for men. Women were lucky to be an afterthought, even given their obvious drawing power. When one tournament offered men more than eight times the winnings of women ($12,500 for the male winner, $1,500 for the female),[13] King had had enough. She and eight others boycotted the tournament and set up their own event in Houston. The rebellion evolved into the Virginia Slims tour in 1971. A number of the top players, including Chris Evert and Evonne Goolagong, stayed with the US Lawn Tennis Association, which had history on its side, but had shown little commitment to the women. For a couple of years, then, there were two women's tours, which was one too many.

The rebels worked hard to make the Slims tour a success, promoting it like mad and even taking tickets at the door; they usually stayed at the homes of local tennis buffs to save money.[14] Today the financials look like rounding errors—a breakthrough moment came in late 1971 when an event offered total prize money of $40,000. But by doing it themselves, the women had proved that there was indeed a market for what they offered; prize money reached $775,000 in 1973, more than twice as much as in 1971.

No one did more than King to make this happen; no one *could* have. In 1973 the two tours consolidated—under the Slims banner. At the same time, the Women's Tennis Association was formed to safeguard women's interests. King, of course, was its first president.[15] In short, King was the making of women's pro tennis, and tennis led the formation of a new culture of sports for women. "Every woman tennis player, every woman athlete should thank her," Chris Evert told ESPN.[16] And since she apparently wasn't busy enough, King established the Women's Sports Foundation, which is still going, and *womenSports* magazine, which is not.

And let's not forget that King was also a superb athlete, winner of 39 Grand Slam titles, 12 of them in singles. Deploying a powerful serve-and-volley game well suited to an era in which three of the four majors were on grass, she was one of the top players in the game for a decade, before balky knees ended her career. She was the first female athlete to earn more than $100,000 a year and the first to be a *Sports Illustrated* Sportsperson of the Year, sharing the award with John Wooden in 1972.

More than anyone else, King shaped the future and the culture of the tour. For example, when the locker room was frosty to the emerging queen of tennis, Chris Evert, King laid down the law. Evert, she said, was going to be great for the sport. Woman up and be nice.[17] It was a gesture that Evert never forgot.

King extended the same generosity to Riggs, the man she once dismissed as a "creep."[18] The two became friends, bonded by their big moment and a love of tennis. When Riggs died in 1995, King called him "a brother and a fellow champion."[19]

In 2006 the National Tennis Center, home to the US Open, was renamed for King; three years later, she received the Presidential Medal of Freedom. The woman who had once infuriated the tennis authorities so much that they threatened to banish her[20] was now a pillar of the establishment.

1974

HANK AARON'S JERSEY

Whereas Babe Ruth traveled the country on a wave of adoration, Hank Aaron's major league journey was more complex. Born in Mobile, Alabama, he played briefly in the Negro Leagues before the Boston Braves bought his contract. As one of the first African Americans to play in the South Atlantic League, the abuse he took was extreme.[1] The only way out was up; he played brilliantly, and by 1954 he had made it to the big leagues, replacing Bobby Thomson—yes, that Bobby Thomson—in the outfield in Milwaukee (where the Braves had migrated in 1953).

Aaron loved Milwaukee—the feeling was mutual—and won his only World Series there in 1957. But from then on his teams were usually mediocre or worse. They reached the playoffs only once—and got skunked by the Miracle Mets of 1969. But year after year Aaron excelled. From 1957 through 1973 he averaged 38 home runs and 110 RBIs a year. In a career that overlapped with that of Willie Mays and Mickey Mantle, who hit bigger home runs in bigger markets, quiet distinction like Aaron's was overlooked.

One way to get a sense of Aaron as a player is to look at the voting for most valuable player. He only won once, in 1957, but he finished in the top dozen 15 times.[2] And his fellow players appreciated his qualities. Curt Simmons, an excellent left-handed pitcher, once said of him, "Trying to sneak a pitch past Hank Aaron is like trying to sneak a sunrise past a rooster." By the early 1970s the whole country had begun to notice, too. At the end of 1972 he had 673 home runs; at the end of 1973, that figure was up to 713. Babe Ruth's record of 714 home runs, one of baseball's most beloved, was about to fall.

For most people, that was fine, even exciting: records are made to be broken. For a vicious minority, though, it was unconscionable for a black man to break this one. Aaron suffered through months of abuse. One typical missive hoped "that youse get good and sick."[3] Another said: "Retire or Die!!!" His children had to be escorted to school.[4] Aaron wasted little time in 1974 getting the thing over with; wearing this jersey, he hit number 714 on his second at-bat of the 1974 season and 715 four days later. But the experience took its toll. "The Ruth chase should have been the greatest period of my life," he wrote, "and it was the worst."[5]

Aaron ended his career with 755 home runs, replacing Ruth's name at the top of the record book. But he didn't erode Ruth's legend. And the same can be said of Aaron. Even though his name is no longer at the top of the home-run table, the legend of Hammerin' Hank is as powerful today—perhaps more so—as when he lofted number 715 into the Atlanta sky.

"I don't want people to forget Babe Ruth," Aaron once said. "I just want them to remember Henry Aaron."

1974

NIKE WAFFLE TRAINER

Legend has it that Isaac Newton lit on the theory of gravity when an apple fell on his head. Alexander Fleming grew penicillin by accident, when he left a mold growing in his lab. The point? Serendipity and inspiration often go hand in hand. Or, in the case of Nike, from foot to foot. The single most important product in Nike's history, the Waffle Trainer, shown below, was the result of one such moment.

In 1971 an obscure company named Blue Ribbon Sports (BRS) paid a local graphic artist $35 to create a logo: she came up with the now-ubiquitous Swoosh. It debuted a new brand name, Nike, named after the Greek goddess of victory. But the most important event for the company that year occurred over the breakfast table of Bill and Barbara Bowerman.

As the coach of the University of Oregon track team (see 1975 entry on Steve Prefontaine) and a cofounder of BRS, Bill Bowerman was constantly tinkering in his workshop, seeking to craft a sneaker with the perfect balance of weight, grip, support, and feel. Now he had something new to think about. Oregon had replaced its cinder track with a urethane one; this was better for athletes, but their spikes would destroy it. On that fateful morning, the bottom of the family's 1930s waffle iron[1] caught his attention. Something like the waffle nubs might grip the track, he thought, without ripping it up.

"So he got up from the table and went tearing into his lab and got two cans of whatever it is you pour together to make the urethane, and poured them into the waffle iron," recalled Barbara Bowerman.[2] Unfortunately, the goo stuck and he couldn't pry the waffle iron open. But the idea stuck just as hard, and further experiments showed potential.

Phil Knight, a former middle distance runner at Oregon, was CEO, but Bowerman was the resident sage—wise enough to know what he didn't know. He enlisted others to help improve the design,

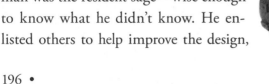

including an orthotist and an orthopedic surgeon.[3] By 1972 the company was cutting waffle soles by
hand, then attaching them to uppers.
Nicknamed the "moon shoes" because the
distinctive patterns they left looked like the imprints the astronauts were
leaving in the lunar dust, these were a giant leap forward in shoe design.

A few athletes wore them at the Olympic Trials and liked them. Next, in
1973, was a limited edition Oregon Waffle, in which the waffle outsole was glued to a
yellow-and-green upper. After further refinement, in 1974 Bowerman earned a patent to
the design, which he described as "an athletic shoe suitable for use on artificial turf . . .
the sole has short, multi-sided polygon-shaped studs which provide gripping edges that
give greatly improved traction."[4] Later that year the Waffle Trainer hit the mass market.[5]

The shoes were light yet gripped any surface with assurance; they also had spring to
them, lessening the pounding that is part of running. The timing was perfect. Millions
of Americans were beginning to jog, and the Waffle Trainer was waiting for them. The
company could barely keep up with demand. The first versions were red, with a white
Swoosh, but Knight thought that the Waffle might do what no other sneaker had—become an item adults would wear all the time. So the company began making blue ones to
go with blue jeans. Sales jumped again, and in 1978, Blue Ribbon Sports finally, and forever, became Nike.[6] The Japanese and European brands that had previously dominated
the market didn't know what had hit them. With the Waffle Trainer, Nike was well and
truly launched. In 1972 company revenues were less than $2 million; a decade later, they
were approaching $700 million.[7] By fiscal 2015 the company founded on a handshake,
with Phil Knight and Bowerman each chipping in $500, had revenues of $30.6 billion.[8]

Bowerman's eureka moment was critical in the making of Nike. He died in 1999, but
is still very much a part of Nike's culture. The company is located on Bowerman Drive,
and one of Nike's 11 maxims, taught to all new employees, is: "Remember the man." The
actual waffle iron was unearthed in 2010, when Bowerman family members were digging
through an old rubbish dump near the workshop (see picture above). Barely recognizable
as a kitchen implement, it is now on permanent display at Nike headquarters.

TONY HAWK'S FIRST SKATEBOARD

When Steve Hawk gave his younger brother this cast-off blue fiberglass skate-board,[1] a Bahne with Cadillac wheels,[2] he could not have known that he was launching his sibling into a lifelong passion—and a fortune. But that is what happened.

Tony Hawk went professional as a 14-year-old in 1982 and earned his first royalty check that year—for 85 cents.[3] By 1993 he had won 73 of 103 competitions.[4] But skateboarding was going through one of its cyclical downturns, and Hawk had blown through some serious money. His wife put him on a $5 a day budget.[5]

Then, in 1995, ESPN changed Hawk's fortunes—and skateboarding—forever. The network had the idea of showcasing "extreme sports"—BMX riding, skateboarding, and motocross, plus oddities like bungee-jumping and street luge. Thus began the X Games. Hawk was already well known in the skating world. When he won the vert contest (for vertical tricks—think ramps and bowls) and placed second in street (in which skaters negotiate courses that mimic urban conditions), he became the face of the sport to mainstream America.

There was some resentment at his status,[6] but Hawk kept the respect of the culture because he kept skating at a high level and invented dozens of tricks, including the nosegrind, the backside ollie-to-tail, and the frontside blunt.[7] The crucial year was 1999. Hawk had decided that these would be his last X Games, and he went out in style. With the television cameras rolling, on his 12th try[8] he completed the first 900—two-and-a-half-midair spins—a trick he had been working on for more than a decade.[9]

Two months later, Activision released *Tony Hawk's Pro Skater* video game; it sold by the zillion and brought the sport to a whole new level of visibility. All of a sudden, Hawk was in demand from magazines and television interviewers who had previously found him—and his sport—easy to ignore. In 2003 he outpolled Kobe, Shaq, and Tiger to win the vote for favorite

male athlete at the Nickelodeon Kids' Choice Awards. And in the ultimate affirmation of twenty-first-century celebrity, there was even a brief reality show, *Tony Hawk's HuckJam Diaries.*[10]

Hawk snagged endorsements with McDonald's, Kohl's, T.J. Maxx, Jeep, Club Med, AT&T, the Gap— even Bagel Bites. There were deals for everything from boards to hoodies to bedding to roller coasters.

Skating culture has always prided itself on being edgy, a kind of an athletic outsider art. So for some die-hards, bringing an extreme sport into the mainstream was akin to consorting with the enemy. It was, at the very least, uncool,[11] an assessment bolstered by the fact that Hawk is associated with vert skating, which lags well behind street in skating cred.

But cozying up to the capitalist machine was also bringing money and attention to the sport. Other skaters—vert and street both—started getting lucrative endorsements, too. A Mountain Dew sticker on a helmet was a small price to pay for not having to work at an office job.

Hawk himself makes no apologies. "I've never changed my value system for money. Ever."[12] In his view, "keeping it core" means representing the sport and its distinctive sensibility well. It does not require honorable indigence. "People don't call you a sell out," he likes to note, "until your stuff finally sells."[13]

PELÉ'S JERSEY FROM THE NEW YORK COSMOS

Officially declared a national treasure in Brazil, Pelé's unofficial role when he came to the United States in 1975 was savior. When he pulled on the jersey of the New York Cosmos of the struggling North American Soccer League (NASL), the hope was that the slightly over-the-hill, 34-year-old legend would bring new fans to soccer. And he did. Before Pelé, the Cosmos played on a scruffy field in a second-rate stadium in one of the more remote areas of New York City. With Pelé, they were able to fill Giants Stadium, peaking at 77,691 for a playoff game in 1977. Five years before, the championship took place on a college field in Long Island and drew maybe 6,000 people.[1]

For a time the Cosmos might have been the most popular sports team in New York, with a blend of style and personality that made it the staple of the back page. "Women, drinking, dancing, and back on the field the next day," remembered goalie Shep Messing fondly. "We transcended everything."[2]

An exaggeration, for sure, but it is true that after Pelé's arrival, the Cosmos players became something like rock stars in cleats. They even had a private table at Studio 54, which was as cool as it got in the mid-1970s.[3] Mick Jagger and Henry Kissinger visited the locker room.[4] And for the first (but not last) time, it was said that the United States was about to become a soccer country, with the game soon to be "on the order of football, baseball, and basketball," a writer for the *New York Times* predicted. Pelé certainly thought so. "I can die now," he said after the Cosmos won the Soccer Bowl in 1977. "I have everything I have wanted from my life in soccer."[5] He went home to Brazil.

But all this obscured some inconvenient truths. Of the 18 teams in the NASL, only one—the Minnesota Kicks—made a profit. Attendance in many markets averaged fewer than 5,000 per game. The rosters, stuffed with an ever-rotating cast of foreigners on their last legs, didn't engage the fans. The press never really got behind the sport once the whole Studio 54 celebrity thing wore thin. "Editors treated it like a leper colony," recalled one New York journalist.[6] Dick Young of the *Daily News* described soccer as "a game for commie pansies in short pants," and he was far from alone in his disdain.[7]

By 1979 attendance was beginning to fall everywhere, including for Cosmos games, and while the league had managed to get a limited television contract with ABC, the ratings were abysmal. In 1980 the once-thriving Philadelphia Fury team attracted fewer than 2,500 fans to a game against Chicago, a reminder of the sad days PP (pre-Pelé). The enthusiasm and deep pockets of owners like Steve Ross (Cosmos) and Lamar Hunt (Dallas Tornado; see 1959 entry on Hunt) could go only so far. Year after year, the losses grew and attendance shrank. In 1980 the league lost $40 million, and the best it could do was narrow that figure down to $25 million in 1983.[8] Celebrities were no longer calling for tickets; the back pages were soccer free again. The league shut down in 1984, done in by overexpansion, poor management, lack of homegrown talent, and most of all, indifference.

For a time, Pelé made the NASL; it could also be argued that he broke it. His three-year, $4.5 million contract[9] was more than the entire payroll of the division (Hank Aaron, for context, was making about $200,000).[10] Franchises began chasing stars—"Everyone had to have a Pelé," said Jack Daley of the San Diego Sockers—driving up costs unsustainably. It's difficult to be churlish about Pelé, who is among the most gracious and likeable of sports figures. And it cannot have been a bad thing for Americans to see him, as well as such great players as Franz Beckenbauer, Johan Cruyff, and Giorgio Chinaglia. Pelé did not make soccer a flagship sport, but he did introduce it to a new generation, many of whom started to play.

It's interesting to compare today's top American soccer league, Major League Soccer, with the NASL. MLS was created after the successful staging of the 1994 World Cup. Lamar Hunt got involved again—at one point, he owned three clubs—but otherwise the cast was completely different and so was the strategy. The league itself owns all the franchises and player contracts in what is known as a "single-entity" structure; franchise owners are, in effect, shareholders in MLS with the right to operate in a given market. This structure has enabled the league to contain costs and grow organically. There is also a salary cap (with some complicated exceptions). Pay is low compared to the Big Three of baseball, basketball, and football but it is hardly terrible (an average of $283,000)[11]. A number of teams have been able to finance soccer-only stadiums. Other than the signing of David Beckham in 2007, the league has avoided trying to buy popularity through short-term celebrity hires; more than half the players were born in the United States or Canada. All in all, MLS is not a spectacular success, but it is on its way to being a solid one. The NASL, by contrast, was briefly spectacular but has to be judged a failure—despite Pelé.

<u>1975</u>

PRE'S ROCK

I n his too-brief career, Steve Prefontaine did the impossible: he made distance running cool to Americans. At the time of his death in 1975, the James Dean of track held every US record from 2,000 meters to 10,000 meters.[1]

There could be a whiff of ghoulishness about Pre's Rock, where he died in a fatal car crash at age 24, but somehow there isn't. His parents were known to visit it, and his friends still do.[2] The sincerity of the visitors who leave totems of their own hard-earned achievements—spikes, ribbons, trophies, socks—can hardly be questioned. Oregon prison inmates carved the granite marker in remembrance of Pre, who organized a running club for them.[3]

Prefontaine came to national attention as a freshman at the University of Oregon, when he made the cover of *Sports Illustrated* as "America's Distance Prodigy." His collegiate career was a litany of triumphs. He won the National Collegiate Athletic Association three-mile four times[4] and also won three cross-country championships. He never lost a college race at any distance over a mile.

But there was more to Pre than his achievements. He had a star quality that no other distance runner in the United State has ever had. Sure, he typically ran from the front, which is high risk and exciting. Yes, his competitiveness was all but tangible. And when he grew that mustache, he added several degrees of sex appeal. What really mattered is that he had a special connection with the fans—they called themselves "Pre's people"—at Oregon's Hayward Field. "The minute Pre hit the field for his jog, there was an undercurrent of enthusiasm in the crowd," recalled former Oregon runner Geoff Hollister. "You could feel the electricity."[5]

Pre's most famous race was one he lost—the 5,000 meters at the 1972 Munich Olympics, run a few days after the terrorist murders of Israeli athletes (see 1972 entry on David Berger). An English commentator noted that Pre was "almost a cult in the United States, sort of an athletic Beatle." But his US record was six seconds slower than the world mark, and the field in the Munich final was strong. He was also two years younger than anyone else and had not competed much internationally. In the final, that inexperience showed.

After an almost embarrassingly slow first 3,400 meters, the last mile was as dramatic as a race can be, and Pre was in the thick of it. Three times in the last 600 meters, he tried to take the lead. Three times, he could not keep it, with Finland's Lasse Viren and Tunisia's Mohamed Gammoudi seeing him off with veteran aplomb. Entirely spent by his efforts, Pre couldn't hang on for the bronze and finished fourth.[6] The judgment, then and later, was that he had had lost a medal not because he wasn't fast enough, but because he had gone for the gold. That decision—to go all out for victory—cost him a place on the podium. But it was pure Pre.

Devastated, it took some time for Pre to recover his drive. Told that Eugene planned to name a street after him, he sneered, "What're they going to call it? Fourth Street?"[7] But he knew he could compete against the best and turned down a $200,000 offer to turn pro, saying he had "unfinished business to take care of." At the Montreal Olympics in 1976, he would be 25, a prime age for distance runners.[8]

His other unfinished business was fighting the Amateur Athletic Union, which decided where he could run and where he couldn't. If Pre wanted to go to a meet with better competition, but the AAU preferred one with more appearance money, he had to go to the latter. Pre and other athletes saw none of that money—except for economy-class travel and $3 a day in expenses. Meanwhile, Soviet-bloc athletes were full-time professionals, and many Europeans received subsidies. "Running doesn't pay your bills," Pre said,[9] in a comment that the grandees of the sport saw as rank ingratitude and probably crypto-communism.

So Pre lived in a trailer and used food stamps. Sometimes he tended bar, and he might have done what many others did, taking money under the table at European meets. In 1973 a local company, Blue Ribbon Sports, gave him a vague $5,000-a-year job as National Director of Public Affairs.[10] Founded by Oregon Coach Bill Bowerman and a former Oregon runner, Phil Knight, the money-losing[11] company thought that linking its obscurity to famous athletes might be a way to raise its game. Pre, with his Oregon roots and national recognition, was a perfect fit. The association remains important to the company, which later changed its name to Nike. A statue of Pre, striding in his Oregon singlet, dominates the entrance to Nike's Prefontaine Hall. "Pre's spirit," said Knight, "is the cornerstone of this company's soul."[12]

Although Prefontaine did not live to see it, by the late 1970s even Congress recognized that the amateur system was a shambles. In 1978 it passed the Amateur Sports Act, which neutered the AAU and gave athletes a voice in governance. By the early 1980s US track athletes could make an honest living from what they did best.

Prefontaine was also one of the sparks who set off the 1970s running boom. Others were his friend Frank Shorter, who won the 1972 Olympic marathon, the first American to do so since 1908; Bill Rodgers, who wore Nike shoes Pre had sent him to win the first of his four Boston Marathons in 1975;[13] and Jim Fixx, author of the 1977 best seller *The Complete Book of Running*. With his intensity and rebelliousness, Prefontaine was the most compelling of these figures. Whether they know it or not, the millions of Americans today running a weekend 5K or 10K, too, are Pre's people.

THRILLA IN MANILA BUTTON

Muhammad Ali is definitely the most famous athlete in history, certainly one of the most beloved, and possibly the most complicated. Once widely regarded as a national disgrace, when he lifted the torch at the Opening Ceremonies of the Atlanta Olympics in 1996, his hands trembling from Parkinson's disease, his transformation into national icon was complete. By then Ali was a figure of respect mixed with sympathy, the controversial elements of his past forgiven, forgotten, or deemed irrelevant.

Ali pioneered a kind of racial militancy before militancy was common; he was anti-Vietnam before that was mainstream. He was a black public figure who didn't pretend to want the approval of white America, and so he didn't care when it was withheld. "I don't have to be what you want me to be," he said. "I'm free to be who I want."[1] And that is what he did. The country was predominantly Judeo-Christian; he would join the Nation of Islam. The public liked its athletes self-effacing; he would call himself "the greatest." Repeatedly.

When Ali defied the draft board in March 1967—even knowing that his military service would be in the form of boxing exhibitions—he paid a heavy price for his act of conscience. His heavyweight title was revoked, his passport seized. For 43 months at the peak of his career, Ali could not fight. He "didn't just change the image that African Americans have of themselves," concluded Arthur Ashe. "He opened the eyes of a lot of white people to the potential of African Americans."[2] After Ali died in June 2016, aged 74, Channing Frye of the Cleveland Cavaliers assessed the fighter's legacy this way: "He just gave the black community a lot of courage and changed our mind-set," Frye told the *New York Times*.[3] Ali showed that "you can voice your opinion and be controversial and still be a champion." Putting Ali in historical context, journalist and critic Wesley Morris called him, "the most important political-cultural figure to survive the deadly tumult of the 1960s and flourish in the 1970s."[4] Bill Clinton gave his eulogy.

But there was a darker side, too. As a young man, Ali's racial rhetoric was sometimes harsh; he could be callous to the women in his life. And there was a mean streak. The Thrilla in Manila in 1975, his third fight against Joe Frazier, showcased Ali at his best and worst.

During Ali's exile, Frazier had taken the heavyweight title; he had also been a reliable ally, repeatedly calling for Ali's reinstatement.[5] Frazier knew he would not be entirely accepted as the champ until he beat Ali. So when Ali's license was finally restored, both men were eager to meet. This would be a bout between two undefeated champions.

At 6 foot 3 and 215 pounds, Ali was known for his speed and footwork; he was often described as a heavyweight with the nimbleness of a lightweight, and he was a genius in defense, picking off opponents' punches with uncanny precision. But he could hit, too; he had knocked out 25 of 31 opponents. At 205 pounds and a little under 6 feet, Frazier was the prototypical slugger, with a left hook of frightening force. He had knocked out 23 of 26.

Between the return of Ali, the contrasting styles of the fighters, and the obvious fact that these were the two finest heavyweights on the planet, interest in the fight was always going to be high. But Ali consciously raised the stakes, casting Frazier as a tool of the white power structure. "Anybody black who thinks Frazier can whup me is an Uncle Tom," he claimed. "Everybody who's black wants me to keep winning."[6] Being cast as the black white hope frustrated and angered Frazier. Apolitical and unpoetic, he could never compete with Ali in a war of words. But he could channel his rage within the four corners of the ring.

Held on March 8, 1971, at Madison Square Garden, this was a "fight of the century" that lived up to its billing. Frank Sinatra was the ringside photographer for *Life* magazine; Burt Lancaster did commentary. And the fight was stupendous. Frazier won the unanimous decision, but Ali won new respect, proving that he could take a punch. In the fifteenth round, Frazier unloaded a left hook to Ali's jaw that referee Arthur

Mercante would say was "as hard as a man can be hit."[7] Ali reeled and went down, flat on his back, his feet flying up with the impact. But he bounced right back up.[8] It might have been the most important moment of the rivalry, signaling his willingness to take the kind of punishment only Frazier could deliver. For his part, Frazier ended up in the hospital. "End of the Ali Legend" read the cover of *Sports Illustrated*.

In retrospect, of course, it was only the end of the beginning, the first chapter in what would become the greatest rivalry in boxing. Chapter 2 took place almost three years later. In the interim, Frazier lost his title to George Foreman, and Ali lost once to Ken Norton. With no belt at stake, there was less hoopla. Ali won a unanimous decision in a good but not great fight to earn a title shot against Foreman. In the famous "Rumble in the Jungle" in Kinshasa, Ali, now 32, recorded an entirely unexpected knockout in the eighth to recapture the title. For his part, Frazier cleared the path to Ali by beating Jerry Quarry and Jimmy Ellis. So the stage was set for chapter 3 on October 1, 1975.

Before their first fight, Ali had ridiculed Frazier for not being black enough. Before the second, he ridiculed him as ignorant. Before the Thrilla, he combined the two elements into one hateful image: a gorilla. He even carried a toy gorilla and would wave or beat it about the head at press conferences. Frazier was "ugly, ugly, ugly!" he shouted. And smelly. And ignorant.[9] Once Ali stood outside Frazier's balcony at 3:30 in the morning and fired a toy pistol in his direction while shouting, "Go back in your hole, gorilla."[10]

Boxing is the most elemental of sports, a form of combat that has existed as long as there have been fists and the will to fight. And on the morning of October 1, 1975, two men stripped each other's will bare, in an unforgettable display of athletic skill and personal courage. Although neither Ali nor Frazier was in his prime, on this day they were at their best. It is widely regarded as the finest fight ever.

The drama came in three acts. For the first three rounds, Ali had his way, landing stinging punches then dancing away. Frazier began to find his rhythm in the fourth. In the sixth, he sent Ali's mouthpiece flying. In the ninth, Ali could be heard howling in pain. After he took a particularly big left to his head in the tenth, Ali told his ringside doctor, "This must be what dying is like."[11]

But Ali never broke. In the twelfth the momentum shifted again. Ali began finding Frazier's head, and Smokin' Joe's right eye began to swell; that was a major problem because he had limited vision in his left eye (something he had kept secret). In the thirteenth Ali's greater range began to tell; while he took some shots, he delivered more. And still Frazier kept coming, propelled by pride and anger and something close to hate. "I had firepower, still. But I no longer had the ability to see clearly. And because of that, I had to step back," Frazier later wrote, "which put me at a distance where I became a target."[12]

The fourteenth round is difficult to watch. Ali hit the target, again and again; Frazier couldn't see what was coming. And still he stayed close, hoping he could land one big blow and knock Ali out. But he couldn't. When the men returned to their corners, both were in a world of hurt. Ali, according to some accounts, wanted to stop; Frazier wanted to go on. But his trainer, Eddie Futch, wouldn't have it. Letting a blind man go into a small ring with the likes of Ali was unconscionable. "Sit down, son," Futch told Frazier. "No one will ever forget what you did here today." And they haven't. Ali was so spent that he collapsed onto the canvas. Frazier had to be guided off. "It was insane in there,"[13] Ali later said. "It was like death. Closest thing to dying that I know of."[14]

The following morning, with the pain dulled but omnipresent, Ali didn't go to his bottomless well of cutting one-liners. Instead, he offered this: "I always bring out the best in the men I fight, but Joe Frazier, I'll tell the world right now, brings out the best in me. I'm gonna tell ya, that's one helluva man, and God bless him."[15] He also told Marvin Frazier, Smokin' Joe's son, to tell his father that he was sorry for the things he had said. But Frazier wouldn't accept a secondhand apology; if Ali had anything to say, he wanted to hear it for himself.

Ali did apologize, in 1991 and again in 2001: "I said a lot of things in the heat of the moment that I shouldn't have said. Called him [Frazier] names I shouldn't have called him. I apologize for that. I'm sorry." It was an imperfect act of contrition—the abuse lasted for years, and bringing a toy gorilla to a press conference was a matter of calculation, not spontaneity—but at least he made it. And Frazier appeared to accept it. "It's time to talk and get together," he said. "Life's too short."

Frazier never did climb out of the well of bitterness, however. His bottomless anger became as ugly as the insults that had provoked it. Watching Ali light the Olympic torch from his modest apartment above his Philadelphia gym, Frazier commented, "I hope he falls in the flame."[16] He took gruesome satisfaction in the idea that his punches might have contributed to Ali's physical decline. As late as 2009, even his cell-phone message reflected his obsession: "My name is Smokin' Joe Frazier, sharp as a razor," it began. And then, clearly referring to Ali and his troubles, it went on, "Yeah, floats like a butterfly, stings like a bee. I'm the man who done the job. He knows, look and see. Call us. Bye, bye."[17]

Neither man was ever the same after Manila. Frazier fought twice more—a loss to Foreman in 1976 and a draw against a second-rater, Jumbo Cummings, in 1981. Ali, however, stayed in the ring for another five years and 10 fights, losing 3 of them. By the early 1980s the signs of Parkinson's began to appear. A degenerative disease, it had taken a terrible toll, and his public appearances became less and less frequent. But he did make his way to Philadelphia for one important occasion: Joe Frazier's funeral in 2011. At one point, he rose and applauded his most important rival.[18]

The gesture was appropriate, because in a way Frazier made Ali. It was the three bouts against Smokin' Joe that revealed Ali as a fighter of rare courage, who could take punch after punch and still have the will and the skill to find a way back. In turn, Ali revealed (and broke) Frazier's heart. Ali's favorite boast was, "I'm the greatest!" He might have been right; it's difficult to say that anyone was ever better than Ali in his prime. But it was Frazier who forced Ali to reach to the bottom of his soul, where true greatness lies.

NANCY LOPEZ'S ROOKIE OF THE YEAR AWARD

It's an unwritten rule: anyone who connects with the gallery and forges a go-for-broke attitude on the golf course must be compared to Arnold Palmer (see 1960 entry on him). But Nancy Lopez probably deserved the comparison more than anyone else. Her followers called themselves "Nancy's Navy,"[1] and like Palmer, she brought new energy and new fans to the game.

In a single remarkable season, 1978, her first full year as a professional, Nancy Lopez made women's golf her own. She won nine titles, including five in a row[2]—one more than the record set by legends Mickey Wright and Kathy Whitworth. She won the last of these in stirring fashion, shooting 32 on the front nine and draining a 25-footer for birdie on the seventeenth to take the lead.[3] Palmer could not have done it better.

For a few months, Lopez pushed women's golf not only onto the sports pages, but onto the front pages.

To this day, Lopez is the only golfer of either sex to win both Rookie of the Year and Player of the Year; she also had the lowest average score and won the Babe Zaharias Trophy as the female athlete of the year.[4] It was a year for the ages, but sporting excellence does not fully account for what became a full-blown phenomenon.

Like Palmer, Lopez had a magic smile and a warmly appealing personality. She signed autographs anywhere and everywhere.[5] She grumbled about her weight and teared up when she spoke of her recently deceased mother. She was both an extraordinary athlete and an everywoman. "She put the LPGA on the map," said Hall of Fame golfer Patty Sheehan. "People just immediately fell in love with her."[6] Lopez had a charm that disarmed. At one US Open, after shooting an appalling 83 and knowing she had missed the cut, she marched down the eighteenth with her putter wrapped in a white towel, waving it in a mock surrender.[7]

Hers was hardly a conventional golf background. Her father, a Mexican immigrant, owned a successful auto body shop in Roswell, New Mexico. He had a three handicap[8] and taught her the game on the local muni.[9] Her swing was the despair of the classicist; she lifted her hands up near the beginning of the stroke; and her backswing was slower than slow,[10] with a loop at the top.[11] But it worked. From tee to green, that swing provided power and accuracy, and her putting sealed the deal.

Like all great athletes, she made it look easy. It wasn't. "I used to putt for hours," she said. "Sometimes I putted so long I couldn't stand up straight when I left the course."[12] She also had the killer instinct of the champ. "There she is, all sweet and smiling," commented her caddie, "then it's all business. She's got that ruthlessness."[13]

After playing on the boys' team in high school, Lopez received the University of Tulsa's first full female athletic scholarship. Two years later she joined the Tour. Lopez was no single-season comet. She won 17 times in her first 50 tournaments[14] and was named Player of the Year in 1979, 1985, and 1988. *Golf* magazine named her "Golfer of the Decade" in 1987,[15] even after she reduced her schedule to raise three daughters. She ended her career with 48 Ladies Professional Golf Association victories, sixth of all time. The only blemish: she never won the US Open, finishing second four times, once as an amateur and once in 1997 at age 40.

Prior to the Lopez tsunami, the women's tour was in threadbare shape. The LPGA didn't hire a commissioner, Ray Volpe, until 1975. He looked at the books and discovered it was bankrupt; the players chipped in to pay the bills. The only source of revenue was taking a percentage of tournament money. By the time Volpe left in 1982, the tournament purse had risen from $750,000 (for the entire tour) to $9 million (it's now $65 million),[16] and the LPGA was selling rights to everything but the bottom of the cup. There is no doubt that the "Lopez effect" contributed significantly to these riches.

In 1996 Australian Karrie Webb was having a great rookie year. Inevitably, she was asked if she saw herself as the next Nancy Lopez. Her response: "There's never going to be a next Nancy Lopez."[17]

LARRY BIRD'S AND MAGIC JOHNSON'S COLLEGE JERSEYS

I n what is still the highest-rated National Collegiate Athletic Association hoops final ever (24.1),[1] Michigan State beat previously undefeated Indiana State 75–64. It wasn't a great game—Michigan State was never in trouble—but it was a memorable one, because it was the first time that Lansing's favorite son, Earvin "Magic" Johnson, faced Larry Bird, the pride of Indiana. It was the only time the college stars met on the court.[2] But that game began one of sport's greatest rivalries—and the most important one in the history of the National Basketball Association.

In 1979 the National Basketball Association was in poor shape. Seventeen of the twenty-three teams were losing money, and several franchises risked being shut down.[3] The Cleveland Cavaliers were so bad and so poorly run they were known as the Cadavers.[4] Few games were televised. One executive said the sport was "regarded as being somewhere between mud wrestling and tractor pulling."[5] The fans were staying away in droves, put off by selfish play on the court and bad behavior off it. Between them, Bird and Johnson would reignite interest in the game and create stirring new chapters in the storied rivalry between the Boston Celtics and the Los Angeles Lakers (see 1962 entry on Bill Russell).

The initial cliché was that Bird, who joined Boston, was the hard-working, blue-collar grinder who played a smart game, and Johnson, who joined the Los Angeles Lakers, the flashy natural. Not the least of their accomplishments was to make nonsense of those racially inflected descriptions.

Bird, who is white, had tons of style; check out his no-look and behind-the-back passes to startled teammates. In a play that Celtics coach Red Auerbach called the best he ever saw,[6] in the first game of the 1981 Finals, Bird missed a shot from the right of the key, got his own rebound, switched the ball from his right to his left hand, and flipped it into the basket before he hit the ground.[7] This was Bird, distilled—the hustle, the spatial awareness, and yes, the flair—in one thrilling sequence.

Johnson, who is black, had tons of substance. He was never a top scorer, but he led the league in assists four times and would be the first man to reach 10,000 of them; he still holds the record for average assists per game (11.2). He had an unparalleled sense of the court, something that enabled him to play point guard, though he was improbably big for the role. As early as the 1980 Finals, Johnson proved just how intelligent his game was. In Game 6, he played every position at one time or another, ending with 42 points, 15 rebounds, 7 assists, and 3 steals. He would be the first rookie to be named most valuable player of the Finals. Lakers' coach Pat Riley would say that Johnson played with "fundamental flamboyance."[8] The exact same description applied to Bird.

Both were 6-foot-9 midwesterners from large families, who grew up competing with their older siblings and learning the value of hard work from their parents. They had a similar attitude to the game that obsessed them. "We weren't about stats," is how Johnson put it. "We were about winning."[9] This attitude transformed the way the game was played, with more passing, more teamwork, and more movement. It was simply more fun to watch. "Just as bad habits are contagious," noted Hall of Famer Chris Mullin, "good habits are, too."[10] Bird and Johnson started this healthy contagion.

A more apt cliché was that they made their teammates better. They led by example, diving for loose balls and playing tenacious defense. They labored to improve and would not tolerate sloppiness or lack of respect for the game. Johnson did all this with a huge smile; Bird was deadpan. But they had the same values, something they came to appreciate midway through their careers, when they became good friends. And while neither would admit it for some time, they also shared another absorbing interest: each other.

Bird would check Johnson's stats first thing; Johnson did the same.[11] He "motivated me like no other," Bird concluded. "I can't get away from Larry," said Johnson.[12] To this day, both say that the first question from fans is always about the other.

Their rivalry defined the NBA for a decade. From 1980 to 1989, one or the other competed in every Final. Over that period, Los Angeles took five titles (1980, 1982, 1985, 1987, and 1988) and the Celtics three (1981, 1984, and 1986).[13] But they didn't play each other for the title until their fifth year. All told, they only played each other 37 times. The Lakers won 22 of these contests.

The NBA did not recover from its many self-inflicted wounds overnight. The 1980 Finals, an excellent matchup between the Lakers and Julius Erving's 76ers, were not televised live. Even in 1984, the first time that Bird and Johnson faced each other for the championship, the series recorded a desultory 8.0 rating; that figure dipped below 7 in 1981, when the Celtics won. But as America grew to appreciate the duo's talents more fully, and as the game became more interesting, that improved to a 15.9 in 1987, their last Final against each other.[14]

The rivalry itself evolved. Bird was the superior player at first; he won the Rookie of the Year award easily, and from 1981 to 1986 finished either first or second in the MVP vote, winning in 1984, 1985, and 1986.[15] Moreover, the Celtics won the first title bout against the Lakers in 1984, a classic duel that went seven games. It marked the eighth time in eight tries that the Celtics had beaten the Lakers in the finals. That was about to change. In 1985 the Lakers finally won—in Boston Garden no less, the first time the Celtics had ever lost a title at home. The Lakers also beat them in 1987, the last great year of the rivalry. Bird and Johnson only played each other a handful of times after that, and never again for the title.

By that point, Johnson was clearly the better player, winning the MVP that year as well as in 1989 and 1990. Foot and back injuries began to slow Bird down—he wouldn't be a first-team all-star after 1988—while Johnson went from strength to strength. The Lakers were better, too. In 1987 and 1988 Los Angeles became the first team to repeat since the 1968–1969 Boston Celtics (of course). They also reached the finals in 1989 and 1991; the Celtics weren't back until 2008.

It looked like Johnson, a fit and healthy 31 in 1991, had at least several more good years ahead of him. He didn't. In November he announced that he had HIV and that he would be retiring. One of the first people he called with the news was Larry Bird.

Johnson returned for the all-star game in February 1992; naturally, he played brilliantly and was named MVP. Four months later, he and Bird were named co-captains of the 1992 "Dream Team" that took the gold medal in the Olympics. At last they were able to do their thing with, rather than against, each other: Johnson feeding Bird, an easy telepathy between the two. They would never compete on the same floor again. It was Michael Jordan's league now.

DONNIE ALLISON'S HELMET FROM THE DAYTONA 500

The day that made NASCAR did not start well. Though the Daytona 500 was a sellout, the rainy and dismal weather on February 18 had left more than a few empty patches in the stands. The Northeast and Midwest had it much worse. Washington, DC, got almost two feet of snow; New York had its coldest day of the century; and four Great Lakes were frozen.

But then—and to this day, NASCAR enthusiasts credit divine intervention—the weather cleared just enough. The race would go on. It was the first time the whole race would be broadcast live, and in a sense the weather was a godsend. A lot of snowbound Americans were not budging from their couches that Sunday afternoon, and there were only a few channels to choose from. So more than 15 million of them tuned in to NASCAR's most important race.[1]

They were bored, at first. To dry the track, the drivers circled the 2.5-mile oval for 15 laps at a stately 85 miles per hour, so the heat of the engines could soak up the moisture. Essentially, viewers were watching the track dry.

The 200-lap race began in earnest on lap 17, when defending Daytona champion Bobby Allison and his older brother, Donnie, shot out to the lead. Fifteen laps later, Bobby's car hit the rear of Donnie's. Both ended up in the soggy infield, and they dragged in Cale Yarborough as well. Even among the conspicuously macho men of NASCAR, Yarborough was known as a tough nut. Now he was furious. He was also three laps behind. But he kept driving, and simmering, and moving up the field as car after car made bad decisions or broke down.

For the viewer at home, the voice of NASCAR, Ken Squiers, was doing his usual excellent job, being both educational and entertaining. By deploying an in-car camera and utilizing low-level angles and other innovative techniques, CBS gave viewers a sense of the speed. It was enough to keep a lot of people watching, rather than cleaning out the basement.

Going into the last lap, Donnie Allison was in front and Yarborough was breathing his fumes. Yarborough made his move on the backstretch, cutting to the inside. Donnie, in NASCAR terminology, "threw a block," not allowing him to pass. "Unh unh unh," Donnie would later recall his thinking at this moment. "You can have all the room you want outside. You're not coming under me off the corner."[2]

Forced almost onto the infield again, Yarborough swung back, tapping Donnie's car with an unmistakable message: get out of the way. Donnie, less than a mile from glory, kept going. And so did Yarborough, steering his car into Donnie's. This time, they traded paint. Their doors locked together, they crashed into the outside wall, then veered across the track and stalled in the infield. Later Yarborough would explain his thinking this way: "I was going to pass him and win the race, but he turned left and crashed me. So, hell, I crashed him back."[3] Now it was down to Darrell Waltrip and Richard Petty, who staged a stirring duel of their own over the backstretch. King Richard won, taking the sixth of his seven Daytona 500s.

The drama was not over, however. A few minutes after the race, Yarborough and Donnie Allison were disputing what had happened at the finish when Bobby drove up (he finished eleventh).[4] Yarborough spotted the man he blamed for the mess on lap 32 and swung his helmet at him, bloodying his face. Bobby crawled through the window and started swinging. He liked to say that Yarborough "started beating on my fist with his nose."[5] Then Yarborough went for a kick, tumbled, and the two began flailing, as Donnie approached, holding this helmet.

Brawling ranked right up there with beer drinking and cheating as hobbies among racers. But this whole thing was new to the great number of Americans stuck at home. And they loved it.

The Fight, as it is known, made NASCAR water-cooler conversation for the first time. Newspapers ran big stories and bigger photos—most of them featuring Donnie and his helmet—and new fans burned up phone lines for tickets. Yarborough and the Allisons were fined, but NASCAR officials had to have been delighted. An exciting finish, a not-too-bad fight, and all on national television. Yarborough later called it "one of the best things [that] ever happened in NASCAR."[6]

Not so good for Donnie. Though he never threw a punch, the famous photo appears to show him about to brain Yarborough with the helmet. It didn't look good, and he began to get threats.[7] His reputation never recovered. Nor did his career. While the two men who fought each went on to take Daytona, Donnie never won another race.[8]

1980

MIKE ERUZIONE'S STICK FROM THE "MIRACLE ON ICE"

"Do you remember where you were when? . . ." The answer to that question, too often, is a tragedy. Not on this occasion. Americans who were awake on the evening of February 22, 1980, can tell you exactly where they were when the boys of winter pulled off this stunning upset.[1]

In sports terms, this was truly miraculous. The Soviet team that came to Lake Placid, New York, for the 1980 Olympics might have been the best hockey team ever. Known for its otherworldly stick handling and elegant passing patterns, it had won gold at the last four Games and also beat pro teams regularly. In the peculiar world of the Olympics, the Soviets were not themselves considered professionals. Soviet officials had argued in the 1950s, when they were negotiating their country's return to the Games, that only capitalists could be professionals. The Olympic authorities were happy to accept this dubious assertion. So the Soviet "amateurs" had no job other than hockey. "It was only work,"[2] remembered goalie Vladislav Tretiak, who said he didn't take a day off in 21 years, not even his wedding day.[3]

The Americans, by contrast, were all in or just out of college. The average age was 22,[4] and they had been playing together for only six months. The team had done well in a series of exhibition matches, but was raw and inexperienced. In a game at Madison Square Garden less than a week before the Olympics began, the Soviets had humiliated them 10–3, and it wasn't that close. The Americans were ranked seventh of the 12 teams entered in the Olympic tournament;[5] At best, the thinking went, they could hope for a bronze.[6]

So it was a nice little story when the Yanks tied third-ranked Sweden in the opening round by scoring a goal with 27 seconds left. Two days later, playing with a pleasing combination of efficiency and exuberance, they administered a 7–3 thrashing of the second-ranked Czechs. "U-S-A, U-S-A," the crowd bellowed, perhaps for the first time.[7]

Now people were taking notice. And when they won their next three games, against Norway (5–1), Romania (7–2), and West Germany (4–2), the hockey bandwagon was rolling. The United States had beaten or tied every team in its part of the draw, coming from behind in four of the contests. Now the team faced the Soviets, who had advanced to the medal round easily.

By definition, for a miracle to happen, there must be divine intervention. The US team seemed to get it when, with a single second left in the first period, Mark Johnson scored on a rebound that Tretiak cleared poorly to tie the game at 2–2. Then came a miracle of misjudgment. Coach Viktor Tikhonov was furious at the last-second lapse. His players said of him that if they ever needed a heart transplant, they wanted Tikhonov's because it had never been used.[8] In this case, he let his anger overrule his judgment. He benched Tretiak, who was considered the best goalie in the world.

The replacement was barely tested in the second period, with the Americans managing only two shots on goal. Jim Craig, on the other hand, made 11 saves, some of them brilliant, but the Soviets snuck one past him during a power play to retake the lead, 3–2.

On their first shot of the third period, eight minutes in, the Americans tied the score. Bedlam in the arena. Eighty-one seconds later, just as the fans were beginning to catch their breath, Captain Mike Eruzione used this stick to score the go-ahead goal.[9]

With 10 minutes left to play, the United States led for the first time, 4–3.

And then something strange happened: the Soviets panicked. They changed lines constantly and played an ugly dump-and-skate game. Though they managed nine shots on goal in the period, Craig stopped them all. As the crowd counted down the final seconds, ABC's Al Michaels asked, "Do you believe in miracles?" And the whole country roared with him, "Yes!"

After one of the more exuberant on-ice celebrations ever seen, the players skated to the locker room to take it all in. They were quiet at first, and some cried. Beating the Soviets on home ice—they had never really believed it was possible.

But they had done it. And then, in a scene so heartwarmingly schmaltzy Jimmy Stewart could not have pulled it off, they sang "God Bless America."[10]

Two days later the team defeated the Finns for the gold medal.[11] Yet again, the Americans had to come from behind, prompting Coach Herb Brooks to give one of the most effective pep talks in history: "If you lose this game," he told the team before the third period, "you'll take it to your F-ing grave."[12] They scored three times and won 4–2.

There are few moments of uncomplicated collective joy. This was one of them. At the time, America was feeling gloomy and uncertain. There were hostages in Iran, gas lines at home, and Soviets in Afghanistan. The country sorely needed a reason to smile.[13] Hockey provided it. When the result was announced at Radio City Music Hall, the audience spontaneously rose to sing the national anthem.[14] Similar scenes played out across the country.

After the Olympics, the Soviet team had some explaining to do. This was not the Stalinist era, so no heads rolled, but the team paid for its silver medals. Tikhonov sent the players to a remote training camp, where they worked out up to four times a day and could only see their families one month a year.[15] The Soviets would not lose another international game for five years.[16]

The Miracle on Ice was a unique moment—and it will stay that way. All the conditions that defined it have changed. The Soviet Union no longer exists, and the United States no longer sends a band of plucky postadolescents out onto the Olympic ice. Professionals have dominated Olympic rosters since the rules were changed in 1998.

Finally, there is the venue. In 1980 Lake Placid was home to about 2,700 people. It had some legacy infrastructure from the Games it had hosted in 1932, and state and federal authorities paid the bills. Still, it is impossible to believe that a modest little village like this will ever again host an Olympics.[17] There were infuriating transportation glitches, and the 1,072 athletes found the Olympic Village, much of which would later be converted into a prison, conspicuously short on charm. Lake Placid pulled it off, though, at a cost of $168.7 million.[18] That would not have paid the laundry bill at Sochi, where the 2014 Games cost an estimated $50 billion.

1980

ERIC HEIDEN'S GOLD RACING SUIT

Considering that relatively few Americans take up their sport, speed skaters have been outsized contributors to US Olympic success. In 1980, dressed in this gold racing suit and skating on an outdoor oval in front of a high school, Eric Heiden won all five speed-skating races, from 500 meters to 10,000 meters. It was the single most dominant performance in the history of the Winter Games. He is still widely considered the best skater of all time.[1] Short-track skater Apolo Ohno is the most medaled US Winter Olympian (eight, from the 2002 through 2010 Games); Bonnie Blair is the most medaled woman (six, five of them gold, from 1988 through 1994).

And then there's Dan Jansen, whose bad luck made him the kind of Olympic icon no one wants to be. The speed skater appeared in four Olympics, competing through tragedy (his sister's death) and spills (twice in 1988) and inexplicable underperformance (fourth and twenty-sixth in two races in 1992). In 1994 he entered the Lillehammer Olympics as the reigning 500-meter champion and world record holder—and finished eighth. But in the kind of ending that even Hollywood might consider too sappy to try, he struck gold in the 1,000, the last race of his career.

1982

THE BALL FROM "THE CATCH"

Once a decade, something happens on the football field that is so memorable, even close to mystical, that it becomes legendary. Think of David Tyree of the New York Giants clutching the ball to his helmet in the 2008 Super Bowl. Or the Music City Miracle of 2000, when the Tennessee Titans recovered an onside kick in the closing seconds and with the help of a handoff and a (much-disputed) lateral, scored the winning touchdown. Or Scott Norwood's wide right from 47 yards at the end of a thrilling Super Bowl in 1991. Or the Immaculate Reception of 1972, when Pittsburgh Steeler quarterback Terry Bradshaw bounced a pass off the hands of Oakland Raiders' great Jack Tatum—and into those of running back Franco Harris, who scooped it up at his knees and rumbled into the end zone. And of course the Ice Bowl (see 1967 entry) and the "greatest game" (see 1958 entry).

For the 1980s, there is "The Catch."

In the 1982 NFC Championship game, the San Francisco 49ers were losing to the Dallas Cowboys. This was a familiar state of affairs; in the 1970s, the Niners had lost to the 'Boys three years in a row in the playoffs. The team really, really did not like Dallas, which was known to many fans as "America's Team" and to the rest of the NFL as insufferable.

But this version of the Niners, which went 13–3, was ready to take the next step. The players were led by their third-year, third-round quarterback, Joe Montana, whom the Cowboys chose not to draft.[1] The take on Montana was that neither his arm nor his physique was big enough for the pros,[2] no matter how many stirring drives he had led during his career at Notre Dame. More to the point, the Niners had beaten Dallas earlier in the year, 45–14. But today, even though the team was playing at home, it hadn't played well. Montana had fumbled once and tossed three interceptions; penalties had hurt, too.

With less than five minutes left, San Francisco started from its own 11-yard line down 27–21. A dozen plays later, it was third and three from the 6, with 58 seconds to play. Montana called Sprint Right Option, in which he was first supposed to look for Freddie Solomon and then for Dwight Clark. The play had clicked earlier, with Solomon scoring. But the Montana-to-Clark option had never worked, not even in practice. "Dwight, be ready," Montana reminded him in the huddle.[3]

Montana took the snap and rolled right, pursued by three defenders. Solomon was not available. So as 750 pounds of angry Cowboys closed in, Montana pump-faked and threw this ball off his back foot to where Clark was supposed to be.

Clark himself was running left to right along the back of the end zone when he saw the ball, tossed so high that to this day many Cowboys believe that Montana was trying to throw it away. Clark ran toward the ball, leaped higher than he ever had, and caught it on his fingertips. Montana, buried under Cowboys, didn't see The Catch. But he heard the stadium explode—and knew. When the point-after put the 49ers ahead, 28–27, the Cowboys had 51 seconds to try to come back. They drove down the field with determination—and then lost a fumble on the Niner 44. Game over.

The Catch marked the beginning of one National Football Conference dynasty—of the 49ers—and the end of another—that of the Dallas Cowboys. San Francisco, which had never won a championship since joining the National Football League in 1950, would go on to win that year's Super Bowl, and three others during the 1980s. The Cowboys, who had been to five Super Bowls in the 1970s, winning twice, would be shut out. Worse, starting in 1986, they would have five straight losing seasons, including a gruesome 1–15 in 1989. Their coach, Tom Landry (see 1967 entry on the Ice Bowl), was fired in early 1989, ending his 29-year reign.

On the other sideline, fellow Hall of Fame coach Bill Walsh would be credited with inventing the West Coast offense, based on quick timing patterns and flexibility, which revolutionized play. He retired in 1989, recognized as one of the most innovative minds in football history.

"Who knows," Montana later speculated, "if [the 49ers] great run would have even happened if we hadn't had that incredible Sunday?"[4] Landry agreed that The Catch marked a decisive turning point: "It was only because of one play—Dwight Clark's catch—that we didn't get back" to the Super Bowl.[5] The loss was that crushing. There have been more spectacular plays in NFL history, and better games. But none has exceeded The Catch for its combination of thrills and consequences. Yet.

1983/1990

CHRIS EVERT'S SHOES AND MARTINA NAVRATILOVA'S WARM-UP JACKET

One was a base-liner, the other a serve-and-volleyer. One was known for her icy on-court demeanor, the other for emotional volatility. One grew up in sunny postwar Florida, the other in Prague, a city made gray with Soviet repression. One was right-handed, the other left-handed. One was straight, the other gay. One never put a foot wrong; the other regularly had to remove her foot from her mouth.

These contrasts shaped, but did not entirely define, the rivalry between Chris Evert and Martina Navratilova. Between 1973 and 1988 the two met on the court 80 times, with Navratilova winning 43 of the matches. On 61 of those occasions they met in the final—and Evert won 36 of those. All told, Evert won 157 tournaments and 18 majors; Navratilova 167 and 18.[1] "Not only did we bring out the best in each other," concluded Navratilova, "but we brought it out for years longer than if either of us had been alone at the top."[2]

There were three distinct phases to the rivalry. In the first, an established Evert swatted aside the young Czech, winning 21 of their first 25 matches. In the second, they tested each other on an equal basis, with Navratilova edging ahead, 15–10. And in the third, Navratilova was the superior player, winning 23 of their last 30 matches. From 1975 to mid-1987, one or the other was ranked number one almost the entire time, with only Evonne Goolagong (2 weeks) and Tracy Austin (23 weeks) interrupting their hegemony.

Those numbers give a sense of the sustained excellence of these players. What elevated this rivalry into the realm of the sublime, however, were two more subtle factors.

First, each woman lifted her game to meet the other. Navratilova's potential was clear from the moment she made her tour debut in 1973. A remarkable all-around athlete, she could rely on her natural gifts to beat most players. But being a plump and undisciplined fast-food junkie was not going to cut it against Evert. "I was in hog heaven," Navratilova recalled of her first few years in the United States after her 1975 defection from Czechoslovakia.[3] Tennis commentator Bud Collins dubbed her "the Great Wide Hope."[4]

Then she got serious about training and nutrition, sculpting her body into a lean and muscular profile. By 1981 she was beating Evert regularly, and beginning in 1982 she was dominant, sweeping Evert in 1983 and 1984. Evert's sneakers pictured below, caked with the red clay of Roland Garros, are from the 1983 French Open, the only Slam she won in this period; it was the fifth of her record seven French titles. Navratilova had lost in the fourth round, her only defeat that entire year.

"It jolted me," Evert admitted of Navratilova's dominance at this time.[5] "It shook me up and it was like, okay, 'What can I do to try to figure out to stay with her?'"[6] So Evert went to work too, hitting the gym to add muscle tone and flexibility. She also worked on her net game and practiced against left-handers.[7] Evert didn't close the gap entirely, but she did narrow it considerably; from mid-1986 until her retirement in 1989, she won 5 of their final 12 contests. Compare their matches from the mid-1970s with, say, their classic French Open final in 1985[8]—probably the greatest of their 80 matches, which Evert won 6–3, 6–7, 7–5—and it's stunning how much better they both became. By raising their game, they raised their sport.

Second, given the stakes and their intensity, the two competed with astonishing decency. Except for a brief period in the early 1980s, when Navratilova thought she needed to dislike Evert to beat her, they stayed friends, which they still are.

Their friendship started early. When Evert burst on the scene as a teenage amateur at the US Open in 1971, many players treated her coolly—"unwelcome in the sorority," in her hurt words.[9] So when a gifted but awkward young Czech player joined the tour a couple of years later, Evert went out of her way to be gracious. It is appropriate that Navratilova won her first Grand Slam title, the French Open doubles in 1975, in partnership with Evert—who then went on to beat her in the singles.

Perhaps the most touching public moment of their friendship occurred in 1986, when Evert bandaged up her knee to play in the Federation Cup in Prague. She could have pleaded injury, but she wanted to be there for her friend. It was Navratilova's first visit back to the country of her birth since her defection 11 years before. The Communist authorities had refused to report on Navratilova's achievements or televise her matches,[10] and she had no idea how she would be received. When Czech player Hana Mandlikova introduced her by name—a simple courtesy that was regarded as politically brave—the crowd roared its welcome. Navratilova teared up. Evert was there to rub her back. But then Evert always had her back. "Even when she beat me," Navratilova would write, "and I'd be sitting in the locker room, depressed, she'd come over to cheer me up."[11]

Navratilova was also supportive.[12] When Evert's first marriage was crumbling, Navratilova invited her to Aspen for a respite—where Evert met Andy Mill, to whom she was married for 18 years. Evert and Navratilova often traveled to tournaments together. Before the 1984 US Open final, they shared pasta and bagels as they waited for the men's match to conclude.[13] Then they played a ferocious 4–6, 6–4, 6–4 match that Navratilova won. "Playing against Chris," said Navratilova, "was always like battling part of your own nature."[14] In perhaps the ultimate compliment from a famously tough competitor, Evert once said, "If I couldn't win the tournament myself, I wanted her to win it."[15] Evert retired in 1989; Navratilova continued to play a little longer. The warm-up jacket pictured on the previous page is from her last major singles championship, Wimbledon in 1990; it was her record ninth singles title there.

For all their differences, the two have many important things in common. They were great sportswomen, in every sense of the word. They both took responsibility for helping to build their sport, working in leadership positions with the Women's Tennis Association and even coordinating their schedules to spread their star power. But the most important thing they share is each other, each an essential half to sport's greatest individual sporting rivalry.

WHEATIES MAGNET WITH MARY LOU RETTON

The moment that American women's gymnastics went from also-ran to global power can be plotted precisely. It occurred in a New York hotel room in 1981. At the end of a long evening, Bela and Marta Karolyi, Romanians who had discovered the great Nadia Comaneci and coached their country's team to Olympic gold in 1976 and 1980, decided to stay in the United States. "The rest of the world laughed at American gymnastics before I came," Bela later said.[1] It's the kind of thing the gregarious and egotistical coach *would* say—and that made him none too popular with his peers. But there is more than a little truth to the statement.

After their defection, the Karolyis' first months in the country were difficult. They struggled with the language and took menial jobs as they worked to get their daughter out of Romania. With the help of friends, they were able to open a small gym in Houston in 1982. Before long, their athletes began to make a name for themselves. One competitor who noticed was Mary Lou Retton, who felt she needed more intense training than she could find in her hometown of Fairmont, West Virginia.[2] She joined the Karolyis' gym in early 1983, aged 15.

Over the next year Retton steadily improved, and in the run-up to the 1984 Los Angeles Olympics, she went on an extraordinary roll, winning major titles in both the United States and overseas. Until, that is, six weeks before the Games, when her knee locked up. After arthroscopic surgery (see 1958 entry) cleared out cartilage, Retton was in the gym the next day.[3] There was just enough time to heal before the Olympics.[4]

Most of the Eastern bloc had stayed away from the Games—tit for tat for the US-led boycott of the 1980 Moscow Olympics. But the Romanians decided to come; they had high hopes for reigning world champion Ecaterina Szabo, whom the Karolyis had also coached, and who was expected to challenge Retton for gold. Bela was not allowed to go on the gym floor, which was reserved for each team's national coach. He wangled a floor pass as an equipment mover, which allowed him to flash signals from behind a barrier.[5]

Women's gymnastics has four events: balance beam, uneven bars, floor exercise, and vault. The scores of each event are added up to determine the winner. With two events left, Szabo was ahead by .15, in large part due to a perfect 10 on the beam. Retton was a performer as much as an athlete, and she was about to go on the mat for the event that rewarded those qualities the most, the floor exercise. To the strains of "Johnny, My Friend"—a song that the Romanians had been known to use—she killed it, tumbling, smiling, and prancing to a 10. Szabo threw down a 9.9 on the bars and was still ahead by .05 as Retton prepared for her last and best event, the vault. Only a 10 would bring her outright victory.

Although she was no more than 4 foot 10, Retton was no pixie. She had the thighs of a speed skater and the shoulders of a linebacker. Her approach to the vault was decidedly aggressive; she sprinted as if she planned to run through it. Her speed gave her the momentum to sail high. Perfectly aligned, she whirled, twisted, and then stuck the landing. Retton flung her arms up, burst into her perfect, albeit crooked, smile, and flew into her coach's arms for the first (but not last) Bela bear hug. Szabo hung her head. She knew, as the crowd knew, as the most ignorant television viewer knew, that this was a 10.

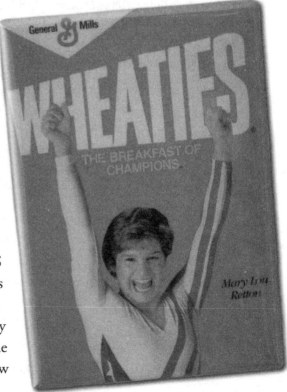

The faultless vault made Retton the first American—in fact, the first non-Eastern European—to win the all-around gold. She picked up three more medals in the individual events, and her gym-mate, Julianne McNamara, won gold on the uneven bars. As a whole, the US team came in second, behind the Romanians, its best performance to date.

Retton's powerful athleticism and bubbly personality made her the breakout star of the 1984 Games. At the end of the year she and fellow

Olympian Edwin Moses were named co-Sportspeople of the Year by *Sports Illustrated*. She also became the first woman to be the face of Wheaties, the "breakfast of champions."

Retton competed for another year and then retired. By that time, streams of little girls had started gymnastics. Just as Retton had been inspired by Nadia Comaneci in 1976, the coming generation of American women was inspired by her.

In large part due to the Karolyis, US women's gymnastics improved by leaps and bounds. From 1952 until 1984 the American women had not won a single medal. That dismal streak ended with Retton. Although the team just missed out on a medal in 1988—a controversial penalty cost them a bronze[6]—it has medaled in every Olympics since, including golds in 1996 and 2012.

Since the early 2000s the less demonstrative (and more popular) Marta Karolyi has played the bigger role on the American national team. The couple also runs a gymnastics camp on their ranch in east Texas; members of the US team train there regularly.[7] Marta Karolyi has said she will retire after the Rio Olympics in 2016. When she does, it will be the end of a glorious era that began in that New York hotel room, when a young couple threw the dice on their future.

1986

JACK NICKLAUS'S DRIVER FROM THE MASTERS

"Nicklaus is gone, done," wrote the golf columnist for the *Atlanta Journal* before the 1986 Masters. "He's 46, and nobody that old wins the Masters."[1] Asked if Nicklaus could win, player Tom Kite replied, "I don't think he can win *any* tournament."[2]

There was ample reason for these judgments. Nicklaus hadn't won a tournament in two years or a major in six. So far in 1986, he had missed three cuts in seven tries, and his best finish was a tie for thirty-ninth.[3] At 46 the Golden Bear was looking distinctly ordinary, with a middle-age paunch and deep lines creasing his face.

Nicklaus did nothing to change anyone's mind during the first round, shooting 74 and missing makeable putts everywhere. He improved to a 71 in the second round, then 69 in the third. With 10 holes to play on Sunday, he was five strokes behind. When he birdied 9, 10, and 11, the patrons—the Masters is too august to have "fans"—began to sense something special was happening. But then he bogeyed 12 and found himself four back once more.

The par five fifteenth changed everything. It was vintage Nicklaus. Needing a birdie, the Bear armed himself with the driver pictured here, addressed the ball—and walloped it almost 300 yards. With about 200 yards to the green, he fired a 4-iron to 12 feet and sank the putt for eagle to get to 7-under. Then he stuffed a drive to a couple of feet on the par-three sixteenth for birdie—it missed being a hole in one by less than an inch—and holed a nasty 18-footer for birdie on the seventeenth to take the lead for the first time. The famous photo of Nicklaus bent at the waist, eyes gleaming, putter held high, is from this moment.

What that image does not capture is the noise that arose at that indelible instant, a spontaneous roar that golfer Nick Price called "the loudest sound I've ever heard on a golf course." At this point the gallery was so excited that Masters decorum slipped. A lady in heels frantically tried to climb a tree, and Nicklaus's own mother was running around to find a better view.[4] Nicklaus himself was in tears.[5]

The emotion came, in part, because all this was happening at Augusta, a place of special memories for him. Back in 1963, when he had challenged the beloved Arnold Palmer here, the patrons had given Nicklaus hell. How dare Blob-O beat America's hero? But he did, becoming the youngest winner of the Masters to that point.[6] Two years later, after his second victory, Bobby Jones, the founder and patron saint of Augusta, offered this benediction: "Jack Nicklaus," he said, "plays a game with which I am not familiar."[7] And now he was on the cusp of winning again. Gathering himself with the help of his son and caddie, Nicklaus gutted out a difficult par on 18. He had finished in 65, shooting 30 on the back nine, and his 279 held up. Nicklaus had won his sixth Masters (the most ever) at 46 (the oldest ever) with a 30 on the last nine (the best ever for the winner).

The GOAT (greatest of all time) designation is always fraught. How does one compare achievement across the arc of time? How many more tournaments could Bobby Jones have won if he had not retired at age 28? What might Ben Hogan have achieved without World War II? Has Tiger Woods faced a deeper talent pool? These are questions to be savored over a single malt on the nineteenth hole.

But some things are not arguable. Jack Nicklaus won 18 majors—all of them at least three times[8]—four more than Tiger Woods. (He also came in second 19 times.) He won 73 tournaments, third behind Sam Snead and Tiger Woods. He was a competitive force for more than 20 years. And he was a true ambassador for his sport, always gracious in victory and dignified in defeat.

Nicklaus had many unforgettable moments on the golf course, but the back nine of Augusta in 1986 was special. He called it "by far the most fulfilling achievement of my career."[9] He never won again, but for one last time, here he was able to reach back to his physical prime, combine it with a quarter century of experience, and forge an unforgettable conclusion.

1987

SMU DOORMAT

U nkind but true: the Southern Methodist University Mustangs have been the doormat of Texas football for 30 years.

From 1980 through 1984, the Mustangs had the best cumulative record in Division I college football (49–9–1); they ranked in the top 12 for four years in a row. The Mustangs went undefeated in 1982 (with one tie), and every Mustang Maniac will tell you Penn State's coronation as national champion that year was at least highway robbery, and quite possibly conspiracy by panty-waisted northerners.

Those halcyon days ended abruptly and have not come close to returning. Since the end of the 1986 season, SMU has had more zero or one-win seasons (seven) than winning ones (four)[1] and has lost more than twice as many games as it has won.[2]

What happened? In February 1987 the National Collegiate Athletic Association revealed that SMU boosters had been systematically violating NCAA rules by paying at least 13 players monthly retainers totaling $61,000 over the previous two years. There is no doubt that this Wild West of cheating lasted much longer, and that the true price tag was much higher. Former SMU linebacker David Stanley told a television interviewer he had been paid a $25,000 bonus and $750 a month.[3]

Not that SMU was an outlier; the entire Southwest Conference was an expensive sinkhole, as were others. In an ESPN documentary, *Pony Excess*, former SMU player Rod Jones boasted that one school offered his family a four-bedroom house. (He turned that down but did accept a car.) A former SMU coach recalled showing a promising recruit $20,000. The response: "That's not even close."

Not only were SMU alumni paying a critical mass of players what amounted to a salary (plus benefits), but these arrangements had been made with the knowledge of a large number of coaches, administrators, and trustees. Then a bunch of them lied about it.

This was not the first or the second or even the fifth time the Mustangs had run into trouble; it was the seventh. The NCAA decided to throw the book at the program.[4] In a

decision that became known as the "death penalty," the NCAA banned SMU from competition for the entire 1987 season and from hosting home games in 1988. SMU also lost various rights in regard to recruiting, television, and hiring. The Mustangs decided not to field a team in 1988, saying it could not be competitive. Which is ironic, because it has rarely been competitive since.

Though the past 30 years have witnessed a long and unseemly stream of collegiate sport scandals, the case of SMU stands out. For one thing, it remains the only Division I team ever to suffer the death penalty.[5] Designed specifically for schools that committed two or more major infractions in a five-year period, the death penalty had only been added to the NCAA's list of sanctions in late 1985. SMU was an experimental sacrifice.

There is no question that the mendacity and cynicism that characterized the SMU saga retain their power to startle. But at least SMU players came away with something tangible from the corruption, in the form of cash-stuffed monthly envelopes, cars, goodies from Neiman-Marcus, livestock, and in at least one case, drug rehab. The same cannot be said of the many college athletes whose bodies are exploited for the greater glory of the U, but who otherwise get no benefit from the association.

The deal is supposed to be straightforward: student athletes get an education in return for participating in sports. In reality, in the "revenue sports"—the NCAA's telling shorthand for football and basketball—academics are routinely mutilated. In 1999 a University of Minnesota secretary revealed that, with the full knowledge of head coach Clem Haskins, she had written some 400 papers for 18 basketball players so that they could stay eligible.[6] Subsequent revelations made it clear that this was a small part of a much bigger mess. "In the two years I was there" in Minnesota, basketball player Russ Archambault said, "I never did a thing."[7]

On every campus, coaches and academic advisers know who the friendly faculty members are and are not shy about enlisting them to coax grades above the cut line. It's hardly a secret. In 1986 the late civil rights leader Julian Bond told *Sports Illustrated* that athletes are "kept from competition in the classroom so they can compete on the playing field, and the time has long passed when something has got to be done."

The NCAA rulebook has become ever more bloated since Bond made those remarks, but the abuses have if anything become more systemic and expensive. In a particularly gruesome example that surfaced in 2011, for 18 years the otherwise well-regarded African and Afro-American Studies Department at the University of North Carolina became an eligibility dump, offering hundreds of no-work, no-show, and no-faculty "paper classes," taken disproportionately by football and basketball players. Sometimes grades were changed[8] or forged; more often, the department administrator central to the scheme was simply told what grade to assign to keep the player eligible.[9] Athletes didn't even have to stay awake, an academic adviser explained to coaches, in one of the more misguided PowerPoint presentations on record.[10]

What may be even more scandalous than such scams are the elaborate and entirely legal dodges (summer classes, extension courses, friendly faculty) designed to keep players academically eligible, even if they are not fulfilling the requirements that would lead them to graduate. That is how Pro Bowl linebacker Dexter Manley managed to be functionally illiterate even after four years at Oklahoma State.[11] When athletes' eligibility runs out, so does official interest in their studies, and scholarships are renewed each year entirely at the discretion of the coach.[12] Break a leg—or just not be very good—and the "student athlete" is out.[13]

Even good students can get mangled by the system. Ravens lineman John Urschel had to fight his academic advisers at Penn State to be able to pursue his passion, mathematics. They suggested he sign up for easier courses.[14] Urschel prevailed, but one has to wonder how many less-committed students have had their education sabotaged this way.

There are other kinds of depredations as well. It's difficult not to hope that there is a particularly hot and smelly locker room in the afterlife for the South Carolina coaches who distributed steroids to their football players in the 1980s.[15] Three later pleaded guilty to drug charges.[16] Former Baylor basketball coach Dave Bliss defamed one of his players, Patrick Dennehy—*after* he was murdered by a teammate. Bliss, fearing that it might be revealed that he had paid part of Dennehy's tuition, asked his players to tell authorities Dennehy was a drug dealer.

Even in terms of pay-for-play, SMU's offenses are beginning to look distinctly small time. Reggie Bush of Southern Cal was sued by his agent for not repaying $290,000 in gifts. When the details came out, Bush had to give back his Heisman.[17] The University of Michigan's men's hoops team provided a distinctive touch. One of its boosters, Ed Martin, paid players nearly $600,000 as a way to launder money from his illegal gambling operations.

But for true creativity, the University of Miami goes to the head of the class. In 1994 federal investigators found that a Miami "academic adviser" had falsified 80 Pell Grant applications, mostly for football players, then kicked back the portion of the $212,000 he hadn't used to buy cocaine. The feds called this "perhaps the largest centralized fraud upon the federal Pell Grant program ever committed."[18]

And if out-of-control boosters led SMU to the gallows, say hello to the starstruck Nevin Shapiro. A 5-foot-5 con artist who was generous with other people's money, Shapiro is serving 20 years for bilking his victims of $930 million. He admitted in a series of prison interviews in 2011 that from 2002 to 2010 he spent millions on Miami football and basketball players. The university, the NCAA concluded in 2013, never noticed because it lacked "institutional control." In addition, some of those involved lied after the fact.

And then there's the Nittany Lions of Penn State. In the wake of what must surely be considered the worst scandal of all—years of sexual abuse by a football assistant coach and not nearly enough done to deal with it—the Nittany Lions got hammered with a $60 million fine, five years' probation, a four-year ban on bowl games, and 40 lost scholarships. Even all that was short of NCAA-induced death (and the penalties were later reduced).[19]

In regard to SMU in 1987, the NCAA could not have been more direct: "The committee's penalties are intended to eliminate a program that was built on a legacy of wrongdoing, deceit, and rule violations." It worked, and ever since—although officials say it ain't so—the NCAA hasn't had the stomach to go there again.

None of this is new. In 1905 *McClure's* magazine published a two-part exposé of college football. The stories of slush funds and non-student athletes sound familiar; in 1929, the Carnegie Foundation published a 350-page report that exhaustively chronicled similar rackets. Unfortunately, a few days later Wall Street crashed, and the country had other things to worry about.

The reality is that the system has been impervious to reform. While NCAA penalties can look tough, the rewards of corruption are much greater than the price of getting caught. In all the cases cited above, except for SMU, the programs lost little in terms of fan support and were generally able to recover quickly. As one coach observed, he was more likely to get fired for losing than for cheating. By one estimate, 30 athletic programs have been eligible for the death penalty since 1987; none has gotten the chop.[20] If being associated with child rape, bilking the feds, and endemic academic fraud don't merit the ultimate NCAA sanction, it is difficult to imagine what will.

Poor SMU. It turns out its biggest mistake was not so much paying athletes, but getting caught at exactly the wrong time.

1988

JOHN MADDEN FOOTBALL VIDEO GAME

John Madden prided himself on being an old-school kind of guy. As a television announcer, he was the oracle of the offensive line.[1] He liked football in the mud and in the cold. His favorite word was "Boom!"

But he was old school, not old-fashioned. Madden was always more than willing to try new techniques on the field, where he won 75 percent of his games—and a Super Bowl—as head coach of the Oakland Raiders. During his 29-year television career, he was one of the first to do live diagrams of plays.

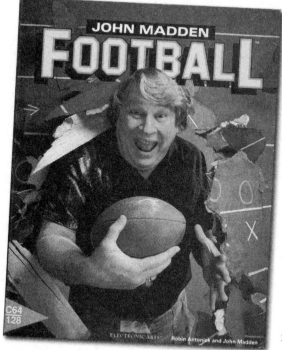

And that helps to explain why, in 1988, Madden became one of the biggest names in video games. In 1984 the head of Electronic Arts (EA), Trip Hawkins, asked Madden to lend his name to a game the company was planning. But the old-school part of Madden hated what EA showed him. Because of technological limitations, the creators could only have seven on a side. "If it's not 11-on-11," Madden stated, "it's not real football."[2] What's more, the demos "didn't have a lot of line play."[3] He would have no part of it. Several years later, computer capabilities had improved enough to meet Madden's standards. In the meantime, the game became known inside EA as an albatross: "Trip's Folly."

But this albatross would fly. Released for the Apple II in 1988, the first version of *John Madden Football* looks laughable now, with clunky cartoon figures bouncing across a dizzying green-and-white field.[4] But it was still the most realistic and sophisticated football game on the market.[5] Based on plays derived from NFL playbooks, each player was rated, including against other players, and the results of one play affected what happened on the next. It sold well enough that EA released a newer, better *John Madden Football* in 1989. This one was designed to work with a new console Sega was producing, the Genesis, which had two joysticks and faster processing. That game—informed by Madden's knowledge and attention to detail—and the console gave birth to the modern sports video game market.

Madden continues to be involved. Developers pick his brain about how to incorporate new kinds of action, and he critiques new plays.[6] The only other constant has been change, which is why *Madden NFL* (as it has been known since 1993) has stayed in the game.[7] Today's versions are immeasurably more sophisticated. The players look like players, not Pac-Men in helmets, and users can craft their own rosters and make their own plays. Data are updated constantly, and everything is interactive.

As a result, *Madden NFL* has become imbedded not only in gaming culture, but also in football culture. The graphics and sound became increasingly sophisticated, and TV began to take tips from the video game, learning how to inject more color and flash.[8] Coaches, too, have taken note. The kinds of things that can be done on *Madden NFL 16* add up to a virtual-reality testing ground. The game is a staple of NFL training camps, and there is even a "*Madden NFL* curse": several players who were featured on the game cover, such as Daunte Culpepper, Peyton Hillis, and Michael Vick, later hit rough patches. Coincidence? Maybe.

1989

PETE ROSE AUTOGRAPHED BASEBALL

Tagged with the derisive nickname "Charlie Hustle" as a rookie, Pete Rose embraced the idea instead, running to first on a walk and flying around the bases with abandon. A career .303 hitter and a key cog in the great Big Red Machine of the 1970s, he made 17 all-star teams, won three batting titles, earned two Gold Gloves, and was voted most valuable player in 1973. His 44-game hitting streak in 1978 was the second-longest in the modern era. He played more games than anyone in history, hit more singles, and made more outs.[1] But to describe Pete Rose by the numbers is like painting by numbers; you get a broad view of an image, but it's crude.

Rose will always be known for three things. First, he loved baseball, and fans loved the way he played it, seeing in his chunky body and not entirely grammatical speech the gritty overachiever he was. His uniform was always dirty, and he would do anything to win. When he left his hometown Cincinnati Reds for the Philadelphia Phillies in 1979, he took his winning spirit with him. The Phillies won their first World Series in 1980, and Hall of Fame third basemen Mike Schmidt would say, "Rose made the difference."[2]

Second, on September 11, 1985, as Cincinnati's player-manager, he lined a clean single to left center for his 4,192st hit, surpassing Ty Cobb for the major league record. He retired with 4,256 of them.

Third, there was the trauma and ugliness of his eviction from the game. As a ballplayer, Rose had a precise sense of what he could and could not do. Off the field, his balance was not as refined. A serious student of the life of Ty Cobb (and the father of a son named Ty), Rose was well aware that the First Commandment of baseball is "Thou shalt not bet." Moreover, every clubhouse has a warning to that effect. But he did it anyway, associating with a crew of uncharming lowlifes to liaise with gamblers.

When Commissioner Bart Giamatti hired an investigator, John Dowd, to look into allegations against Rose, Dowd found significant evidence that Rose, denials to the contrary, had indeed bet on the Reds while he was playing and managing. Rose and

Giamatti made a deal that major league baseball would not formally declare that he had bet on baseball, but Rose would agree that baseball had "a factual basis to the penalty imposed on him."[3] Rose would be placed on the ineligible list—the punishment set out in Rule 21 (d)[4]—and could apply for reinstatement after at least a year. Eight days later, Giamatti died.

For more than 14 years Rose continued to deny that he had bet on baseball. In 2004 he confessed, sort of. In *My Prison Without Bars*, one of the worst sports memoirs ever written—and that is a rich vein to mine—he admitted that he had bet, but never on the Reds to lose. "I'm sure that I'm supposed to act all sorry or sad or guilty now that I've accepted that I've done something wrong," he wrote. "But you see, I'm just not built that way."[5] The gracelessness of the apology, if that is what it was, did not impress. Rose continues to be barred from the game and from the Hall of Fame.

The Hit King, as Rose styles himself, has long made his living by signing his autograph at card shows. He charges a premium to write one sentence—"I'm sorry I bet on baseball."

CAMDEN YARDS

Camden Yards revolutionized the modern architecture of baseball. In fact, "counterrevolution" may be the better term, because it represented a return to older design principles: build downtown, for baseball only, with seats close to the field, and to reflect and honor the urban landscape.

Those were the hallmarks of America's pioneer modern ballparks, Shibe Park in Philadelphia and Forbes Field in Pittsburgh, which both opened in 1909. They were constructed of steel and concrete, a big improvement over the earlier jury-rigged wooden firetraps held together by spit and chewing gum. Shibe Park was a beaux arts masterpiece where owner/manager Connie Mack had his office in a cupola. Forbes was tucked into the city's Oakland neighborhood with understated style.

Pittsburgh, to its eternal credit, has preserved Forbes Field's home plate, imbedded in the floor of Posvar Hall at the University of Pittsburgh, and a large portion of the outfield wall, complete with ivy and the distance markings—an incredible 457 feet to left-center. Pilgrims can thus pay homage to one of baseball's greatest moments: Bill Mazeroski's home run to win game seven of the 1960 World Series. Shibe Park, abandoned in 1970 and razed six years later, has vanished altogether, save for a few bricks. Phillies Hall of Fame outfielder and broadcaster Richie Ashburn almost melted when he thought of the place: "It looked like a ballpark. It smelled like a ballpark. It had a feeling and a heartbeat, a personality that was all baseball."[1]

Both cities replaced these urban icons with ghastly, multipurpose stadiums featuring artificial turf and cutouts around the bases. Described perfectly by baseball writer Roger Angell as "grassless and graceless,"[2] these cookie-cutter fields of screams wore out their welcome quickly, but not before other cities followed suit, including great baseball towns that really should have known better, such as St. Louis and Cincinnati. Houston, Minnesota, Montreal, Seattle, and Toronto played in domes, which were even worse. Even the stadiums that didn't follow the blueprint just weren't very good. San Francisco's

Candlestick Park was notorious for swirling winds that made it almost unplayable at times. Shea Stadium could rock, but it aged quickly, and not well.

Ironically, Baltimore's predecessor to Camden Yards, Memorial Stadium, was not bad at all: excellent atmosphere, a good field, pretty good sightlines. It was homey. But the economics of baseball were changing, and Memorial could not deliver them; the Orioles had had their eye on a downtown field for years.

After flirting with some seriously banal ideas, and prodded by Baltimore Orioles officials, the designers hearkened back to the golden age of baseball architecture, 1909 to 1923,[3] going as far as measuring the angles and distances of the old parks to discern their golden mean. After distilling the best of the old, they added modern improvements. Some of the old parks had vast foul territory, for example, which meant a lot of cheap outs and that fans were far from the action. Camden Yards kept them close. Plumbing, amenities, training facilities, and food were much better. There are no view-blocking columns.

The field is walkable from downtown and just blocks from Babe Ruth's birthplace. Somewhere in center field his father ran a saloon;[4] the Ruth family privy was discovered during excavations.[5] The architects honored the city's industrial roots by incorporating the former B & O warehouse, the longest building on the East Coast, into the design. That decision was controversial at the time;[6] in retrospect, it was the genius of the obvious. Camden Yards would be much, much less without the warehouse dominating the right field skyline.

It's true that the expensive luxury boxes may draw the wrong kind of customer. And there were some other imperfections, such as seats that didn't orient toward home plate and an out-of-scale video screen.[7] On the whole, though, the place was a miracle. Likeable and functional, it was a throwback that didn't reek of preciousness. It just worked.

And from the moment it opened in 1992, everyone in baseball recognized that.[8] With too many cities proving amenable to throwing tax dollars at baseball billionaires, a building boom ensued. Since 1992, 20 major league ballparks have been built; 18 of them reflect the Camden Yards imprint.[9] Brick is big. Quirkiness is carefully designed. Steel trusses are de rigeur.

Camden Yards was so influential it arguably made retro the new cookie-cutter. (To visit the homes of the Washington Nationals and the New York Mets is to feel déjà vu all over again.) Even so, the fact remains that these parks are much better than what they replaced and are all good places to watch, and play, the game.

Camden Yards itself has seen more mediocrity than greatness on the field, but it has hosted two truly historic moments. The first occurred on September 6, 1995, when Cal Ripken played his 2,131st consecutive game, breaking Lou Gehrig's record. Naturally the hometown hero hit a home run—and Eddie Murray, one of Ripken's closest friends, hit his 500th in the same game.

The second happened on April 29, 2015, when the Orioles and Chicago White Sox played a game with an official attendance of zero. In the wake of a death in police custody, unrest and disturbances had been flaring up around Baltimore for days. Camden Yards was not immune. A few days before, fans had been locked in after a game due to what the scoreboard referred to as "an ongoing public safety issue outside the park."[10] Because city leaders were skittish about a big public gathering at such a fraught time, the teams agreed to play in an empty stadium. There can be no better, or worse, demonstration that the Elysian fields of sports can never be separated from what happens outside the lines.

JACKIE JOYNER-KERSEE'S SHOE

"Someday, this little girl is going to be the First Lady of something," the matri-arch said when her granddaughter was born in 1962.[1] Such predictions are common from grandparents. This one, however, came true, because that infant, Jacqueline Joyner-Kersee, became the first lady of track-and-field.

And perhaps more than that. Although it's tricky—indeed, impossible—to compare athletes across generations, either Babe Didrikson Zaharias or Jackie Joyner-Kersee is surely America's greatest female athlete. The former was accomplished in more sports; the latter excelled in two sports in an era when the competition was much tougher. Call it a toss-up.

Joyner-Kersee was born in East St. Louis when it was a bustling blue-collar town. But the factories closed, and the middle class fled. When she was growing up, it was, and remains, a very tough place. But she had strict parents—a 10:00 p.m. curfew, no makeup, and no dating until she was 16. "The complete list of [my mother's] rules would fill this book,"[2] Joyner-Kersee recalled ruefully in her autobiography. In addition, a nearby community center[3] provided activities, including dance, art, a library, and sports for the active youngster. She also found a good coach, Nino Fennoy, at a young age. All this provided a foundation for excellence. In high school she was a top student as well as captain of the basketball and volleyball teams. She earned a hoops scholarship to the University of California Los Angeles, where she insisted that she also be allowed to compete in track.

Joyner-Kersee was a gifted basketball player, starting for four years; like Didrikson, she was named an all-American. But she had more room to grow on the track. Entering UCLA as a long jumper, at the suggestion of assistant coach (and future husband) Bob Kersee, she took up the heptathlon. She would never give up the long jump; she adored the purity of it. A one-time world record holder, she won an Olympic gold medal in the event in 1988, plus bronze in 1992 and 1996. Her personal best of 24 feet, 6¾ inches is still the American standard.

But it was in the heptathlon that Joyner-Kersee found her true calling. The event has seven elements—the 100-meter hurdles, high jump, shot put, 200 meters, long jump, javelin, and 800 meters—and the variety allowed her to display her wide-ranging athleticism. About 5 foot 10 and 150 pounds, she had the build for the strength events, while still being lithe enough for the sprints. At the 1984 Olympics she finished a close second; if she had run the last event, the 800 meters, just a third of a second faster, she would have won.[4] She would not lose again for almost a dozen years.

Over that period she won gold medals in Seoul in 1988 and Barcelona in 1992 and four world championships.[5] She was the first woman to score more than 7,000 points; her world record of 7,291 still stands. Sometimes she won all seven elements. In 1986 Joyner-Kersee won the Sullivan Award as the country's top amateur and also won the Jesse Owens Award in both 1986 and 1987 as the best track athlete. In 2001 she was named the top collegiate athlete of the previous 25 years.[6] Her six Olympic medals tie her with Allyson Felix for the most ever by an American woman in track-and-field. In recognition of all this, in 2013 the award for best female track athlete was renamed after her.[7]

Jackie Joyner-Kersee was part of the first generation of women athletes to benefit fully from the forces changing sports.[8] Thanks to Title IX, there were athletic scholarships available that allowed her to build her skills. And beginning in 1981 the rules governing amateurism softened; this meant that after graduating from UCLA, she could support herself through sponsorships and endorsements and thus extend her career. Her last major event was in 2000; the shoe pictured here dates from 1993.

Light and composed of man-made fibers, it's interesting to compare it to the leather one that Mae Faggs wore (see 1952 entry on the Tigerbelles) or even to the first modern American track shoe (see 1974 entry on the Nike Waffle Trainer).

Since leaving competition, among other things, Joyner-Kersee has founded a community center in East St. Louis[9] that offers many of the same kinds of programs from which she benefited so much. And her first coach, Nino Fennoy, has led East St. Louis high school girls to 16 state championships.[10] Perhaps somewhere among them is the next first lady of US track.

1995/2009

GENO AURIEMMA'S FIRST CHAMPIONSHIP TROPHY AND PAT SUMMITT'S 1,000TH VICTORY BALL

For 12 years, it was a wonderfully nasty rivalry. When the women of the Universities of Connecticut and Tennessee played basketball against each other, the stakes were always high, the games often close.

A few months after their first nationally televised clash in January 1995, the UConn Huskies brushed the Lady Vols aside, 70–64, to complete an undefeated season and win the team's first national championship (see trophy on page 253). The following year Tennessee got a most satisfying revenge, beating UConn in overtime in the Final Four, in one of the greatest games in hoops history. Four times, the teams met in the National Collegiate Athletic Association final; four times, UConn won.

Then there were the coaches, two of the legends of the sport. Geno Auriemma of UConn and Pat Summitt of Tennessee began as relatively friendly rivals but became relatively unfriendly ones, to the extent that in 2007, Summitt canceled all regular-season games. She suspected UConn was committing recruiting violations;[1] she was also upset that Auriemma had called her Lady Vols the "evil empire." Since then, the teams have only met in the NCAA tournament.

Of course the two coaches had a great deal in common. "We both lived the game," Summitt would write, "as if it was in us on a cellular level."[2] Both were brilliant, intense, dedicated coaches who did not tolerate fools, bad officiating, stupid questions, or sloppy play. They both had exemplary records when it came to the academic accomplishments of their players. Both were natural alphas, not inclined to cede, or share, status as leaders of the sport.

Born on a family farm in rural Tennessee, Pat Head Summitt was raised on a diet of hard work and rectitude. Her career covered the entire modern history of women's hoops. She grew up with the six-player, half-court game in high school and played in the first national college tournament as well as on the first US Olympic team, which won the silver medal in 1976.

Hired to coach Tennessee in 1974, she was paid $250, and also did the laundry and drove the team van. To pay for new uniforms, the team sold doughnuts.[3] But Summitt began to build a reputation; in 1984, she coached the US Olympic team to a gold medal. By then she had perfected The Stare, a piercing look that was intimidating even to see on television.

In her 38-year tenure as head coach (1974–2012), Summitt never had a losing season. Her teams made every NCAA tournament, winning the national championship six times between 1987 and 1998—including the last three in a row. She began to be referred to as the "John Wooden of women's basketball"; Wooden won 10 titles with UCLA from 1964 to 1975. In 2009 Summitt became the first Division I hoops coach to win 1,000 games, an achievement commemorated with this ball. By the time she retired in 2012, she had won more games (1,098) than any other basketball coach, male or female; gone to 18 Final Fours; and won eight titles. From 1985 to February 2016, the Lady Vols were never out of the top 25—a record 565 weeks.[4] In 2000 she was named the Naismith Women's Collegiate Coach of the Century; John Wooden won the award for men.

Auriemma comes from a very different background. He emigrated from Italy as a boy and grew up outside Philadelphia. His first college coaching job was as an assistant for the women's team at St Joseph's in Philadelphia; his sense of humor is spiked with distinctly Philly barbs. He also worked at Immaculata coach Cathy Rush's (see 1972 Immaculata Mighty Macs entry) summer hoops camps;[5] Rush helped him get the post as an assistant at the elite University of Virginia women's program. After four years he was ready to run his own show and became head coach at UConn in 1985. Those Huskies were a hangdog bunch, with only one winning season in 11 years. By 1991 they were in the Final Four, and in 1995 they won it all. Huskies teams have gone undefeated five more times under Auriemma, at one point winning 90 games in a row, breaking Wooden's record of 88.[6] He also coached the American women to gold in the 2012 Olympics. In 2016, the Huskies won their fourth title in a row, and eleventh under Auriemma, breaking Wooden's record, and appear primed to keep going.

UConn–Tennessee is the only women's team rivalry that has approached anything like the intensity and interest characteristic of those in the men's game, such as Duke–North Carolina. Summitt herself referred to it as an "absolute masterpiece."[7] Like any great rivalry, UConn and Tennessee pushed each other, and the game itself, to greater excellence. From 1995 to 2010, one or the other won 12 of 16 NCAA championships, and all but two Final Fours over that period featured at least one of them.

The contest has lost some of its edge because UConn has been so dominant of late; Tennessee hasn't won since 2008. The renewed friendship between Auriemma and Summitt has also taken the venom out of it. But the most important reason it will never be the same is that Summitt will not be part of it. In 2011, at age 59, she was diagnosed with early onset Alzheimer's. She retired after that season—a personal tragedy and a terrible loss to the game she loved. When she died in June 2016, all of basketball—and all of Tennessee—mourned. Pat Summitt was, literally, a game-changer.

PIECE OF FLOOR FROM MICHAEL JORDAN'S "LAST SHOT" WITH THE BULLS

As a freshman at North Carolina, Michael Jordan sank the game-winning shot in the 1982 National Collegiate Athletic Association finals. As an Olympian, he won gold medals in 1984 and 1992. As a professional, he won six titles with the Chicago Bulls. As an individual, he won the Rookie of the Year, five most valuable player awards, and ten scoring titles. And as a commercial icon, he's unmatched.

Even so, failure is a crucial element of the Jordan story—something confirmed by the man himself. "I've missed more than 9,000 shots in my career," he said in a 1998 commercial. "I've lost almost 300 games. Twenty-six times I've been trusted to take the game-winning shot and missed. I've failed over and over and over again in my life."[1]

Jordan hated failure, but he never feared it, which is why he was always in position to take the final shot and wanted to. And he channeled the sting of failure into greatness. In his induction speech into the Basketball Hall of Fame, he reminded the coach who didn't name him to the high school varsity, "You made a mistake, dude."[2] In the National Basketball Association, his rivals noticed how he improved his jump shot, ball-handling, and defense.[3]

Jordan's commercial success, too, was built on a willingness to fail. In his first contract with Nike, he insisted on having his own brand. If it was a dud, it would be a personal and highly public dud. The first Air Jordan rang up $130 million in sales in 1985.[4] That put Nike, which had been struggling, back on track. Now in its thirtieth edition,[5] the brand continues to dominate the sneaker market.

The best advertising, however, was on the court. Jordan was wearing the first Air Jordans when he scored 63 points in the playoffs against one of the NBA's greatest teams, the 1986 Celtics. The Bulls lost in double-overtime, but Larry Bird was so awed he called his rival "God disguised as Michael Jordan."[6] After six years when he played brilliantly but his team always failed to win the big one, the Bulls broke through in 1991 for the first of three consecutive titles.

The one failure Jordan did not convert into success was on the baseball field. He retired from the NBA in October 1993—a year marked by the murder of his father, James—to try to make it to the majors. With the AA Birmingham Barons, though, he hit only .202 in 127 games[7] and committed 11 errors in the outfield. He returned to the Bulls in March 1995. In his fifth game back, he scored 55 points. With Jordan fully committed again, Chicago won three straight championships, in 1996, 1997, and 1998, matching the "three-peat" that had preceded his baseball interlude.

His greatest moment with the Bulls was his last. Chicago was up three games to two in the 1998 finals, but was playing in front of a tough Utah Jazz crowd. Due to injuries and illness, the Bulls were not at full strength, and Jordan had carried the team. Late in the fourth quarter, though, his exhaustion showed; at one point, he missed four straight jumpers.[8]

With 41.9 seconds left, the Jazz were up 86–83, after a three-pointer from the estimable John Stockton. In less than five seconds, Jordan drove to the basket and scored, to close the gap to one. Stockton took the ball back up court; with about 16 seconds left, he passed inside to Karl Malone. From behind, Jordan swatted the ball out of Malone's hands, recovered it, and dribbled up court with complete assurance. At 10 seconds, Jordan made his move, driving right, nudging Utah's Byron Russell left, then stepping back via a lovely crossover dribble to create space. From the

top of the key, he paused, set, and with perfect form, hit the game-winner. (A fragment of that floor is seen on the previous page.) The Bulls had their sixth title in eight years.

Seven months later, in January 1999, Jordan announced his retirement. It felt right. His last shot was the perfect ending to an epic career, and most of the key members of the team, including coach Phil Jackson, would not be back for the 1998–1999 season. But Jordan couldn't stay away. He returned to play for two frustrating years with the Washington Wizards in 2001–2003. Then he retired for good.

Jordan did much more than rack up trophies. He changed the NBA. He joined the league at precisely the right time. The advent of Larry Bird and Magic Johnson had lifted the league from the depths of near-irrelevance (see 1979 entry on them). But the combination of Jordan, new leadership, and new technology launched the NBA to new heights.

The new leader was David Stern, who became commissioner in 1984. He had a good reputation with the players and helped to negotiate an antidrug policy and a revenue-sharing structure in 1983; these agreements stabilized the league's finances and improved its reputation.[9] As commissioner, Stern was brilliant in leveraging new technology, meaning new kinds of television. Cable TV, particularly the emergence of ESPN and regional networks, ensured more complete American coverage and added a generous new source of revenues. Satellite technology enabled the game to find new fans overseas. In 1986 people in about three dozen countries could see NBA games; a decade later, that number had increased to 175.[10] For much of this global audience, Jordan *was* the NBA. Stern would always remember being in China in 1990 when a local guide earnestly told him how much she liked the "red oxen."[11]

"Michael changed the world," concluded Bill Walton, the former UCLA and NBA star. Like many things said about Jordan, that seems over the top. But he was the greatest player ever, and is still the most famous. It's quite a legacy, and the ultimate affirmation of his belief that his willingness to try, and fail, "is why I succeed."[12]

BALL FROM THE 1999 WOMEN'S WORLD CUP

In a familiar scene, there were 90,000 roaring fans in the Rose Bowl, and across the country, 40 million people scarfed down nachos and wings as they cheered their team in the big game. But there was one big difference: the game that provoked all this—the final of the 1999 World Cup—was being played by women.

The US women's team was a soccer power. Led by a veteran core, it had won the first World Cup in 1991 and finished third in 1995. Posters of Michelle Akers, Julie Foudy, Mia Hamm, Kristine Lilly, Carla Overbeck, and Brianna Scurry were on the bedroom walls of girls all over the country.

Then they won the Olympics in 1996, beating reigning World Cup champion Norway in overtime to reach the final. But television barely covered the women's games, only managing to air limited tape-delayed highlights. In the stirring final against a resolute Chinese side, the United States won 2–1 before more than 76,000 enthralled fans,[1] and the players emerged as genuine stars, even though television managed only to air a few minutes of that, too.[2]

Olympic gold was the perfect preparation for the 1999 World Cup. When the United States had won the right to host the event, the leaders of FIFA, the international soccer federation, thought to make it a cozy little affair, clustered in second-tier venues on the East Coast.[3] Maybe the games could get a little coverage at the far end of the cable spectrum. This was largely the same FIFA that had insisted that the women play 40-minute halves during the 1991 World Cup; 45 minutes, they decreed, would be too much for the gals.[4]

The American players, however, were not interested in hosting a mini-me World Cup, and they forced people to listen. The members of the national team were an appealing bunch, lacking the criminal records and sense of entitlement that filled too many sports pages. It didn't hurt one bit that they were attractive—"babe city" in David Letterman's words. Many had been playing together for years, often under difficult conditions, and there was a palpable cohesiveness and team-first spirit. At the same time, they were brimming with competitive fire. The team's sports psychologist remembered that blood spilled, literally, during a game that required them to grab spoons or be eliminated.[5] Put it all together, and the result was a group portrait of pleasing hues. Not unlike the pioneers of the women's tennis tour, the soccer players worked hard to promote their sport, giving clinics and signing autographs. That helped to build grassroots enthusiasm for the Cup.

As a result of the charm offensive, it gradually began to occur to the powers that be that while this soccer team was discernibly female, which was too bad, it might be worth a little more attention. After all, the US women actually won things, something that could not be said of their male counterparts. And with 7.5 million American girls registered to play,[6] maybe those 10,000-seat venues were a little unambitious. So soccer went for it, booking the Boston, Chicago, New York, and Washington pro football stadiums, plus the Stanford stadium and smaller venues in Portland and San Jose. The goal was to sell 312,000 tickets, a guesstimate that was wildly wrong. Half a million tickets were gone before the first kick.[7]

The tournament became a phenomenon, and this wasn't just an American show. Early-round matches like Mexico–Italy attracted more than 50,000 spectators; even North Korea–Denmark sold out. Best of all, the US women played with the verve and charisma they had been displaying for years, beating a strong German squad 3–2 in the quarterfinals. Against Brazil in the semis, goalkeeper Scurry had her best game of the tournament, keeping an aggressive offensive team out of the goal in a 2–0 victory.

By the time of the final against China on July 10, World Cup fever had spread; even the most macho sports bars tuned in to the final. There have been better games. The action clustered around midfield, as both teams played tightly, afraid to make a blunder. China's goalkeeper had to make only four saves in regulation; Scurry made two. But there was also intensity, some superb passing—and one heart-stopping moment in extra time, when China connected on a header that defender Kristine Lilly just barely managed to kick away. After 120 minutes, the score was 0–0.

So it would come down to penalty kicks. The first four kicks, two from each team, were good. On the fifth kick, though, Scurry anticipated Liu Ying's intention and made an excellent save low and to her left. If the final three Americans could convert, the World Cup would be theirs. The Chinese did not make it easy, with their last two players both finding the back of the net. It came down to Brandi Chastain. She lined up slightly to the right of the ball, took four short steps, stroked through with her left, and lined a shot high into the right corner. Unstoppable. Goal, match, and Cup to the Americans. Plus, the unforgettable image of Chastain ripping off her team jersey, revealing a black sports bra and stellar abs.

Signed by most of the US team, the slightly scuffed ball pictured here was used in that memorable World Cup. The images are of the places where games were held: the Statue of Liberty for New York; the Capitol for Washington, DC; a circuit map for San Jose, the heart of Silicon Valley. It is an all-American artifact for an all-American triumph, both on and off the field.

While the US women's team has continued to excel in international competition, winning Olympic gold medals in 2004, 2008, and 2012, and another World Cup title in 2015, that performance has not translated into professional success. A women's pro soccer league kicked off in 2001 but closed after three seasons and $100 million in losses.[8] Another began in 2009 and folded in 2012; a third is hanging in there.[9] Whether the problem is that the athletes are female, or that the game is soccer, or that the sports calendar is crowded, or that this is just one of those things Americans only care about every few years, women's pro soccer hasn't found its footing. But the girls of summer, circa 1999, gave American fans the most remarkable three weeks in the history of women's team sports. So far.

TIGER WOODS'S SCORECARDS FROM THE US OPEN

In his finest performance in his best year, Tiger Woods won the US Open at Pebble Beach by 15 shots—the largest margin of victory in a major.[1] Shooting 65–69–71–67, as these scorecards show, he led from start to finish and tied the Open scoring record at 272.[2] When Woods won the British Open the following month—setting a course record at 19 under par—he became, at age 24, the youngest man to win all four majors. And when he followed that with the PGA and then the 2001 Masters, he owned all four modern major trophies at the same time. Over the four tournaments, he showed not only skill but true grit. At the PGA, he had to sink a six-footer on the last hole to force a playoff. At the Masters, the back nine was a nail-biter until he pulled ahead for good on the sixteenth.

It was not a Grand Slam, because Woods did not win all four within a calendar year. But the Tiger Slam is still the most remarkable achievement in modern golf. Only Ben Hogan, in 1953, won as many as three majors in a row. Woods's record in 2000 might be the most dominant ever. He entered 20 events, won 9, and finished in the top three 14 times.

Remarkable, but not surprising. Tiger Woods had been on golf's radar for almost his entire life. As a toddler he showed off his form on the *Mike Douglas Show*, where he also managed to upstage Bob Hope. Woods won three Junior Amateurs and three US Amateurs. At age 16 he became the youngest man to compete in a tour event. Like the man he has spent

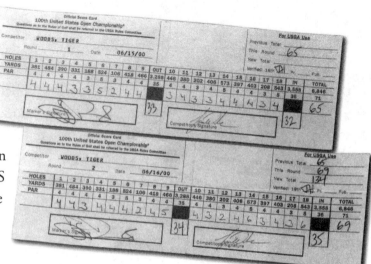

his life chasing, Jack Nicklaus, Woods won his first major, the 1997 Masters, while still the reigning US Amateur champion.

That triumph had particular meaning, because the Masters tournament had been all-white until the year of Woods's birth, 1975, when 40-year-old Lee Elder became the first black man to play in the tournament. Charlie Sifford and Pete Brown, despite two tour victories each, were never invited. Bobby Jones (see 1930 entry), the creator of the Masters and regarded as one of the great gentlemen of the game, was, for better and in this case, for worse, a man of his place and time; he never addressed this injustice before his death in 1971. The club itself didn't have a black member until 1990.

The Masters was hardly unique in its attitude. From 1934 to 1961 the bylaws of the Professional Golfers Association of America restricted membership to "professional golfers of the Caucasian race." Teddy Rhodes had to sue to earn his way into the US Open in 1948.

Woods had teed up at Augusta as an amateur in 1995 and 1996, when he played a practice round with Jack Nicklaus and Arnold Palmer. But 1997 was his first major as a professional. Initially he looked rattled, shooting a 40 on the front nine. Then he settled down and played some of the most dominating golf ever seen, shooting a 30 on the back nine and then 66–65–69 to finish at 18 under (a course record), 12 shots ahead (another record) at age 21 years, 3 months (ditto). A student of the history of the game, Woods acknowledged those who came before him. "I wasn't the pioneer," he said. "Charlie Sifford, Lee Elder, Ted Rhodes: those are the guys who paved the way."[3] Nicklaus marveled at what he saw: "He's taking the course apart."[4]

From 1997 through 2010, Woods dominated the game, ending every year ranked first (11 times) or second (3 times).[5] He also made a record 142 consecutive cuts.[6] In 2008 he won his fourteenth and bravest major, taking the US Open on the nineteenth playoff hole while in pain from a balky knee.

At that point, Woods was 34 and looked likely to surpass Nicklaus's record of 18 major triumphs. Although he was Player of the Year in both 2009 and 2013, he hasn't won a major since that Open. Personal troubles and injuries have taken a toll, and the rise of young talent like Jason Day, Rory McIlroy, and Jordan Spieth has raised the degree of difficulty. Once the most intimidating figure in the sport, Woods ended the 2015 season ranked 416th.

But however Woods's career plays out, he has created an enduring legacy. Handsome, personable, multiethnic, and supremely skilled, he brought a new audience to golf, and with it, more television coverage and a lot more money.

He also changed the game itself. In the wake of his 1997 victory, the mandarins of the Masters were not pleased at how ordinary Woods made their precious course look. They immediately set about "Tiger-proofing" Augusta, lengthening numerous holes and adding rough, bunkers, and trees all over;[7] the course is 500 yards longer now than it was in 1997.[8] Other courses have done the same.

This points to an issue that golf has not yet come to grips with. Balls fly farther. Clubs have improved. Players are fitter and stronger. In 1996 the longest driver, John Daly, averaged 288.8 yards[9] off the tee, a figure that would no longer rank in the top 100. Some of the world's greatest courses, designed in a different era, could be overwhelmed by the modern power game. And yet who wants a world in which St. Andrews and Merion could become obsolete?[10]

LANCE ARMSTRONG'S BIKE FROM THE TOUR DE FRANCE

"Everybody wants to know what I'm on. What am I on? I'm
 on my bike, busting my ass six hours a day."[1]

"I didn't take performance-enhancing drugs, I didn't ask anyone else to take
 them and I didn't condone or encourage anyone else to take them."[2]

"Anyone who thought I would go through four cycles of chemo
 just to risk my life by taking EPO was crazy."[3]

"How many times do I have to say it? It can't be any clearer
 than 'I've never taken drugs.' How clear is that?"[4]

All lies, of course. According to the US Anti-Doping Agency's report released in October 2012, Lance Armstrong led "a massive team doping scheme, more extensive than any previously revealed in professional sports history."[5] He was banned from competition for life and stripped of his seven Tour de France titles. Once a secular saint who hung out with U2's Bono, dated Sheryl Crow, and chatted with presidents, he was named the most disliked athlete in America in 2013.[6]

Armstrong's fall was extreme because he plummetted from such a height. After he claimed his first of seven straight Tour titles in 1999, less than three years after being diagnosed with testicular cancer, the *New York Times* lauded his "resoundingly positive image" for an event that had been so decimated the year before with doping arrests that it became known as the "Tour de Dopage." When *Sports Illustrated* named him Sportsman of the Year in 2002, the magazine noted that much of the public saw Armstrong as "more than an athlete. He's become a kind of hope machine."[7] Two years later, a poll named him "the best sports role model of the last 50 years."[8]

In 2000 he used this bike, a Trek 5500, on some of the flatter stages of the Tour, including the final run into Paris; made mostly of carbon fiber, it weighs less than four pounds.[9] Armstrong eventually finished more than six minutes ahead of Jan Ullrich of Germany. His second victory in a row, it secured his status as a truly great cyclist and seemed to confirm that doping was not essential to winning.

That was how it seemed at the time. In fact, Armstrong had been doping since the mid-1990s.[10] Even after the dam of lies broke, he could not bring himself to face the consequences of his actions. His defense, as told to Oprah Winfrey in January 2014: "All 200 guys that started the race broke the rules."

He had a point. Cycling in this era was drenched in drugs; every Tour winner but one from 1996 to 2010 has been implicated.[11] Armstrong also benefited from the see-no-evil mentality of the authorities, a blindness encouraged not only by the money Armstrong brought to the sport, but perhaps also by his donations to the official anti-doping program. As late as 2011, Hein Verbruggen, the president of the international cycling federation, was adamant: "Lance Armstrong has never used doping. Never, never, never."[12]

What made Armstrong so toxic was not just the doping and the lying, but the malevolence with which he defended himself. Given that he had doped for years, why did he go out of his way to ruin those who had said he did? David Walsh, a Sunday *Times* (of London) reporter, was vilified as a "little troll"[13] and sued for libel. Cyclist Christophe Bassons was bullied out of the sport. Betsy Andreu, wife of teammate Frankie Andreu, was ridiculed as a "crazy bitch" and an "ugly liar." Emma O'Reilly, a former masseuse for his team, was tangled in lawsuits and referred to as a "whore" with a drinking problem who lied for money.[14] And then there's the vicious campaign against Greg LeMond, now the only American winner of the Tour de France (1986, 1989, 1990). LeMond was forced to apologize[15] and saw his business interests in cycling undermined[16] when he questioned Armstrong's relationship with Michele Ferrari, an Italian doctor[17] convicted of sporting fraud in 2001.[18] Ferrari was so notorious he became known as "Dr. Evil."[19] As Betsy Andreu put it, "The doping is bad, but Lance's abuse of power is worse."[20]

At the same time Armstrong was wrecking these people's lives, he was also working hard to raise money for his cancer foundation, Livestrong; many cancer patients have called him an inspiration. "He saved my life because he started Livestrong," said cancer survivor Laurey Matson, "and he helped a lot of other people all over the world."[21] Such a judgment cannot be dismissed. Moreover, Armstrong appears to have been humbled by events. No longer the crass bully he was in his prime,[22] he has apologized, publicly and privately, to many of the people he harmed. But none of this can excuse the astonishing breadth and depth of his deceit as a sportsman.

2003

YAO MING BOBBLEHEAD

Yao Ming was literally born to be a basketball player. Chinese Communist Party officials coaxed his parents—both of them tall and accomplished hoopsters—to marry, with the explicit intention of raising an athlete who would make his country proud.[1] Improbably, the strategy worked. In 2002 the Houston Rockets made the 22-year-old Shanghai Sharks center their top pick, the first time a number 1 draft choice had come from overseas. "Houston, I am come!" Yao announced.[2]

He came, saw, and conquered. Texans instantly took to the gentle giant with the soft shooting touch and shy smile. This bobblehead hints at the affection—such promotions are given to successful, likeable players, not surly benchwarmers. (And appropriately, it was made in China.)

In 2003 Yao became the first Chinese player to make the National Basketball Association all-star team,[3] and over an eight-year career, he averaged 19 points and 9.2 rebounds a game.[4] In a larger sense, however—and everything about the 7-foot-6 Yao has to be seen on a larger scale—he was the human face of the NBA's commitment to globalize the game.

China and the NBA were a natural fit, even though it took a century to make the match. James Naismith (see 1891 entry) created the game at the YMCA's international training school; Christian missionaries took the game with them as they fanned out around the world. Beginning in the 1890s, the game sank deep roots in China. "You can just feel what the game means to them," a Christian missionary wrote to Naismith in the 1930s. "It cannot be described or pictured; it cannot be told; it must be seen."[5] To this day, a visitor can venture to the dustiest backwater, and there will likely be nets. Even during the Cultural Revolution, in which foreign influences were ruthlessly squashed, hoops kept going.[6] The game is that imbedded into the culture.[7]

After the NBA began regular broadcasts to China, Chinese youths took to American hoops in a big way, and Yao became the nation's most popular athlete. Apple, Gatorade, McDonald's, Toyota, Visa, and other global companies signed him up. His first all-star game would be available to half the world's population.[8] Outside the Olympics and the World Cup, no sport had ever had that kind of reach. In 2010, a year before Yao retired due to chronic ankle and foot injuries, *Sports Illustrated* called him the "most influential NBA player since Michael Jordan."[9]

The story of Yao, then, is the story of globalization. Or one of them; different sports are taking different routes. The NBA remains popular in China, but few Chinese players have made it to the show—six total and none in 2016. An overambitious (and politically naïve) plan to start a mini-NBA in China fell flat. But on opening day of the 2015–2016 season, there were more than 100 foreign-born players on NBA rosters, from countries as diverse as Argentina, Bosnia and Herzegovina, Cameroon, the Dominican Republic, Israel, Russia, Senegal, Sweden, and Turkey.[10] That is 20 times as many players as in 1993. Dozens of Americans have also played in the Chinese Basketball Association.

Other American sports leagues have embraced globalization. Unlike the case of China, though, this has more to do with growing the talent pool than expanding the audience. In 1975, 7 percent of Major League Baseball players were born outside the United States; by opening day in 2015, that figure was 26.5 percent.[11] Most are from Latin America, but Australia, Brazil, Japan, the Netherlands, and South Korea are all represented as well. Nearly half of minor leaguers are foreign born.

Hockey, too, has outgrown its North American roots. As recently as the 1970s, more than 90 percent of NHL players were born in Canada; now about half are.[12] Players from the Czech Republic, Finland, Russia, Slovakia, and Sweden comprise a quarter of NHL rosters.[13]

2004

CURT SCHILLING'S BLOODY SOCK

In truth, it wasn't much of a rivalry. From 1921, when the New York Yankees won their first World Series, through 2003, the Bronx Bombers had won 26 World Series. The Red Sox's tally over that period was zero; their last championship was in 1918, when Babe Ruth was their star pitcher (see 1932 entry). The Sox traded Ruth before the 1920 season, a gruesome mistake that their fans would later deem the "Curse of the Bambino." Rarely were the two teams good at the same time, and when they were, as in 1949, 1978, and 1999, New York always won the big game. This was a rivalry in the way that a nail is a rival to a hammer: it may be a very good nail, but its destiny is to get pounded.

So in 2003, when the American League championship series went to a seventh game, only the route to the usual result was different. Boston manager Grady Little left a tired Pedro Martinez in the game. The Yankees tied the score in the eighth and won it in the eleventh. That off-season, the Red Sox added starting pitcher Curt Schilling, a brilliant postseason performer, to the roster, as well as adding relief depth. The Yankees signed Alex Rodriguez.

In 2004 the rivalry was for real, as both teams were expected to contend. Scalpers got improbable prices even for spring-training games. But for a three-month stretch, the Sox were mired in mediocrity. After a 13-inning thriller on July 1, when Yankee shortstop Derek Jeter sacrificed his face to catch a foul ball (while his Boston counterpart, Nomar Garciaparra, sat on the bench, seemingly uninterested in the goings-on),[1] the Sox were 8.5 games back.[2] It looked like wait 'til next year yet again. Instead, the Sox shed former fan favorite Garciaparra at the trading deadline to improve clubhouse chemistry and defense, and the team began to gel. Boston went 42–18 from August on[3] and swept the Angels in the division series.

And then, just as abruptly, the momentum stopped. The Sox dropped their first three games to the Yankees in the league championship series, capped by a 19–8 shellacking. Boston mourned. "Soon it will be over," wrote Bob Ryan of the *Boston Globe*, "and we will spend another dreary winter lamenting this and lamenting that."[4] One likely lament: the injury to Schilling, who had torn the sheath on a tendon in his right ankle against the Angels. Not that Schilling's ankle was likely to matter. No team in baseball history had ever come back from 3–0 to win a postseason series; only two had even forced a sixth game.

In the ninth inning of Game 4, the Yankees had a one-run lead with the incomparable Mariano Rivera on the mound. Uncharacteristically, Rivera walked the lead-off batter. Then pinch-runner Dave Roberts stole second base. He scored on a single to tie the game. The Sox had life. More important, they had David Ortiz, who won the game with a twelfth-inning home run. In a thrilling Game 5, Ortiz came through again, this time singling home the winning run in the bottom of the fourteenth.

With the Yankees now ahead three games to two, it was Schilling's turn to play the hero. But in order to pitch, he needed to be able to push off his damaged right leg. Red Sox physicians thought they could create a kind of sling on which the tendon could rest; nothing like this had been tried before, so they experimented on a cadaver.[5] When the procedure appeared to work, they brought the idea to Schilling. He agreed to try. The doctors applied a local anesthetic, incised the pitcher's right ankle, and created what was essentially an artificial sheath.[6]

As Schilling warmed up before Game 6, the sutures began to tear, and blood seeped through the white stocking. But the Yankees did little to add to Schilling's discomfort, getting only four hits off him—and never, curiously, trying to bunt. "I mean, if you're looking at a wounded duck," mused Sox infielder Kevin Millar, "why not?"[7] Boston won 4–2, to tie the series, and took the decisive seventh game 10–3. The Sox went on to sweep an excellent Cardinals team to win Boston's first World Series since 1918. The "Curse of the Bambino" was truly and completely dead. The Sox would also win the Series in 2007 and 2013.

Facing financial difficulties[8] after his video game company went under,[9] Schilling sold the bloody sock at auction in 2013.[10] But while the sock itself has disappeared into private hands, the "bloody sock game" will endure forever. This red badge of courage stands for the 2004 Red Sox's defining qualities—grit and a willingness to take calculated risks—that added up to the greatest comeback in sports history.

2005

FORREST GRIFFIN'S GLOVES FROM
THE ULTIMATE FIGHTER 1

The premise of the first Ultimate Fighting Championship (UFC) in 1993 was simple: match a specialist in one martial art—say, karate—against an expert in another, such as sumo. Then rake in the profits by selling the action on pay-per-view television. When one fighter kicked a sumo wrestler, spraying two teeth into the crowd and imbedding two into his feet, a sport was born. Okay, it wasn't a sport then; it was a spectacle. But it certainly is a sport now.

To clarify: UFC is a trademark. The sport is mixed martial arts (MMA). But UFC has become almost synonymous with its creation, having bought out most of its rivals. For those who don't like a helping of pain with their competition, MMA can be hard to watch. But it is not all about the blood. MMA fighters are remarkable athletes, needing strength, speed, stamina, flexibility, technique, and courage.

In regular matches, the contestants fight three rounds of three minutes each, though few run that long. More often, a contestant surrenders by tapping the mat. Championships can go five rounds. The barefoot fighters employ a range of techniques, including boxing, karate, jiu-jitsu (particularly the Brazilian variety), Muay Thai, savate, sumo, and wrestling. They compete in a 750-square-foot, octagon-shaped ring, with a six-foot, padded, chain-link fence. Three judges score each fight, and a referee keeps things semiorderly.[1]

In the early days almost anything went, except eye gouging and below-the-belt shots. There were no weight classes and no time limits. When US senator John McCain referred to MMA as "human cockfighting,"[2] in 1996, it was difficult to disagree.

And he was not alone. Though MMA found an audience from the start, critics did not have to look far to find evidence to stoke their sense of outrage. Here is how one fighter described his work: "I was hitting him to the brain stem, which is a killing blow. And when he covered up, I swing back, with upswings, to the eye sockets, with two knuckles and a thumb."[3] Dozens of states banned MMA; many cable stations refused to air the fights.

By 2000 the UFC had begun to rein in its blood-and-gore image, implementing weight classes, toning down the to-the-death marketing, and outlawing practices such as "fishhooking"[4]—plunging a finger into any orifice and pulling. That year New Jersey decided to allow MMA, imposing regulations that remain the basis of current standards.[5] There would be no more flying teeth; fighters must wear mouth guards.

But the founders were sick of it all; in 2001 they sold the rights to the name and everything else for $2 million to Zuffa (Italian for "fight"), a company established for the purpose by casino moguls Frank and Lorenzo Fertitta (81 percent), and Dana White, who managed a couple of UFC fighters. Frank Fertitta became the low-profile CEO, White the extremely high-profile president.

The new owners saw two important things. First, MMA was shabby, operating in sad, badly lit venues that no celebrity would set foot in. And second, it had to grow up. "No-holds-barred" cage fighting appealed to a certain subset of young men, but it was never going to impress state regulators. Lorenzo Fertitta could attest to that; he was a member of the Nevada State Athletic Commission.

White set about improving operations, while the Fertittas kept paying the bills as they began to make their case to state athletic commissions. Nevada signed up, and with that, the cable operators came back.[6] UFC40, in 2002, attracted a healthy 150,000 pay-per-view purchases and a good deal of media attention.

It was a big step toward recovery, but MMA was not quite off the mat. Noticing the popularity of reality TV, the Fertittas pitched a series to Spike TV, a new cable channel directed at young men. UFC would pay all the costs of the first season of what became *The Ultimate Fighter* (*TUF*); each episode would not only showcase the usual too-many-people-in-one-house nastiness, but also an MMA fight. The last men standing would fight a final. Spike leaped at the idea of getting free content, and *TUF* became a hit. When fighter Forrest Griffin faced off against Stephan Bonnar on April 9, 2005, there was a built-in audience for the first live broadcast of a UFC fight.

It was an instant classic. Going three full rounds, the fighters displayed the brutal glory of MMA at its best. Before an audience of 2.6 million viewers, Griffin won on a 29–28 decision.

These are the gloves he used in the bout that is commonly referred to as "the fight that saved the UFC." The circle was complete. Begun as a made-for-pay-TV exhibition, UFC secured its future because it became a made-for-reality-TV one.

The numbers watching pay-per-view fights soared on the back of *TUF*'s success, and MMA was well and truly launched. By 2008 it had joined the mainstream of American sports. And not just in the United States: The biggest bouts are broadcast to 140-plus countries, and MMA leagues exist on every continent except Antarctica. None of this would have happened without the critics, who forced UFC to change from a bloody spectacle to a real athletic contest. "We ran toward the regulation, not away from it," White later said. "In a way, McCain created the sport. If he hadn't pushed, it would not have become a sport now."[7] In March 2016, New York legalized MMA, making it legal in all 50 states; four months later, the Fertittas and White sold their interest in the sport for $4 billion.

And MMA is not just for men, either. Ronda Rousey, an Olympic bronze medalist in judo, became the first woman to sign with UFC in 2012.[8] She rode her signature armbar move to the bantamweight title. In 2015 the previously undefeated Rousey was dethroned by boxer Holly Holm in an upset that confirmed that women's fights could score, too.[9] Then Holm lost a classic five-rounder to veteran Miesha "Cupcake" Tate, after leading most of the fight. Tate, whose background is in wrestling, has lost to Rousey twice before. So the plot thickens, to everyone's profit.

Mixed martial art fights are not for everyone, and certainly not for those who cannot stand the sight of blood, but they are no longer anything like human cockfighting. In fact, the man behind that memorable phrase, John McCain, now says that if MMA had existed back in his days as a boxer at the Naval Academy, he would have tried it.

2007

MITCHELL REPORT

Pity George Mitchell. The former senator from Maine had played a huge role in bringing something like peace to Northern Ireland in the late 1990s. But the terrorists on both sides of that hideous conflict were models of reason and cooperation compared to the challenge he took on in 2006: determining the nature and extent of performance-enhancing drug use in major league baseball.

As heads swelled and records fell in the 1990s and early 2000s, baseball's drug culture went essentially unchallenged. This was a systemic failure. The players' union was ferociously against testing for performance-enhancing drugs (PEDs), casting it entirely as a privacy issue, when it was a health, safety, and equity issue as well. Baseball executives were more than willing to look the other way as the game attempted to recover from the self-inflicted wound of the 1994 strike. The great majority of journalists contrived not to notice that acne—a common side effect of steroid use—was spreading across many a muscled torso. Not that the players would have talked, anyway; baseball's code of omertà rivaled that of cycling (see 2000 entry on Lance Armstrong). The fans didn't appear all that interested, either.

Even so, the evidence was accumulating. In 2000 there were several incidents in which drug paraphernalia was found in clubhouses.[1] Former most valuable player Ken Caminiti admitted to his own steroid abuse in 2002[2] and suggested that as many as half the players were on something. Baseball did manage to institute an anonymous testing program the next year; of the 1,438 tested, 104 failed, a tribute not only to a certain lack of wit, but perhaps to a perception that the system was not to be taken seriously.[3] Although feeble, this modest program can be seen in retrospect as the beginning of the end for steroids, or at least of open and rampant abuse. In 2004, a stronger system was instituted.

Still, the drip, drip, drip of suspicion and innuendo continued. A number of players had to testify to a grand jury about the notorious BALCO laboratory in the San Francisco Bay area, which was implicated in the convictions of numerous athletes, including track's Marion Jones and cycling's Tammy Thomas. The deeply unpopular former player Jose Canseco not only admitted to juicing, but implicated others in his books.[4] There were numerous reports of players receiving PEDs through dodgy Internet pharmacies.[5] In early 2006 two persuasive and well-researched books, *Juicing the Game* by Howard Bryant and *Game of Shadows* by Mark Fainaru-Wada and Lance Williams, made it obvious to all but the willfully blind that baseball had a problem.

Using steroids for sports was not only illegal under federal law, but had also been specifically prohibited by baseball since 1991.[6] Maybe it was time to do something. Enter Mitchell, hired to conduct an independent investigation.

Mitchell had no subpoena power, and received little cooperation (only 68 of 500 former players contacted talked, for example, and only one active one). The union was unhelpful, advising the players not to speak with the senator.[7] But he plodded ahead, and with the help of some clubhouse dealers, dropped this 409-page bombshell at the end of 2007.

Although the report fell well short of proof beyond a reasonable doubt in its specifics, the cumulative effect was damning. And it named almost 90 names, some of them big, including Barry Bonds, Roger Clemens, Mark McGwire, and Rafael Palmeiro—all of them once-certain Hall of Famers.[8]

REPORT TO THE COMMISSIONER OF BASEBALL
OF AN INDEPENDENT INVESTIGATION INTO
THE ILLEGAL USE OF STEROIDS AND OTHER
PERFORMANCE ENHANCING SUBSTANCES
BY PLAYERS IN MAJOR LEAGUE BASEBALL

GEORGE J. MITCHELL

DLA PIPER US LLP

December 13, 2007

The baseball establishment was naturally shocked and appalled at the Mitchell Report's central finding: that "for more than a decade there has been widespread illegal use of anabolic steroids and other performance enhancing substances."[9] The American public decided to get outraged, too. In retrospect, however, the biggest impact of the Mitchell Report may have been on the players.

For years they had resisted action on PEDs. As in cycling, drugs thrived in baseball because of a sense that this was a closed culture that made its own rules. After Mitchell, the culture seemed to change. From that point on, few players have seemed willing to defend, even tacitly, the indefensible. What they knew better than anyone was that this was not a victimless crime. For every player who dopes to get that little extra pop to stay in the game—and that describes a large number of users—there is someone riding the bus in the minors not getting his chance.

Baseball will never be drug-free. In this, it is no different than any other segment of society. But in large part due to the Mitchell Report and the changes it provoked, PEDs can no longer be taken with impunity.

2008

MICHAEL PHELPS'S SWIM CAP

Associated with prosperity and good fortune, the number 8 is auspicious in Chinese culture. So it is appropriate that the Beijing Olympics will always be associated with the number 8. The Games took place in 2008; the Opening Ceremonies started at 8:08 on August 8. And for the only time in Olympic history, an athlete won eight gold medals.

Beijing was not Michael Phelps's first Olympics, nor his last. At age 15 in Sydney in 2000, he finished a strong fifth in the 200-meter butterfly and posted a stunning last 50 meters[1] that hinted at something special. A few months later he became the youngest man to set a world swimming record. In Athens in 2004, he won eight medals (six gold and two bronze), tying the mark for the most in a single Olympics. In London in 2012, Phelps added four more golds and two silvers.

But nothing could compare to Beijing. Phelps had set an audacious goal: break Mark Spitz's 1972 record of seven gold medals. To achieve it, he would have to race 17 times in nine days, in all four strokes.

He almost didn't make it. Like any great drama, there were hairbreadth escapes. In the second event, the 4 x 100-meter freestyle relay, in which Phelps swam the first leg, the whole thing looked in jeopardy. Going into the last length, America's fourth swimmer, Jason Lezak, was eight-tenths of a second[2] behind.[3] But as another great American athlete put it, it ain't over 'til it's over (see 1956 entry on Yogi Berra). This wasn't over.

Lezak made a good turn, then swam near the lane line to draft off the French swimmer who was leading, Alain

Bernard. With about 20 meters left, the American found another gear and began to close. He hit the wall in perfect form, his arm extended to the fullest extent—and out-touched Bernard by eight one-hundredths of a second.[4] Lezak had turned in a miraculous 46.06 split, the fastest ever.[5] Phelps had his second gold—and an image for the ages, as he let out a vein-popping bellow to the roof of the Water Cube.

A few days later Phelps had to make his own Hail Mary in the last 50 meters. The event was the 100-meter butterfly, the only individual event he was swimming in which he did not own the world record. Milorad Čavić, a Californian who represented Serbia, took a .62-second lead into the turn. Phelps, always known as a fearsome closer, narrowed the gap. With five meters left, though, he was still a little behind. But Čavić lifted his head[6] as he glided to the finish. Phelps stayed in form and added one more stroke. It was just enough to win—by .01, or less than an inch. That was gold medal number 7. He collected his eighth the next day, in almost routine fashion, in the 4 x 100-meter medley relay, as the American team chopped 1.3 seconds off the world record. His final tally: eight for eight, with seven world records.

Phelps had a physique made for swimming: large feet, a long torso, and a 76-inch wingspan. "He did very well in the gene pool," his longtime coach Bob Bowman liked to say.[7] He loved to win and, perhaps more important, hated to lose. At the peak of his peak, he didn't seem to mind the drudgery of looking at the bottom of a pool five hours a day, 365 days a year. He had that certain extra something that separates the sublime from the merely excellent.

But in other eras, he could have had all this and still fallen short, through bad luck and human error. Phelps benefited from the perfection of timing, in the form of the electronic touch pads that record the end of the race. These take the human element out of determining winners, and as American swimmer Lance Larson could attest, that can make all the difference.

At the 1960 games, Larson and Australian John Devitt finished 1–2 in the 100-meter freestyle. But who was first? Devitt thought it was Larson, and graciously congratulated him. Larson also thought he had won, and happily splashed around the pool. The three timers assigned to each lane consulted their scorecards; they split 3–3 on the finish. Then they looked at their stopwatches. The three timers for Davitt recorded the identical time: 55.2, and the three for Larson had him at 55.0, 55.1, and 55.1. The electronic timer, used as a backup, also had Larson ahead.

At this point, the chief judge, Henry Runströmmer, stepped in.[8] Under Olympic rules, he had no standing in the matter. Nevertheless, he declared that Larson swam 55.2 and that Devitt had won. He came to this conclusion, he said, because he had seen the finish. True enough, but he was five lanes away, and at an angle.[9] The Americans appealed for years, but the result stood.

Better timekeeping technology became a priority after that. Electronic touch pads got their first Olympic workout in Tokyo in 1964[10] and became standard in 1968.[11] When Phelps out-touched Čavić, he had precise timing devices and underwater cameras to make sure it held up.

As of the end of 2015, Phelps has twice as many gold medals (18) as any other athlete. His 22 total medals are 10 more than any other man has.[12] The numbers deliver a definitive judgment: he is the greatest Olympian of all time.

2009

VENUS WILLIAMS'S DRESS AND SERENA WILLIAMS'S SHOES FROM WIMBLEDON

Individually, each is great. Together, they are the finest sibling act in any sport, at any time, on any planet.

Venus, the elder by 15 months, was the first to greatness, winning both Wimbledon and the US Open in 2000 and 2001, and the Olympic gold in singles in 2000. In mid-2002 she was the top-ranked player in the world—until Serena toppled her. Venus won three more Wimbledons after Serena's ascendency, giving her a total of seven majors (and seven runners-up). Since the open era began in 1968, only seven women have won more.

Serena, however, has made her sister's achievements look almost pedestrian. As of July 2016, she has won 22 majors—tied with Steffi Graf for the most in the open era—and at the tennis old age of 34, she looks like she could keep racking them up for years. Given that the game is more globalized than ever, it's hard not to conclude that she is the greatest player ever. Venus would be in anyone's top 20.[1]

In 2001, when Venus met Serena in the finals of the US Open, it was the first time siblings had competed for a US Open title, and the first time since 1884 in the final of any kind of Slam.[2] The match was broadcast nationally in prime time, also a first. Venus won in straight sets. Afterward, she sounded ambivalent. "I always want Serena to win," she said. "I'm the bigger sister. I'm the one who takes care of her. I make sure she has everything even if I don't. I love her. It's hard." For the reserved Venus, this was as expressive as anything she ever said publicly, and was obviously heartfelt.

And then the two went on a binge, meeting in the finals of five of the next seven majors, including four in a row. Serena won all four to complete the first "Serena Slam" in 2002–2003 (four straight majors, but not in the same calendar year). All told, through 2015 the sisters had faced each other 27 times, with Serena leading 16–11, including a

6–2 mark in major finals. They were both brilliant at the same time for a time, but this never developed into a true rivalry. Watching them play each other was an uncomfortable experience. Many of their matches were one-sided and error-strewn, with Serena visibly holding herself back from her usual fist-pumping, screaming aggression. They never apologized for beating each other, but they never relished it, either.[3]

They much preferred playing *with* each other. In the runup to Rio, they had a perfect Olympic record, winning doubles golds in 2000, 2008, 2012; they were also 14 for 14 in Slam finals.[4] Several times, they won a doubles title together after dueling in the singles.

In a sense, their greatest achievement was maintaining their extraordinary bond despite both wanting the same thing, fiercely. Tennis was a Williams family affair, something the five sisters and their parents did together; there is even a picture of Venus pushing Serena in a stroller onto a court.[5] They grew up playing against each other every day. Venus was the first to reach a Grand Slam final,[6] and she dominated their early matches, winning five of the first six. But when Serena was the first to win a major, the 1999 US Open, Venus was visibly shattered.[7]

For their entire lives to that point, Serena had played catch-up. It was Venus who was profiled as a 10-year-old in *Sports Illustrated* and the *New York Times*,[8] Venus who brought agents to the door, Venus who got the first big endorsements. As Serena once put it, in a comment that hints at the complex dynamics of the sisterhood, "Ever since I was young, even when I came on tour, it was Venus, Venus, Venus, Venus. Oh, and the little sister."[9]

But from 2002 on, the little sister took over. The turning point may have been psychological as much as anything. In May 2003 Serena noted, "I had to realize that I wasn't Venus. I used to want to be her—not like her, but *be* her—and I think that held me back."[10] With that separation came greatness.

Serena's journey has been signposted with stops and starts, injuries and ailments, listlessness and passion, slumps and dominance, graciousness and the opposite. She's been ranked Number 1 half a dozen different times and has sunk as low as 139. In 2006 Chris Evert chided her for not wholly committing herself to tennis. Prior to the 2007 Australian Open, Serena was dubbed a "lost cause." She won that championship and then took the US Open as well. There has also been tragedy—the murder of an older sister, Yetunde, in 2003—and a medical scare for Serena in the form of blood clots in both lungs in 2011. In addition there have been a few on-court foul-mouthed outbursts, including the classic threat to shove a ball down an offending lineswoman's throat in 2009.

The most recent phase of Serena's career has been the most remarkable one. After a humiliating first-round exit in the French Open in 2012, she got angry, and fit. No one had ever questioned her competitiveness on the court, only her commitment off it. At age 30, when most players are thinking about what's next, she won 102 of her next 107 matches, plus a gold medal in singles in the 2012 London Olympics.

Then came another letdown. In the first three Slams of 2014, she didn't make it as far as the fourth round, and in the second round of the Wimbledon doubles, she lurched and staggered, unable to hit a serve. "She can't even pick up a ball," noted an incredulous Evert.[11] Mercifully, the sisters retired after three very strange games; Serena blamed a viral infection. On the verge of being written off yet again, she then ripped off her second "Serena Slam" in what may have been the most dominating stretch of her remarkable career. None of it was easy. At the Australian Open in 2015, she vomited during the match; at the French, she played with the flu.[12]

Although both are still competing, the Williamses have more past than future, and it is possible to have some perspective on their achievements. Going beyond the numbers, impressive as they are, what can be said is that for a full decade, the sisters dominated their sport. That cannot be said of any other pair of siblings.

Considered that way, it does seem as if this is a story that has not been given its due. There are several possible reasons for this. The obvious one is that they are black, and tennis is still an overwhelmingly white sport. Other than the Williamses, the only other African American woman to win a major is Althea Gibson, who won four from 1956 to 1958. There is some talent coming up, including Madison Keys, Sloane Stephens, and Taylor Townsend, but there may be lingering, even unconscious resistance to seeing African Americans as the face of the sport.

A second factor is that tennis is declining in popularity in the United States. Outside a few big events, there isn't much coverage of the sport, period. Ironically, the sisters would get more attention if American men were doing better, thus raising the profile of the game. A third factor is that in commercial terms, the most successful endorsers seem to be graciously bland. So in 2014, blond, willowy, and European Maria Sharapova—who does bland nicely—made $10 million more in endorsements[13] than Serena, who hadn't lost to her since 2004. Serena can do gracious, but bland is not one of her many gifts. Perhaps none of this mattered; it seems more likely that it all did.

In 2009 the sisters met at Wimbledon. Serena wore the shoes pictured here; Venus wore the dress on the opposite page. It was their last showdown in a major final. Venus was the two-time defending champion and had beaten Serena the previous year for the title. This time, Serena won 7–6, 6–2. As late as 2010, the sisters were ranked one and two in the world. That year, however, Venus was diagnosed with an auto-immune disease, Sjogren's syndrome;[14] between that, a balky hip, and the calendar,[15] she has not been in the top five since January 2011.

But she is still the big sister. When Serena had her bizarre breakdown at Wimbledon in 2014, Venus was there, putting her arm over her sister's shoulder and gently escorting her off the court—just as she had helped her onto it, 30-plus years before.

FIRST BASE FROM ARMANDO GALARRAGA'S "IMPERFECT GAME"

The best umpires don't get noticed. So June 2, 2010, was a bad day when Jim Joyce, a 22-year vet whom players considered one of the game's best,[1] became a star.

It was the top of the ninth, and the Detroit Tigers were leading the Cleveland Indians 3–0; Detroit's Armando Galarraga (career record to that point: 20–18) was three outs from pitching a perfect game. The hitter was Mark Grudzielanek, a 15-year veteran, who at age 40 had lost a little bat speed. Center-fielder Austin Jackson was playing him slightly toward right, and shallow. Galarraga's fastball was a little high and a little flat. Grudzielanek lined it to deep left-center—exactly where Jackson wasn't. Jackson sprinted after it, with his back to the plate. Just as he reached the warning track, he stretched out his glove—and the ball landed in it.[2] It was the play of the game, maybe of the year, and was uncannily similar to Willie Mays's famous catch in the 1954 World Series. Every no-hitter seems to have one improbable defensive gift. Now Galarraga had his.

The next batter hit a routine grounder to shortstop. One out to go. Up came Jason Donald, the Indians' light-hitting rookie shortstop. A fastball on the outside corner for a strike, a slider outside for a ball. Donald anticipated another pitch outside and got it, poking it toward the right side of the infield. First baseman Miguel Cabrera ranged far to his right, almost halfway to second base, then squared and threw toward the bag. Hustling over, Galarraga gloved the ball and stomped the bag pictured here with his right foot.

He and Cabrera threw up their arms in triumph.

Then Joyce swung his arms wide and yelled: "Safe!" Galarraga's arms came down to the top of his head. He smiled, incredulous. Then he collected himself and calmly got the last out. Joyce was used to being yelled at by managers, abused by players, and booed by hometown partisans, so he was not unduly bothered that the crowd, and the Tigers, were giving him a hard time. His job was to "call 'em as he sees 'em," and as he saw it, Donald got to the bag first. But the shadow of a doubt was deepening. As he walked off the field, Joyce was a worried man. On a monitor in the umpires' locker room, he saw what everyone else had: he had blown the call on the last out of what should have been the twenty-first perfect game in history.

And if Galarraga's best moment was his smile and his professionalism in inducing a twenty-eighth out, in the next few minutes, Joyce would have his own. "No, I did not get the call correct," he said. "I kicked the shit out of it."[3] And he remembered the victim of his mistake: "I feel like I took something away from the kid and I don't know how to give it back." Then he cried.[4] Even the Detroit press could not beat him up after that. When the reporters left the locker room, Joyce made one request to Tiger manager Jim Leyland, who had come by to comfort him: he wanted to see Galarraga. Still distraught and tearful, Joyce managed to tell the pitcher, "I am so sorry, Armando. I don't know what else to say." And Galarraga found the right answer: "Nobody's perfect."

This is perhaps the only time a terrible call ended up being a feel-good story, but the grace under pressure the two men showed made it just that. The two protagonists became something like folk heroes. At the following night's game, Galarraga handed the lineup card to Joyce, who was working home plate. They shook hands—and the crowd cheered. One blown call, two class acts.

The incident played an important role in baseball's expansion of instant replay, restricted at the time to disputed home-run calls. In the aftermath of the imperfect game, Commissioner Bud Selig said he would think again.[5] Selig himself was cool to instant replay, and so were many players[6] and managers.[7] But it became faintly ridiculous that everyone in the stadium with a smartphone had access to instant replay—but not the umpires. Beginning in 2014, Major League Baseball agreed.

FRAGMENT OF THE AUBURN OAKS

College football, for all its manifold problems (see 1987 entry on SMU), maintains its attraction for a simple reason: it's fun. There are dozens of traditions that to outsiders are hokey but to fans are as important as anything that happens on the field.

Watching 90,000 University of Wisconsin fans jump to "Jump Around" between the third and fourth quarters is thrilling. The University of Hawaii's version of the "haka" may not be entirely accurate, but it's very cool. And only the stony-hearted could fail to be stirred by the pregame march of the Army Cadets and Navy Midshipmen. Or by Florida State's Chief Osceola galloping into the stadium on Renegade, his trusty steed, then planting a flaming spear at midfield. The Ivy Leaguers at Penn throw toast onto the field before the fourth quarter.

Then there is sound. Drumlines and battles of the bands are regular features of football at historically black universities; the sound-off between Grambling's Tiger Marching Band and Southern University's Human Jukebox is a highlight of the annual Bayou Classic in New Orleans. The routines of marching bands at large schools like Ohio State have become so intricate that they have become YouTube sensations.[1]

Then there are the chants. From Kansas: "Rock, chalk, Jayhawk!" From Alabama: "Rammer jammer, yellow hammer, give 'em hell, Alabama!" At Bethany College in Kansas, home to teams once known as the Terrible Swedes, students shout, "Rockar! Stockar! Thor och hans bockar!"[2] To hear 100,000-plus fans belt out Michigan's fight song—perhaps the best in all football—is to get goosebumps. Tennessee has a bluetick coonhound, Smokey, trained to howl after the Volunteers score.

But a coonhound is a comparatively minor member of the zoo of mascots associated with the college game. Colorado has Ralphie the buffalo. Louisiana State and Memphis both have tigers (caged, thank heavens), and Yale has had Handsome Dan bulldogs since 1889. Georgia also has a bulldog, Uga; after its death, it gets interred in a special marble vault near the stadium. There have been nine more Ugas since the first one. Navy has a goat mascot that really should get combat pay, because it keeps getting kidnapped. Army has a mule and Air Force a falcon, named Mach 1. Texas has a longhorn steer called Bevo. Baylor has two black bears, sisters named Judge Lady and Judge Joy, and South Carolina a red-breasted black gamecock, Sir Big Spur.

All this makes autumn Saturdays a uniquely American spectacle in college towns across the country. The only thing better is rivalry week, when an additional set of traditions kicks in, often in the form of a useless and ugly totem to the winner.

Oklahoma and Texas compete in the Red River shootout for the Golden Hat. Brigham Young University and Utah State compete for an old wagon wheel; Indiana and Purdue for an oak bucket; Notre Dame and USC for a made-in-Ireland shillelagh; Maine and New Hampshire for a musket; and Union and Rensselaer Polytechnic for a remarkably ugly set of red clogs called the "Dutchmen's shoes." The men of Concordia and St. Olaf fight for a troll made of Norwegian moss.

Perhaps the most famous totem is the axe head mounted on a wooden plaque that Stanford and the University of California have traded back and forth since 1899. Stanford students used the original axe to decapitate a blue-and-gold Cal effigy; Cal students stole the tool and kept it in a bank vault for the next 30-odd years, until Stanford stole it back in a daring heist.[3] Barring the occasional theft—and the score in that regard is 4–3 Stanford—the winner of the Big Game gets the axe, and the score is etched onto the plate under the axe head.

But every time the axe changes possession, the owner rubs out the score of the 1982 game—the one that featured The Play. In that game, Stanford had scored with four seconds left to take a 20–19 lead. On the kickoff, Cal lateraled five times before threading through the Stanford marching band to score the winning touchdown. All Stanford fans swear that at least one lateral was illegal and possibly two. So when Stanford has the axe, it changes the score to 20–19; when Cal has the axe, it restores the score to 25–20.

There is no way to define what the most intense collegiate rivalry is, but Auburn–Alabama has to be near the top. The annual Iron Bowl between the teams in November is the most important date on the state's calendar; the other 364 days, Auburn–Alabama is pretty important too. Auburn fans deride Alabama as a home for spoiled, lazy rich kids spending daddy's money and whiling away afternoons under the magnolia trees.

Bama fans ridicule Auburn as a cow college for folks with dirt between their toes and gaps between whatever teeth they have. In the words of one caller to Paul Finebaum's popular sports radio show, "I ain't got no love for them West Georgia coon-dog buzzard inbred toenail lickers."[4]

The University of Alabama has the edge in the Iron Bowl (44–35–1 through 2015) and also in pedigree; it was the home of Bear Bryant, the legendary coach who led the Crimson Tide to six national titles from 1958 to 1982 and also played a key role in the racial integration of the university. Joe Namath played for Bama. For its part, Auburn has Nova, a golden eagle that swoops down over the stadium before games. It had Bo Jackson. And it has "rolling the corner." After important victories, Auburn fans go to the corner of College and Magnolia Streets and throw toilet paper onto two oak trees. Like many college traditions, the ritual sounds more than a little cheesy. Auburn loves it.

All this is great fun, until someone gets the stupids. That's what happened in 2010. In that year's Iron Bowl, Auburn quarterback Cam Newton led the Tigers to victory after falling behind 24–zip—the biggest Auburn Iron Bowl comeback ever. In Auburn, the game is known as "the Cam-back"; in Tuscaloosa it's "the collapse." The Tigers went on to win the national championship.

And a man named Harvey Almorn Updyke of Dadeville got angry. Even in Alabama, Updyke's allegiance is extreme. His children are named Bear Bryant and Crimson Tyde, and he once said that he thought about Bama football 18 hours a day.[5] Distressed by the Cam-back, Updyke bought some herbicide, drove to

Auburn, and poisoned the 85-year-old oaks. Then in January 2011, identifying himself as "Al from Dadeville," he called into Finebaum's show to brag that the trees are "not dead yet, but they definitely will die."[6] The former Texas state trooper was no criminal mastermind; he was quickly arrested and convicted of criminal mischief, desecration, and damaging agriculture.[7]

In April 2013 Auburn had to euthanize the trees; the cow college has experts on soil and tree health, but too much poison had been at work for too long. Even the miracle of Alabama fans sending $50,000 to help save the trees[8] could not halt their decline. But it didn't seem right to just toss trees that had been the site of so much joy. So the university chopped them up and sold the splinters, one of which is shown on the opposite page, with the proceeds going to the scholarship fund.

Auburn got its revenge on the field in 2013 in perhaps the greatest Iron Bowl ever. With one second left, and the score tied at 28, top-ranked Alabama tried a 57-yard field goal. The kick fell just short. Near the back of the end zone, with no time on the clock, Auburn's Chris Davis caught the ball—and ran it back 109 astonishing yards. Auburn won 34–28—and also ended Bama's quest for a third straight national title.

The play, known as the "Kick Six," was a triumph that took less than 20 seconds. Fifteen months later came another triumph that was months in the making: Two 35-foot live oaks were planted at Toomer's Corner. Another 30 trees, grown from acorns of the original oaks, were planted nearby.

2013

STUFFED ANIMAL LEFT AFTER THE BOSTON MARATHON BOMBING

At 2:49 p.m. on April 15, 2013, more than 5,600 of the 23,000-plus runners who had started that morning were moving toward the finish line of the Boston Marathon. These were ordinary people who had sacrificed time and their ordinary vices to try to do something extraordinary. As they plodded along, they were lifted by the encouragement of spectators who appreciated their efforts—people like the Richard family, who were there to cheer on friends.

And then there was an explosion, from a bomb in a knapsack placed near where the family stood. Eight-year-old Martin Richard was killed, his six-year-old sister would lose a leg, his mother would lose sight in one eye, and his father's eardrums were ruptured. About 200 yards away, another pressure-cooker bomb killed Krystle Marie Campbell and Lu Lingzi. More than 260 others were injured.

The bombers were two Kyrgyzstan-born, Massachusetts-raised brothers, Tamerlan and Dzhokhar Tsarnaev. During the ensuing manhunt, which all but shut down the city and several nearby towns, the two shot and killed a Massachusetts Institute of Technology police officer, Sean Collier. In an ensuing firefight,

Tamerlan Tsarnaev was killed, and another police officer, Richard Donahue, was fatally wounded. Four days after the bombing, Dzhokhar Tsarnaev was found, wounded and hiding in a boat. He was eventually convicted on 30 federal counts, ranging from murder to the use of weapons of mass destruction.

Boston is the world's oldest marathon, and perhaps its most beloved (see 1967 entry on Kathrine Switzer). It began in 1897[1] as part of the celebrations associated with a new state holiday, Patriots' Day, which commemorates the Revolutionary War battles of Lexington and Concord. The race is barnacled with tradition, from the "scream tunnel" at Wellesley to Heartbreak Hill and olive wreaths for the winners. The Red Sox always play a morning game, so marathoners run by Fenway Park during the action. Patriots' Day is as much a rite of spring as Memorial Day is of summer.

In the aftermath of the bombing, the city's motto was "Boston Strong." Red Sox slugger David Ortiz became an unlikely laureate of the city's emotions. "This jersey that we wear today, it doesn't say 'Red Sox.' It says 'Boston,'" he told a Fenway crowd the day after Tsarnaev was captured. "This is our f—ing city!"[2] That was Boston Strong, in a slightly profane nutshell.

But Boston has a softer side, too. Right after the explosions, people began leaving small tokens of grief and remembrance. What began as a ripple became a veritable tide of mementoes, eventually spreading across several blocks. There were lots of running shoes, but also flags, balloons, crosses, and flowers. And stuffed animals by the score.

It is an image of sweet innocence—like the smile of Martin Richard.[3]

MASSILLON TIGERS' BABY FOOTBALL

Devotion to Massillon Tigers football can last from the cradle to the grave—literally. For more than 50 years, every boy born in Massillon, Ohio, has received an orange-and-black football in his hospital crib, courtesy of the booster club. (Recently, some baby girls have also been graced.) On the other end of life's journey, a local funeral home offers Tiger-themed urns and caskets.[1]

There is a certain historic justice to this, because Ohio was the cradle of professional football. There was an active, if disorganized, pro game in the state by the early 1900s, and 4 of the original 10 teams in what became the National Football League[2] were from Ohio: Akron, Canton, Cleveland, and Dayton.[3]

Canton is home to the Pro Football Hall of Fame and also to the McKinley Bulldogs, half of one of high school football's oldest and fiercest rivalries, with the Massillon Tigers. Massillon won the Ohio professional championship in 1904, 1905, and 1906, the latter a satisfying victory against Canton.

After 1906 there was a period of disarray, due to scandals and financial difficulties. But the pro game in Ohio revived, and with it, the rivalry. This time, Canton had the edge. With Jim Thorpe (see 1912 entry) often in the backfield, competing against Massillon's Knute Rockne (see 1925 entry on the modern football),[4] Canton won titles in 1916, 1917, and 1919.

As professional franchises migrated to bigger urban areas in the 1920s, the football focus in Ohio shifted to the high schools. Canton's schoolboys took the pro team's nickname, the Bulldogs, and Massillon's did the same, becoming the Tigers. The two have been fighting like cats and dogs ever since, with Massillon taking home the coveted Victory Bell 68 times to McKinley's 53, with five ties.[5] Massillon was the training ground for Hall of Fame coach Paul Brown, who played on the high school team, then coached it from 1932 to 1941, going 80–8–2 and winning six state championships.[6] It was on Brown's watch that the Booster Club was formed and the stadium built. Its address: Paul Brown Drive. The Tigers kept going after he left. A 1951 newsreel, *Touchdown Town*, called Massillon the "Number 1 grid city in America," where "football is more than a sport. It's a cult, a religion, a civic enterprise that knows no season and bounces its merry way 365 days a year." That sums it up nicely.

The Tiger spirit manifests itself in many ways. Paul Brown Stadium can hold almost 20,000 people. And if often needs to, which is remarkable given that Massillon's population is only about 32,000. There is also a privately funded, 80,000-square-foot indoor practice center[7] and a state-of-the-art turf field. It is not unheard of to "red-shirt" a Massillon eight-grader so that he has an additional year to grow before entering high school.[8]

For nonplayers, there are a marching band and a cheerleading squad (also hotly contested). For the adults, there are several social clubs devoted to the team. Radio shows, newspapers, pulpits, and barbershop habitués talk up the Tigers constantly. "The identity of the town is what takes place at the high school," is the way one coach put it in 1999.[9] That is still the case, and the most important thing that happens at the high school happens on Friday nights in the fall.

The towns of Canton and Massillon have had their share of trouble. Both towns have struggled to find new sources of prosperity since heavy industry declined in the 1970s and 1980s. Through it all, football has been a source of civic spirit and cohesion—albeit one that puts a heavy burden on the shoulder pads of teenagers.

It's fair to ask whether football is *too* important to the town. In the grand scheme of things, maybe being obsessed with, say, nanotechnology might be wiser. But it is only right to acknowledge that having football to rally around has given places like Massillon a sense of pride not easily nurtured and difficult to replace. Say what you will about putting football at the heart of the city, at least Massillon has a beating heart.

"Four things will always be in Massillon," one fan put it: "pride, courage, hard work, and Massillon football."[10]

2016

CTE-RELATED BRAIN SCANS

Mike Webster was a born center. That was his position on the great Pittsburgh Steelers teams of the 1970s, on which he anchored the offensive line in four Super Bowl victories. As a team leader, he was in the center of the action in the locker room.[1] And posthumously, Iron Mike was at the center of the discovery of chronic traumatic encephalopathy (CTE) in football players.

After years of behavioral and physical decline—at one point, the Hall of Famer was living in a truck and stunning himself with a Taser to get to sleep[2]—Webster died in 2002. He had played for 17 years and in 340 National Football League games.[3] At his autopsy, the forensic pathologist Bennet Omalu decided to "fix" his brain—that is, prepare it for further analysis. Omalu was shocked at what he saw. Webster was only 50 when he died. His brain, however, looked like that of an 85-year-old man with Alzheimer's.[4]

After more study, Omalu concluded that Webster had suffered from CTE, a neurodegenerative condition caused by repeated blows to the head. Symptoms include dementia, depression, aggression, and memory loss. In 2005 Omalu wrote an article to that effect, concluding, "This case highlights potential long-term neurodegenerative outcomes in retired professional National Football League players subjected to repeated mild traumatic brain injury."[5]

Medical researchers believe that repeated trauma causes the buildup of the tau protein, in the form of neurofibrillary tangles. In people with CTE, these tangles, which look like skeins of yarn, accumulate in distinct areas.[6] Think of them as little brown nooses that strangle nerves in the brain, including those that govern mood and cognitive functions such as memory and reasoning.[7] The image on the left shows a healthy brain section; the one on the right is of a former football player and shows signs of CTE. The bright patches indicate excessive deposits of tau proteins.

In a sense, none of this should have been surprising. "Dementia pugilistica"—the formal name for boxers who are "punch drunk"—has been studied since the 1920s.[8] It

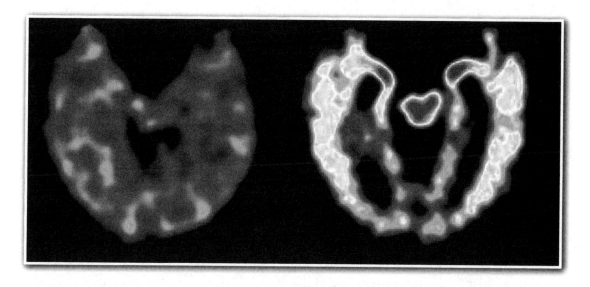

doesn't stretch common sense to think that when football players get hit in the head, they too might suffer brain damage. But the NFL challenged—indeed, attacked—studies and scientists that found a link between football and brain trauma. Three doctors associated with the league—none of them neuropathologists—demanded that Omalu's 2005 paper be retracted,[9] saying that his understanding of CTE was "completely wrong."[10]

For years[11] the league's own research was positively chipper.[12] A series of papers reported that even after three concussions, there was no decline in brain function,[13] and that much higher rates of dementia didn't really mean anything.[14] In one NFL-funded study, the authors made the assertion, surprising to every fan with a television, that "professional football players do not sustain frequent repetitive blows to the brain on a regular basis."[15] When the NFL retirement board approved partial disability payments to Mike Webster, however, it stated that his cognitive injuries were due to "head injuries he suffered as a football player."[16] Even after that, the league refused to admit any such thing, at least publicly.[17]

Beginning around 2007 the NFL changed course, creating concussion protocols and setting up a fund to help pay the medical bills of former players with dementia. In late 2009 the league conceded that concussions, as well as the accumulation of nonconcussive hits, could lead to long-term health problems.[18] In 2015 the NFL settled a class-action suit on behalf of almost 6,000 former NFL players, agreeing to financial compensation for those diagnosed with CTE, Lou Gehrig's disease, Parkinson's, Alzheimer's, and dementia.[19] The total cost could go north of $1 billion. But it was only in March 2016 that the NFL formally acknowledged a connection between the traumatic brain injuries that could be sustained by players and CTE.

Chronic traumatic encephalopathy is not fully understood, and at this time it can only be diagnosed posthumously. The how and why of incidence are unknown. There may be other factors, such as genetics, medical history, or steroid use, that could help to explain why some people develop it while others do not. What can be said with some confidence is that CTE is associated with repeated blows to the head, and that therefore football players and boxers are at much higher risk. The NFL players have been asked to donate their brains to research, and the evidence to date is devastating: almost all the donated brains (87 of 91, or 96 percent) show some degree of CTE.

2016

SPECIAL OLYMPICS MEDALS

Sports occupy an ambiguous place in the social landscape. They provide pleasure to tens of millions of Americans and can help people get and stay healthy. At their finest, they create instances of beauty that are a form of physical art. On the other hand, sports have also provided a setting for greed, exploitation, prejudice, and corruption.

But one unambiguously positive trend has been that more and more people have been able to experience the positive dimensions of sports. One important moment occurred in 1968 in Chicago, when 1,000 young people from 26 states competed in three sports (track, floor hockey, and swimming) in the first Special Olympics. Now there are 4.5 million participants, from 180 countries.[1]

The idea behind the Special Olympics was to improve the general fitness and social skills of intellectually disabled children. And that is still largely the point; communities and parents put on 80,000 local events a year. In addition, the Special Olympics World Games are held every two years, alternating between summer and winter. There are 32 sports (25 summer,[2] 7 winter), and participants compete against others of similar ability.

In 2015 in Los Angeles, 6,500 people competed at the most recent Summer Games; the Opening Ceremonies were held in the Coliseum, and ESPN was on hand.

These medals come from several such events. Christopher Byrne of New Jersey,[3] who has been competing in the Special Olympics since the first meet in 1968, won a gold in ice skating at the 1989 Winter Games in Reno (left); a bronze in track-and-field at the 1991 Summer Games in Minneapolis (middle); and another skating gold at the 1993 Winter Games in Salzburg, Austria (right).

The Special Olympics were the inspiration of Eunice Kennedy Shriver, younger sister not only of John F. Kennedy but also of Rosemary Kennedy, who was intellectually disabled. Not everyone considered the event a good idea. Skeptics were concerned that the children (and at first the Special Olympics were for children only) would become frustrated by defeat or downhearted by the difficulty of learning a sport. While not every participant has loved the experience, the overwhelming lesson of the Special Olympics is that bringing sports to more people is a good thing, helping to build confidence and improve health. Besides, the games are fun.

The Paralympics are another example of how people who were once shut out of sports have found ways to get into them. In the United States, disabled World War II veterans took to the idea of wheelchair basketball.[4] By 1949[5] there were wheelchair basketball tourneys, and in 1957 the first National Wheelchair Games took place, offering track, darts, Ping-Pong, and archery, as well as hoops.[6]

Three years later, Rome held the first Paralympics. It wasn't big—400 men[7] from 23 countries in eight sports[8]—and it was exclusively for wheelchair athletes, but it was a start. The Winter Paralympics began in 1976.[9] Over time the Paralympics have broadened in scope, and the rules have been standardized. There are 10 disability categories; in addition, athletes are assessed on their degree of impairment to make the competition as comparable as possible. The standard of performance has risen markedly. The best Paralympians are world-class athletes; check out the ripped upper bodies of top wheelchair marathoners, who can finish a 26.2-mile course in less than 90 minutes.

In ironic proof of how the Paralympics have come of age, they even attract scandal and controversy on a regular basis, just like every other kind of sport. There have been flunked drug tests,[10] classification disputes,[11] sex scandals,[12] and arguments over money and technology. South African sprinter Oscar Pistorius was the photogenic face of the Paralympics in 2012, when he became the first amputee runner to also compete in the conventional Games. Three years later, he was convicted of killing his girlfriend.[13]

On the whole, though, the story has to be seen as one of genuine progress, with more physically disabled people participating in sports, and more nondisabled people appreciating their skills. More than 4,300 athletes (1,523 of them women) from 164 countries participated in the London Paralympics in 2012.[14]

ACKNOWLEDGMENTS

One of the small pleasures of writing this book has been talking to people all over the country about their passion. Almost everyone I spoke to caught the idea immediately; for those who didn't, all I had to do was ask, "What exhibit makes people stop and say, 'That's cool!'?" Then they got it—and almost all shared my enthusiasm. So I'd like to thank all those who keep America's many wonderful small museums going and who have been so helpful to me. Ditto, of course, to the professional staffs at various halls of fame, sports organizations, and the Smithsonian.

Christopher Hunt was a helpful reader on an early version, and my brothers Cullen and Finn Murphy read the final draft. Brendan Murphy and Meg Murphy Nash read specific entries and improved them. My brother-in-law, Cary Sleeper, did brilliant photography for many items. My sister Cullene Murphy did the same with her image of Mike Eruzione's stick. Another sister, Byrne Sleeper, helped keep me sane and reasonably cheerful throughout; yet another, Siobhan Grogan, helped me celebrate the end of it all with a weekend in Mexico City. My mother made a point of *not* asking about the book with such determination that I almost felt sorry for her, but I know she was always rooting for me, which is all that matters. And my late father, John Cullen Murphy, introduced me to the joy of sports.

My friends were wonderfully patient with how I could find a link between almost any topic of conversation and an item in the book. I consider this a neat party trick (and one, in fact, that I can keep playing). I suspect they might be less enthusiastic. Even so, their interest, even if some of it was feigned, kept me going.

For a variety of boring reasons, this book had to be written relatively quickly. I could never have finished if my colleagues at McKinsey had not supported me to a degree far above any reasonable expectation.

This is my third book. Each time, I have ventured to Thailand near the end of the ordeal for sun, sustenance, and friendship at the home of Gretchen Worth and her four-legged friends. Thanks, yet again.

Finally, thanks to my agent, Rafe Sagalyn, for selling the idea, and then for liking it, and to the staff at Perseus, who turned a jigsaw puzzle of words and pictures into a handsome book.

NOTES

CIRCA 1100–STATUE OF A CHUNKEY PLAYER

1. Stewart Culin, *Games of the North American Indians* (New York: Dover Publications, 2012), 421.

2. William R. Iseminger, *Cahokia Mounds: America's First City* (Charleston, SC: The History Press, 2010), 85.

3. James Adair, *The History of the American Indians* (London: Printed for Edward and Charles Dilly, 1775), 401.

4. Quoted in Culin, *Games of the North American Indians*, 513.

5. Adam King, ed., *Southeastern Ceremonial Complex: Chronology, Content, Contest* (Tuscaloosa: University of Alabama Press, 2007), 242.

6. Timothy R. Pauketat, *Cahokia: Ancient America's Great City on the Mississippi* (New York: Viking, 2009), 42.

7. Ibid., 44.

8. Timothy R. Pauketat, "America's First Pastime," *Archaeology Magazine* 62, no. 5 (September–October 2009), archive.archaeology.org/0909/abstracts/pastime.html.

9. Timothy Pauketat, "Cahokia: A Pre-Columbian American City," *History Now* (n.d.), http://www.gilderlehrman .org/history-by-era/american-indians/essays/cahokia-pre-columbian-american-city.

10. "Cahokia: America's Forgotten City," *National Geographic* [January 2011], http://ngm.nationalgeographic .com/2011/01/cahokia/burmeister-photography.

11. Cahokia Mounds State Historic Site, http://ww.cahokiamounds.org/learn/.

12. "Cahokia: America's Forgotten City."

LATE 1600s–OLDEST AMERICAN "LAWN BOWLE"

1. Nancy Struna, "Puritans and Sport: The Irretrievable Guide to Change," *Journal of Sport History* 4, no. 1 (1977): 9.

2. "Early Modern Olympians: Puritan Sportsmen in 17th-Century England and America," *Canadian Journal of History* (Autumn 2008): 261.

3. "Katherine Nanny Naylor: A Personal Story from Colonial Boston," *Cross Street Backlot*, Massachusetts Historical Commission, 2014, http://www.sec.state.ma.us/mhc/mhcarchexhibitsonline/crossstreetbacklot.htm.

4. *Common-place: The Journal of Early American Life* 16, no. 1 (Fall 2015), http://www.common-place.org/vol -03/no-04/boston/. Partisans of Jamestown, Virginia, might dispute the assertion. In May 1611 Thomas Dale arrived in Jamestown to lead the settlement, which was struggling with hunger despite living in a fertile land rich in fish and game. Dale was disgusted to find that other than "some few seeds put into a private garden or two," little planting had been done. Instead, he complained, the colonists were busy at "their daily and usuall works, bowling in the streetes." Archaeologists have unearthed small clay balls that might have been used for such play,

but they also might have been used for cooking. So the use of that artifact is ambiguous, while that of the ball from Mrs. Naylor's privy is not.

5. Struna, "Puritans and Sport," 11.

6. George Francis Dow, *Every Day Life in the Massachusetts Bay Colony* (New York: Dover Publications, 1988), 110.

7. Ann-Eliza Lewis, "A Recreation to Great Persons: Bowling in Colonial Boston," *Northeast Historical Archaeology* 27, no. 1 (1998): 131, http://digitalcommons.buffalostate.edu/cgi/viewcontent.cgi?article=1162&context=neha.

8. Ann-Eliza Lewis, "Boston's Curious Bowling History," *Cultural Resource Management* 23, no. 10 (2000): 29, http://npshistory.com/newsletters/crm/crm-v23n10.pdf.

1823–SOUVENIR FROM THE GREAT MATCH RACE

1. Equivalent to more than $900,000 in 2015.

2. John Eisenberg, *The Great Match Race: When North Met South in America's First Sports Spectacle* (Boston: Houghton Mifflin, 2006), 72.

3. Melvin Adelman, *A Sporting Time: New York City and the Rise of Modern Athletics, 1820–70* (Urbana-Champaign: University of Illinois Press, 1986), 34.

4. Daniel Russell, "American Eclipse: Glen Cove Thoroughbred," n.d., www.glencoveheritage.com; www.bloodlines.net.

5. An Old Turfman (Cadwallader Colden), "The Great Match Race," *American Turf Register and Sporting Magazine* 2 (September 1830): 3–12.

6. By way of comparison, today's Belmont, the longest of the Triple Crown races at 1.5 miles, is regarded as a test of endurance.

7. Eisenberg, *The Great Match Race*, 147.

8. International Museum of the Horse, "Intersectional Match Races," n.d., http://www.imh.org/exhibits/online/intersectional-match-races.

9. Eisenberg, *The Great Match Race*, 161, 170.

10. Ibid., ix.

11. Ibid., 171, 173.

12. Ibid., 197.

13. Ibid., 233.

PRE-1845–LACROSSE STICK

1. An Englishman in colonial Virginia might have been referencing lacrosse when he wrote in 1612 of "[a] kind of exercise they have often amongst them much like that which boyes call bandy in English." William Strachey, *The Historie of Travaile into Virginia Britannia* (London: Printed for the Hakluyt Society, 1849), 77. But the reference is vague. On the other hand, Strachey's reference to "the exercise of football" is spot on, describing a game recognizably soccer-ish. Quoted in Culin, *Games of the North American Indians*, 513.

2. Peter Bailey Lund, "European Discovery and Development," in *Lacrosse: A History of the Game*, n.d., http://www.e-lacrosse.com/laxhist4.htm.

3. Peter Bailey Lund, "The American Indian Game," in *Lacrosse: A History of the Game*, n.d., http://www.e-lacrosse.com/laxhist3.htm.

4. Thomas Vennum Jr., "The History of Lacrosse," *About the Sport: History*, n.d., http://www.uslacrosse.org/about-the-sport/history.aspx.

5. Lissa Edwards, "Deadly Lacrosse Game in Mackinac Straits at Fort Michilimackinac in 1763," *MyNorth*, May 16, 2010, http://mynorth.com/2010/05/deadly-lacrosse-game-in-mackinac-straits-at-fort-michilimackinac-in-1763/.

6. Frances Eyman, "Lacrosse and the Cayuga Thunder Rite," *Expedition Magazine* (Summer 1964): 16.

1851–STERN ORNAMENT FROM THE *AMERICA*

1. A brother, Edward, founded the Stevens Institute of Technology in Hoboken. The school would help to design a number of defenders of the America's Cup. In another cultural context, the Stevens family owned the land in Hoboken (they owned most of Hoboken) where the murdered Mary Rogers was found in 1841. This famous unsolved mystery was the inspiration for Edgar Allan Poe's story, "The Mystery of Marie Roget."

2. Thomas R. Neblett, *Civil War Yacht: Chronicles of the Schooner* America (Mustang, OK: Tate Publishing & Enterprises, 2009), 37.

3. "Arrival of the American Clipper Yacht 'America,' of the New York Yacht Club," *Illustrated London News* 19, no. 508 (August 9, 1851), 173.

4. Charles Boswell, *The* America: *The Story of the World's Most Famous Yacht* (New York: D. McKay Co., 1967), 29.

5. Thomas Lawson and Winfield Thompson, *The Lawson History of the America's Cup* (Southampton, UK: Ashford Press Publishing, 1986 [first published in 1902]), 16.

6. Quoted in Neblett, *Civil War Yacht,* 77.

7. Royal Yacht Squadron, "About RYS: The Yacht America," n.d., https://www.rys.org.uk/about/the-yacht-america/.

8. Lawson and Thompson, *Lawson History of the America's Cup,* 29.

9. Herbert L. Stone and William H. Taylor, *The America's Cup Races* (Princeton, NJ: D. Van Nostrad Co., 1958).

10. Neblett, *Civil War Yacht,* 241.

11. John Rousmaniere, *The Low Black Schooner: Yacht* America, *1851–1945* (Mystic, CT: Mystic Seaport Museum, 1986).

12. Neblett, *Civil War Yacht,* 211.

13. Ibid., 252.

14. Ibid., 85.

1853–SOIL FROM THE ELYSIAN FIELDS

1. "Knickerbocker Rules," http://www.baseball-almanac.com/rule11.shtml.

2. "Doc Adams," Society for American Baseball Research, n.d., http://sabr.org/bioproj/person/14ec7492.

3. Quoted in John Thorn, *Baseball in the Garden of Eden: The Secret History of the Early Game* (New York: Simon & Schuster, 2011), 26.

4. "Daniel Lucius 'Doc' Adams—Long Overlooked Baseball Pioneer," *MLB Reports*, July 25, 2012, http://mlbreports.com/2012/07/25/docadams/.

5. Richard Sandomir, "Founding Rules of 'Base Ball' Sell for $3.26 Million in Auction," *New York Times*, April 24, 2016.

6. Monica Nucciarone, "Alexander Cartwright," Society for American Baseball Research, n.d., http://sabr.org/bioproj/person/09ed3dd4.

7. Monica Nucciarone, *Alexander Cartwright: The Life Behind the Baseball Legend* (Lincoln and London: University of Nebraska Press, 2009), 159.

8. The Baseball Reliquary, "Soil Sample from Elysian Fields," n.d., http://www.baseballreliquary.org/about/collections/soil-sample-from-elysian-fields/.

9. Ibid.

10. Mike Pesca, "The Man Who Made Baseball's Box Score a Hit," NPR, July 30, 2009, http://www.npr.org/templates/story/story.php?storyId=106891539; "Henry Chadwick," National Baseball Hall of Fame, n.d., http://baseballhall.org/hof/chadwick-henry.

1860—ABRAHAM LINCOLN'S HANDBALL

1. David Herbert Donald, *We Are Lincoln Men: Abraham Lincoln and His Friends* (New York: Simon & Schuster, 2003), 13.

2. David Fleming, "The Civil Warrior," *Sports Illustrated*, February 6, 1995, http://www.si.com/vault/1995/02/06/133235/the-civil-warrior-on-the-us-frontier-young-abe-lincoln-was-a-great-wrestler----and-sportsman.

3. Douglas L. Wilson and Rodney O. Davis, eds., *Herndon's Informants* (Urbana and Chicago: University of Illinois Press, 1998), 554.

4. *Journal of the Illinois State Historical Society* (June 1954): 60.

5. David Levinson and Karen Christensen, *Encyclopedia of World Sport: From Ancient Times to the Present* (New York, Oxford: Oxford University Press, 1999), 164.

6. Brand Whitlock, *Abraham Lincoln* (Boston: Small, Maynard & Company, 1916), 104.

1870—SPORTSMAN'S HALL

1. For a good idea of what this might have looked like, see episode 4 of *The Knick* on Cinemax.

2. Quoted in Martin Kaufman and Herbert J. Kaufman, "Henry Bergh, Kit Burns, and the Sportsmen of New York," *New York Folklore Quarterly*, 28, no. 1 (March 1972): 23.

3. James William Buel, *Mysteries and Miseries of America's Great Cities: Embracing New York, Washington City, San Francisco, Salt Lake City, and New Orleans* (St. Louis and Philadelphia: Historical Publishing Co., 1883), 49.

4. "The Band-Box of the Late Kit Burns," *New York Times*, January 2, 1871.

1889—JOHN L. SULLIVAN'S DUMBBELL

1. Richard Hoffer, "Fisticuffs John L. Sullivan & Jake Kilrain in The Outlaw Brawl That Started It All: How 75 Rounds of Bare-fisted Boxing in 1889 Crowned America's First Superstar and Transformed the Face of Sport," *Sports Illustrated*, May 6, 2002. http://www.si.com/vault/2002/05/06/8101527/fisticuffs-john-l-sullivan--jake-kilrain-in-the-outlaw-brawl-that-started-it-all-how-75-rounds-of-barefisted-boxing-in-1889-crowned-americas-first-superstar-and-transformed-the-face-of-sport.

2. $259,495 in 2015 dollars.

3. Hoffer, "Fisticuffs."

4. Christopher Klein, *Strong Boy: The Life and Times of John L. Sullivan, America's First Sports Hero* (Guilford, CT: Lyons Press, 2013), 153.

5. Nat Fleischer, *John L. Sullivan: Champion of Champions* (New York: Putnam, 1951), 120–122.

6. Hoffer, "Fisticuffs."

7. Ibid.

8. Michael Woods, "125 Years Ago Today, John L. Sullivan Stopped Jake Kilrain in Round 75," *The Sweet Science*, July 8, 2014, http://www.thesweetscience.com/news/articles/18924-125-years-ago-today-john-l-sullivan-stopped-jake-kilrain-in-round-75.

9. Christian Stone, "Sullivan's Last Stand," *Sports Illustrated*, October 27, 1992, http://www.si.com/vault/1992/10/27/127455/then--now-100-years-ago-sullivans-last-stand.

10. Fleischer, *John L. Sullivan*, xi.

1890–ISAAC MURPHY'S SILK PURSE

1. National Museum of Racing and Hall of Fame, "Isaac B. Murphy," 2014, https://www.racingmuseum.org/hall-of-fame/isaac-b-murphy.

2. His given name was Isaac Burns; after his mother's death, he changed it to her maiden name, Murphy.

3. Katherine C. Mooney, *Race Horse Men: How Slavery and Freedom Were Made at the Racetrack* (Cambridge, MA: President and Fellows of Harvard College, 2014), 41.

4. "Running Unfinished Races," *New York Times*, August 20, 1885.

5. $266,060 in 2015 dollars.

6. Edward Hotaling, *The Great Black Jockeys: The Lives and Times of the Men Who Dominated America's First National Sport* (n.p.: Prima Lifestyles, 1999), 255.

7. Jim Bolus, "Honest Isaac's Legacy: The Greatest U.S. Jockey of the 19th Century Was a Black Man, Isaac Murphy," *Sports Illustrated*, April 29, 1996, http://www.si.com/vault/1996/04/29/212372/honest-isaacs-legacy-the-greatest-us-jockey-of-the-19th-century-was-a-black-man-isaac-murphy.

8. "Freeland's Famous Jockey: Joe Cotton's Owner Tells How He First Taught the Boy to Ride," *New York Times*, August 20, 1885.

9. Pellom McDaniels III, *The Prince of Jockeys: The Life of Isaac Burns Murphy* (Lexington: University Press of Kentucky, 2013), 353.

10. Ibid., 362.

11. Hotaling, *The Great Black Jockeys*, 269.

12. Bolus, "Honest Isaac's Legacy."

13. Arthur Ashe, *A Hard Road to Glory: A History of the African-American Athlete, 1619–1918* (New York: Warner Books, 1988), 50.

14. Hotaling, *The Great Black Jockeys*, 326.

15. Ashe, *A Hard Road to Glory*, 47.

16. Charles Hirshberg, "Pilloried at the Post," *Sports Illustrated*, June 26, 2006, http://www.si.com/vault/2006/06/26/8380584/pilloried-at-the-post-.

17. Hotaling, *The Great Black Jockeys*, 327.

18. Arthur Ashe and Arnold Rampersand, *Days of Grace* (New York: Ballantine Books, 1993), 174.

1891–JAMES NAISMITH'S ORIGINAL RULES OF BASKETBALL

1. Rob Rains, with Helen Carpenter, *James Naismith: The Man Who Invented Basketball* (Philadelphia: Temple University Press, 2009), 36.

2. Kansapedia, Kansas Historical Society: http://www.kshs.org/kansapedia/james-naismith/12154.

3. James Naismith, *Basketball: Its Origin and Development* (New York: Association Press, 1941), 37.

4. Ibid., 44–55.

5. The Y can also take credit for volleyball, which was invented by William Morgan of the Holyoke YMCA, about 10 miles from Springfield. Morgan was seeking to create a less strenuous game for older men; he called it "mintonette" (see Rains, *James Naismith*, 61).

6. Tony Ladd and James Mathisen, *Muscular Christianity: Evangelical Protestants and the Development of American Sport* (Grand Rapids, MI: Baker Books, 1999), 61, 63.

7. Ibid., 21. Another apostle of muscular Christianity was Amos Alonzo Stagg, who was a contemporary of Naismith's at Springfield. A former theology student at Yale, Stagg considered joining the ministry, but decided to reach men's souls through sports instead; he played in the first game of hoops. In 1892 he went to the University of Chicago, where he became the first nationally known football coach, famous for inventing the huddle and the T-formation.

8. Naismith, *Basketball*, 115.

9. Ibid., 163.

10. Sister of art historian Bernard Berenson.

11. Ralph Melnick, *Senda Berenson: The Unlikely Founder of Women's Basketball* (Amherst: University of Massachusetts Press, 2007), 1.

12. *Sports Illustrated*, March 22, 1993.

13. Melnick, *Senda Berenson*, 23.

14. Ibid., 81.

15. The first women's intercollegiate game took place in 1895, between Berkeley and Stanford.

1892–RECORD OF PAYMENT FOR FIRST PROFESSIONAL FOOTBALL PLAYER

1. Allen Barra, "The First Pro Football Player Wasn't Just First; He Was Also Great," *The Atlantic*, November 12, 2012, http://www.theatlantic.com/entertainment/archive/2012/11/the-first-pro-football-player-wasnt-just-first-he-was-also-great/265102/.

1892–SAFETY BICYCLE

1. Richard Harmon, "Progress and Flight: An Interpretation of the American Cycle Craze of the 1890s," *Journal of Social History* (Winter 1971–1972): 236.

2. This was the English-made Rover; see David Herlihy, *Bicycle: The History* (New Haven, CT: Yale University Press, 2004), 235.

3. Ibid., 246, 252.

4. Sidney Aronson, "The Sociology of the Bicycle," *Social Forces* (March 1952): 305.

5. Arabella Kenealy, "Woman as Athlete," *Nineteenth Century*, (April 1899): 635–645.

6. Bella Bathurst, *The Bicycle Book* (New York: HarperCollins, 2011), 104.

7. Aronson, "Sociology of the Bicycle," 308.

8. Mrs. Reginald De Koven, "Bicycling for Women," *Cosmopolitan* 19 (August 1895): 392–394.

9. E. B. Turner, FRCS, "A Report on Cycling in Health and Disease," *British Medical Journal*, June 6, 1896.

10. Harmon, "Progress and Flight," 240.

11. Herlihy, *Bicycle*, 294.

12. A.M. Godfrey, "Cycling Clubs and Their Spheres of Action," *Outing*, July 1897, 4.

13. Aronson, "Sociology of the Bicycle," 310.

14. Herlihy, *Bicycle*, 300.

15. Frances E. Willard, updated February 16, 2016, https://www.aoc.gov/capitol-hill/national-statuary-hall-collection/frances-e-willard.

16. Frances Willard, *A Wheel Within a Wheel: How I Learned to Ride a Bicycle* (London: Hutchinson & Co., 1895), 25.

17. Ibid., 75.

1909–THE YARD OF BRICKS AT THE INDIANAPOLIS MOTOR SPEEDWAY

1. *The Indiana Historian* (December 1996): 3.

2. Jay F. Hein and Allison Melangton, "In Prospect," *American Outlook* (Winter 2011), http://www.americanoutlook.org/in-prospect1.html.

3. https://www.lincolnhighwayassoc.org/info/.

4. "Yard of Bricks & Panasonic Pagoda," n.d., https://www.indianapolismotorspeedway.com/at-the-track/yard-of-bricks-pagoda/yard-of-bricks.

1910—ANNIE OAKLEY'S RIFLE

1. Shirl Kasper, *Annie Oakley* (Norman and London: University of Oklahoma Press, 1992), 43.

1912—JIM THORPE'S RESTORED OLYMPIC GOLD MEDALS

1. Ron Flatter, "Thorpe Preceded Deion, Bo," ESPN.com, n.d., https://espn.go.com/sportscentury/features /00016499.html.

2. "Jim Thorpe Is Dead On West Coast at 64," *New York Times*, March 29, 1953, http://www.nytimes.com /learning/general/onthisday/bday/0528.html; Joseph D. O'Brian, "The Greatest Athlete in the World," *American Heritage* 43, no. 4 (July/August 1992), http://www.americanheritage.com/content/greatest-athlete-world.

3. "Jim Thorpe Named Greatest in Sport; Top Athlete in Half-Century Poll," *New York Times*, February 12, 1950.

4. O'Brian, "The Greatest Athlete in the World."

5. Kate Buford, *Native American Son: The Life and Sporting Legend of Jim Thorpe* (New York: Knopf, 2010), 163–164.

6. Alfred E. Senn, *Power Politics, and the Olympic Games* (Champaign, IL: Human Kinetics, 1999), 31.

7. O'Brian, "The Greatest Athlete in the World."

8. Allen Guttmann, *The Games Must Go On: Avery Brundage and the Olympic Movement* (New York: Columbia University Press, 1984), 28.

9. Quoted in Robert Shaplen, "Amateur," *New Yorker*, July 23, 1960.

10. Andrew Denning, "Alpine Skiing and the Winter Games—An Olympic Problem? 1936–1972," December 2010, 9, 11, 12, https://doc.rero.ch/record/22121/files/Denning_final_report.pdf_attachment_.pdf.

11. Taps Gallagher and Mike Brewster, *Stolen Glory: The U.S., the Soviet Union, and the Olympic Basketball Game That Never Ended* (Beverly Hills, CA: GM Books, 2012).

12. "Pennsylvania Town Named for Jim Thorpe Can Keep Athlete's Body," *CBS News*, October 23, 2014, http://www.cbsnews.com/news/pennsylvania-town-named-for-jim-thorpe-can-keep-athletes-body/.

1913—FRANCIS OUIMET'S IRONS, BALL, AND SCORECARD FROM THE US OPEN

1. Herbert Warren Wind, *The Story of American Golf* (New York: Knopf, 1975), 73.

2. Mark Frost, The Greatest Game Ever Played: Harry Vardon, Francis Ouimet, and the Birth of Modern Golf (Hyperion E-book, 2002), 92.

3. Rick Reilly, "The Longest Long Shot: September 18–20, 1913, Francis Ouimet Wins the U.S. Open," *Sports Illustrated*, November 29, 1999, http://www.si.com/vault/1999/11/29/270654/the-longest-long-shot -september-18-20-1913-francis-ouimet-wins-the-us-open.

4. Frost, *Greatest Game Ever Played*, 371.

5. "Ouimet World's Golf Champion," *New York Times*, September 21, 1913.

6. Wind, *Story of American Golf*, 76.

7. David Owen and Joan Bingham, eds., *Lure of the Links: Great Golf Stories* (New York: Atlantic Monthly Press, 1997), 4.

8. Wind, *Story of American Golf*, 86.

9. Bobby Jones and O. B. Keeler, *Down the Fairway* (New York: Minton, Balch, 1927), 38–39.

10. Frost, *Greatest Game Ever Played*, 468.

1921—RADIO BROADCAST OF THE DEMPSEY-CARPENTIER FIGHT

1. John Lardner, "Boyle's Thirty Acres and the Revolution," *New Yorker*, November 4, 1950, 135.

2. Thomas Myler, "Georges Carpentier, the Orchid Man," *Boxing Digest*, January 2010, 28.

3. Mappen, Marc, "Jerseyana," *New York Times*, June 9, 1991.

4. Skip Myslenski, "30 Acres of Romance, Hokum and Balderdash," *Sports Illustrated*, December 16, 1968, http://www.si.com/vault/1968/12/16/551662/30-acres-of-romance-hokum-and-balderdash.

5. Lardner, "Boyles Thirty Acres and the Revolution," 136.

6. There were other connections: Abe Attell, a gambler implicated in the 1919 World Series fix, was present at the negotiations to set up the match. (Dempsey got $300,000; Carpentier, $200,000.) Gene Tunney fought on the undercard. He would later whip Carpentier and take the title from Dempsey. Mike Jacobs, a ticket broker, helped to finance the event; he would become Joe Louis's manager.

7. To see the whole fight, go to Norman Marcus, "George Carpentier: The 'Orchid Man'," July 23, 2012, http://www.boxing.com/georges_carpentier_the_orchid_man.html.

8. Ibid.

9. "First Program Broadcast by KDKA Six Years Ago; Pioneer Station Went on the Air Nov. 2, 1920, with Election Returns—Many Broadcasting Records Are Credited to Pittsburgh Station," *New York Times*, October 31, 1926, http://query.nytimes.com/gst/abstract.html?res=9905E6D91639E633A25752C3A9669D946795D6CF.

10. Mark Frost, *The Grand Slam: Bobby Jones, America, and the Story of Golf* (New York: Hyperion, 2004), 180.

11. Vintage Radio and Communications Museum of Connecticut, http://www.radiomuseum.org/r/rca_aeriola _sr_1.html.

12. Glen Jeansonne, with David Luhrssen, *A Time of Paradox: America Since 1890* (Lanham, MD: Rowman & Littlefield, 2006), 196.

1925—THE MODERN FOOTBALL

1. Jim Morrison, "The Early History of Football's Forward Pass," *Smithsonian Magazine*, December 28, 2010, http://www.smithsonianmag.com/history/the-early-history-of-footballs-forward-pass-78015237/?no-ist.

2. Sally Jenkins, *The Real All-Americans: The Team That Changed a Game, a People, and a* Nation (New York: Doubleday, 2007), 234.

3. Ibid., 245.

4. *2015 Official NFL Record and Fact Book* (New York: National Football League, 2015), 357.

5. John J. Miller, *The Big Scrum: How Teddy Roosevelt Saved Football* (New York: HarperCollins, 2011), 218.

6. Dan Revsine, *The Opening Kickoff: The Tumultuous Birth of a Football Nation* (Guilford, CT: Lyons Press, 2014), 207.

7. Karen Croake Heisler, *Fighting Irish: Legends, Lists, and Lore* (Champaign, IL: Sports Publishing, 2006), 46; Miller, *Big Scrum*, 206.

8. *New York Times*, November 2, 1913.

9. Jenkins, *Real All-Americans*, 336.

10. Thanks to John J. Miller for the description.

11. Scott Oldham, "Bombs Away," *Popular Mechanics*, October 2001, 64–67.

12. Ibid.

1920s—TAD LUCAS'S RIDING BOOTS

1. "Tad Lucas," n.d., Pro Rodeo Hall of Fame, http://www.prorodeohalloffame.com/inductees/by-category /notableslifetime-achievement/tad-lucas/.

2. "Lucas, Barbara," *Encyclopedia of the Great Plains*, ed. David J. Wishart (Lincoln: University of Nebraska, 2011), http://plainshumanities.unl.edu/encyclopedia/doc/egp.sr.034.

3. Teresa Jordan, *Cowgirls: Women of the American West* (Lincoln: University of Nebraska Press, 1992), 200.

4. Sylvia Gann Mahoney, "Rodeos," *Handbook of Texas Online*, Texas State Historical Association, 2010, https://tshaonline.org/handbook/online/articles/llr01.

5. Women's Professional Rodeo Association, "66 Years of Women in Rodeo," n.d., http://www.wpra.com/pdfs/2014_Wrangler_NFR.pdf.

1925—STATISTICS FROM RED GRANGE'S NFL DEBUT

1. Pro Football Hall of Fame, "Grange's Debut on Thanksgiving," January 1, 2005, http://www.profootballhof.com/news/grange-s-debut-on-thanksgiving/. Playing both ways, he ran for 92 yards, threw six passes, and intercepted one.

2. Red Grange (with Ira Morton), *The Galloping Ghost: The Autobiography of Red Grange* (Wheaton, IL: Crossroads Communications, 1981), 44.

3. Herbert Warren Wind, ed., *The Realm of Sport* (New York: Simon & Schuster, 1966), 319.

4. John M. Carroll, *Red Grange and the Rise of Modern Football* (Champaign: University of Illinois Press, 1999), 78.

5. It was initially known as the American Professional Football Association; the National Football League became its name in 1922.

6. "Red Grange," *ESPN SportsCentury*, July 9, 1999.

7. Carroll, *Red Grange and the Rise of Modern Football*, 99.

8. Jim Reisler, *Cash and Carry: The Spectacular Rise and Hard Fall of CC Pyle, America's First Sports Agent* (Jefferson, NC: McFarland, 2009), 71.

9. Ibid., 70.

10. George A. Halas, "My Forty Years in Pro Football," *Saturday Evening Post*, November 30, 1957, 108.

11. Carroll, *Red Grange and the Rise of Modern Football*, 113.

12. "Grange's Two Days Here Yield $370,000; Gets $300,000 to Act in Movie; Other Sums for Endorsing Numerous Trade Articles. EARNINGS NEARLY $500,000 Likely to Roll Up $1,000,000, He Defends Turning 'Pro' as Grasping Opportunity," *New York Times*, December 8, 1925, http://query.nytimes.com/gst/abstract.html?res=9406E2DE113AEF3ABC4053DFB467838E639EDE.

13. "Grange Is Booed by Boston Fans; Displays Poor Form, Is Stopped at Every Turn, Gaining Only 20 Yards as Bears Lose, 9-6; 15,000 in the Stands Brave Cold to See Star and Do Not Hesitate to Express Disappointment—Steam Rollers Win," *New York Times*, December 10, 1925, http://query.nytimes.com/gst/abstract.html?res=9F06EFDB1539E633A25753C1A9649D946495D6CF.

14. John Underwood, "Was He the Greatest of All Time?," *Sports Illustrated*, September 4, 1985, http://www.si.com/vault/1985/09/04/643872/was-he-the-greatest-of-all-time.

15. Dave Anderson, "The Bear Who Really Was One," *New York Times*, November 2, 1983, http://www.nytimes.com/1983/11/02/sports/sports-of-the-times-the-bear-who-really-was-one.html.

1926—HELEN WILLS'S LEATHER TRAVEL BAG

1. Lisa Dillman, "Tennis: Helen Wills Moody Roark Attracts Attention Again, Thanks to Martina," *Los Angeles Times*, June 26, 1988, http://articles.latimes.com/1988-06-26/sports/sp-8410_1_helen-wills-moody.

2. Gary Morley, "Suzanne Lenglen: The First Diva of Tennis," *CNN*, June 6, 2013, http://edition.cnn.com/2013/06/06/sport/tennis/suzanne-lenglen-french-open-tennis/.

3. Larry Engelmann, *The Goddess & the American Girl: The Story of Suzanne Lenglen and Helen Wills* (Oxford: Oxford University Press, 1988), ix.

4. She withdrew from the quarterfinals in 1924.

5. Sarah Pileggi, "The Lady in the White Silk Dress," *Sports Illustrated*, September 13, 1982, http://www.si.com/vault/1982/09/13/624724/the-lady-in-the-white-silk-dress.

6. Engelmann, *Goddess & the American Girl*, 157.

7. A few bits and pieces can be seen at *Suzanne Lenglen vs Helen Wills—1926 Cannes, France*, January 11, 2009, https://www.youtube.com/watch?v=8HSsH7V3Ml8.

8. Helen Wills, *Fifteen-Thirty: The Story of a Tennis Player* (New York and London: Charles Scribner & Sons, 1937), 94.

9. Engelmann, *Goddess & the American Girl*, 179.

10. *Time*, February 9, 1948.

11. Robin Finn, "Helen Wills Moody, Dominant Champion Who Won 8 Wimbledon Titles, Dies at 92," *New York Times*, January 3, 1998, http://www.nytimes.com/1998/01/03/sports/helen-wills-moody-dominant -champion-who-won-8-wimbledon-titles-dies-at-92.html.

12. *Saturday Evening Post*, April 4, 1931, 70.

13. *Saturday Evening Post*, June 17, 1933, 80.

1929—AMELIA EARHART'S GOGGLES

1. Patricia Sullivan, "Pioneering Pilot Elinor Smith Sullivan Dies at 98," *Washington Post*, March 24, 2010, http://www.washingtonpost.com/wp-dyn/content/article/2010/03/23/AR2010032303758.html.

2. "Breaking Through the Clouds—The Story," nd., http://www.breakingthroughtheclouds.com/noframes .asp?f=story.html.

3. Gene Nora Jessen, "1929 Air Race," 1999, http://www.ninety-nines.org/the_1929_air_race.htm.

4. Susan Butler, *East to the Dawn*, media tie-in ed. (New York: Da Capo Press, 2009), 231.

5. "Goggles. Flying. Amelia Earhart," Smithsonian National Air and Space Museum, http://airandspace.si .edu/collections/artifact.cfm?object=nasm_A19580054000.

6. Victoria Garrett Jones, *Amelia Earhart: A Life in Flight* (New York and London: Sterling, 2009).

1930—BILL TILDEN'S TENNIS RACKET

1. Tilden never played in Australia, and its tourney was not considered a major at the time. The French was for French players only until 1925; he did not compete at Wimbledon from 1922 through 1926.

2. Australia, however, had a remarkable run: from 1950 through 1967, it won fifteen of eighteen Davis Cups.

3. Marshall Jon Fisher, *A Terrible Splendor: Three Extraordinary Men, a World Poised for War, and the Greatest Tennis Match Ever Played* (New York: Crown, 2009), 128.

4. *New York Times*, August 29, 2009.

5. Caryl Phillips, ed., *The Right Set: A Tennis Anthology* (New York: Vintage, 1999), 64; Fisher, *A Terrible Splendor*, 33.

6. Fisher, *A Terrible Splendor*, 120.

7. "Bill Tilden," International Tennis Hall of Fame, n.d., https://www.tennisfame.com/hall-of-famers /inductees/bill-tilden/.

8. Fisher, *A Terrible Splendor*, 249, 251–252.

9. Frank Deford, *Big Bill Tilden: The Triumphs and the Tragedy* (New York: Simon & Schuster, 1976), p.167.

10. Fisher, *A Terrible Splendor*, 249.

11. Ibid., 258.

12. *Time*, June 15, 1953.

1930—BOBBY JONES'S PUTTER, CALAMITY JANE

1. Bobby Jones and O. B. Keeler, *Down the Fairway* (New York: Minton, Balch, 1927), 108.

2. "The Amazing Mr. Jones," n.d., http://themajorsofgolf.com/features/the-amazing-bobby-jones/.

3. Mark Frost, *The Grand Slam: Bobby Jones, America, and the Story of Golf* (New York: Hyperion, 2004), 382.

4. Bill Fields, "Jones Had a Trusted Partner in His Putter," *ESPN*, March 5, 2009, http://sports.espn.go.com/golf/news/story?id=3954571.

5. Herbert Warren Wind, *The Story of American Golf* (New York: Knopf, 1975), 201.

6. Frost, *The Grand Slam*, 393.

7. A number of these can be seen on YouTube at https://www.youtube.com/results?search_query=how+i+play+golf+bobby+jones+.

8. Stephen Lowe, "De-marbleizing Bobby Jones," *Georgia Historical Quarterly* 83, no. 4: 670.

9. Jones, Robert Tyre, Jr., Lt, Col., n.d., http://airforce.togetherweserved.com/usaf/servlet/tws.webapp.WebApp?cmd=ShadowBoxProfile&type=BattleMemoryExt&ID=42538.

10. Ron Fimwrite, "The Emperor Jones," *Sports Illustrated*, April 11, 1994, http://www.si.com/vault/1994/04/11/130825/the-emperor-jones-bobby-joness-reign-over-golf-from-1923-to-1930-was-absolute-but-he-proved-just-as-masterly-off-the-course-as-he-was-on-it.

1932–BABE DIDRIKSON'S UNIFORM

1. "Babe Zaharias Dies; Athlete Had Cancer," *New York Times*, September 28, 1956, http://www.nytimes.com/learning/general/onthisday/bday/0626.html.

2. Benjamin Rader, *American Sports: From the Age of Folk Games to the Age of Televised Sports*, 2nd ed. (Englewood Cliffs, NJ: Prentice Hall, 1990), 125.

3. Bruce Kidd, "Women's Olympic History," *CAAWS Action Bulletin* (Spring 1994), http://www.caaws-womenatthegames.ca/olympics/2004/history/womens_games.cfm.

4. Jaime Schultz, *Qualifying Times: Points of Change in U.S. Women's Sport* (Champaign: University of Illinois Press, 2014), 78.

5. Rich Wallace and Sandra Neil Wallace, *Babe Conquers the World: The Legendary Life of Babe Didrikson Zaharias* (Honesdale, PA: Calkins Creek, 2014), 64.

6. Ian Jobling, "The Women's 800 Meters Track Event Post 1928: Quo Vadis?," *Journal of Olympic History* 14 (March 2006): 43–47.

7. Roger Robinson, "'Eleven Wretched Women': What Really Happened in the First Olympic Women's 800m," *Running Times*, May 14, 2012, http://www.runnersworld.com/running-times-info/eleven-wretched-women.

8. Ibid.

9. Quoted in Francis Edward Abernethy, ed., *Legendary Ladies of Texas* (Denton: University of North Texas Press, 1994), 179.

10. William Oscar Johnson, "Babe Part 2," *Sports Illustrated*, October 13, 1975, http://www.si.com/vault/1975/10/13/613267/babe-part-2.

11. http://www.babedidriksonzaharias.org/?page_id=74.

12. Babe Didrikson Zaharias and Harry Paxton, *This Life I've Led: My Autobiography* (New York: Robert Hale,1956), 184.

13. Abernethy, *Legendary Ladies of Texas*, 119.

14. Susan E. Cayleff, "The 'Texas Tomboy': The Life and Legend of Babe Didrikson Zaharias," *OAH Magazine of History* (Summer 1992): 29.

15. The Vare Trophy, given to the golfer with the lowest stroke average, is named after her.

16. "Ora Washington," Women's Basketball Hall of Fame, n.d., http://www.wbhof.com/OWashington.html.

17. Quoted in Pamela Grundy and Susan Shackleford, *Shattering the Glass: The Remarkable History of Women's Basketball* (New York: New Press, 2005), 59.

18. Cecile Houry, "American Women and the Modern Summer Olympic Games: A Story of Obstacles and Struggles for Participation and Equality" (PhD diss., University of Miami, 2011), 127.

1932–BABE RUTH'S "CALLED SHOT" BAT

1. Leigh Montville, *The Big Bam: The Life and Times of Babe Ruth* (New York: Random House, 2006), 310.

2. See this video of part of the action at http://m.mlb.com/video/topic/6479266/v3218817/bb-moments -32-ws-gm-3-babe-ruths-called-shot.

3. Robert W. Creamer, *Babe: The Legend Comes to Life* (New York: Simon & Schuster, 1974), 364.

4. Quoted in ibid., 367.

5. Babe Ruth (as told to Bob Considine): *The Babe Ruth Story* (New York: E. P. Dutton, 1948), 194.

6. Quoted in Larry Getlen, "Journalist Debunks Babe Ruth's Legendary 'Called Shot," *New York Post*, February 1, 2014, http://nypost.com/2014/02/01/chicago-journalist-debunks-babe-ruths-called-shot/.

7. Quoted in Creamer, *Babe*, 365.

8. In 1998, *Sporting News* ranked him first in a list of baseball's 100 best; in 1999, ESPN ranked him the second -greatest athlete in North American history, behind Michael Jordan.

9. Allan Wood, "Babe Ruth," Society for American Baseball Research, n.d., http://sabr.org/bioproj/ person/9dcdd01c.

1935–PROGRAM FROM THE FIRST NIGHT BASEBALL GAME

1. *Time*, August 6, 1930.

2. Quoted in David George Surdam, *Wins, Losses, and Empty Seats: How Baseball Outlasted the Great Depression* (Lincoln and London: University of Nebraska Press, 2011), 220.

3. Frank Graham, *The New York Giants* (New York: Putnam, 1952), 47.

4. John Thorn, Pete Palmer, and Larry Gershman, *Total Baseball* (Kingston, NY: Total Sports, 2001), 75, 76.

5. Surdam, *Wins, Losses, and Empty Seats*, 318.

6. *Time*, June 3, 1935.

7. Surdam, *Wins, Losses, and Empty Seats*, 227, 229.

8. Ibid., 229.

9. Ibid., 240.

10. "Famous Firsts: Night Games," *Baseball Almanac*, n.d., http://www.baseball-almanac.com/firsts/first10 .shtml.

11. John Drebinger, "Majors Raise Limit of Home Night Games to 14, Except for 21 at Washington," *New York Times*, February 4, 1942, 24; except in New York City, where night games were banned as making the city too visible to German U-boats; John Drebinger, "Dodgers Defeat Giants in Twilight Game Raising $59,859 for Navy Relief," *New York Times*, May 9, 1942, 16.

12. Shane Tourtellotte, "Day for Night," *The Hardball Times*, May 9, 2012, http://www.hardballtimes.com/day -for-night/.

CIRCA 1935–DUKE KAHANAMOKU'S SURFBOARD

1. Peter Westwick and Peter Neushul, *The World in the Curl: An Unconventional History of Surfing* (New York: Crown, 2013), 14.

2. Ben Marcus, "From Polynesia, with Love: The History of Surfing from Captain Cook to the Present," n.d., http://www.surfingforlife.com/history.html.

3. James Cook, Charles Clerke, John Gore, and James King, *A Voyage to the Pacific Ocean* (n.p., 1784), 3:147.

4. Westwick and Neushul, *World in the Curl*, 14–22.

5. *New Yorker*, August 24, 1992, 42.

6. "Surfing Heroes," n.d., http://www.clubofthewaves.com/surf-culture/surfing-heroes.php.

7. Ellie Crowe, *Surfer of the Century* (New York: Lee & Low Books, 2007), 13.

8. "About Duke," n.d., http://www.dukekahanamoku.com/about-duke/.

9. *New York Times*, February 16, 1920.

10. Westwick and Neushul, *World in the Curl*, 46.

11. Michael Scott Moore, *Sweetness and Blood: How Surfing Spread from Hawaii and California to the Rest of the World, with Some Unexpected Results* (New York: Rodale, 2010), 147.

12. Matt Warshaw, *The Encyclopedia of Surfing* (Orlando, FL: Harcourt, 2005), 309.

13. "Duke Kahanamoku and The Superhuman Rescue," WaterWays, June 14, 2015, http://www.theinertia.com/surf/duke-kahanamoku-and-the-superhuman-rescue/.

14. Michael Beschloss, "Duke of Hawaii: A Swimmer and Surfer Who Straddled Two Cultures," *The Upshot*, August 22, 2014, http://www.nytimes.com/2014/08/23/upshot/duke-of-hawaii-a-swimmer-and-surfer-who-straddled-two-cultures.html

15. "Kahanamoku, Duke," n.d., http://encyclopediaofsurfing.com/entries/kahanamoku-duke.

16. "Kahanamoku Given 'Beach Boy' Funeral," *New York Times*, January 29, 1968, http://query.nytimes.com/gst/abstract.html?res=9F05E4D81038E134BC4151DFB7668383679EDE.

1936—JESSE OWENS'S BATON FROM THE 4 X 100-METER RELAY

1. Here are some examples of how the story is usually told: Russell Baker, "Sunday Observer; Good Bad Sports," *New York Times*, February 1, 1976, http://query.nytimes.com/gst/abstract.html?res=9E0CE5DD163FE23BA15752C0A9649C946790D6CF: "[Hitler] blatantly snubbed Owens, a black man, for making a hash of Hitlerian theory about Aryan supremacy."

Ebony, September 1988, 120: "Jesse Owens delivered the most convincing blow in the fight for Black legitimacy in athletics. With Adolph Hitler looking on, Owens almost single-handedly debunked the German leader's self-proclaimed doctrine of Aryan supremacy."

Ebony, September 1988, 144: "The story of an incredible moment of truth when the son of a sharecropper and the grandson of slaves temporarily derailed the Nazi juggernaut and gave the lie to Hitler's theories on Aryan (read: White) supremacy."

Phil Taylor, "Flying in the Face of the Fuhrer: August 3–9 1936, Jesse Owens Dominates the Berlin Olympics," *Sports Illustrated*, November 29, 1999, http://www.si.com/vault/1999/11/29/270661/flying-in-the-face-of-the-fuhrer-august-3-9-1936-jesse-owens-dominates-the-berlin-olympics: "As he [Owens] raced past his competitors, he was more idea than man, a charcoal rebuttal to Nazi notions of Aryan supremacy."

"Revolutionary Moments in Sports," *Sports Illustrated*, April 26, 2010, http://www.si.com/more-sports/photos/2010/04/26-1revolutionary-moments-in-sports#2: "Olympics in Berlin as a showcase for Nazi Germany and the racial inferiority of African-Americans among ethnic groups."

Larry Schwartz, "Owens Pierced a Myth," ESPN, 2000, https://web.archive.org/web/20000706211910/http://espn.go.com/sportscentury/features/00016393.html: "In one week in the summer of 1936, on the sacred soil of the Fatherland, the master athlete humiliated the master race."

2. Mack Robinson, Jackie's older brother, won the silver medal in this event.

3. The image is available at http://www.olympic.org/Assets/MediaPlayer/Photos/TOM%20TREASURES/Jesse%20Owens/960/Jesse-Owens-et-Luz-Long.jpg.

4. Jeremy Schaap, *Triumph: The Untold Story of Jesse Owens and Hitler's Olympics* (Boston: Houghton Mifflin, 2007). Schaap notes that technically, Owens also set records in the 200-meter dash and 200-meter hurdles. The metric distances are slightly shorter, but Owens ran the longer distance faster than anyone had ever run the metric ones.

5. Arnd Kruger and William Murray, eds., *The Nazi Olympics: Sport, Politics, and Appeasement in the 1930s* (Champaign: University of Illinois Press, 2003), 49.

6. David K. Wiggins, *Glory Bound: Black Athletes in a White America* (Syracuse: Syracuse University Press, 1997), 66–67; Allen Guttmann, *The Olympics: A History of the Modern Games*, 2nd ed. (Urbana and Chicago: University of Illinois Press, 2002), 60.

7. See, for example, Carolyn Marvin, "Avery Brundage and American Participation in the 1936 Olympic Games," *Journal of American Studies* 16, no. 1 (1982): 91, http://repository.upenn.edu/cgi/viewcontent.cgi?article =1073&context=asc_papers.

8. The AAU's vote was close: 58.25 to 55.75.

9. Guy Walters, *Berlin Games: How Hitler Stole the Olympic Dream* (London: John Murray, 2012), 195.

10. Williams earned a degree in mechanical engineering from Berkeley. He later became an instructor of the Tuskegee Airmen, who would prove their mettle in the skies above Nazi Germany.

11. Archie F. Williams, "The Joy of Flying: Olympic Gold, Air Force Colonel, and Teacher," University of California Black Alumni Series, 1993, http://texts.cdlib.org/view?docId=kt0v19n496&doc.view=entire_text.

12. LuValle earned a PhD in chemistry and math from Caltech, working under Nobel laureate Linus Pauling.

13. James LuValle, "An Olympian's Oral History," 1988, http://library.la84.org/6oic/OralHistory/OH LuValle.pdf.

14. Arthur J. Daley, "Owens Captures Olympic Title, Equals World 100-Meter Record; Beats Metcalfe in 0:10.3 as U.S. Takes Lead in Men's Track and Field," *New York Times*, August 4, 1936, http://query.nytimes .com/gst/abstract.html?res=9C00E7DA1E3FEE3BBC4C53DFBE66838D629EDE.

15. He later joined the Dutch Nazi Party and served time in prison after the war for crimes committed during the occupation.

16. William Shirer, *The Nightmare Years* (Boston: Little, Brown, 1984), 234.

17. Quoted in Walters, *Berlin Games*, 221.

18. Rounding out the African American contingent were four boxers and two weight lifters, but they won no medals; Wiggins, *Glory Bound*, 73.

19. Quoted in the *Guardian*, December 21, 2011.

20. "Top Honors Captured by Germany as Olympic Games Are Concluded; Reich Gained More Medals in Berlin Than Any Other Country—Intense Nationalism Gave Its Entries Inspirational Lift," *New York Times*, August 17, 1936, http://query.nytimes.com/gst/abstract.html?res=9C07E1D8143CE53ABC4F52DFBE66838 D629EDE.

21. Kruger and Murray, *The Nazi Olympics*, 21.

22. "Berlin 1936: Television in Germany," n.d., http://www.tvhistory.tv/1936_German_Olympics_TV _Program_English.JPG.

23. Frederick William Rubien, ed., *Report of the American Olympic Committee: Games of the XIth Olympiad, Berlin, Germany, August 1 to 16, 1936* (n.p.: American Olympic Committee, 1937).

24. Report of the German Olympic Committee.

25. According to an account from a Swiss Olympian, Paul Martin, that extended to sex. Martin said there was a "love garden" in the corner of the village to which specially chosen maidens were given passes in order to sport with the athletes—but only the white ones. They got the Olympian's identification before sex; if they got pregnant, the state rewarded them. Thus would the Reich's racial stock be improved. When it comes to the Nazis and race, almost anything is conceivable. Still, the sourcing of this anecdote seemed too thin to include in the text, but the story is too interesting not to mention. From David Clay Large, *Nazi Games: The Olympics of 1936* (New York: WW Norton, 2007), 182–183.

26. William J. Baker, *Jesse Owens: An American Life* (Champaign: University of Illinois Press, 2006), 35.

27. Henry A. Slaughter, "Calls for Fair Play; Reader Would Welcome Tolerance 'in Fact' Here," *New York Times*, August 15, 1936, http://query.nytimes.com/gst/abstract.html?res=9B07E6D91130E13BBC4D52 DFBE66838D629EDE.

28. There were American Olympians who had previously won more medals, but either in lightly contested sports or in Olympics with few participants. For example, Marcus Hurley won four golds and a bronze in cycling in the 1904 Olympics, and Anton Heida won five golds and a silver in gymnastics. Only twelve countries

participated in the 1904 Games, however, which were a poorly organized sideshow to the St. Louis World's Fair, and Americans accounted for 526 of the 651 athletes. Owens's achievement in a bigger, more competitive environment is clearly more impressive.

29. Arthur Pincus, "50 Years Later, Bitter Memories of the Berlin Games," *New York Times*, August 10, 1986, http://www.nytimes.com/1986/08/10/sports/50-years-later-bitter-memories-of-the-berlin-games.html.

30. Baker, *Jesse Owens*, 107.

31. See images at http://www.businessinsider.com/photos-of-abandoned-olympic-village-in-berlin-2015-3 ?op=1.

1936—THE *HUSKY CLIPPER*

1. See entries on the 1980 Olympic hockey team and the 1954/1955 Indiana state basketball champions.

2. Daniel James Brown, *The Boys in the Boat: Nine Americans and Their Epic Quest for Gold at the 1936 Berlin Olympics* (New York: Viking, 2013), 286.

3. Michael J. Socolow, "Six Minutes in Berlin," Slate, [July 23, 2012], http://www.slate.com/articles/sports /fivering_circus/2012/07/_1936_olympics_rowing_the_greatest_underdog_nazi_defeating_american_olympic _victory_you_ve_never_heard_of_.html.

4. Daniel James Brown, *"The Boys in the Boat"*, June 12, 2013, https://www.youtube.com/watch?v=blb3k8 VTsTM.

5. *Saturday Evening Post*, June 19, 1937.

6. Dan Raley, "Events of the Century," *Seattle Post-Intelligencer*, December 21, 1999, http://www.seattlepi.com /sports/article/Events-of-the-century-3835569.php.

7. Brown, *The Boys in the Boat*, 346.

8. http://www.huskycrew.com/audio-video/BobMoch1936%2010-02.mp3; about 19:00.

9. Brown, *The Boys in the Boat*, 350.

10. "Washington Rowing: The 1936 Olympic Team," Husky Crew, n.d., http://www.huskycrew.com /Husky%20Crew%201936%20-%20The%20Boys%20In%20The%20Boat.htm.

11. The times were United States 6:25.4; Italy 6:26; Germany 6.26.4.

12. Alvin Ulbrickson with Richard L. Neuberger, "Now! Now! Now!" *Colliers*, June 26, 1937, 21.

13. Discussion of *The Boys in the Boat*, University of Washington Athletics, n.d., http://www.gohuskies.com /ViewArticle.dbml?DB_OEM_ID=30200&ATCLID=209853072.

1938—TOWEL THROWN INTO THE RING AT THE FIGHT BETWEEN JOE LOUIS AND MAX SCHMELING

1. Paul L. Montgomery, "Boxing; Schmeling Still Battles to Grasp the Past," *New York Times*, June 19, 1988, http://www.nytimes.com/1988/06/19/sports/boxing-schmeling-still-battles-to-grasp-the-past.html.

2. One estimate is that two out of three southerners were rooting for Joe Louis; see David Margolick, *Beyond Glory: Joe Louis vs Max Schmeling, and a World on the Brink* (New York: Knopf, 2005), 12, 141, 263.

3. Ibid., 171.

4. *Joe Louis: America's Hero Betrayed* (HBO documentary film, first aired February 23, 2008); 10:00.

5. *Joe Louis vs Max Schmeling, II*, January 23, 2013, https://www.youtube.com/watch?v=OSE281i5gNM; the fight starts at 6:40. Under US rules, throwing in the towel did not end the fight, and the ref tossed it back—but stopped the fight a few seconds later on his own authority.

6. "The Fight That Didn't Shake Their World," *Financial Times*, September 30, 2005, http://www.ft.com/intl /cms/s/2/8586e528-31d8-11da-9c7f-00000e2511c8.html.

7. Interview with Maya Angelou, 1992, for *The Great Depression*, Washington University Film and Media Archive, Henry Hampton Collection.

8. Margolick, *Beyond Glory*, 334.

9. *Joe Louis: America's Hero Betrayed*; 1:04:05

10. Edward Hotaling, *The Great Black Jockeys: The Lives and Times of the Men Who Dominated America's First National Sport* (Roseville, CA: Prima Lifestyles, 1999), 326–327.

11. Mark Kram, *Ghosts of Manila: The Fateful Blood Feud Between Muhammad Ali and Joe Frazier* (New York: HarperCollins, 2001), 63.

12. *Joe Louis: America's Hero Betrayed*; 28:35.

13. Margolick, *Beyond Glory*, 109.

1943–1954—HANDBOOK FROM THE ALL-AMERICAN GIRLS PROFESSIONAL BASEBALL LEAGUE

1. Merrie Fidler, *The Origins and History of the All-American Girls Professional Baseball League* (Jefferson, NC: McFarland, 2006), 23.

2. A worker in an explosives factory made about $1 an hour; see https://fraser.stlouisfed.org/scribd/?title _id=4294&filepath=/docs/publications/bls/bls_0819_1945.pdf#scribd-open, page 1.

3. There were cases when women would fill in due to resignations or financial troubles; see Fidler, *Origins and History of the All-American*, 162.

4. Patricia I. Brown, *A League of My Own: Memoir of Pitcher for the All-American Girls Professional Baseball League* (Jefferson, NC: McFarland, 2003), 41.

5. Clement C. GrawOzburn, "The Women of the All-American Girls Professional Baseball League: Pioneers in Their Own Right," *UW-L Journal of Undergraduate Research* 7 (2004): 5.

6. Jack Fincher, "The 'Belles of the Ball Game' Were a Hit with Their Fans," *Smithsonian Magazine*, July 1989, 92.

7. Fidler, *Origins and History of the All-American*, 196.

8. Ibid., 196, 174.

9. Carol Pierman, "Baseball, Conduct, and True Womanhood," *Women's Studies Quarterly* 33, nos. 1–2 (Spring 2005): 68–85.

10. Barbara Gregorich, *Women at Play: The Story of Women in Baseball* (San Diego, CA: Harcourt Brace, 1993), 86.

11. Fincher, "The 'Belles of the Ball Game,'" 89.

12. Gregorich, *Women at Play*, 92.

13. "The All American Girls Professional Baseball League," SeanLanham.com, n.d., http://seanlahman.com /baseball-archive/womens-baseball/.

14. Sam Carr, "Before A League of Their Own," National Baseball Hall of Fame, n.d., http://baseballhall.org /discover/baseball-history/there-is-crying-in-baseball.

1945—10TH MOUNTAIN DIVISION PARKA

1. *Fire and Ice: The Winter War of Finland and Russia*, August 13, 2013, https://www.youtube.comwatch?v =PMa3w8L92Xs.

2. Captain Thomas P. Govan, *Training for Mountain and Winter Warfare*, Study No. 23, 1946, http://www .skitrooper.org/agf.htm#BM1.

3. William Johnson, "Phantoms of the Snow," *Sports Illustrated*, February 8, 1971, http://www.si.com /vault/1971/02/08/554283/phantoms-of-the-snow.

4. *Mountain Fighters* (documentary, 1943).

5. Kenny Moore, *Bowerman and the Men of Oregon* (New York: Rodale, 2006), 69.

6. Charles Wellborn, *Official History of the 86th Mountain Infantry in Italy* (86th Headquarters Company, 1945), 7, http://10thmtndivassoc.org/86th/.

7. Peter Shelton, *Climb to Conquer* (New York: Scribner, 2003), 2; for an example of what these patrols were like, see Wellborn, *Official History of the 86th Mountain Infantry*, 4–5.

8. Shelton, *Climb to Conquer*, 139.

9. Ibid., 184.

10. John Imbrie, *Chronology of the 10th Mountain Division in World War II* (n.p.: National Association of the 10th Mountain Division, Incorporated, 2004), 29, http://www.10thmtndivassoc.org/chronology.pdf.

11. Tom Jenkins, "Assault on Riva Ridge," *American History*, December 2001, 52.

12. *Sports Afield*, January 2002, 46.

13. Charles Sanders, *The Boys of Winter: Life and Death in the U.S. Ski Troops During the Second World War* (2005), 201.

14. One of Vail's most popular runs is called Riva Ridge.

15. Shelton, *Climb to Conquer*, 233.

16. Ibid., 139.

17. Bill Pennington, "The Legacy of the Soldiers on Skis," *New York Times*, March 10, 2006, http://www.nytimes.com/2006/03/10/travel/escapes/10ski.html.

1947–JACKIE ROBINSON'S JERSEY

1. Kostya Kennedy, "Keeper of the Flame," *Sports Illustrated*, April 16, 2012, http://www.si.com/vault/2012/04/16/106181606/keeper-of-the-flame.

2. Jackie's older brother Mack was also a great athlete, finishing second to Jesse Owens in the 200 meters in the 1936 Olympics.

3. Arthur Ashe, *A Hard Road to Glory* (New York: Warner Books, 1988), 41.

4. Robert Lipsyte and Peter Levine, *Idols of the Game: A Sporting History of the American Century* (Atlanta, GA: Turner Publishing, 1995), 174.

5. William Kashatus, "Baseball's Noble Experiment," *American History*, March/April 1997, 32.

6. Herbert Warren Wind, ed., *The Realm of Sport* (New York: Simon & Schuster, 1966), 62.

7. Jimmy Breslin, *Branch Rickey* (New York: Viking, 2011), 57.

8. Ibid., 77.

9. Arnold Rampersad, *Jackie Robinson: A Biography* (London: Random House, 1997), 164.

10. Earl Brown, *Amsterdam News*, April 19, 1947.

11. Ibid.

12. SABR Biography Project, http://sabr.org/bioproj/person/bb9e2490.

13. Bill James, *The New Bill James Historical Baseball Abstract* (New York: Simon & Schuster, 2001), 361.

14. *Sports Illustrated*, April 15, 2015.

15. Kashatus, "Baseball's Noble Experiment," 32.

16. Ira Berkow, "The Doors Were Open, But Reception Was Hostile," *New York Times*, April 13, 1987, http://www.nytimes.com/1987/04/13/sports/the-doors-were-open-but-reception-was-hostile.html.

17. Jackie Robinson (as told to Alfred Duckett), *I Never Had It Made* (New York: Putnam, 1972), 91.

18. Ibid., 7.

19. Lipsyte and Levine, *Idols of the Game*, 179.

20. Rampersad, *Jackie Robinson*, 16.

21. Ibid., 551.

22. Robinson, *I Never Had It Made*, 250.

1949–ORIGINAL ICE-RESURFACING MACHINE

1. "Sun Valley, Idaho: History," n.d., http://www.gonorthwest.com/Idaho/central/Sun-Valley/svhistory.htm.

2. Christian Roman, *Times Minute: Origins of the Ski Lift* (video), *New York Times Magazine*, February 21, 2014, http://www.nytimes.com/video/multimedia/100000002726690/times-minute-origins-of-the-ski-lift.html.

3. James Surowiecki, *The Wisdom of Crowds* (New York: Anchor Books, 2005), 242.

4. See a video showing the 1946 version at *Bowling's Electric Brain (1946)—The World's First Automatic Pinsetter*, February 20, 2012, https://www.youtube.com/watch?v=DogVYVOqMNg.

5. Old Bowling, http://oldbowling.com/.

6. Andrew Hurley, *Diners, Bowling Alleys, and Trailer Parks: Chasing the American Dream in the Postwar Consumer Culture* (New York: Basic Books, 2001), 143.

7. Paul Harber, "Putting the Cart before the Horse?," April 18, 1998, http://www.greensandgo.com/history.htm.

8. "The Zamboni Story," n.d., http://zamboni.com/about/zamboni-archives/the-zamboni-story/.

9. Ibid.

10. Matthews Shaer, "Remembering Frank Zamboni, the original 'Iceman'," *Christian Science Monitor*, January 16, 2013, http://www.csmonitor.com/Technology/2013/0116/Remembering-Frank-Zamboni-the-original-Iceman-video.

11. "The Zamboni Machine Genealogy," n.d., http://www.zamboni.com/wp-content/uploads/2014/09/Timeline-2013_updated1.jpg.

12. "Fun Facts," Zamboni, n.d., http://zamboni.com/about/fun-facts/.

13. *Los Angeles Times*, June 4, 1988.

14. Charlie Brown quotes, ThinkExist.com, n.d., http://thinkexist.com/quotation/there-are-three-things-in-life-that-people-like/565998.html.

1952—TIGERBELLE MAE FAGGS'S SHOES FROM THE HELSINKI OLYMPICS

1. Until 1968, the official name was Tennessee Agricultural & Industrial State University. For the purposes of this book, I credit a medal to any woman who competed for TSU, even if she was not a student at the time.

2. Ed Temple, with B'Lou Carter, *Only the Pure in Heart Survive* (Nashville, TN: Broadman Press, 1980), 19.

3. Patrick B. Miller and David Wiggins, *Sport and the Color Line: Athletes and Race Relations in 20th-Century America* (New York and London: Routledge, 2004), 253.

4. John C. Walker and Malina Iida, eds., *Better Than the Best: Black Athletes Speak, 1920–2007* (Seattle and London: University of Washington Press, 2010).

5. Tracey Salisbury, "First to the Finish Line: The Tennessee State Tigerbelles 1944–1994" (PhD diss., University of North Carolina/Greensboro, 2009).

6. "Tennessee State University: An Olympic Tradition," n.d., http://www.tsu-alumni.org/olympic.htm#med; this tally includes Ralph Boston's medals. He was a TSU student, but obviously not a Tigerbelle.

7. Ibid. The exception was Willye B. White, who left TSU after a year for rebelling against Temple's strict rules, including no riding in cars. White was the first American to compete in five Olympics (1956 through 1972). A long jumper/sprinter, she won a silver medal in the 4 x 100-meter relay with two other Tigerbelles.

8. The graduation rate for all Tigerbelles from 1944 to 1994 was between 85 and 90 percent, depending on how it is calculated (Salisbury, "First to the Finish Line," 231).

9. Karen Rosen and Doug Williams, "Ed Temple," Team USA Hall of Fame, n.d., http://www.teamusa.org/HOF-Class-of-2012-Home/HOF-Class-of-2012-Ed-Temple.

10. *Wilma Rudolph*, October 2, 2009, https://www.youtube.com/watch?v=q4C5l11QnEQ; Wilma Rudolph, *Wilma* (New York: New American Library, 1977), 38.

11. Ibid., 17.

12. Ibid., 81.

13. Rob Bagchi, "50 Stunning Olympic Moments No. 35: Wilma Rudolph's Triple Gold in 1960," *The Guardian*, June 1, 2012, http://www.theguardian.com/sport/blog/2012/jun/01/50-stunning-olympic-moments-wilma-rudolph.

14. David Maraniss, *Rome 1960: The Summer Olympics That Stirred the World* (New York: Simon & Schuster, 2009).

15. "Honoring Wilma Rudolph," *New York Times*, November 19, 1994, http://www.nytimes.com/1994/11/19/sports/honoring-wilma-rudolph.html.

16. "Like Nothing Else in Tennessee," *Sports Illustrated*, November 14, 1960.

17. Temple and Carter, *Only the Pure in Heart Survive*, 29.

18. David K. Wiggins and R. Pierre eds., *Rivals: Legendary Matchups That Made Sports History* (Fayetteville: University of Arkansas Press, 2010), 347.

19. Salisbury, "First to the Finish Line," 208.

20. Jackie Joyner-Kersee (with Sonja Steptoe), *A Kind of Grace: The Autobiography of the World's Greatest Female Athlete* (New York: Warner Books, 1997), 85.

1952–MAGAZINE COVER FEATURING TOMMY KONO

1. "Who Is Tommy Kono?," n.d., http://www.tommykono.com/.

2. *Tommy Kono Speaks,* series promo, August 24, 2014, https://www.youtube.com/watch?v=H4jDsFe-rqo.

3. Burkhard Bilger, "The Strongest Man in the World," *New Yorker*, July 23, 2012, http://www.newyorker.com/magazine/2012/07/23/the-strongest-man-in-the-world.

4. Joseph R. Svinth, "Tommy Kono," January 2000, http://ejmas.com/pt/ptart_svinth_0100.htm.

5. "Tommy Kono," *Sports Reference*, n.d., http://www.sports-reference.com/olympics/athletes/ko/tommy-kono-1.html.

6. Frank Litsky, "Tommy Kono, Weight-Lifting Champion Raised in Internment Camp, Dies at 85," *New York Times*, April 30, 2016.

7. Svinth, "Tommy Kono."

8. "Tommy Tmnio Kono," *Lift Up*, n.d., http://www.chidlovski.net/liftup/l_galleryResult.asp?a_id=274.

1954/1955–MILAN HIGH SCHOOL LETTER JACKET AND OSCAR ROBERTSON'S CRISPUS ATTUCKS JERSEY

1. Wood had also coached at French Lick, where another Indiana hoops legend, Larry Bird, was born in 1956.

2. Greg Guffy, *The Greatest Basketball Story Ever Told: The Milan Miracle, Then and Now* (Bloomington: Indiana University Press, 1993), 49.

3. *1954 IHSAA State Championship Milan v.s Muncie Central*, September 28, 2014, https://www.youtube.com/watch?v=aZ1_4YCGiLw; go to about 32:50.

4. Bob Cook, "Crispus Attucks High, 60 Years Later: Race and the 'Hoosiers' Sequel Never Made," *Forbes*, December 29, 2014, http://www.forbes.com/sites/bobcook/2014/12/29/crispus-attucks-high-60-years-later-race-and-the-hoosiers-sequel-never-made/.

5. Wayne Drehs, "The Forgotten Hoosiers," ESPN, February 26, 2009, http://sports.espn.go.com/blackhistory2009/news/story?id=3932017.

6. IHSAA Boys Basketball State Champions, http://www.ihsaa.org/Sports/Boys/Basketball/StateChampions/tabid/124/Default.aspx.

7. *New York Times*, May 22, 2015.

8. Drehs, "Forgotten Hoosiers."

9. The movie clip is available for comparison, at https://www.youtube.com/watch?v=A0QTBAWc3tM.

10. Drehs, "Forgotten Hoosiers."

1955–PAINTING OF STILLMAN'S GYM

1. A. J. Liebling, *Just Enough Liebling: Classic Work by the Legendary "New Yorker" Writer* (New York: North Point Press, 2005), 370.

2. Edward Rohrbough, "The Tough and Tender at New York's Stillman's Gym," *Honolulu Record*, November 21, 1957, 4, http://www.hawaii.edu/uhwo/clear/HonoluluRecord/articles/v10n17/The%20Tough%20And%20Tender%20At%20New%20Yorks%20Stillmans%20Gym.html.

3. John Garfield, "Stillman's Gym: The Center of the Boxing Universe," *WAIL! The CBZ Journal* (2001), http://cyberboxingzone.com/boxing/w0502-jg.htm.

4. Budd Schulberg, *Sparring with Hemingway* (Chicago: I. R. Dee, 1995), 64.

5. Angelo Dundee and Bert Sugar, *My View from the Corner: A Life in Boxing* (New York: McGraw Hill, 2007), 27.

6. *New Yorker*, May 11, 1929, 25.

7. Mike Casey, "The Recollections of Whitey Bimstein," February 1, 2013, http://www.boxing.com/the_recollections_of_whitey_bimstein.html.

8. Franklin Foer and Marc Tracy, eds., *Jewish Jocks: An Unorthodox Hall of Fame* (New York and Boston: Twelve, 2012), 33.

9. "Louis Watches Pastor; Sees Workout at Stillman's Gym—Conn Boxes Five Rounds,"*New York Times*, August 2, 1940, http://query.nytimes.com/gst/abstract.html?res=9406E5DF1638E532A25751C0A96E9C946193D6CF.

10. "Champ and Chump," *The Economist*, May 5, 2005, http://www.economist.com/node/3935978.

11. Howard M. Tuckner, "Final Bell Tolls for Stillman's and Owner Doesn't Care; Garage Will Replace Boxing Landmark on 8th Avenue," *New York Times*, February 8, 1959, http://query.nytimes.com/gst/abstract.html?res=9B05E2D81738EF3BBC4053DFB4668382649EDE.

1956—YOGI BERRA'S CATCHER'S MITT

1. "Yogi Berra," Baseball-Reference.com, n.d., http://www.baseball-reference.com/players/b/berrayo01.shtml.

2. "Most Seasons on a World Series Winning Team," n.d., http://www.baseball-reference.com/leaders/leaders_most_rings.shtml.

3. "Yogisms," n.d., http://yogiberramuseum.org/just-for-fun/yogisms/.

4. Rob Fleder, ed., *Sports Illustrated: Fifty Years of Great Writing; 50th Anniversary, 1954–2004* (New York: Liberty Street, 2004), 36.

5. Yogi Berra, as told to T. Paxton, "Everything Happens to Me," *Saturday Evening Post*, April 29, 1950.

6. Tom Verducci, "Remembering the Great American Life of Yankees Legend Yogi Berra," September 23, 2015, http://www.si.com/mlb/2015/09/23/yogi-berra-new-york-yankees-catcher-dies-90-obituary#.

7. *Time*, October 22, 1956, 81.

8. The owner of the White Sox, Chuck Comiskey, ranked him third in this regard, for example. See *Saturday Evening Post*, June 15, 1957, 37.

9. Fleder, *Sports Illustrated: Fifty Years of Great Writing*, 41.

10. Verducci, "Remembering the Great American Life of Yankees Legend Yogi Berra."

1958—FIRST MODERN ARTHROSCOPE

1. Hans Passler and Yuping Yang, "The Past and the Future of Arthroscopy," in *Sports Injuries: Prevention, Diagnosis, Treatment and Rehabilitation*, ed. M. N. Doral et al., 5–13 (Heidelberg, Germany: Springer, 2012).

2. Sung-Jae Kim and Sang-Jin Shin, "Technical Evolution of Arthroscopic Knee Surgery," *Yonsei Medical Journal* 40, no. 6 (1999): 569.

3. R. W. Jackson, "Memories of the Early Days of Arthroscopy: 1965–1975," *Arthroscopy: The Journal of Arthroscopic and Related Surgery* 3, no. 1 (1987): 1–3.

4. Marlene DeMaio, "Giants of Arthroscopic Surgery," *Clinical Orthopaedics and Related Research* (August 2013), http://www.ncbi.nlm.nih.gov/pmc/articles/PMC3705061/#CR18.

5. Lorraine Bigony, "Arthroscopic Surgery: A Historical Perspective," *Orthopaedic Nursing* (November/December 2008): 349.

6. William Oscar Johnson, "A Man Who Gets All the Breaks," *Sports Illustrated*, February 21, 1983, http://www.si.com/vault/1983/02/21/627228/a-man-who-gets-all-the-breaks.

7. Jane E. Brody, "Knee Microsurgery: Boon to Some, But Overuse Is a Growing Concern," *New York Times*, February 25, 1986, http://www.nytimes.com/1986/02/25/science/knee-microsurgery-boon-to-some-but-overuse -is-a-growing-concern.html.

8. Passler and Yang, "The Past and the Future of Arthroscopy," 12.

9. "Tommy John Surgery: All-Time List," MLB Reports, n.d., http://mlbreports.com/tj-surgery/.

10. "Tommy John FAQ," n.d., PitchSmart, http://m.mlb.com/pitchsmart/tommy-john-faq.

11. Stephanie Apstein, "Tommy John Casualties," *Sports Illustrated,* July 6, 2015, http://www.si.com /vault/2016/02/11/tommy-john-casualties.

1958—ARTIFACTS FROM THE "GREATEST GAME"

1. Three were coaches: Tom Landry, defensive coach of the Giants; Vince Lombardi, the offensive coach for the Giants; and Weeb Ewbank, head coach of the Colts.

2. Lou Sahadi, *Johnny Unitas: America's Quarterback* (Chicago: Triumph Books, 2004), 15.

3. Larry Schwartz, "Unitas Led Colts to Win in NFL's Greatest Game," ESPN Classic, June 21, 2004, http:// espn.go.com/classic/s/unitasjohnnyadd.html. Mackey would later be diagnosed with CTE (see 2016 entry).

4. Frank Litsky, "Pro Football: There Were Better Games. None More Important," *New York Times*, December 16, 1998, http://www.nytimes.com/1998/12/16/sports/pro-football-there-were-better-games-none-more-important.html.

5. $38,745 in 2015 dollars; the Colts' owner, Carroll Rosenbloom, matched this. The winning share of the 2015 Super Bowl was $165,000. Unitas was making $17,550 in 1958; Ameche, who made $20,000, was the highest paid Colt. Marchetti was making $11,250.

6. Jack Cavanaugh, *Giants Among Men: How Robustelli, Huff, Gifford, and the Giants Made New York a Football Town and Changed the NFL* (New York: Random House, 2008), 178.

7. For highlights of the game, see *Johnny Unitas Defeats New York Giants in 1958 Pro-grid Championship*, January 9, 2012, https://www.youtube.com/watch?v=LG3mjPaIwSk.

8. Cavanaugh, *Giants Among Men*, 181.

9. Mark Bowden, *The Best Game Ever: Giants vs. Colts, 1958, and the Birth of the Modern NFL* (New York: Atlantic Monthly Press, 2008), 208.

10. Michael MacCambridge, *Lamar Hunt: A Life in Sports* (Kansas City, MO: Andrews McMeel Publishing, 2012), 115; Dave Anderson, "Sports of *The Times*: A New York-Baltimore History Lesson for the N.F.L.," *New York Times*, January 21, 2001, http://www.nytimes.com/2001/01/21/sports/sports-of-the-times-a-new-york -baltimore-history-lesson-for-the-nfl.html.

1959—STATUE OF LAMAR HUNT

1. Gerald Eskenazi, "Lamar Hunt, a Force in Football, Dies at 74," *New York Times*, December 15, 2006, http://www.nytimes.com/2006/12/15/sports/football/15hunt.html?_r=0.

2. Michael MacCambridge, *Lamar Hunt: A Life in Sports* (Kansas City, MO: Andrews McMeel Publishing, 2012), prologue.

3. Ibid.

4. Eskenazi, "Lamar Hunt, a Force in Football."

5. Eric Allen Hall, *Arthur Ashe: Tennis and Justice in the Civil Rights Era* (Baltimore, MD: Johns Hopkins University Press, 2014), 149.

6. MacCambridge, *Lamar Hunt*, ch. 14.

7. Ibid., ch. 15.

8. "The Legacy of Lamar Hunt," FC Dallas, n.d., http://www.fcdallas.com/club/legacy.

9. MacCambridge, *Lamar Hunt*, epilogue.

1960–PETE ROZELLE'S TYPEWRITER

1. *Sports Illustrated*, January 21, 1980.

2. Michael MacCambridge, *America's Game: The Epic Story of How Pro Football Captured a Nation* (New York: Anchor Books, 2004), 144.

3. Ibid., 148.

4. Kenneth Rudeen, "Sportsman of the Year," *Sports Illustrated*, January 6, 1964, http://www.si.com/vault /1964/01/06/608138/sportsman-of-the-year.

5. Peter King, Paul Zimmerman, Austin Murphy, and Michael Silver, "The Path to Power: How Did Pro Football Become, at Century's End, the Titan of American Sports?," *Sports Illustrated*, August 30, 1999, http:// www.si.com/vault/1999/08/30/265643/the-path-to-power-how-did-pro-football-become-at-centurys-end-the-titan -of-american-sports-eight-landmarks-one-from-each-decade-of-the-nfls-existence-were-critical-to-its-success.

6. MacCambridge, *America's Game*, 106.

7. Dale L. Cressman and Lisa Swenson, "The Pigskin and the Picture Tube," *Journal of Broadcasting and Electronic Media* (September 2007): 492.

8. $73.1 million and $214.4 million in 2015 dollars, respectively.

9. Rudeen, "Sportsman of the Year."

10. MacCambridge, *America's Game*, xvii.

11. Larry Felser, *The Birth of the New NFL* (Guilford, CT: Lyon's Press, 2008), 97.

12. MacCambridge, *America's Game*, 230.

13. Felser, *Birth of the New NFL*, 8.

1960–ARNOLD PALMER'S VISOR FROM THE US OPEN

1. "1960 US Open at Cherry Hills," n.d., http://www.arnoldpalmer.com/experience/exhibits/1960_usopen_ cherryhills.aspx.

2. Herbert Warren Wind, *Following Through* (New York: Ticknor & Fields, 1985), 201.

3. Ibid., 204.

4. Jack Nicklaus and Ken Bowden, *Jack Nicklaus: My Story* (New York: Simon & Schuster, 1997), 34.

5. $115,460 and $15,635 in 2015 dollars, respectively.

6. *Saturday Evening Post*, June 18, 1960 (with Will Grimsley).

7. $28,063 in 2015 dollars.

8. Mike Walker, "After Arnold Palmer Came to St. Andrews in 1960, American Golf Was Never the Same Again," *Golf,* July 15, 2010/December 1, 2014, http://www.golf.com/tour-and-news/after-arnold-palmer-came -st-andrews-1960-american-golf-was-never-same-again.

9. Jay Busbee, "How Arnold Palmer Changed Golf Forever," July 17, 2013, http://sports.yahoo.com/news/ golf--how-arnold-palmer-changed-golf-forever-084900662.html.

10. Thomas Hauser, *Thomas Hauser on Sports: Remembering the Journey* (Fayetteville: University of Arkansas Press, 2013), 64.

11. $647,366 in 2015 dollars.

12. Ray Cave, "Sportsman of the Year: Arnold Palmer," *Sports Illustrated*, January 9, 1961, http://www.si.com /vault/1961/01/09/578878/sportsman-of-the-year-arnold-palmer.

1962–BILL RUSSELL'S 10,000-REBOUND BALL

1. Aram Goudsouzian, "Bill Russell and the Basketball Revolution," *American Studies* (Fall–Winter 2006): 65.

2. Gilbert Rogin, "'We Are Grown Men Playing a Child's Game'," *Sports Illustrated*, November 18, 1963, http://www.si.com/vault/1963/11/18/594385/we-are-grown-men-playing-a-childs-game.

3. Bill Russell with Alan Steinberg, *Red and Me: My Coach, My Lifelong Friend* (New York: HarperCollins, 2009), xi.

4. In the same draft, the Celtics also took K. C. Jones, who did not compete that year because of a military commitment. This may have been the most successful draft in NBA history—all three made the Hall of Fame.

5. Bob Ryan, "Timeless Excellence," *NBA Encyclopedia*, playoff ed., n.d., http://www.nba.com/encyclopedia /players/bill_russell.html.

6. "Bill Russell," Basketball-Reference.com, n.d., http://www.basketball-reference.com/players/r/russebi01 .html.

7. Wilt Chamberlain had 10, including the top 7, and Jerry Lucas had 1. Chamberlain also had more rebounds (23,924) and a slightly higher per game average (22.9).

8. Lew Freedman, *Dynasty: Auerbach, Cousy, Havlicek, Russell, and the Rise of the Boston Celtics* (Guilford, CT: Globe Pequot Press, 2011), 84.

9. William F. Russell and Taylor Branch, *Second Wind: The Memoirs of an Opinionated Man* (New York: Random House, 1979), 140.

10. Ibid., 129; Brown died in 1964.

11. Randy Roberts, *"But They Can't Beat Us": Oscar Robertson and the Crispus Attucks Tigers* (Champaign, IL: Sports Publishing; [Indianapolis, IN]: Indiana Historical Society, 1999), 73.

12. Russell and Branch, *Second Wind*, 202.

13. Freedman, *Dynasty*, epilogue. Russell's attitude has been less unyielding since. When the Celtics moved out of the Garden into new premises in 1995, he went to the grand opening, and when the city unveiled a statue of him downtown in 2013, he went to that, too.

1966—MARVIN MILLER'S UNION CONTRACT

1. Robinson would change his mind, telling a federal court in 1970: "Anything that is one-sided is wrong in America. The reserve clause is one-sided in favor of the owners and should be modified to give the player some control over his destiny." See Mary Kay Linge, *Jackie Robinson: A Biography* (Westport, CT: Greenwood Press, 2007), 146.

2. Tom Verducci, "[Forty for the Ages]: 7: Marvin Miller," *Sports Illustrated*, September 19, 1994, http://www .si.com/vault/1994/09/19/132057/7-marvin-miller#.

3. Larry Burke and Peter Thomas Fornatale, *Change Up: An Oral History of 8 Key Events That Shaped Modern Baseball* (New York: Rodale, 2008), 103.

4. In 2015 dollars, $47,740 to $68,200.

5. Burke and Fornatale, *Change Up*, 103.

6. "May 23, 1970: Second CBA Brings Impartial Arbitrator to Baseball," MLBPlayers.com, May 23, 2016, http://mlb.mlb.com/pa/news/article.jsp?ymd=20160523&content_id=179790802&vkey=mlbpa_news&fext=.jsp.

7. Brad Snyder, *A Well-Paid Slave: Curt Flood's Fight for Free Agency in Professional Sports* (New York: Viking, 2006), 81.

8. *Flood v. Kuhn*, 407 U.S. 258 (1972), https://supreme.justia.com/cases/federal/us/407/258/case.html.

9. Robert F. Burk, *Marvin Miller: Baseball Revolutionary* (Urbana: University of Illinois Press, 2015), 173.

10. Ibid., 180.

11. Ibid., 178.

12. "MLBPA Info: Frequently Asked Questions," MLBPlayers.com, n.d., http://mlb.mlb.com/pa/info/faq .jsp#minimum.

13. Ibid.

14. Malcolm Gladwell, "Annals of Business: Talent Grab," *New Yorker*, October 11, 2010, 87.

15. Vin Getz, "Major League Baseball's Average Salaries 1964–2010," Sports List of the Day, December 5, 2011, http://sportslistoftheday.com/2011/12/05/major-league-baseballs-average-salaries-1964--2010/. In 2015 dollars, $17,664 in 1966 is equivalent to $129,392; $245,000 in 1982 is $602,563.

16. "MLBPA Info: Frequently Asked Questions."

17. $46.5 million in 2015 dollars.

18. New York Yankees, "The Business of Baseball: 2015 Ranking," *Forbes*, n.d., http://www.forbes.com/teams /new-york-yankees/.

1967—KATHRINE SWITZER'S BIB FROM THE BOSTON MARATHON

1. Roberta "Bobbi" Gibbs, "A Run of One's Own," Running Past, n.d., runningpast.com/gibb_story.htm. With a time of 3:21, Gibbs finished in the top third of the field. She also ran unregistered in 1967, finishing an hour ahead of Switzer, and in 1968, and as a registered runner in 1983, 1996, and 2001.

2. Kathrine Switzer, *Marathon Woman: Running the Race to Revolutionize Women's Sports* (New York: Carroll & Graf, 2007), 73.

3. "Famed Runners Kathrine Switzer, Roger Robinson to Speak at AHS, Auburn Citizen," October 12, 2014, http://kathrineswitzer.com/about-kathrine/kathrine-switzer-faqs/F.

4. "Boston Marathon History: Participation," n.d., http://www.baa.org/races/boston-marathon/boston -marathon-history/participation.aspx.

5. "Kathrine Switzer, the Woman Behind Those Numbers," n.d., http://www.261fearless.org/about-261-and -kathrine-switzer/.

6. "Boston Marathon Yearly Synopses (1897–2013)," [2014], http://www.johnhancock.com/bostonmarathon /mediaguide/5-racesynopsis.php.

7. Switzer, *Marathon Woman*, 116.

8. Ibid., 217.

1967—BENCH FROM THE ICE BOWL

1. Mary Kornely, "The Ice Bowl," *Wisconsin Weather Stories*, n.d., http://weatherstories.ssec.wisc.edu/stories/ice bowl.html.

2. Shirley Povich, "Even at Top, Lombardi Looked Up," *Washington Post*, September 4, 1970, http://www .washingtonpost.com/wp-srv/sports/longterm/general/povich/launch/lombardi.htm.

3. Michael MacCambridge, *America's Game: The Epic Story of How Pro Football Captured a Nation* (New York: Anchor Books, 2004), 243.

4. Jerry Kramer, *Instant Replay: The Green Bay Diary of Jerry Kramer,* ed. Dick Schaap (New York: World Publishing, 1968), 256.

5. David Claerbaut, *Bart Starr: When Leadership Mattered* (Dallas, TX: Taylor Trade, 2012), 185.

6. *Sports Illustrated,* July 7, 2011.

7. *Vince Lombardi: A Football Life—The Ice Bowl*, March 10, 2015, https://www.youtube.com/watch?v=FhNn 7ENixBY.

8. Kramer, *Instant Replay,* 259.

9. David Maraniss, *When Pride Still Mattered: A Life of Vince Lombardi* (New York: Simon & Schuster, 1999), 427.

10. The Packers also won three in a row in 1929, 1930, and 1931. No one else has done so.

1968—STATUE OF TOMMIE SMITH AND JOHN CARLOS

1. Harry Edwards, *The Revolt of the Black Athlete* (New York: Free Press, 1969), 59.

2. Dave Zirin and John Wesley Carlos, *The John Carlos Story: The Sports Moment That Changed the World* (Chicago: Haymarket Books, 2011), 82, 85.

3. Ibid., 91.

4. Harry Edwards put one vote at 13 in favor of competing, 12 against, and one undecided; *The Revolt of the Black Athlete*, 98.

5. David Zirin, *A People's History of Sports in the United States* (New York: New Press; distr. by Norton, 2008), 174.

6. Zirin and Carlos, *The John Carlos Story*, 100.

7. Norman would pay for his support. Widely criticized back in Australia, he was left off the 1972 Olympic team, though he was still the country's best sprinter, and wasn't even invited to the Sydney Olympics in 2000. The US team made him their guest. When he died in 2006, Smith and Carlos traveled to Australia to serve as pallbearers.

8. Smith himself makes the military connection. See Tommie Smith and David Steele, *Silent Gesture: The Autobiography of Tommie Smith* (Philadelphia: Temple University Press, 2007), 139.

9. The iconography of the various elements is somewhat disputed. Carlos does not mention the scarf; Smith says he wore it to represent black pride. See Kevin Witherspoon, *Before the Eyes of the World: Mexico and the 1968 Olympic Games* (DeKalb: Northern Illinois University Press, 2008), 131. In addition, both men take credit for the idea of the glove.

10. *63: Black Power Salute*, April 6, 2014, https://www.youtube.com/watch?v=QCNkW2kNcjw.

11. Smith and Steele, *Silent Gesture*, 173.

12. See the BBC coverage from that evening at *1968 Olympics: The Black Power Salute*, July 20, 2012, https://www.youtube.com/watch?v=jnvCiKUlLAw, at about 39:10.

13. "American Olympic Medal Winners Suspended for Black Power Salutes," *New York Times*, October 18, 1968.

14. Michael Llewellyn Smith, *Days of 1896: Athens and the Invention of the Modern Olympic Games* (New York: Greekworks.com, 2005), 108.

15. "An Olympian's Oral History: Monique Berlioux," 2015, http://library.la84.org/6oic/OralHistory/OH Berlioux.pdf, 40.

16. Ibid., 41.

17. Ibid.

18. Smith, *Days of 1896*, 172. In a truly Orwellian and entirely characteristic post-Games twist, Brundage urged the Mexican authorities not to mention or show the moment in their official report. The Mexicans ignored him.

19. "The Show Goes On," *New York Times*, September 6, 1972, http://timesmachine.nytimes.com/times machine/1972/09/06/81957931.html?pageNumber=51.

20. Michael Janofsky, "A Departure from the Past," *New York Times*, April 9, 1990, http://www.nytimes.com/1990/04/09/sports/a-departure-from-the-past.html.

21. *Olympics Games Mexico 68: Vera Caslavska*, May 17, 2009, https://www.youtube.com/watch?v=lksI8O8_u7M; go to the 2:30 mark.

22. In 1985, to his credit, IOC president Juan Antonio Samaranch insisted on seeing her in order to give her the Olympic Order, and thereafter the restrictions loosened; Janofsky, "A Departure from the Past."

23. Simon Burnton, "50 Stunning Olympic Moments No. 41: Emil Zatopek the Triple-Gold Winner," *The Guardian*, June 22, 2012, http://www.theguardian.com/sport/blog/2012/jun/22/50-olympic-stunning-moments-emil-zatopek.

24. Tal Pinchevsky, *Breakaway: From Behind the Iron Curtain to the NHL—The Untold Story of Hockey's Great Escapes* (New York: Wiley, 2012), 37.

25. Tomas Bouska and Klara Pinerova, interview with Augustin Bubnik, in *Czechoslovak Political Prisoners* (published by author, 2009), 97–113.

26. Like Čáslavská, Sohn bowed his head during the Japanese anthem; he also covered the Japanese flag on his jersey with the oak plant given to all winners. South Korea, and Sohn, eventually turned the tables neatly. In

1948 he led the first independent South Korean team at the London Olympics, and in 1988 he lit the torch at the opening ceremonies in Seoul.

27. The People's Republic had a small delegation in 1952; arriving late, it only competed in one event.

28. "Tommie Smith," *SportsLetter Interviews* 18, no. 5 (April 2007), http://library.la84.org/SportsLibrary/SL Interviews/TommieSmith.pdf.

29. "Olympics a Stage for Political Contests, Too," WBUR, February 28, 2008, http://www.wbur.org/npr /87767864.

1968/1975—ARTHUR ASHE'S RACKETS

1. $95,480 and $40,920 in 2015 dollars, respectively.

2. Prize money, United States Tennis Association, http://www.usopen.org/en_US/about/history/prizemoney.html.

3. $1.6 million in 1979 dollars is $5.23 million in 2015 dollars.

4. $1.49 million in 2015 dollars; Eric Allen Hall, *Arthur Ashe: Tennis and Justice in the Civil Rights Era* (Baltimore, MD: Johns Hopkins University Press, 2014), 208.

5. Peter Bodo, *Ashe vs Connors: Wimbledon 1975; Tennis That Went beyond Centre Court* (London: Aurum Press, 2015), ch. 9.

6. Aimee Lewis, "Wimbledon: How Arthur Ashe Became Only Black Man to Win Title," BBC Sport, June 25, 2015, bbc.com/sport/tennis/33228456.

7. Quoted in Bodo, *Ashe vs Connors*, epilogue.

8. Paul Fein, *Tennis Confidential: Today's Greatest Players, Matches, and Controversies* (Washington, DC: Brassey's, 2002), ch. 21.

9. Bodo, *Ashe vs Connors*, ch. 10.

10. Ray Kennedy, "Howard Head Says 'I'm Giving Up the Thing World'," *Sports Illustrated*, September 29, 1980, http://www.si.com/vault/1980/09/29/825010/howard-head-says-im-giving-up-the-thing-world-the -inventor-of-the-revolutionary-head-ski-and-prince-racket-has-decided-that-the-world-will-have-to-wait-for-a -better-snorkel-at-66-hes-geared-down-savoring-life-and-trying-to-quotr; Howard Head Papers, 1926–1991, Archives Center, National Museum of American History, http://amhistory.si.edu/archives/d8589.htm.

11. *Ski* magazine, November 20, 2006.

12. 1976: Prince Classic, http://www.princetennis.com/inside-prince/history/1976/.

13. *Engineering and Technology*, August 2013.

14. Arthur Ashe (with Arnold Rampersand), *Days of Grace* (New York: Random House, 1993), 109.

15. Ibid., 148.

16. Bodo, *Ashe vs Connors*, ch. 5.

17. Ashe, *Days of Grace*, 292.

1968—ROBERTO CLEMENTE BASEBALL CARD

1. Diana Nelson Jones, "Saint Roberto Clemente?: Former Pittsburgh Pastor Seeks Sainthood for the Pirates Great," *Pittsburgh Post-Gazette*, January 11, 2015, http://www.post-gazette.com/local/pittsburgh-history /2015/01/11/Saint-Roberto-Clemente-Richard-Rossi-Pirates/stories/201501110144.

2. *ESPN Deportes Presents The Clemente Effect*, November 24, 2014, https://www.youtube.com/watch?v=GM nvizAoDUI, at 43:15.

3. Stew Thornley, "Roberto Clemente," Society for American Baseball Research, n.d., http://sabr.org/bioproj /person/8b153bc4#sdendnote9sym.

4. The metric is "total zone runs"; see BaseballProjection.com for an explanation.

5. Puerto Rico's Hiram Bithorn debuted in the major leagues with the Cubs in 1942.

6. *Sports Century—Roberto Clemente*, December 10, 2012, https://www.youtube.com/watch?v=APaxP5e0Lqg, at 10:00.

7. David Maraniss, *Clemente: The Passion and Grace of Baseball's Last Hero* (New York: Simon & Schuster, 2006), 2.

8. *ESPN Deportes Presents The Clemente Effect*, at 17:00.

9. Kal Wagenheim, *Clemente!* (New York: Praeger, 1973), 186.

10. Wagenheim, *Clemente!*, 25.

11. *Sports Illustrated*, March 7, 1966.

12. Maraniss, 220, 232.

13. Ibid., 272.

1969—GAME BALL FROM SUPER BOWL III

1. Michael MacCambridge, *America's Game: The Epic Story of How Pro Football Captured a Nation* (New York: Anchor Books, 2004), 253.

2. Paul Zimmerman, "Baltimore Colts vs. New York Jets, Super Bowl III: So, Joe Said It Was So," *Sports Illustrated*, January 2, 1989, http://www.si.com/vault/1989/01/02/119175/baltimore-colts-vs-new-york-jets-super -bowl-iii-so-joe-said-it-was-so-the-colts-were-the-nfls-new-standard-bearer-but-few-figured-the-afl-could-win -its-first-title-an-exception-was-joe-namath.

3. "Jets Likely to Use Same Starting Team Against Colts That Played Raiders; Three Will Face Difficult Tasks," *New York Times*, January 5, 1969, http://query.nytimes.com/gst/abstract.html?res=9A0DE0D7123BE 73ABC4D53DFB7668382679EDE.

4. Mark Kriegel, *Namath: A Biography* (New York: Viking, 2004), 268.

5. Ibid., 269.

6. Richard Sandomir, "Super Bowl III Revisited, on ESPN," *New York Times*, September 9, 1997, http://www .nytimes.com/1997/09/09/sports/super-bowl-iii-revisited-on-espn.html.

7. MacCambridge, *America's Game,* 255.

1970—BOBBY ORR'S KNEE BRACE

1. Herbert Warren Wind, "Orr Country," The Sporting Scene, *New Yorker*, March 27, 1971, 109.

2. Ibid., 109, 113.

3. S. L. Price, "The Ever Elusive, Always Inscrutable and Still Incomparable Bobby Orr," *Sports Illustrated*, March 2, 2009, http://www.si.com/vault/2009/03/02/105783066/the-ever-elusive-always-inscrutable -and-still-incomparable-bobby-orr.

4. Bobby Orr, *My Story* (New York: Putnam, 2013), back cover.

5. *Legends of Hockey—Bobby Orr*, April 23, 2009, https://www.youtube.com/watch?v=k74iUt5bKNs.

6. Mark Mulvoy, "NHL," *Sports Illustrated*, October 21, 1974, http://www.si.com/vault/1974/10/21/618527/nhl.

7. Stephen Brunt, *Searching for Bobby Orr* (Toronto: Knopf Canada, 2006), 114.

8. Ibid., 259.

9. Orr, *My Story*, 151.

10. Ibid., 156.

11. Russ Conway, *Game Misconduct: Allan Eagleson and the Corruption of Hockey* (Toronto: MacFarlane Walter & Ross; Buffalo, NY: Distributed in the U.S. by General Distribution Services, 1997), 137–148; Orr, *My Story*, 152–153.

12. Michael Farber, "Man on a Mission Russ Conway's Investigative Work May Bring Down a Hockey Power Broker," *Sports Illustrated*, February 19, 1996, http://www.si.com/vault/1996/02/19/210076/man-on-a-mission

-russ-conways-investigative-work-may-bring-down-a-hockey-power-broker; Conway, *Game Misconduct*; see chs. 3 and 4 for examples related to disability.

13. Ibid.

14. Ron Base, "Bobby Orr, Me, and the Mystery of Alan Eagleson," October 17, 2013, https://ronbase .wordpress.com/2013/10/17/bobby-orr-me-and-the-mystery-of-alan-eagleson/.

1970—YELLOW BLAZER FROM *MONDAY NIGHT FOOTBALL*

1. Michael MacCambridge, *America's Game: The Epic Story of How Pro Football Captured a Nation* (New York: Anchor Books, 2004), 276.

2. "The Titan of Television," *Sports Illustrated*, August 16, 1994, http://www.si.com/vault/1994/08/16/131802 /on-august-16-1954-sports-illustrated-published-its-first-issue-and-in-the-four-decades-since-the-world-of -sports-has-been-transformed-the-author-traces-the-path-through-those-40-years-by-way-of-four-men-and-a -mall-chapter-one-th.

3. MacCambridge, *America's Game*, 276.

4. Marc Gunther and Bill Carter, *Monday Night Mayhem* (New York: Beech Tree Books, 1988), 29.

5. $52.6 million in 2015 dollars.

6. William Johnson, "TV Made It All a New Game," *Sports Illustrated*, December 22, 1969, http://www.si .com/vault/1969/12/22/618805/tv-made-it-all-a-new-game.

7. Gunther and Carter, *Monday Night Mayhem*, 35.

8. Ibid., 22.

9. Neil Amdur, "The Television Dollars Foster New Perceptions," *New York Times*, October 30, 1982, http:// www.nytimes.com/1982/10/30/sports/the-television-dollars-foster-new-perceptions.html.

10. Bruce Newman, "Howard Cosell," *Sports Illustrated*, September 19, 1994, http://www.si.com/vault /1994/09/19/132042/22-howard-cosell.

11. Amdur, Television Dollars Foster New Perceptions."

12. *New York Times*, September 8, 2011.

1971—GOLF CLUB USED ON THE MOON

1. "Golf History and the USGA Museum," n.d., http://www.usgamuseum.com/about_museum/news_events /news_article.aspx?newsid=177.

2. Mark Aumann, "Remembering Alan Shepard's Lunar Golf Shots, 44 Years Later," *Golf Buzz*, February 26, 2015, http://www.pga.com/news/golf-buzz/feb-6-1971-alan-shepard-plays-golf-moon.

3. *Golf on the Moon*, August 24, 2006, https://www.youtube.com/watch?v=KZLl3XwlAIE.

4. Shephard gives more detail on the incident at *Alan Shepard—Last Interview (1998)*, May 15, 2015, https:// www.youtube.com/watch?v=kF3SuruDCwE; go to about 1:02:50.

5. Neal Thompson, *Light This Candle: The Life and Times of Alan Shepard* (New York: Three Rivers Press, 2007), 450.

1971—PING-PONG DIPLOMACY SOUVENIR PADDLES

1. Xu Guoqi, *Olympic Dreams: China and Sport, 1895–2008* (Cambridge, MA: Harvard University Press, 2008), 117.

2. Ibid., 129; Nicholas Griffin, *Ping-Pong Diplomacy: The Secret History of the Game That Changed the World* (New York: Scribner, 2014), 186.

3. "Ping-Pong Diplomacy," *New York Times*, April 10, 1971, http://query.nytimes.com/gst/abstract.html ?res=9804E6D81530E73BBC4852DFB266838A669EDE.

4. Zhaohui Hong and Yi Sun, "The Butterfly Effect and the Making of 'Ping-Pong Diplomacy'," *Journal of Contemporary China* 9, no. 25 (2000): 432.

5. Ibid.; Xu, *Olympic Dreams*, 134–135.

6. Xu, *Olympic Dreams*, 137.

7. Hong and Sun, "The Butterfly Effect," 440.

8. Griffin, *Ping-Pong Diplomacy*, 151–161.

9. Ibid., 265.

10. Ruth Eckstein, "Ping-Pong Diplomacy: A View from Behind the Scenes," *The Journal of American-East Asian Relations* 2, no 3 (Fall 1993): 328; Hong and Sun, "The Butterfly Effect," 442.

11. Griffin, *Ping-Pong Diplomacy*, 269–270.

1972–MEMORIAL TO DAVID BERGER

1. Brian Cazeneuve, "The American Cleveland-Born and -Bred, David Berger Followed His Olympic Dream to Israel, and Death in Munich," *Sports Illustrated*, August 26, 2002, http://www.si.com/vault/2002/08/26/328153/the-american-cleveland-born-and-bred-david-berger-followed-his-olympic-dream-to-israel-and-death-in-munich.

2. For some footage of Berger in competition, see *David Berger—Israeli Olympian*, June 10, 2012, https://www.youtube.com/watch?v=xyzqiFejiOQ.

3. Cazeneuve, "The American Cleveland-Born and -Bred, David Berger."

4. *One Day in September (Documentary film 1999)*, February 3, 2016, https://www.youtube.com/watch?v=p8VHxcb8kFA, at 21:00.

5. Mike Brewster and Taps Gallagher, *Stolen Glory: The U.S., the Soviet Union, and the Olympic Basketball Game That Never Ended* (Beverly Hills, CA: GM Books, 2012), ch. 24.

6. David Binder, "9 Israelis on Olympic Team Killed with 4 Arab Captors as Police Fight Band That Disrupted Munich Games," *New York Times*, September 6, 1972, https://www.nytimes.com/learning/general/onthisday/big/0905.html.

7. *The Official Report of the Organizing Committee for the Games of the XXth Olympiad Munich 1972* (Munich: Pro Sport Munchen, 1973), 1:35, http://library.la84.org/6oic/OfficialReports/1972/1972s1pt1.pdf.

8. *New Yorker*, August 21, 2000, 163.

9. "Tragedy in Munich," David Berger National Memorial, n.d., http://www.nps.gov/dabe/tragedy-in-munich.htm.

10. *Official Report of the Organizing Committee*, 1:38.

11. David Berger Memorial, Mandel Jewish Community Center of Cleveland, http://www.mandeljcc.org/david-berger-memorial/mandel/.

1972–SILVER MEDAL FROM THE US-USSR MEN'S BASKETBALL FINAL

1. David K. Wiggins and R. Pierre Rodgers, eds., *Rivals: Legendary Matchups That Made Sports History* (Fayetteville: University of Arkansas Press, 2010), 351.

2. Erving had signed a pro contract. Thompson was too young. Walton had a foot injury.

3. *1972 Olympic Gold Medal Basketball Issues and What Happened to the Medals*, January 4, 2011, https://www.youtube.com/watch?v=RwZuPi4cbyg.

4. Brewster and Gallagher, *Stolen Glory*, ch. 26.

5. Ibid., ch. 27.

6. Neil Amdur, "Basketball or Chaos?," *New York Times*, September 10, 1972, http://www.nytimes.com/packages/html/sports/year_in_sports/09.10.html.

7. Gary Smith, "A Few Pieces of Silver," *Sports Illustrated*, June 15, 1992, http://www.si.com/vault /1992/06/15/126660/robbed-of-gold-medals-in-munich-the-72-us-olympic-basketball-team-will-not-betray-its -principles-for----a-few-pieces-of-silver.

8. Randy Harvey and Sergeii L. Loiko, "Untarnished Gold: Controversy? What Controversy? Soviets Still Feel They Deserved Basketball Victory in 1972," July 18, 1992, http://articles.latimes.com/1992-07-18/sports /sp-3572_1_soviet-union-s-basketball.

9. *1972 Olympics Basketball Final USA–USSR*, September 6, 2012, https://www.youtube.com/watch?v=NuB m0PRt23I; see 1:10:45.

10. Brewster and Gallagher, *Stolen Glory*, ch. 26.

1972–IMMACULATA MIGHTY MACS UNIFORM

1. Julie Byrne, *O, God of Players: The Story of the Immaculata Mighty Macs* (New York: Columbia University Press, 2003), 108.

2. Much of this description is derived from Byrne, *O, God of Players*, particularly chs. 1 and 2.

3. *ESPN Mighty Macs*, September 19, 2009, https://www.youtube.com/watch?v=8bztw90sAQA.

4. Benjamin G. Rader, *American Sports: From the Age of Folk Games to the Age of Televised Sports* (Englewood Cliffs, NJ: Prentice Hall, 1990), 323.

5. *Sports Illustrated*, May 28, 1973, 93.

6. Selena Roberts, *A Necessary Spectacle: Billie Jean King, Bobby Riggs, and the Tennis Match That Leveled the Game* (New York: Crown, 2005), 162.

7. *Sports Illustrated*, May 28, 1973, 93.

8. Pat Summitt, *Sum It Up* (Waterville, ME: Thorndike Press, 2013), 73; her team at the University of Tennessee/Martin walked around town with a big glass piggy bank asking for donations.

9. Partisans of West Chester University will object. The Golden Rams did win a national tournament in 1969, but this was an invitational. The AIAW's 1972 tournament is generally regarded as the beginning of the modern women's hoops era. Sorry.

10. Joan Hult and Marianna Trekell, eds., *A Century of Women's Basketball: From Frailty to Final Four* (Reston, VA: National Association for Girls and Women in Sport, 1991), 310–311.

11. Pamela Grundy and Susan Shackelford, *Shattering the Glass: The Remarkable History of Women's Basketball* (New York: New Press, 2005), 161.

12. *Immaculata Commemorative Magazine* (Spring 2011), http://uc.immaculata.edu/magazine/spring2011/.

13. Byrne, *O, God of Players*, 181.

14. *Immaculata Commemorative Magazine*.

15. Byrne, *O, God of Players*, 185.

16. Welch Suggs, *A Place on the Team: The Triumph and Tragedy of Title IX* (Princeton, NJ: Princeton University Press, 2005), 113.

17. Ibid., 123.

18. Ibid., 140.

19. John Irving, "Wrestling with Title IX," *New York Times*, January 28, 2003, http://www.nytimes .com/2003/01/28/opinion/wrestling-with-title-ix.html?pagewanted=all; Suggs, *A Place on the Team*, 125, 129, 135–136, 139.

20. Greta Cohen, ed., *Women in Sport: Issues and Controversies* (Newbury Park, CA: Sage, 1993), 61.

21. Joe Marshall, "On and Up with the Mighty Macs," *Sports Illustrated*, February 3, 1975, http://www.si .com/vault/1975/02/03/616188/on-and-up-with-the-mighty-macs.

22. *Cathy Rush's Basketball Hall of Fame Enshrinement Speech*, February 17, 2012, https://www.youtube.com/watch?v=wd2OgJy8KmE.

1973—NAIL FROM SECRETARIAT'S SHOE

1. Lawrence Scanlan, *The Horse God Built: The Untold Story of Secretariat, the World's Greatest Racehorse* (New York: Thomas Dunne Books/St. Martin's Press, 2007), 15.

2. Raymond Woolfe Jr., *Secretariat* (Radnor, PA: Chilton Book, 1974), 28.

3. Scanlan, *Horse God Built*, 13.

4. Woolfe, *Secretariat*, 37.

5. Ibid., 39.

6. *Sports Illustrated*, October 16, 1989.

7. *Sports Illustrated*, June 4, 1990.

8. William Nack, "Secretariat," *Sports Illustrated*, September 19, 1994, http://www.si.com/vault/1994/09/19/132047/17-secretariat.

9. Scanlan, *Horse God Built*, 151.

10. Ibid., 155.

11. *Secretariat—Documentary* [ESPN], May 26, 2012, https://www.youtube.com/watch?v=Lhfi6zOLdK4, at 12:00.

12. This was not straightforward. The track's electronic timing device broke down. Clockers from the *Daily Racing Form* and in the press all gave him the record; the official clocker did not. In 2012, however, the Maryland Racing Commission reviewed the evidence and voted to change the official time to 1:53, a record.

13. Whitney Tower, "Putting a New Light on the Derby," *Sports Illustrated*, April 30, 1973, http://www.si.com/vault/1973/04/30/615640/putting-a-new-light-on-the-derby.

14. "Ask Penny," n.d., http://www.secretariat.com/ask-penny/.

15. The race can be seen at *Secretariat—Belmont Stakes 1973*, May 5, 2011, https://www.youtube.com/watch?v=V18ui3Rtjz4.

1973—BILLIE JEAN KING'S DRESS AND BOBBY RIGGS'S JACKET FROM THE "BATTLE OF THE SEXES"

1. Neil Amdur, "Riggs Defeats Mrs. Court, 6–2, 6–1; No Resemblance Credits Soft Touch Riggs Beats Mrs. Court in 57 Minutes, 6–2, 6–1 Aussies Plan Rematch," *New York Times*, May 14, 1973, http://query.nytimes.com/gst/abstract.html?res=9E01E7DC133DE630A45757C1A9639C946290D6CF.

2. Tom LeCompte, *The Last Sure Thing: The Life and Times of Bobby Riggs* (Easthampton, MA: Black Squirrel Publishing, 2003), 313.

3. Bobby Riggs, with George McGann, *Court Hustler* (New York: Signet, 1974), 17–19.

4. LeCompte, *Last Sure Thing*, 359.

5. Billie Jean King, with Kim Chapin, *Billie Jean* (New York: Harper & Row, 1974), 177–178.

6. Ed Leibowitz, "How Billie Jean King Picked Her Outfit for the Battle of the Sexes Match," *Smithsonian Magazine* September 2003, http://www.smithsonianmag.com/arts-culture/how-billie-jean-king-picked-her-outfit-for-the-battle-of-the-sexes-match-89938552/?no-ist.

7. Bud Collins, *The Bud Collins History of Tennis: An Authoritative Encyclopedia and Record Book* (New York: New Chapter Press, 2010), 167.

8. Neil Amdur, "Mrs. King Defeats Riggs, 6-4, 6-3, 6-3, Amid a Circus Atmosphere," *New York Times*, September 20, 1973, http://www.nytimes.com/learning/general/onthisday/big/0920.html#article.

9. Billie Jean King, with Frank Deford, *Billie Jean* (New York: Viking Press, 1982).

10. Neil Amaur, "Take that, Gents!" *New York Times*, September 21, 1973.

11. Jesse Greenspan, "Billie Jean King Wins the 'Battle of the Sexes,' 40 Years Ago," *History in the Head-lines*, September 20, 2013, http://www.history.com/news/billie-jean-king-wins-the-battle-of-the-sexes -40-years-ago; Kate Torgovnick May, "'I Beat Bobby Riggs Because I Respected Him': Billie Jean King Talks the Battle of the Sexes at TEDWomen2015," *TEDBlog*, May 29, 2015, http://blog.ted.com/billie-jean -king-on-the-battle-of-the-sexes-at-tedwomen-2015/.

12. Susan Ware, *Game, Set, Match: Billie Jean King and the Revolution in Women's Sports* (Chapel Hill: University of North Carolina Press, 2011), 44.

13. Roberts, *A Necessary Spectacle*, 76.

14. Grace Lichtenstein, "Perfume in the Locker Room; Chrissie and Rosie and the Arm and Billie and Wendy," *New York Times Magazine*, May 27, 1973, 28, http://query.nytimes.com/gst/abstract.html?res=9B0CE0 DD123DE63ABC4F51DFB3668388669EDE.

15. "About the WTA," n.d., http://www.wtatennis.com/scontent/article/2951989/title/about-the-wta.

16. *"This Week" Sunday Spotlight: Billie Jean King*, September 22, 2013, https://www.youtube.com/watch?v =MyMtOwwtJW0.

17. Roberts, *A Necessary Spectacle*, 85.

18. Greenspan, "Billie Jean King Wins."

19. *Sports Illustrated*, November 6, 1996.

20. King and Chapin, *Billie Jean*, 76.

1974—HANK AARON'S JERSEY

1. Tom Stanton, *Hank Aaron and the Home Run That Changed America* (New York: HarperCollins, 2004), 22.

2. "Hank Aaron," Baseball-Reference.com, n.d., http://www.baseball-reference.com/players/a/aaronha01 .shtml.

3. Bill Johnson, "Hank Aaron," Society for American Baseball Research, n.d., http://sabr.org/bioproj/person /5a36cc6f.

4. Jen Christensen, "Besting Ruth, Beating Hate: How Hank Aaron Made Baseball History," CNN, [April 2014], http://www.cnn.com/interactive/2014/04/us/hank-aaron-anniversary/.

5. Hank Aaron, with Lonnie Wheeler, *I Had a Hammer: The Hank Aaron Story* (New York: HarperCollins, 1991), 141.

1974—NIKE WAFFLE TRAINER

1. "Found: The Waffle Iron That Inspired Nike," National Public Radio, March 3, 2011, http://www.npr .org/2011/03/03/134239745/Found-The-Waffle-Iron-That-Inspired-Nike.

2. "The Nike Waffle Outsole," Nike corporate communication, n.d.

3. Kenny Moore, *Bowerman and the Men of Oregon* (Emmaus, PA: Rodale, 2006), 315.

4. US Patent Office, "Athletic shoe for artificial turf," (Washington, DC, filed 1972, granted 1974), http:// www.google/patents/US3793750.

5. This was not the first Bowerman/Nike shoe. The Cortez had come out a few years before; it had a wide heel, thick sole, good arch support, raised heel, and cushioned innersole. Runners loved the Cortez and it sold well; it, too, was important in the development of the company. But at the time the company (then called Blue Ribbon Sports) was still in business with the Onitsuka Company, the Japanese firm it had been working with since 1964, distributing Tiger shoes to the American market (see Moore, *Bowerman and the Men of Oregon*, 183–184, 314–315). In the movie *Forrest Gump*, the title character wears Cortez sneakers when he runs across the country.

6. Phil Knight, *Shoe Dog: A Memoir by the Creator of Nike* (New York: Scribner, 2016), 240.

7. "Nike, Inc., 1981 Annual Report," n.d.;" Nike, Inc., 1982 Annual Report," n.d. All of Nike's annual reports can be found at http://investors.nike.com/investors/news-events-and-reports/.

8. "Nike, Inc. Reports Fiscal 2015 Fourth Quarter and Full Year Results," June 25, 2015, http://news.nike.com/news/nike-inc-reports-fiscal-2015-fourth-quarter-and-full-year-results.

1975—TONY HAWK'S FIRST SKATEBOARD

1. Tony Hawk and Pat Hawk, *How Did I Get Here? The Ascent of an Unlikely CEO* (Hoboken, NJ: Wiley, 2010), 11.

2. Ben Marcus, *The Skateboard: The Good, the Rad, and the Gnarly* (2011), 197.

3. Hawk and Hawk, *How Did I Get Here?*, 13.

4. "Bio," Tony Hawk, n.d., http://tonyhawk.com/bio/.

5. Marcus, *Skateboard*, 194.

6. Tony Hawk, with Sean Mortimer, *Hawk: Occupation Skateboarder* (New York: HarperCollins, 2001).

7. *TransWorld Skateboarding*, September 2008, 166.

8. Tony Hawk and Sean Mortimer, "My Last X Games," in *Tony Hawk: Professional Skateboarder* (New York: ReganBooks, 2002).

9. The trick can be seen at *Tony Hawk 900*, July 23, 2008, https://www.youtube.com/watch?v=e4QGnppJ-ys. Hawk also did the first 720.

10. Marcus, *Skateboard*.

11. Mark Levine, "The Birdman," The Sporting Scene, *New Yorker*, July 26, 1999, 73, http://www.newyorker.com/magazine/1999/07/26/the-birdman.

12. *Tony Hawk—Who You Callin' A Sellout?*, January 27, 2015, https://www.youtube.com/watch?v=2wv-SppeJCs.

13. "Tony Hawk on Selling Out Without Being a Sellout," *Entrepreneur*, May 2, 2012, http://www.entrepreneur.com/video/223459.

1975—PELÉ'S JERSEY FROM THE NEW YORK COSMOS

1. *New Yorker*, September 12, 1977.

2. Gavin Newsham, *Once in a Lifetime: The Incredible Story of the New York Cosmos* (New York: Grove Press; [Berkeley]: Distributed by Publishers Group West, 2006), 129.

3. Jonathan Mahler, "Disco Inferno: When the Cosmos Ruled the Town," *New York Times*, July 2, 2006, http://www.nytimes.com/2006/07/02/nyregion/thecity/02cosm.html?_r=0.

4. David Segal, "The New York Cosmos Want to Take the Field Again," *New York Times Magazine*, April 17, 2011, http://www.nytimes.com/2011/04/17/magazine/mag-17Cosmos-t.html.

5. Newsham, *Once in a Lifetime*, 138.

6. Ibid., 35.

7. Mahler, "Disco Inferno."

8. Newsham, *Once in a Lifetime*, 239.

9. Gerald Eskenazi, "Prospects for Cosmos Take a Bullish Turn," *New York Times*, June 5, 1975, 43.

10. Segal, "New York Cosmos Want to Take the Field Again."

11. *Forbes*, July 20, 2015.

1975—PRE'S ROCK

1. Kenny Moore, *Bowerman and the Men of Oregon* (Emmaus, PA: Rodale, 2006), 328.

2. Daniel Wojcik, "Pre's Rock: Pilgrimage, Ritual, and Runners' Traditions at the Roadside Shrine for Steve Prefontaine," in *Shrines and Pilgrimage in Contemporary Society: New Itineraries into the Sacred*, ed. Peter Jan Margry (Amsterdam: University of Amsterdam Press, 2008), 212, 222.

3. Ibid., 210.

4. "Steve Prefontaine," USA Track & Field, https://www.usatf.org/HallOfFame/TF/showBio.asp?HOFIDs =130.

5. Tom Jordan, *Pre: The Story of America's Greatest Running Legend* (Emmaus, Pa.: Rodale, 1997), 41.

6. The last four laps can be seen at *HD-Steve Prefontaine 1972 5000m Final (English Commentary)*, June 2, 2014, https://www.youtube.com/watch?v=_iKt8_pkHgY.

7. Phil Knight, *Shoe Dog: A Memoir by the Creator of Nike* (New York: Scribner, 2016), 240.

8. *Fire on the Track—The Steve Prefontaine Story, Part 4*, December 22, 2011, https://www.youtube.com/watch ?v=BlFjD9HcXmw&index=4&list=PL3D26589E58850FF6.

9. Ibid.

10. Phil Knight, *Shoe Dog: A Memoir by the Creator of Nike* (New York: Scribner, 2016), 240.

11. Donald Katz, "Triumph of the Swoosh," *Sports Illustrated*, August 16, 1993.

12. Donald Katz, *Just Do It: The Nike Spirit in the Corporate World* (New York: Random House, 1994), 64.

13. Jordan, *Pre*, 101.

1975–THRILLA IN MANILA BUTTON

1. Robert Lipsyte and Peter Levine, *Idols of the Game: A Sporting History of the American Century* (Atlanta: Turner Publishing, 1995), 246.

2. Thomas Hauser, "The Importance of Muhammad Ali," *History Now*, n.d., http://www.gilderlehrman.org /history-by-era/civil-rights-movement/essays/importance-muhammad-ali.

3. Michael Powell, "In Muhammad Ali, an Example of a Truer Kind of Bravery in Sports," *New York Times*, June 4, 2016.

4. Wesley Morris, "Muhammad Ali Evolved From a Blockbuster Fighter to a Country's Conscience," *New York Times*, June 4, 2016.

5. *HBO Thrilla in Manila Documentary*, March 6, 2013, https://www.youtube.com/watch?v=dUQNKb_1xlc, at 13:45.

6. Thomas Hauser, *Muhammad Ali: His Life and Times* (New York: Simon & Schuster, 1991), 221.

7. Ibid., 229.

8. Mark Kram, *Ghosts of Manila: The Fateful Blood Feud Between Muhammad Ali and Joe Frazier* (New York: HarperCollins, 2001), 149.

9. Ibid., 169.

10. "About Toy Gun, Girlfriend: Ali 'Explains,'" *The Victoria Advocate*, September 23, 1975, https://news .google.com/newspapers?nid=861&dat=19750923&id=shJZAAAAIBAJ&sjid=VUYNAAAAIBAJ&pg=5235,42 84583&hl=en.

11. William Nack, "'The Fight's Over, Joe'," *Sports Illustrated*, September 30, 1996, http://www.si.com/vault /1996/09/30/208924/the-fights-over-joe-more-than-two-decades-after-they-last-met-in-the-ring-joe-frazier-is -still-taking-shots-at-muhammad-ali-but-this-time-its-a-war-of-words.

12. Joe Frazier, with Phil Berger, *Smokin' Joe* (New York: Macmillan, 1996), 164.

13. *The Sporting News*, June 25, 2001.

14. Mark Kram, "'Lawdy, Lawdy He's Great'," *Sports Illustrated*, October 13, 1975, http://www.si.com/vault /1975/10/13/613261/lawdy-lawdy-hes-great.

15. Ibid.

16. Kram, *Ghosts of Manila*, 30.

17. HBO, *Thrilla in Manila*, 1:27:25.

18. Jeré Longman, "Philadelphia and the Boxing World Pay Tribute to Frazier," *New York Times,* November 15, 2011, http://www.nytimes.com/2011/11/15/sports/philadelphia-and-the-boxing-world-pay-tribute-to-frazier.html.

1978–NANCY LOPEZ'S ROOKIE OF THE YEAR AWARD

1. Grace Lichtenstein, "Burning Up the Links; with Her Long Drives, Putts and Sex Appeal, Nancy Lopez Has Become the New Charismatic Headliner of Women's Golf: Swinging Along with Nancy Lopez," *New York Times Magazine,* July 2, 1978, http://query.nytimes.com/gst/abstract.html?res=9D04E7 DD1E31E632A25751C0A9619C946990D6CF.

2. Annika Sorenstam tied this mark in 2005.

3. "Record 5th for Miss Lopez; Seventh Victory of Year Nine Holes; Four Birdies,"*New York Times,* June 19, 1978, http://query.nytimes.com/gst/abstract.html?res=9B06E4DF1131E632A2575AC1A9609C946990D6CF.

4. *New York Time*s, July 13, 1978.

5. Jim Burnett, *Tee Times: On the Road with the LPGA* (New York: Scribner, 1997), 90.

6. *Investors' Business Daily*, February 27, 2013.

7. Richard Lapchick, ed., *100 Trailblazers: Great Women Athletes Who Opened the Doors to Future Generations* (Morgantown, WV: Fitness Information Technology, 2009), 185.

8. Marc Myers, "Golfer Nancy Lopez on Being a Daddy's Girl," *Wall Street Journal*, June 9, 2015, http://www .wsj.com/articles/golfer-nancy-lopez-on-being-a-daddys-girl-1433865127.

9. Lichtenstein, "Burning Up the Links."

10. Burnett, *Tee Times*, 20.

11. Gordon S. White Jr., "Golf's Blazing Rookie Pro; Nancy Marie Lopez Woman in the News Her Swing Criticized on Course at Age 8 Won Collegiate Title," *New York Times*, May 31, 1978, http://query.nytimes.com /gst/abstract.html?res=9A02E3D91030E632A25752C3A9639C946990D6CF.

12. Burnett, *Tee Times*, 89.

13. Nancy Lopez, with Peter Schwed, *The Education of a Woman Golfer* (New York: Simon & Schuster, 1979), 188.

14. John Papanek, "Out of the Swing of Things," *Sports Illustrated*, June 9, 1980, http://www.si.com/vault /1980/06/09/824718/out-of-the-swing-of-things-somehow-nancy-lopez-melton-slipped-out-of-the-groove-and-a -lot-of-folks--but-not-her-rivals--hope-she-gets-back-in.

15. "Nancy Lopez," LPGA, n.d., http://www.lpga.com/players/nancy-lopez/81218/bio.

16. Roger Vaughan, *Golf, the Woman's Game* (New York: Stewart, Tabori & Chang, 2001), 127.

17. Burnett, *Tee Times*, 126.

1979–LARRY BIRD'S AND MAGIC JOHNSON'S COLLEGE JERSEYS

1. "Highest-rated televised NCAA basketball national championship games from 1975 to 2015," n.d., http:// www.statista.com/statistics/219645/ncaa-basketball-tournament-games-by-tv-ratings/.

2. The Johnson jersey is a replica.

3. N. R. Kleinfield, "How One Man Rescued Basketball, and Its Bottom Line," *New York Times*, March 4, 1990, http://www.nytimes.com/1990/03/04/business/how-one-man-rescued-basketball-and-its-bottom-line.html.

4. Vince McKee, *The Cleveland Cavaliers: A History of the Wine & Gold* (Charleston, SC: The History Press, 2014), 33.

5. David Halberstam, *Playing for Keeps: Michael Jordan and the World He Made* (New York: Broadway Books, 2000), ch. 9.

6. John Papanek, "Gifts That God Didn't Give," *Sports Illustrated*, November 9, 1981, http://www.si.com/vault/1981/11/09/826097/gifts-that-god-didnt-give-larry-bird-was-blessed-with-his-height-but-lots-of-work-made-him-the-nbas-most-complete-player-since-oscar-robertson.

7. *Larry Bird (18-21-9) vs. Moses Malone (8-15-3) 1981 Finals Gm 1—Bird Clutch*, November 6, 2015, https://www.youtube.com/watch?v=cmTJwLU3ZM0, at 3:20.

8. *Sports Illustrated*, June 22, 1987.

9. David K. Wiggins and R. Pierre Rodgers, eds., *Rivals: Legendary Matchups That Made Sports History* (Fayetteville: University of Arkansas Press, 2010), 70.

10. Jack McCallum, "Leaving a Huge Void," *Sports Illustrated*, March 23, 1992, http://www.si.com/vault/1992/03/23/126207/leaving-a-huge-void-magic-johnson-larry-bird-nba.

11. Wiggins and Rodgers, *Rivals*, 71.

12. Larry Bird and Earvin "Magic" Johnson, with Jackie MacMullan, *When the Game Was Ours* (Boston: Houghton Mifflin Harcourt, 2009), v and x.

13. The Philadelphia 76ers won in 1983 and the Detroit Pistons in 1989.

14. "National Basketball Association Nielsen Ratings," n.d. Gutenberg.us/articles/national_basketball_association_nielsen_ratings.

15. Wiggins and Rodgers, *Rivals*, 82.

1979—DONNIE ALLISON'S HELMET FROM THE DAYTONA 500

1. Ryan McGee, *ESPN Ultimate NASCAR: 100 Defining Moments in Stock Car Racing History* (New York: ESPN Books, 2007), 103.

2. *A Perfect Storm: The 1979 Daytona 500 (2015)*, February 13, 2015, http://www.youtube.com.

3. Mark Bechtel, *He Crashed Me So I Crashed Him Back: The True Story of the Year the King, Jaws, Earnhardt, and the Rest of NASCAR's Feudin', Fightin' Good Ol' Boys Put Stock Car Racing on the Map* (New York: Little, Brown, 2011).

4. *Sports Illustrated*, January 28, 1998.

5. Peter Golenbock, *Miracle: Bobby Allison and the Saga of the Alabama Gang* (New York: St. Martin's Griffin, 2007), 166.

6. Dave Caldwell, "Recalling a Fight, and Titles," *New York Times*, October 26, 2008, http://www.nytimes.com/2008/10/26/sports/othersports/26nascar.html?_r=0.

7. Ed Hinton, *Daytona: From the Birth of Speed to the Death of the Man in Black* (New York: Warner Books, 2001), 10.

8. Unnoticed at the time, a promising young driver named Dale Earnhardt finished a creditable eighth place. He would win Rookie of the Year in 1979 and go on to become a legend, winning 76 races, including Daytona in 1998. And Daytona is also where the legend died. In third place on the final turn of the final lap, a couple of car lengths behind his son, Earnhardt veered left near the infield and then sharply right, slamming nose first into the retaining wall at 160 miles per hour. His skull fractured, he did not survive the drive to the hospital. That day is forever known as "Black Sunday." If The Fight is the day that made NASCAR, Black Sunday is the day it got really serious about safety. In the wake of Earnhardt's death, NASCAR imposed a series of new regulations, including the mandatory use of head and neck restraints.

1980—MIKE ERUZIONE'S STICK FROM THE "MIRACLE ON ICE"

1. This game took place at 5:00 p.m.; ABC television naturally wanted to push it to prime time, but the Soviets said no. As a result, the game was televised *after* its conclusion, on a tape delay. So all those people who remember where they were when the United States won probably remember where they were when they saw it, not when it was actually played.

2. *Do You Believe in Miracles? The Story of the 1980 U.S. Hockey Team* [2001], April 25, 2015, https://www .youtube.com/watch?v=f-K-mm8Bqik.

3. Wayne Coffey, *The Boys of Winter: The Untold Story of a Coach, a Dream, and the 1980 U.S. Olympic Hockey Team* (New York: Crown, 2005), 39.

4. Les Krantz, *Not Till the Fat Lady Sings: The Most Dramatic Sports Finishes of All Time* (Chicago: Triumph Books, 2003), 11.

5. Jim Naughton, "Russia Routs U.S. in Hockey by 10-3; Soviet Coach Puzzled Soviet Six Routs U.S. by 10-3 Spectacular Goal," *New York Times*, February 10, 1980, http://query.nytimes.com/gst/abstract.html ?res=9E01E4D61538E432A25753C1A9649C94619FD6CF.

6. E. M. Swift, "A Reminder of What We Can Be," *Sports Illustrated*, December 22, 1980, http://www.si.com/ vault/1980/12/22/106775781/a-reminder-of-what-we-can-be.

7. Al Michaels, with L. Jon Wertheim, *You Can't Make This Up: Miracles, Memories, and the Perfect Marriage of Sports and Television* (New York: William Morrow, 2014), 109.

8. *Sports Illustrated*, January 26, 2015.

9. After the game, Eruzione tossed the stick into the stands—and his brother caught it. Eruzione later wrote the score of the game on the upper handle.

10. Swift, "A Reminder of What We Can Be."

11. Because of the complexities of the Olympic tournament in 1980, which was a round-robin, not single elimination, if the United States had lost to Finland, it would have finished fourth.

12. Michaels, *You Can't Make This Up,* 120.

13. *Do You Believe In Miracles?* (see note 2).

14. Dudley Clendinin, "U.S. Hockey Victory Stirs National Celebration; Nation Is Jubilant Over Victory the Boys from Minnesota Lincoln Center Chimes In," *New York Times*, February 25, 1980, http://query.nytimes .com/gst/abstract.html?res=9506E2DA103EE732A25756C2A9649C94619FD6CF.

15. *Red Army*, May 25, 2015, https://www.youtube.com/watch?v=lBi2GicxYiE.

16. Coffey, *Boys of Winter*, 247.

17. Its victory in the bidding process, however, was not a surprise; it was the only bidder.

18. *XIII Olympic Winter Games, Lake Placid 1980: Final Report*, February 13–24, 1980, http://www.olympic. org/Documents/Reports/Official%20Past%20Games%20Reports/Winter/EN/1980_Lake_Placid.pdf; equivalent to $487.4 million in 2015 dollars.

1980–ERIC HEIDEN'S GOLD RACING SUIT

1. See, for example, the ranking from a Dutch sports magazine at this Web site: http://wayback.archive.org /web/20060714135102/http://www.teamsupportsystems.com/schaatslijst/lijst_m_allround_top10.htm.

1982–THE BALL FROM "THE CATCH"

1. Michael MacCambridge, *America's Game: The Epic Story of How Pro Football Captured a Nation* (New York: Anchor Books, 2004), 337.

2. Tom Friend, "Montana, Cool to the End, Says Goodbye," *New York Times*, April 19, 1995, http://www.ny times.com/1995/04/19/sports/pro-football-montana-cool-to-the-end-says-goodbye.html?mtrref=query.nytimes .com&gwh=D35B1F87ACFFA0F96760746BE08A9C42&gwt=pay.

3. *"The Catch" & the Birth of a 49ers' Dynasty/"The Timeline: A Tale of Two Cities"/NFL Network*, December 15, 2015, https://www.youtube.com/watch?v=14CKs0rY0jE.

4. Gary Myers, *The Catch: One Play, Two Dynasties, and the Game That Changed the NFL* (New York: Crown, 2009), xi.

5. Ibid., 68.

1983/1990–CHRIS EVERT'S SHOES AND MARTINA NAVRATILOVA'S WARM-UP JACKET

1. "Martina Navratilova," International Tennis Hall of Fame, n.d., https://www.tennisfame.com/hall-of-famers/inductees/martina-navratilova/; "Chris Evert," International Tennis Hall of Fame, n.d., https://www.tennisfame.com/hall-of-famers/inductees/chris-evert/.

2. *Sports Illustrated*, August 28, 1989.

3. *Sports Century Martina Navratilova Part 2*, September 17, 2014, https://www.youtube.com/watch?v=FiIvMcxFz9k.

4. Larry Schwartz, "Martina Was Alone on Top," n.d., http://espn.go.com/sportscentury/features/00016378.html.

5. Johnette Howard, *The Rivals: Chris Evert v. Martina Navratilova, Their Epic Duels and Extraordinary Friendship* (London: Yellow Jersey, 2005), 232.

6. *Sports Century Martina Navratilova.*

7. Howard, *Rivals*, 235.

8. Evert won 6–3, 6–7, 7–5.

9. David K. Wiggins and R. Pierre Rodgers, eds., *Rivals: Legendary Matchups That Made Sports History* (Fayetteville: University of Arkansas Press, 2010), 113.

10. Frank Deford, "Yes, You Can Go Home Again: Martina Navratilova Went Home to Czechoslovakia and Found Fans Plentiful at the Federation Cup," *Sports Illustrated*, August 4, 1986, http://www.si.com/vault/1986/08/04/113755/yes-you-can-go-home-again-martina-navratilova-went-home-to-czechoslovakia-and-found-fans-plentiful-at-the-federation-cup.

11. *Sports Illustrated*, August 28, 1989.

12. Robin Finn, "Tennis: Legendary Rivals and Close Friends; Evert and Navratilova Reunite on Court," *New York Times*, May 6, 1998, http://www.nytimes.com/1998/05/06/sports/tennis-legendary-rivals-and-close-friends-evert-and-navratilova-reunite-on-court.html?mtrref=query.nytimes.com&gwh=0396E7D05FEE5A502C9FFA565BD6176D&gwt=pay.

13. *New York Times*, September 9, 1984.

14. Caryl Phillips, eds., *The Right Set: The Faber Book of Tennis* (New York: Vintage Books, 1999), 181.

15. *Sports Illustrated*, August 28, 1989.

1984–WHEATIES MAGNET WITH MARY LOU RETTON

1. "Bela Karolyi Quotes," n.d., http://www.brainyquote.com/quotes/quotes/b/belakaroly539244.html.

2. Mary Lou Retton and Bela Karolyi, with John Powers, *Mary Lou: Creating an Olympic Champion* (New York: McGraw-Hill, 1986), 21–23.

3. *Mary Lou Retton—Olympic Gold (Part 1)*, October 6, 2010, https://www.youtube.com/watch?v=4sSuTdsjxTI.

4. Retton and Karolyi, *Mary Lou*, 123.

5. Ibid., 146.

6. Bela Karolyi and Nancy Ann Richardson, *Feel No Fear* (New York: Hyperion, 1994), 180.

7. Anne Marie Tiernon, "Karolyi Camp: Exclusive Look Inside Building an Olympic Dynasty, WTHR, July 23, 2015, http://www.wthr.com/story/29606887/gymnastics-legend-martha-karolyi-to-step-down-as-us-team-coordinator.

1986–JACK NICKLAUS'S DRIVER FROM THE MASTERS

1. Jeff Babineau, "1986 Masters: 'Nobody That Old Wins the Masters'," *Golfweek*, April 4, 2011, http://archives.golfweek.com/news/2011/mar/25/1986-masters-nobody-old-wins-masters/.

2. Ron Furlong, "Jack Nicklaus and the 1986 Masters: A Look Back 25 Years Later," *Bleacher Report*, March 2, 2011, http://bleacherreport.com/articles/619550-jack-nicklaus-and-the-1986-masters-a-look-back-25-years-later.

3. Jack Nicklaus, *My Story* (New York: Simon & Schuster, 1997), 435.

4. Guy Yocom, "Speaking of Miracles," *Golf Digest*, January 18, 2011, http://www.golfdigest.com/story/jack-nicklaus-1986-yocom.

5. Herbert Warren Wind, "Nicklaus All the Way Back," The Sporting Scene, *New Yorker*, June 2, 1986, http://www.newyorker.com/magazine/1986/06/02/nicklaus-all-the-way-back.

6. Tiger Woods and Jordan Spieth have since won the Masters at a younger age.

7. Frank Deford, "Still Glittering After All These Years," *Sports Illustrated*, December 25, 1978, http://www.si.com/vault/1978/12/25/826315/still-glittering-after-all-these-years-for-20-glorious-years-from-his-first-us-amateur-win-in-1959-to-his-third-british-open-victory-in-july-jack-nicklaus-has-dominated-the-world-of-golf.

8. Six Masters (1963, 1965, 1966, 1972, 1975, 1986), five PGAs (1963, 1971, 1973, 1975, 1980), four US Opens (1962, 1967, 1972, 1980), and three British Opens (1966, 1970, 1978). He also won two US Amateurs.

9. Nicklaus, *My Story*, 445.

1987—SMU DOORMAT

1. "Year-by-Year Statistics," SMU, 2015, http://grfx.cstv.com/photos/schools/smu/sports/m-footbl/auto_pdf/2015-16/misc_non_event/06-Records2015-02.pdf.

2. The cumulative record from 1989 through 2016 is 95–215–3.

3. ESPN documentary, *Pony Excess*, n.d., http://espn.go.com/30for30/film?page=pony-excess.

4. David Whitford, *A Payroll to Meet* (New York: Macmillan, 1989), preface.

5. Under a previous set of rules, the University of Kentucky men's basketball team suffered something like the death penalty in 1952–1953 for point shaving and the University of Louisiana/Lafayette men's hoops team did also for a truly spectacular mix of academic fraud and pay-for-play violations from 1973 to 1975. In the modern death penalty era (post-1985), Tulane and the University of San Francisco self-administered something like the death penalty, voluntarily shutting down their men's hoops programs for a time (for payments, cheating, and gambling). So did the University of Western Kentucky in regard to its men's and women's swimming and diving teams (for hazing).

6. University of Minnesota Twin Cities Public Infractions Report, October 24, 2000, http://news.minnesota.publicradio.org/features/199903/11_newsroom_cheating/infractionsreport.shtml.

7. *Cincinnati Enquirer*, March 11, 1999.

8. Jay M. Smith and Mary Willingham, *Cheated: The UNC Scandal, the Education of Athletes, and the Future of Big-Time College Sports* (Herndon, VA: Potomac Books, 2015), 46, 145.

9. Kenneth L. Wainstein, A. Joseph Jay III, and Colleen Depman Kukowski, "Investigation of Irregular Classes in the Department of African and Afro-American Studies at the University of North Carolina at Chapel Hill," October 16, 2014 (hereinafter Wainstein Report), 38–39, http://3qh929iorux3fdpl532k03kg.wpengine.netdna-cdn.com/wp-content/uploads/2014/10/UNC-FINAL-REPORT.pdf.

10. To see the slide, go to page 22 of the Wainstein Report: http://3qh929iorux3fdpl532k03kg.wpengine.netdna-cdn.com/wp-content/uploads/2014/10/UNC-FINAL-REPORT.pdf.

11. "Senate Panel Hears Manley Tell of Learning Disability," *New York Times*, May 19, 1989, http://www.nytimes.com/1989/05/19/sports/senate-panel-hears-manley-tell-of-learning-disability.html.

12. "A Trail of Tears: The Exploitation of the College Athlete," *Florida Coastal Law Review* XI: 650.

13. "The Shame of College Sports," *The Atlantic*, October 2011, http://www.theatlantic.com/magazine/archive/2011/10/the-shame-of-college-sports/308643/.

14. Emily Kaplan, "Baltimore Hustle," *Sports Illustrated*, August 24, 2015, http://www.si.com/vault/2016/02/11/baltimore-hustle.

15. Bruce Selcraig, "As Blue as the Grass," *Sports Illustrated*, October 24, 1988, http://www.si.com/vault/1988/10/24/118719/as-blue-as-the-grass-new-charges-of-wrongdoing-make-glum-times-glummer-for-kentucky-basketball.

16. *New York Times*, November 8, 1989.

17. George Dohrmann, "Troy Burning," *Sports Illustrated*, June 21, 2010, http://www.si.com/vault/2010/06/21/105951544/troy-burning.

18. Alexander Wolff, "Broken Beyond Repair: An Open Letter to the President of Miami Urges Him to Dismantle His Vaunted Football Program to Salvage His School's Reputation," *Sports Illustrated*, June 12, 1995, http://www.si.com/vault/1995/06/12/203859/broken-beyond-repair-an-open-letter-to-the-president-of-miami-urges-him-to-dismantle-his-vaunted-football-program-to-salvage-his-schools-reputation.

19. Michelle Brutlag Hosick, "Executive Committee Restores Penn State Football Postseason, Scholarships," NCAA, September 8, 2014, http://www.ncaa.org/about/resources/media-center/news/executive-committee-restores-penn-state-football-postseason-scholarships.

20. "Top 10 Infamous NCAA Sanctions: 1. The Death Penalty," Real Clear Sports, May 17, 2013, http://www.realclearsports.com/lists/infamous_ncaa_sanctions/smu_football.html. Two minor ones are Division II Morehouse University men's soccer and Division III MacMurray College's men's tennis.

1988—*JOHN MADDEN FOOTBALL* VIDEO GAME

1. John Madden, with Dave Anderson, *All Madden: Hey, I'm Talking about Pro Football!* (New York: HarperCollins, 1996), 145.

2. Patrick Hruby, "The Franchise: The inside Story of How '*Madden NFL*' Became a Video Game Dynasty," ESPN, n.d., http://sports.espn.go.com/espn/eticket/story?page=100805/madden.

3. *Former NFL Coach John Madden*, December 9, 2010, https://www.youtube.com/watch?v=FYMVLimSV08.

4. See an image from the first year at "Top 25 Features in *Madden NFL* History," August 2, 2013, https://www.easports.com/madden-nfl/news/2013/madden-football-history.

5. This video gives an idea of how it worked: *"John Madden Football" for the Apple II*, April 14, 2011, https://www.youtube.com/watch?v=8EbPghLpK6c.

6. Tom Bissell, "Kickoff: *Madden NFL* and the Future of Video Game Sports," Grantland, January 26, 2012, http://grantland.com/features/tom-bissell-making-madden-nfl/.

7. Steven L. Kent, *The Ultimate History of Video Games: From Pong to Pokemon and Beyond—The Story Behind the Craze That Touched Our Lives and Changed the World* (Roseville, CA: Prima Publishing, 2001), 266.

8. Jeff Jensen, "Videogame Nation: These Are Your Father's [and Your Grandma's] Videogames—America's $6.35 Billion Obsession Has Hollywood Salivating," *Entertainment Weekly*, December 6, 2002, 24, http://www.ew.com/article/2002/12/06/videogame-nation.

1989—PETE ROSE AUTOGRAPHED BASEBALL

1. American League and National League, Baseball-Reference.com, n.d., http://www.baseball-reference.com/.

2. Dave Kindred, "Philadelphia Didn't Appreciate Schmidt as It Should Have," *Los Angeles Times*, January 22, 1995, http://articles.latimes.com/1995-01-22/sports/sp-22932_1_mike-schmidt.

3. Rose/Giamatti Agreement, [August 23, 1989], http://seanlahman.com/files/rose/agreement.html.

4. Jeffrey Standen, "Pete Rose and Baseball's Rule 21," *NINE: A Journal of Baseball History and Culture* 18, no. 2 (Spring 2010): 135.

5. Pete Rose and Rick Hill, *My Prison Without Bars* (Emmaus, PA: Rodale Press, 2004), 320.

1992–CAMDEN YARDS

1. Josh Leventhal, *Take Me Out to the Ballpark* (New York: Black Dog & Leventhal, 2006), 48.

2. Roger Angell, "The Pit and the Pendulum," *New Yorker*, May 21, 1990, http://www.newyorker.com/magazine /1990/05/21/the-pit-and-the-pendulum.

3. Specifically, from the building of Shibe and Forbes through the first Yankee Stadium.

4. Matt Lupica, *The Baseball Stadium Insider: A Dissection of All Thirty Ballparks, Legendary Players, and Memorable Moments* (Kent, OH: Black Squirrel Books, 2015), 53.

5. "Baseball: Ruth Outhouse Found in Ball Park," *New York Times*, February 11, 1992, http://www.nytimes .com/1992/02/11/sports/baseball-ruth-outhouse-found-in-ball-park.html.

6. Peter Richmond, *Ballpark: Camden Yards and the Building of an American Dream* (New York: Simon & Schuster, 1993), 139.

7. Ibid., 257.

8. There were critics. In "Field of Kitsch" in *New Republic* (August 17, 1992; https://newrepublic.com/article /62280/field-kitsch), Nicholas Dawidoff derided Camden Yards as an "instant antique." But the thing is, baseball fans *like* kitsch.

9. An exception is the new Yankee Stadium (2009), which chose instead to replicate the lines of the old one, built in 1923. A wise choice, of course, but the consensus is that there is a certain something lacking in the new, grandiose stadium, whose over-the-top commercialism is also off-putting. The Miami Marlins went with a more contemporary, show-biz, Miami-cool kind of vibe, complete with a many-colored sculpture, featuring pink flamingos and flying fish; it lights up when the Marlins hit a home run. It has not had much use.

10. Alec Brzezinski, "Freddie Gray Protest Outside Camden Yards Turns Violent," *Sporting News*, April 25, 2015, http://www.sportingnews.com/mlb/story/2015-04-25/freddie-gray-protest-camden-yards-violent -mlb-baltimore-orioles-baseball.

1993–JACKIE JOYNER-KERSEE'S SHOE

1. Neil Cohen, *Jackie Joyner-Kersee* (Boston: Little, Brown, 1992), 10.

2. Jackie Joyner-Kersee, with Sonja Steptoe, *A Kind of Grace: The Autobiography of the World's Greatest Female Athlete* (New York: Warner Books, 1997), 22.

3. Geri Harrington, *Jackie Joyner-Kersee: Champion Athlete* (New York: Chelsea House, 1995), 27.

4. Cohen, *Jackie Joyner-Kersee*, 58.

5. "Jackie Joyner-Kersee at a Glance [and] . . . in Depth," n.d., http://jackiejoynerkersee.com/CSEP%20 -Jackie%20Joyner%20Kersee%20Bio%20-%20Final.pdf.

6. "PLUS: AWARDS; Joyner-Kersee Named Top Athlete," *New York Times*, April 24, 2001, http://www.ny times.com/2001/04/24/sports/plus-awards-joyner-kersee-named-top-athlete.html.

7. "Jesse Owens Award," USA Track & Field, n.d., http://www.usatf.org/statistics/Annual-Awards/TF/Jesse OwensAward.aspx.

8. Jennifer H. Lansbury, *A Spectacular Leap: Black Women Athletes in 20th Century America* (Fayetteville: University of Arkansas Press, 2014), 200–210.

9. Ramona Shelburne, "Jackie Joyner-Kersee: 'Never Forget Where You Come From'," ESPN, October 10, 2014, http://espn.go.com/espnw/w-in-action/article/11673532/never-forget-where-come-from.

10. "Records and History: Girls Track & Field Records Menu," IHSA, n.d., http://www.ihsa.org/Sports Activities/GirlsTrackField/RecordsHistory.aspx.

1995/2009—GENO AURIEMMA'S FIRST CHAMPIONSHIP TROPHY AND PAT SUMMITT'S 1,000TH VICTORY BALL

1. David K. Wiggins and R. Pierre Rodgers, eds., *Rivals: Legendary Matchups That Made Sports History* (Fayetteville: University of Arkansas Press, 2010), 236.

2. Pat Summitt, *Sum It Up* (Waterville, ME: Thorndike Press, 2013), 244.

3. Jere Longman, "1998 N.C.A.A. Tournament: Tennessee Redefining the Women's Game," *New York Times*, March 26, 1998, http://www.nytimes.com/1998/03/26/sports/1998-ncaa-tournament-tennessee-redefining -the-women-s-game.html.

4. Jere Longman, "Tennessee, a Cornerstone of the Women's Poll, Falls Out of the Top 25," *New York Times*, February 23, 2016, http://www.nytimes.com/2016/02/23/sports/ncaabasketball/tennessee-lady-vols-top-25.html.

5. Harvey Araton, "Game's Present Yields Floor to Its Past Before a UConn Win," *New York Times*, January 4, 2015, http://www.nytimes.com/2015/01/05/sports/ncaabasketball/games-present-yields-floor-to-its-past-before -uconn-defeats-st-johns.html.

6. The longest streak is 131 games, set by the Flying Queens of Wayland Baptist College in Plainview, Texas, from 1953 to 1958. The team got its name from a local basketball-crazy benefactor who flew them to their games. There was no college tournament during this era, but the Flying Queens won four straight AAU titles from 1954 to 1957. In 1958, led by Nera White, the first woman inducted into the Naismith Basketball Hall of Fame, Nashville Business College (NBC) broke the streak in the AAU semifinals, winning that year and also in 1960. Wayland won in 1959 and 1961. Beginning in 1962, though, NBC went on a great run, winning eight straight titles, beating Wayland in the finals each time. See Pamela Grundy and Susan Shackelford, *Shattering the Glass: The Remarkable History of Women's Basketball* (New York: New Press, 2005), 95–101; and Skip Hollandsworth, "Hoop Queens," *Texas Monthly*, April 2013, http://www.texasmonthly.com/the-culture/hoop-queens/.

7. Summitt, *Sum It Up*, 243.

1998—PIECE OF FLOOR FROM MICHAEL JORDAN'S "LAST SHOT" WITH THE BULLS

1. *Michael Jordan—"Failure,"* February 16, 2012, https://www.youtube.com/watch?v=GuXZFQKKF7A.

2. *Michael Jordan's Basketball Hall of Fame Enshrinement Speech*, February 21, 2012, https://www.youtube .com/watch?v=XLzBMGXfK4c

3. Sam Smith, *There Is No Next* (New York: Diversion Books, 2014), 107.

4. David Remnick, ed., *The Only Game in Town: Sportswriting from* The New Yorker (New York: Random House, 2010), 160. The original article appeared in 1998.

5. Matt Dollinger, "Air Power," *Sports Illustrated*, February 1, 2016, http://www.si.com/vault/2016/02/11/air -power.

6. "'God Disguised as Michael Jordan'," NBA Encyclopedia, playoff ed., n.d., http://www.nba.com/history /jordan63_moments.html.

7. "Michael Jordan," Baseball-Reference.com, n.d., http://www.baseball-reference.com/register/player.cgi?id =jordan001mic.

8. David Halberstam, *Playing for Keeps: Michael Jordan and the World He Made* (New York: Broadway Books, 2000), ch. 9.

9. Ibid.

10. Walter Lafeber, *Michael Jordan and the New Global Capitalism* (New York: Norton, 2002), 79.

11. Smith, *There Is No Next*, 48.

12. *Michael Jordan—"Failure."*

1999—BALL FROM THE 1999 WOMEN'S WORLD CUP

1. George Vecsey, "Women's Soccer: 76,481 Fans, 1 U.S. Gold," August 2, 1996, http://www.nytimes.com /1996/08/02/sports/women-s-soccer-76481-fans-1-us-gold.html.

2. David Wangerin, *Soccer in a Football World* (Philadelphia: Temple University Press, 2008), 295.

3. Jere Longman, *The Girls of Summer: The U.S. Women's Soccer Team and How It Changed the World* (New York: HarperCollins, 2000), 30.

4. Ibid., 57.

5. Ibid., 22.

6. *The Economist*, June 26, 1999, 35.

7. Wangerin, *Soccer in a Football World*, 297.

8. Graham Hays, "WUSA Collapse Leaves Void in Sports," ESPN FC, September 15, 2013, http://www.espnfc.com/story/277363.

9. Jacob Pramuk, "For US Soccer Wages, Women Still Fall Far Short of Men," CNBC, July 6, 2015, http://www.cnbc.com/2015/07/06/for-us-soccer-wages-women-still-fall-far-short-of-men.html.

2000–TIGER WOODS'S SCORECARDS FROM THE US OPEN

1. In second place is old Tom Morris's 13-stroke win in the British Open in 1862, against a field of six.

2. Rory McIlroy broke the record, shooting a 268 in 2011.

3. David Westin, "1997: Tiger Tracks into History with Masters Win," Masters, March 24, 2012, http://www.augusta.com/masters/story/history/1997-tiger-tracks-history-masters-win.

4. "45 Great Moments in Golf," *Golf*, n.d., http://www.golf.com/tour-and-news/45-great-moments-golf.

5. Official World Golf Ranking, "Tiger Woods," n.d., http://www.owgr.com/en/Ranking/PlayerProfile.aspx?playerID=5321.

6. From February 1998 to May 2005.

7. *Sports Illustrated*, April 4, 2006.

8. Bob Harig, "'Tiger-Proofing' Augusta Took a Toll on All," ESPN, April 1, 2011, http://espn.go.com/golf/masters11/columns/story?columnist=harig_bob&page=110329-RTTMasters.

9. "Driving Distance: Y-T-D-statistics through Diners Club Matches, Dec[ember] 15, 1996," http://www.pgatour.com/stats/stat.101.1996.html.

10. "America's 100 Greatest Golf Courses," *Golf Digest*, January 2015, http://www.golfdigest.com/gallery/americas-100-greatest-golf-courses-ranking.

2000–LANCE ARMSTRONG'S BIKE FROM THE TOUR DE FRANCE

1. *Lance Armstrong Ad—I'm on My Bike, What Are You On?* [Nike commercial, 2001], August 18, 2014, https://www.youtube.com/watch?v=fxnqHvEbGnc.

2. Juliet Macur, *Cycle of Lies* (New York: HarperCollins, 2014), 289.

3. Lance Armstrong with Sally Jenkins, *Every Second Counts* (New York: Broadway Books, 2004).

4. November 30, 2005, deposition of Lance Armstrong in lawsuit brought by SCA Promotions; see video of his testimony at https://www.youtube.com/watch?v=sC7bH_6S7gs.

5. United States Anti-Doping Agency, "Report on Proceedings under the World Anti-Doping Code and the USADA Protocol," 2012, http://cdn.velonews.competitor.com/files/2012/10/Reasoned-Decision.pdf, 5.

6. Michael McCann, "My Dance with Lance," *Sports Illustrated*, March 11, 2013, http://www.si.com/vault/2013/03/11/106296024/my-dance-with-lance.

7. Rick reily, "Sportsman of the Year: Lance Armstrong," *Sports Illustrated*, December 16, 2002.

8. "50 Years of Sports in America," *Sports Illustrated*, September 27, 2004, http://www.si.com/vault/2004/09/27/8186830/50-years-of-sports-in-america.

9. Trek 5500 bicycle used by Lance Armstrong in the 2000 Tour de France, National Museum of American History, http://americanhistory.si.edu/collections/search/object/nmah_1294955.

10. He says as much in *The Armstrong Lie*, August 16, 2015, https://www.youtube.com/watch?v=g40HoNEPdj8.

11. David Walsh, *Seven Deadly Sins: My Pursuit of Lance Armstrong* (New York: Atria Books, 2013); the exception is Carlos Sastre, who won the Tour in 2008.

12. Reed Albergotti and Vanessa O'Connell, *Wheelmen: Lance Armstrong, the Tour de France, and the Greatest Sports Conspiracy Ever* (New York: Gotham Books, 2013), 267.

13. Quoted in *Sports Illustrated*, July 29, 2007.

14. Emma O'Reilly, *The Race to Truth* (London: Transworld, 2014), prologue; see ch. 24 for Armstrong's exact words.

15. Bill Gifford, "Greg LeMond vs. The World," *Men's Journal*, July 2008, http://www.mensjournal.com/magazine/greg-lemond-vs-the-world-20130318?page=7.

16. David Epstein, "Kathy LeMond: Armstrong Embarrassed, Not Truly Sorry," *Sports Illustrated*, January 18, 2013, http://www.si.com/more-sports/2013/01/18/lance-armstrong-admission-kathy-lemond-reaction.

17. Quoted in Alexander Wolff, "A Massive Fraud Now More Fully Exposed," *Sports Illustrated*, October 22, 2012, http://www.si.com/vault/2012/10/22/106246058/a-massive-fraud-now-more-fully-exposed.

18. Albergotti and O'Connell, *Wheelmen*, 143, 195.

19. William Fotheringham, *Cyclopedia: It's All about the Bike* (Chicago: Chicago Review Press, 2011), 127; O'Reilly, *Race to Truth*, ch. 9.

20. *The Armstrong Lie*, at 1:36:15.

21. Michael Hall, "The Man Who Fell to Earth," *Texas Monthly*, March 2013, http://www.texasmonthly.com/articles/the-man-who-fell-to-earth/.

22. O'Reilly, *Race to Truth*, epilogue.

2003—YAO MING BOBBLEHEAD

1. Brook Larmer, *Operation Yao Ming* (New York: Gotham Books, 2005), xx.

2. Ibid., 243.

3. He was not the first to play in the NBA, however. Mengke Bateer played for the Denver Nuggets and Wang Zhizhi played for the Dallas Mavericks.

4. "11: Ming Yao,' NBA.com/Stats, n.d., http://stats.nba.com/player/#!/2397/.

5. Larmer, *Operation Yao Ming*, ch. 1.

6. *The Year of the Yao, Part 2*, December 25, 2011, https://www.youtube.com/watch?v=EOON9n312bE, at 2:20.

7. Helen Gao, "From Mao Zedong to Jeremy Lin: Why Basketball Is China's Biggest Sport," *The Atlantic*, February 22, 2012, http://www.theatlantic.com/international/archive/2012/02/from-mao-zedong-to-jeremy-lin-why-basketball-is-chinas-biggest-sport/253427/.

8. Larmer, *Operation Yao Ming*, 289.

9. L. Jon Wertheim, "The Full Measure of Yao," *Sports Illustrated*, December 6, 2010, http://www.si.com/vault/2010/12/06/106012870/the-full-measure-of-yao.

10. "NBA Rosters Feature 100 International Players for Second Consecutive Year," NBA Communications, October 27, 2015, http://pr.nba.com/nba-international-players-2015-16-rosters/?ls=iref:nbahpts.

11. "Opening Day Rosters Feature 230 Players Born Outside the U.S.," MLB.com, April 6, 2015, http://m.mlb.com/news/article/116591920/opening-day-rosters-feature-230-players-born-outside-the-us.

12. "NHL Nationality Breakdown from 191718 to 201516," n.d., http://www.quanthockey.com/TS/TS_PlayerNationalities.php.

13. "NHL International: Where Players Come from and How Much They Make," *Hockey News*, October 8, 2014, http://www.thehockeynews.com/blog/nhl-international-where-players-come-from-and-how-much-they-make/.

2004—CURT SCHILLING'S BLOODY SOCK

1. Dan Shaughnessy, *Reversing the Curse: Inside the History-making Red Sox Championship Season* (Boston: Houghton Mifflin, 2005), 133.

2. "Events of Thursday, July 1, 2004," Retrosheet, http://www.retrosheet.org/boxesetc/2004/07012004.htm.

3. "The 2004 Boston Red Sox," Retrosheet, http://www.retrosheet.org/boxesetc/2004/TBOS02004.htm.

4. "Even by Their Standards, This Is a New Low," *Boston Globe*, October 17, 2004, http://www.boston.com/sports/baseball/redsox/articles/2004/10/17/even_by_their_standards_this_is_a_new_low/.

5. W. Laurence Coker, *Baseball Injuries: Case Studies, by Type, in the Major Leagues* (Jefferson, NC: McFarland, 2013), 103.

6. A picture of his postsurgical ankle is available at "Curt Schilling Tweets Gross Picture from Bloody Sock Game," Extra Mustard, *Sports Illustrated*, November 12, 2014, http://www.si.com/extra-mustard/2014/11/12/curt-schilling-bloody-sock-game-tweet.

7. Allan Wood and Bill Nowlin, *Don't Let Us Win Tonight: An Oral History of the 2004 Boston Red Sox's Impossible Playoff Run* (Chicago: Triumph Books, 2014).

8. Abby Goodnough, "Trouble in Rhode Island for Boston Baseball Hero Trying Out a New Game," *New York Times*, May 20, 2012, http://www.nytimes.com/2012/05/21/us/curt-schillings-business-trouble-in-rhode-island.html.

9. Sean Williams, "What Curt Schilling's Bankruptcy Can Teach Us," Motley Fool, October 15, 2013, http://www.fool.com/investing/general/2013/10/15/curt-schilling-bankruptcy-can-teach-us.aspx.

10. "Curt Schilling's Bloody Sock Sells for $92,613 at Auction," *USA Today*, February 24, 2013, http://www.usatoday.com/story/sports/mlb/2013/02/24/curt-schilling-bloody-sock-sells-at-auction/1942457/.

2005—FORREST GRIFFIN'S GLOVES FROM *THE ULTIMATE FIGHTER 1*

1. "Rules and Regulations," n.d., http://www.ufc.com/discover/sport/rules-and-regulations.

2. See, for example, Robert J. Szczerba, "Mixed Martial Arts and the Evolution of John McCain," *Forbes*, April 3, 2014, http://www.forbes.com/sites/robertszczerba/2014/04/03/mixed-martial-arts-and-the-evolution-of-john-mccain/#2515da91a3b6.

3. L. Jon Wertheim, *Blood in the Cage: Mixed Martial Arts, Pat Miletich, and the Furious Rise of the UFC* (Boston: Houghton Mifflin Harcourt, 2009), 96.

4. L. Jon Wertheim, "The New Main Event," *Sports Illustrated*, May 28, 2007, http://www.si.com/vault/2007/05/28/100052951/the-new-main-event.

5. New Jersey State Athletic Control Board, "Law and Public Safety," [2002], http://www.state.nj.us/lps/sacb/docs/martial.html.

6. Wertheim, *Blood in the Cage*, 147.

7. Ibid.

8. Luke Thomas, "Dana White Confirms Ronda Rousey Has Signed with UFC," November 16, 2012, http://www.mmafighting.com/2012/11/16/3654894/dana-white-confirms-ronda-rousey-signed-ufc-mma-news.

9. Erik Hedegaard, "Ronda Rousey: The World's Most Dangerous Woman," *Rolling Stone*, May 28, 2015, http://www.rollingstone.com/sports/features/ronda-rousey-the-worlds-most-dangerous-woman-20150528; Wertheim, *Blood in the Cage*, 150.

2007—MITCHELL REPORT

1. The Mitchell Report, 22, http://mlb.mlb.com/mlb/news/mitchell/report.jsp?p=22.

2. Tom Verducci, "Is Baseball in the Asterisk Era?," *Sports Illustrated*, March 15, 2004, http://www.si.com/vault/2004/03/15/365144/is-baseball-in-the-asterisk-era-new-questions-about-steroids-have-cast-doubt-on-the-legitimacy-of-the-games-power-hitting-records.

3. John Schlegel, "The Timeline of the 'List'," July 30, 2009, http://mlb.mlb.com/news/print.jsp?ymd =20090730&content_id=6157972&fext=.jsp&c_id=mlb.

4. Jose Canseco, *Juiced: Wild Times, Rampant 'Roids, Smash Hits, and How Baseball Got Big* (New York: It Books, 2006).

5. *Sports Illustrated*, March 7, 2007.

6. "The Steroids Era," ESPN, December 5, 2012, http://espn.go.com/mlb/topics/_/page/the-steroids-era; Mitchell Report, 18, http://mlb.mlb.com/mlb/news/mitchell/index.jsp.

7. "Event Timeline," MLB, n.d., http://mlb.mlb.com/mlb/news/drug_policy.jsp?content=timeline; see entries from March to November 2007; Mitchell Report, 13–14.

8. See http://www.baseball-reference.com/friv/mitchell-report-players.shtml.

9. George J. Mitchell, "Report to the Commissioner of Baseball of an Independent Investigation into the Illegal Use of Steroids and Other Performance Enhancing Substances by Players in Major League Baseball," December 13, 2007, Executive Summary, http://files.mlb.com/mitchrpt.pdf.

2008–MICHAEL PHELPS'S SWIM CAP

1. Paul McMullen, *Amazing Pace: The Story of Olympic Champion Michael Phelps from Sydney to Athens to Beijing* (Emmaus, PA: Rodale, 2006), xi.

2. Barry Svrluga, "Men's 4x100 Freestyle Relay: Some Numbers," *Washington Post*, August 11, 2008, http:// voices.washingtonpost.com/olympics/2008/08/mens_4x100_freestyle_relay_som.html.

3. *Gold Medal Moments: Michael Phelps Makes History in 2008*, July 16, 2012, https://www.youtube.com /watch?v=nLhTCwor1YQ.

4. "Lezak Runs Down French to Win Relay Gold for U.S," ESPN, August 11, 2008, http://sports.espn.go .com/oly/summer08/swimming/news/story?id=3528865.

5. See https://search.yahoo.com/yhs/search?p=4x100+freestyle+relay+2008+olympics&ei=UTF-8&hspart =mozilla&hsimp=yhs-002.

6. Phelps makes this point in an interview, "The Golden Boy," *60 Minutes*, September 20, 2010, https://www .youtube.com/watch?v=zJ_LXsPFens.

7. *Sports Illustrated*, December 29, 2003.

8. David Maraniss, *Rome 1960: The Summer Olympics That Stirred the World* (New York: Simon & Schuster, 2009), 130–138.

9. See http://www.sports-reference.com/olympics/summer/1960/SWI/mens-100-metres-freestyle.html.

10. John Findling and Kimberly Pelle, eds., *The Encyclopedia of the Modern Olympic Movement* (Westport, CT: Greenwood Press, 2004), 169.

11. "Timekeeping at the Olympic Games," n.d., http://www.swatchgroup.com/en/services/archive/london _2012/timekeeping_at_the_olympic_games_1.

12. Among women, the Soviet gymnast Larisa Latynina has 18 medals, 9 of them gold.

2009–VENUS WILLIAMS'S DRESS AND SERENA WILLIAMS'S SHOES FROM WIMBLEDON

1. In 2012, for example, the Tennis Channel did a series on the 100 greatest players of all time. Venus was the eighth-ranked woman (http://www.tigerdroppings.com/rant/more-sports/tennis-channels-100-greatest -tennis-players-of-all-time/32467108/).

2. The only other was at the first Wimbledon in 1884, when Maud Watson beat Lillian Watson, in what was really the championship of west London.

3. They did play the occasional good, even great, match: of these, the Wimbledon final in 2008 (7–5, 6–4 to Venus); the US Open quarterfinal in 2008 (7–6, 7–6 to Serena); and the 2015 US Open quarterfinal (6–2, 1–6, 6–3 to Serena) stand out.

4. They are not the only African American sisters to excel in doubles. From 1938 to 1941 and 1944 to 1953, Margaret and Roumania Peters won 14 American Tennis Association doubles titles. The ATA ran tennis for black Americans, because the USTA would not allow whites to play blacks. In 1946 Roumania beat Althea Gibson for the ATA singles title. Gibson then won the next 10 straight.

5. Serena Williams with Daniel Paisner, *On the Line* (New York: Grand Central Publishing, 2009), 9.

6. The 1997 US Open; she is the only unseeded female finalist in the Open era.

7. L. Jon Wertheim, *Venus Envy: A Sensational Season on the Women's Tour* (New York: HarperCollins, 2001), 9.

8. Sonja Steptoe, "Child's Play," *Sports Illustrated*, June 10, 1991, http://www.si.com/vault/1991/06/10/124343 /childs-play-tennis-newest-pixie-is-named-venus-at-age-10-she-dreams-of-flying-to-jupiter-others-have-earthier -hopes-for-her.

9. *New York Times Magazine*, August 19, 2007.

10. L. Jon Wertheim, "The Serena Show," *Sports Illustrated*, May 26, 2003, http://www.si.com/vault /2003/05/26/343652/the-serena-show-serena-williams-who-defends-her-french-open-title-next-week-is-now-tenniss -biggest-star-and-no-one-could-be-happier-on-the-grand-stage.

11. *Serena Williams Disoriented While Serving at Wimbledon Doubles Match*, July 1, 2014, https://www.you tube.com/watch?v=d1ovzG5SZDQ.

12. S. L. Price, "Serena Williams," *Sports Illustrated*, December 21, 2015, http://www.si.com/vault/2016/02/11 /serena-williams.

13. Kurt Badenhausen, ed., "The World's Highest-Paid Athletes," *Forbes*, June 10, 2015, http://www.forbes.com /athletes/.

14. "Venus Williams: What Is Sjogren's Syndrome?," ABC News, September 1, 2011, http://abcnews.go.com /Health/w_MindBodyNews/venus-williams-sjogrens-syndrome/story?id=14426884.

15. See http://www.coretennis.net/tennis-player/venus-williams/221/ranking.html.

2010—FIRST BASE FROM ARMANDO GALARRAGA'S "IMPERFECT GAME"

1. "Joyce Tops Survey; Players Nix Replay," ESPN, June 13, 2010, http://sports.espn.go.com/mlb/news /story?id=5281467.

2. A video of Jackson's catch is available at *Austin Jackson INCREDIBLE Over-the-Shoulder Catch*, December 1, 2010, https://www.youtube.com/watch?v=BACyz2SSoT0. A video of Mays's catch is available at *Willie Mays Famous Catch*, October 2, 2008, https://www.youtube.com/watch?v=gUK9lG-7HTc.

3. Joyce's comments are available at *Umpire Jim Joyce's Apology for His Call That Ruined Armando Galarraga's Perfect Game*, June 5, 2010, https://www.youtube.com/watch?v=Dp8ST0WidfA.

4. Armando Galarraga and Jim Joyce, *Nobody's Perfect: Two Men, One Call, and a Game for Baseball History* (New York: Atlantic Monthly Press, 2011), 217.

5. Paul Clemens, "Nearly Perfect in Detroit," *New York Times*, June 4, 2010, http://www.nytimes.com/2010/06 /05/opinion/05clemens.html.

6. "Joyce Tops Survey; Players Nix Replay," ESPN, June 13, 2010, http://sports.espn.go.com/mlb/news/story ?id=5281467.

7. Phil Taylor, "Play It Again, Bud," *Sports Illustrated*, August 30, 2010, http://www.si.com/vault/2010 /08/30/105976962/play-it-again-bud.

2010—FRAGMENT OF THE AUBURN OAKS

1. 1.5 million views for this one; see *Ohio State Marching Band "Hollywood Blockbusters" Themed Halftime Show vs Penn State—10/26/13*, October 27, 2013, https://www.youtube.com/watch?v=GxhWyaD_SUQ.

2. Stan Beck and Jack Wilkinson, *College Sports Traditions: Picking Up Butch, Silent Night, and Many Others* (Lanham, MD: Scarecrow, 2013), 359.

3. *Handbook of Stanford University* (Palo Alto, CA: Published by the Stanford Axe Committee, 2012–2013), 8, http://web.stanford.edu/group/axecomm/cgi-bin/wordpress/wp-content/uploads/2013/04/2012-Stanford-Handbook-PDF.pdf.

4. Reeves Wiedeman, "King of the South," *New Yorker*, December 10, 2012, http://www.newyorker.com/magazine/2012/12/10/king-of-the-south.

5. Wright Thompson, "The Life and Times of Harvey Updyke," ESPN, May 24, 2011, http://espn.go.com/college-football/columns/story?id=6575499.

6. Wiedeman, "King of the South."

7. "Harvey Updyke Receives 3 Years," ESPN, March 25, 2013, http://espn.go.com/college-football/story/_/id/9086566/harvey-updyke-sentenced-3-years-auburn-tree-poisoning.

8. Tommy Tomlinson, "Something Went Very Wrong at Toomer's Corner," *Sports Illustrated*, August 15, 2011, http://www.si.com/vault/2011/08/15/106097882/something-went-very-wrong-at-toomers-corner.

2013–STUFFED ANIMAL LEFT AFTER THE BOSTON MARATHON BOMBING

1. "Globe Coverage of the First Boston Marathon," April 20, 1897, http://www.boston.com/zope_homepage/sports/marathon_archive/history/1897_globe.htm.

2. *Big Papi David Ortiz "This Is Our Fuckin City!" Boston Strong*, April 20, 2013, https://www.youtube.com/watch?v=eGMJeVHXsL0.

3. What became known as the "Makeshift Memorial" was taken down in June. Most of the items were collected and are in storage.

2015–MASSILLON TIGERS' BABY FOOTBALL

1. Heitger Funeral Service, http://www.heitger.com/content.php?sid=70491&ssid=156621.

2. *2015 Official NFL Record and Fact Book*, 356–357.

3. The others were the Hammond Pros and Muncie Flyers (Indiana); the Rochester (New York) Jeffersons; and the Rock Island Independents, the Decatur Staleys, and the Racine Cardinals (Illinois). Later that year, the Buffalo (New York) All-Americans, the Chicago Tigers, the Columbus (Ohio) Panhandles, and the Detroit Heralds also joined the league.

4. *2015 Official NFL Record and Fact Book*, 356–357.

5. Gary Vogt, Massillon Tiger Football Booster Club historian.

6. He went on to Ohio State and then to Cleveland, where he became so identified with the team that it was named after him.

7. David K. Wiggins and R. Pierre Rodgers, eds., *Rivals: Legendary Matchups That Made Sports History* (Fayetteville: University of Arkansas Press, 2010), 192.

8. *Go, Tigers! Massillon, Ohio: Where They Live, Breathe and Eat Football* (New York: New York Video Group, 2001).

9. Ibid.

10. Wiggins and Rodgers, *Rivals*, 195.

2016–CTE-RELATED BRAIN SCANS

1. Mark Fainaru-Wada and Steve Fainaru, "How the NFL Worked to Hide the Truth about Concussions and Brain Damage," *Scientific American*, March 7, 2014, http://www.scientificamerican.com/article/how-the-nfl-worked-to-hide-the-truth-about-concussions-and-brain-damage-excerpt/.

2. Ben Reiter, "Brain Trust," *Sports Illustrated*, December 28, 2015, http://www.si.com/vault/2016/02/11/brain-trust.

3. Gary M. Pomerantz, *Their Life's Work: The Brotherhood of the 1970s Pittsburgh Steelers, Then and Now* (New York: Simon & Schuster, 2013), 303.

4. Adam Hadhazy, "Concussions Exact Toll on Football Players Long After They Retire," *Scientific American*, September 2, 2008, http://www.scientificamerican.com/article/football-concussions-felt-long-after-retirement/.

5. Bennet I. Omalu et al., "Chronic Traumatic Encephalopathy in a National Football League Player," *Neurosurgery* 57, no. 1 (July 2005): 128.

6. "What Is Tau and Its Role in Chronic Traumatic Encephalopathy?" [interview with Dr. Ann McKee], n.d., http://www.brainline.org/content/multimedia.php?id=4115.

7. "Chronic Traumatic Encephalopathy," Psychiatry Neuroimaging Laboratory, n.d., http://pnl.bwh.harvard.edu/education/what-is/chronic-traumatic-encephalopathy/.

8. Christine M. Baugh, Clifford A. Robbins, Robert A. Stern, and Ann C. McKee, "Current Understanding of Chronic Traumatic Encephalopathy," *Current Treatment Options in Neurology* 16 (2014): 306, http://www.bu.edu/cte/files/2009/10/Baugh-CTE-review-2014.pdf.

9. Jeanne Marie Laskas, "Bennet Omalu, Concussions, and the NFL: How One Doctor Changed Football Forever," *GQ*, September 14, 2009, http://www.gq.com/story/nfl-players-brain-dementia-study-memory-concussions.

10. "League of Denial: The NFL's Concussion Crisis," *Frontline*, October 8, 2013, http://www.pbs.org/wgbh/frontline/film/league-of-denial/, at 42:30.

11. Jason M. Breslow, "NFL Concussion Settlement Wins Final Approval from Judge," Frontline, April 22, 2015, http://www.pbs.org/wgbh/frontline/article/nfl-concussion-settlement-wins-final-approval-from-judge/.

12. Peter Keating, "Doctor Yes," ESPN, April 15, 2009, http://espn.go.com/espnmag/story?id=3644940.

13. Ibid.

14. Alan Schwarz, "N.F.L. Acknowledges Long-Term Concussion Effects," *New York Times*, December 20, 2009, http://www.nytimes.com/2009/12/21/sports/football/21concussions.html.

15. Breslow, "NFL Concussion Settlement."

16. *League of Denial*, at 20:15.

17. Steve Fainaru and Mark Fainaru-Wada, "Mixed Messages on Brain Injuries," ESPN, November 16, 2012, http://espn.go.com/espn/otl/story/_/page/OTL-Mixed-Messages/nfl-disability-board-concluded-playing-football-caused-brain-injuries-even-officials-issued-denials-years.

18. George Vecsey, "A Decade of Disillusion in U.S. Sports," *New York Times*, December 22, 2009, http://www.nytimes.com/2009/12/21/sports/21iht-SRUS.html.

19. NFL Concussion Settlement Program, https://nflconcussionsettlement.com/.

2016—SPECIAL OLYMPICS MEDALS

1. Special Olympics, "What We Do," n.d., http://www.specialolympics.org/Sections/What_We_Do/What_We_Do.aspx.

2. Special Olympics, http://www.la2015.org/sports.

3. The author's cousin.

4. National Veterans Wheelchair Games, http://wheelchairgames.org/history/. Britain was actually the first; the 1948 Stoke Mandeville Games, which took place after the London Olympics that year, are considered a precursor to the Paralympics.

5. Maurice Smith, "The Beginning of Wheelchair Sports," *Wheelchair News*, October 24, 2013, http://www.karmanhealthcare.com/blog/2013/10/24/beginning-wheelchair-sports/.

6. Karen DePauw and Susan Gavron, *Disability Sport* (Champaign, IL: Human Kinetics, 2005), 83.

7. Harriet May Savitz, *A History of Wheelchair Sports* (n.p.: Backinprint.com, 2006), 47; women began competing in 1962.

8. Paralympic Movement, http://www.paralympic.org/rome-1960.

9. "Paralympics—History of the Movement," n.d., http://www.paralympic.org/the-ipc/history-of-the-movement.

10. James Montague, "The Thin Line: Paralympic Classification Causes Controversy," CNN, August 31, 2012, http://www.cnn.com/2012/08/31/sport/london-2012-paralympics-classification-arlen/index.html.

11. Richard Aikman, "Chin Denied Silver as Medal Fiasco Worsens," *Guardian*, September 14, 2008, http://www.theguardian.com/sport/2008/sep/14/paralympics2008.

12. "Jordanian Paralympians Pull Out of London Games after Sexual Assault Charges in Northern Ireland," *Daily Telegraph* (London), August 23, 2012, http://www.telegraph.co.uk/sport/olympics/paralympic-sport/9494310/Jordanian-Paralympians-pull-out-of-London-Games-after-sexual-assault-charges-in-Northern-Ireland.html.

13. Zandi Shabalala, "'Blade Runner' Pistorius Found Guilty of Murder on Appeal," MSN News, December 3, 2015, http://www.msn.com/en-us/news/world/blade-runner-pistorius-found-guilty-of-murder-on-appeal/ar-AAfYaxl?li=BBnbfcL.

14. "Participation Numbers: London 2012 Paralympic Games," n.d., http://www.paralympic.org/ipc_results/reports/participation2pdf.php?sport=all&games=2012PG&gender=.

CREDITS

INDEX

Cait Murphy is an editor at McKinsey & Company, working most often on issues relating to energy and the environment. In addition, she has written freelance for publications including the *Atlantic*, *American Heritage*, *Washington Post*, and the *Financial Times*. Murphy previously worked for the *Asian Wall Street Journal*, the *Economist*, and *Fortune*. A lifelong sports fan and mediocre athlete, she lives in New York City.

10/16